Social and economic history of England

edited by Asa Briggs

Medieval England — Rural society and economic change 1086-1348

Edward Miller
Master of Fitzwilliam College, Cambridge
and
John Hatcher
University Lecturer in History
and Fellow of Corpus Christi College, Cambridge

Longman
London and New York

Longman Group Limited
Longman House, Burnt Mill, Harlow
Essex CM20 2JE, England
Associated companies throughout the world

*Published in the United States of America
by Longman Inc., New York*

© Longman Group Limited 1978

First published 1978
Second impression, with corrections, 1980
Third impression 1985

Library of Congress Cataloging in Publication Data

Miller, Edward, 1915–
  Medieval England.

  (Social and economic history of England)
  Bibliography: p. 275
  1. England–Social conditions. 2. England–Social life and customs–Medieval period, 1066–1485.
3. England–Economic conditions. I. Hatcher, John, joint author. II. Title. III. Series.
HN386.A8M54 1978   309.1′42′02   77- 21445
ISBN 0-582-48547-9

Type photoset in 10 point Times
Produced by Longman Group (FE) Ltd
Printed in Hong Kong

Contents

Abbreviations

(As used in Notes and Bibliography)

Agric. Hist.	*Agricultural History*
Agric. Hist. Rev.	*Agricultural History Review*
B.L.	British Library
	(formerly the British Museum)
Bishop Swinfield's	*Roll of the Household Expenses of*
Household Book	*Richard de Swinfield*
Brit. Acad. Rec. Soc. Econ. Hist.	British Academy Records of Social
	and Economic History
C.R.	*Court Rolls*
Cart. Osen.	*Cartulary of Oseney Priory,*
	ed. H. E. Salter
D.B.	*Domesday Book seu Liber*
	Censualis
Danelaw Documents	*Documents Illustrative of the Social*
	and Economic History of the
	Danelaw
E.H.R.	*English Historical Review*
Econ. H.R.	*Economic History Review*
Eng. Hist. Docs	*English Historical Documents*
Feudal Aids	*Inquisitions and Assessments*
	Relating to Feudal Aids
Guisborough Chartulary	*Cartularium Prioratus de Gyseburne*
J. Econ. Hist.	*Journal of Economic History.*
P. and P.	*Past and Present*
P.R.O.	Public Record Office
P.R.O. Chancery Inq. p.m.	Public Record Office, Chancery
	Inquisitiones post mortem
Proc. Brit. Acad.	*Proceedings of the British Academy*
Regesta	*Regesta Regum Anglo-*
	Normannorum
Rot. Hundr.	*Rotuli Hundredorum*
Sussex Custumals.	*Custumals of the Sussex Manors*
	of the Archbishop of Canterbury
T.R.H.S.	*Transactions of the Royal*
	Historical Society
U.P.	University Press
V.C.H.	*Victoria County History*

Preface and acknowledgements

In the writing of this book we have had to face certain difficulties and have accumulated many obligations. To take the difficulties first, recent years have seen radical changes in local government boundaries and in our currency. We have none the less felt it appropriate, in a study of the medieval countryside, to attribute places to the historic counties or other districts in which they then lay. Sums of money have also been expressed in medieval terms, in which twelve pennies made a shilling, twenty shillings a pound, and thirteen shillings and fourpence a mark. As to obligations, we have listed in the notes and bibliography the works of many scholars on whose labours we have heavily drawn, although even since this book went to press others have appeared which we regret came too late for us to use. Miss Barbara Harvey's magisterial study of the Westminster Abbey estates is a salient example. Some obligations call for more explicit acknowledgement. We are grateful to the Economic History Review for permission to reproduce the statistics from articles by D. L. Farmer published in the *Economic History Review,* 2nd series, **9**(1956), **10**(1957) and **22**(1969); to Mrs Gillian Baker, Miss Brenda Magurran and Mrs Audrey Stone for turning so many untidy drafts into acceptable copy; and to Dr E. J. King for reading an early draft of the whole work and making many helpful suggestions. Finally, we wish to record a special indebtedness, extending over many years, to Professor M. M. Postan. No-one in our generation has done so much to enlarge our understanding of the medieval English countryside, and we are fortunate in being among the beneficiaries of his work. At the same time, of course, responsibility for our conclusions is solely our own.

E. M.
J. H.

Cover photographs:
Ripon Cathedral (Aerofilms Ltd.). Addit Ms 28162 and Royal Ms 2B vii f. 78V (both from the British Library).

Introduction

Many problems face the student who seeks to understand a society different in time and structure from his own, and for the student seeking to understand medieval society these problems are magnified by the inadequacies of the surviving sources. Apart from the fact that, with the passage of time, many have simply perished, the period known as the Middle Ages was one of restricted literacy when many things that we would record in writing were a matter of oral transactions that have left no record for remote generations. *What* happened, therefore, is frequently in doubt, so that it is hardly surprising that *why* or *how* it happened should be the subject of lively controversy. This does not mean, however, that we should abandon the effort to discover what happened and why and how; and generations of scholars have done a very great deal to provide answers, even though some of them are debatable, to precisely these questions. It is the object of this study to introduce the reader to some of the fruits of their labours.

Life and death

At the same time, precisely because the medieval environment is an unfamiliar one, it may prove useful to pass in review certain features of medieval life that provide the starkest contrasts to life in our own times. To begin with there was the very precariousness of life, deriving above all from man's dependence on the weather and his vulnerability to disease. Most of the inhabitants of the medieval west were small-scale peasant farmers equipped only with a backward technology and mainly dependent for their daily consumption upon their own fields and livestock. The quality and quantity of the harvest, therefore, was always of paramount consequence to them; the harvest was largely determined by the vagaries of the weather; and its yield in turn was also a major influence on levels of employment and activity in sections of the economy far removed from agriculture. A poor harvest meant less to eat and less to sell for the peasant household; a really bad harvest might compel many peasant households to buy food in order to survive, to starve their livestock of fodder, even to slaughter some animals. At the same time meagre yields meant high prices, so that all those who had to buy food had less income over for the purchase of manufactured articles and non-essential products. Consequently excessive cold, drought, high winds and, worst of all, wet summers adversely affected labourers, craftsmen, merchants as well as peasant farmers; and a succession of harvest failures might provoke a crisis which embraced all branches of the economy.

Poor harvests affected adversely the physical as well as the economic health of the nation. Starvation in the medical sense was probably relatively rare, particularly in the countryside, but prolonged shortages led to widespread malnutrition among substantial sections of society. Malnutrition enhanced susceptibility to disease and reduced the ability to fight it to such an extent that the undernourished must frequently have died from relatively minor afflictions like colds, influenzas and mild fevers. Food shortages also forced hungry people to consume rotting meat or mildewed grain, which might engender fatal attacks of food-poisoning. Not all mortality, of course, stemmed from dearth or harvest failure. Diseases such as typhus and dysentery, which attacked all age groups, were caused for the most part by lack of clean water, adequate sanitation and personal hygiene; smallpox, measles, diphtheria and scarlet fever affected mainly the young; and winter brought fatal bouts of pulmonary diseases like influenza and pneumonia, and tuberculosis (the 'white plague' of later centuries) may sometimes have reached epidemic proportions. The frequency and virulence of all these diseases were heightened by an almost complete ignorance of preventive and curative measures, while accidents or injuries resulting in cuts or broken bones often led to permanent disabilities or even to death through lack of, or inexpert, treatment.

Not surprisingly expectations of life were very low by modern English standards, but such indications as we have need to be considered in historical perspective. The population trend is determined by fertility as well as mortality and, as the experience of the major part of our period demonstrates, a relatively low expectation of life can frequently coincide with population increase. It is necessary to use such vague terms as 'high' and 'low' since figures derived from medieval data are evidently debatable; but possibly we may take as a right order of magnitude the estimate that at birth even the children of gentry and noble families might on average have expected a life span of no more than twenty-two to twenty-eight years.[1] Once the early years had been surmounted, prospects of survival improved, but having reached his twenties the man of gentle status could still not expect to reach his fifties, nor the poor man to live beyond his early forties. Not surprisingly, therefore, the opinion was that *senectus*, seniority or age, had its commencement at forty-five.[2] These figures have perforce been drawn from the latter part of our period when the long rise in population was drawing to a close or even being reversed; but bad as they appear they reflect a society which was markedly healthier and with a better life-expectancy than that which followed in the years after the coming of plague in 1348.

The violence of medieval society also contributed to the uncertainty and brevity of life. The records of law courts, of course, afford a very one-sided picture of the times; but throughout the period which here concerns us they are unanimous in their testimony that men were swift to defend their rights by force and, when quarrels arose, to resort to the knife or other weapon that most of them seem to have carried. Individual violence, moreover, was complemented by the activities of gangs of bandits, some of which appear to have acted in defiance of the law for years on end. A study of these phenomena in the West Midlands, for example, leads to the sombre conclusion that 'excessive violence was characteristic of the epoch' and that the machinery of the common law was ineffective in curbing it.[3] Nor is there reason to believe that part of the country in any way exceptional. In such circumstances it is hardly surprising that the Statute of Winchester (1285) alleged that 'from day to day robberies, murders, burnings be more often committed than they have been heretofore' and complained bitterly that jurors 'rather suffer felonies done to strangers to pass unpunished than to indict the offenders of whom great part be people of the same district'.[4] In fact, however, the ineffectiveness of the law to deal with violent crime was not due alone to the partiality of jurors for their neighbours. No small number of those suspected escaped arrest: 125 persons accused of murder and other killings, for example, were reported to have fled rather than stand trial at the Warwick Assizes in 1306. Furthermore, for those who were tried the rate of conviction was low: it amounted only to five out of the thirty-six persons indicted for felony at the Worcester gaol delivery in 1304.[5] Finally, at this time, when Edward I had much need of men for his armies in Scotland, even those who were convicted might obtain pardons for all manner of crimes, including homicides, in return for a period of military service.[6] No less than seventeen of the reputed Worcestershire felons in 1304 produced royal pardons.

The effects of civil wars and civil disturbances must be added to those of criminal violence. The impact of such disturbances have often been exaggerated in the past, and in particular their impact on the country as a whole; but we must beware of going to the opposite extreme by minimizing excessively their consequences. We need to bear in mind that between the Norman Conquest and the Black Death there was only a single period of more than thirty years of internal peace. Regions were very unevenly affected, but some were badly enough hit on occasion. One chronicler of Stephen's reign speaks of 'villages . . . standing lonely and almost empty', and the fields whitening unreaped with a magnificent harvest because the peasantry had fled or perished of famine. Another, referring to Henry II's time, speaks of the 'horror and carnage' that prevailed when William the Lion of Scotland and his Galloway men descended on northern England in 1174.[7] It will never be possible to count the casualties of these episodes, but at least for northern England two of them involved a very heavy toll of life: the devastation wrought by Danish, Scottish and Norman armies in 1069–70 and, much later, by the Scots alone in the early decades of the fourteenth century.[8]

Dependence

If death was omnipresent in these centuries, and much in men's thoughts, so was the dependence of man upon man. Social, economic, political, even legal relations were rooted in personal dependence. Forms and practice varied widely from century to century and from one part of the country to another; but there is a real sense in which society, as Maitland put it, had taken 'a pyramidal or conical shape'.[9] It was a society of lords and men, often described by the adjective 'feudal'; but its basic features are more important than the epithets applied to it. At its apex was the king, with the mightiest noblemen or barons just below him, lesser barons still further below, and so on down to the base constituted by the mass of the peasantry. Each tier in this hierarchy was composed of the 'men' of the tiers above, a relationship of personal dependence enshrined in the notion of homage. At one level, by an oath of homage, a knight might become the 'man' of a baron; at another level the body of manorial peasants who faced their lord (or his representative) in the manor court were that lord's 'homage', his 'men' in a somewhat less elevated sense. Furthermore, the tiers in the pyramid were linked by an intricate network of services and obligations, some arising from the personal dependence of man on lord. At the same time, these services and obligations were also based on the giving and receiving of land, so that the 'man's' dependence on his lord was reinforced by the fact that, in relation to that lord, he was also a dependent tenant.

Dependence, personal and tenurial, was the cement of society and entailed a whole gamut of obligations. At one end of the scale the relationship of baron to king or knight to baron obliged the dependant to defend his lord's interests, to serve him in war, in the last resort to lay down his life for him. The virtues of prowess and loyalty[10] were the marks of the good 'man' of the chivalric orders. The obligations of the majority of men, however, and in particular of that very large section of the peasantry deemed to be 'unfree', were of a very different sort. For many of them a principal duty was the provision of compulsory and regular labour on their lord's home farm over and above a wide range of other constraints: the payment of rents in money and kind, attachment for life to their holding, the need to secure their lord's permission to marry or educate their children, and submission to their lord's power to tax them and sit in justice on them. These were some of the marks of the condition called serfdom or villeinage; but it was a condition that must be distinguished from slavery. Heavy as the villein's obligations might be, they were limited, largely by custom; and as a member of the lord's homage in the manor court the villein might have the opportunity of participating in the declaration of what the custom of that manor was. Further, once he had paid what he owed and done those services incumbent on him, what remained of the fruits of his land and labour were his own. Not all of the peasantry were villeins, of course, and the burdens sustained by tenants who were 'free' were normally substantially lighter than the villein's burdens. Even the freeholder, however, had some obligations, even if they were merely nominal; freehold in the modern sense did not exist in the Middle Ages, for all land was held of someone else who, in virtue of his lordship, was entitled to demand rent and service from its holder.

This social order may be regarded in one respect as a response to the uncertainties of the time. Generations of intermittent invasion and internal warfare throughout the post-Carolingian West moved great landowners to seek security by enlisting fighting men in their service and buying their fidelity by endowing them with land. At the same time, uncertain communications and commerce fostered a prudent desire for self-sufficiency: lords reserved home farms for their own use to ensure the provisioning of their households, and, in order to guarantee their cultivation, bound their tenantry to these demesnes and the performance of compulsory labour on them. Uncertainty also imposed on lords a duty to offer protection to their tenantry and afford them access to justice through the medium of seignorial courts. These were features of an order well enough suited to extremely unsettled times. For that very reason the establishment of a better peace, the expansion of production and the growth of trade – all characteristics of the central Middle Ages – created tensions in the order inherited from the age of invasions. The institutions of 'feudal' society, and the serfdom that was a basic feature of the rural order, had to be modified or adapted to fit new circumstances.

Inequalities

The inhabitants of medieval England, then, were by no means all tied to the precarious and extremely arduous life of the small subsistence farmer. The economic standing of individuals was, in fact, marked by gross inequalities, a characteristic shared by the economic order with most other facets of contemporary society. In the period under review England produced many distinguished men of letters – theologians, philosophers and lawyers such as William of Ockham, Roger Bacon, Robert Grosseteste, Ranulf Glanville and Henry Bracton; and her rapidly developing literary genius was shortly to culminate in the poetry of Langland, Chaucer and Gower. In remembering these literary giants, however, we must not forget that the majority of Englishmen at that time were illiterate, for it is doubtful whether one in ten of the population could read or write, and still fewer could do so with facility. This sort of contrast between the few and the many is to be perceived everywhere. In building, for example, castles and still more the great churches demonstrate the immense technical and artistic potential of the time, but these represent the exceptional survival of exceptional structures. Stone buildings were a relative rarity in this period, so much so that in conveyances a stone house will be so described to mark its distinctiveness from the ordinary house of wood or wood and daub. Of the latter sort of buildings few survived for more than a generation or so; they were so impermanent in their nature that the men of Bamburgh dismantled them and carried the timbers into the castle when Scottish raiders came, and they can have offered only rudimentary shelter from cold and wind and rain.[11] We are a far cry here from the majesty of Rievaulx or Fountains, of Lincoln or Ely.

Economic disparities were no less omnipresent. The most obvious juxtaposition is that between the mass of the peasantry, seated upon subsistence family farms, and the landowning churchmen and lay feudatories whose large possessions permitted them, in the expansive climate of the thirteenth century, to become producers of commodities on a grand scale. Here the poverty of the many contrasted sharply with the great wealth enjoyed by the few. At the same time, the romantic trades in exotic goods that were plied between continents are no less to be distinguished from the humdrum commerce, often in penny packets, in daily necessities; and the skilled crafts fashioning luxury articles from scarce and expensive materials from those making ordinary goods for ordinary men.

We must not, however, make these distinctions too sharp. Even the greatest of landowners, and even in the thirteenth century when their enterprise was fully commercialized, relied in part upon their own lands to provide directly for some part of their needs. Conversely, even the poorest peasant farmer was debarred from concentrating solely on producing just enough from his land to feed his family. In addition he needed to raise money to meet his cash obligations to his lord. Some of this cash might come from seizing the occasional opportunity to earn wages, but the rest had to be raised by selling some part of the product of his land. These surpluses of peasant agriculture, surpluses that were in a sense 'contrived', helped to feed those who did not produce their own food or not enough food for their needs – merchants, craftsmen, priests possibly, even landlords. Over and above, the money the peasant earned by marketing produce, however reluctantly, and paid over in rents and fines and taxes and tithes, contributed to those accumulations of wealth which made possible the building of cathedrals and castles, sustained the edifice of learning, and supported the luxury trades and industries.

The inequalities of medieval society were recognized by the men of the time and justification was found for them in notions of hierarchy and degree, a set of relationships between man and man which was held to enjoy divine approval. At its simplest this doctrine distinguished men according to their role or function, and it divided society into three 'estates': those who prayed, those who fought and those who toiled. The essentials of this scheme were set out with admirable brevity by Abbot Aelfric of Eynsham writing two generations before the Norman Conquest:

'*The throne stands on these three supports:* laboratores, bellatores, oratores. Laboratores *are they who provide us with sustenance, ploughmen and husbandmen devoted to that alone.* Oratores *are they who intercede for us to God and promote Christianity among Christian peoples in the service of God, as spiritual toil, devoted to that alone for the benefit of us all.* Bellatores *are they who guard our boroughs and also our land, fighting with weapons against the oncoming army.*[12]

Inevitably, reality was apt to depart from this simple ideal. According to the author of a poem, probably dating from the early thirteenth century, the fault at that time lay with the clergy, for the devil had taken 'by surprise the richest of those whom God divided into three in order to maintain the land and the laws in lawfulness. . . . Whatever may be true of the layfolk, the clerks are lost'. We are told, however, that the villein was performing his allotted task satisfactorily, for 'the more he labours with his hands the happier and healthier is he; he will never tire'.[13] A somewhat later commentator, Bartholomew Anglicus, held a markedly less sanguine view of the peasant's lot, seeing him as being 'held low with divers and contrary charges and travails among wretchedness and woe'. Bartholomew, none the less, immediately makes plain that he is not advocating any improvement in the conditions of the peasantry, still less any change in the social order, for he adds that 'when they be not held low with dread, their hearts swell, and wax stout and proud, against the commandments of their sovereigns – Dread maketh bond men and women meek and low, and goodly love maketh them stout and despiteful.'[14]

The concept of a society consisting of three exclusive but harmoniously dependent parts becomes progressively more divorced from reality as we move further from the times of Aelfric. Not only was 'discord' created by the worldliness of the clergy, by the growing dominance of money over service in the relations between lord and vassal, and by the opposition of some members of the peasantry to the impositions of their lords, but a new 'estate' was rising, composed of merchants, lawyers, managers and industrialists, which did not fit easily into the old system. Consequently although Chaucer in his *Prologue to the Canterbury Tales* introduces us to an 'estate' society, it is far more complex than that envisaged in earlier times. The old simple tripartite division is still there, exemplified by the three idealized portraits of parson, knight and ploughman; but the new and more complex social structure is also exemplified by a long list of more or less reprehensible personages, including not only quasi-ecclesiastical functionaries but a serjeant at law, a merchant, a sailor, a cook, a manciple, a doctor, a reeve, a haberdasher, a carpenter, a weaver, a dyer, and a tapestry-maker. The society of King Edward's England had a richer diversity than the society of the England King William conquered.

The forces of change

The dominant theme of the social and economic history of England between the Norman Conquest and the Black Death may be summed up in a single word: expansion. Throughout that period, or most of it, the frontiers of settlement were being moved forward. Vast areas of hitherto unused or under-used moorland and woodland and marshland were being brought into productive use at the same time as existing farmland was being exploited more intensively. New towns and industries were being established; old towns and industries were expanding; and trade was extended in its scope and its scale. In brief, in virtually every sector of the economy more and more was being produced and more and more was being exchanged. This increase of activity in some sense reflected a parallel growth of population, so that not only was activity heightened but more and more hands were engaged in it.

The reality of economic expansion during these generations does not necessarily imply that the community as a whole became progressively more prosperous. England's medieval experience in this respect is one that is not uncommon in the history of pre-industrial societies, in many of which an expansion of aggregate production has failed to coincide with genuine economic growth, involving a rise in average real incomes per head. In this connection, the primitive techniques and the emphasis on subsistence in the medieval peasant economy was basically important: in the absence of significant technological advances the amount of land available per head largely determined the level of output per head, and consequently the standard of living of the great rural majority. For this reason, the tendency in England, before the eighteenth century, so far as the peasantry was concerned, was for a high population level to coincide with lower living standards and a lower population level to coincide with higher living standards.

The growth of population between the eleventh and end of the thirteenth century was pushing the country into the first of these two situations. In the earlier part of the period it is likely enough that increases in production more than compensated for the increase in the number of mouths to be fed, if only because unused land was still relatively plentiful. In the latter part of the period, on the other hand, signs appear which suggest that production may have been failing to keep pace with continued population growth. In such circumstances the standards of living of very large sections of the community were almost inevitably forced downwards in the absence of sufficiently major developments in other sectors of the economy that might have offered relief to overcrowding in the countryside. As things were, the tendency for wide circles of countrymen to find their incomes falling was also apt to have the effect of undermining those influences which, at the height of medieval expansion, had favoured the burgeoning of the non-agricultural elements in the economy.

To say more than this at this stage would be to plunge even deeper into the troubled waters of historical controversy. As we shall see, while the fact of population growth is not disputed, the rate at which it grew has been vigorously debated. Not surprisingly, therefore, the extent (if any) of the decline in the standard of living has proved no less a bone of contention. Some scholars envisage the majority of thirteenth-century peasants as 'smallholders leading a wretched existence on an inadequate number of acres' and the degree of over-population to have been such eventually 'as to push the death-rates to a punishing height'.[15] Others view the outcome of medieval expansion with greater optimism. For one, 'far from suffering from over-population England was a prosperous country in all but the worst years'; and for another, 'in the

ENGLAND & WALES

Counties

Scale of miles

0 10 20 30 40 50 60 70 80

Tarset ·

Newminster ·

Tynemouth ·

Newcastle ·

Durham ·

Holme Cultram ·

Carlisle ·

SCOTLAND

CUMBERLAND

WESTMORLAND

Gosforth ·

Furness ·

Cockersand ·

Lancaster ·

Whalley ·

LANCASHIRE

NORTHUMBERLAND

DURHAM

Guisborough ·

Rievaulx ·

Whitby ·

Fountains ·

Bolton ·

York ·

Wakefield ·

Y O R K

Hull ·

Chester ·

CHESHIRE

FLINT

DENBIGH

CARNARVON

MERIONETH

ANGLESEY

ISLE OF
MAN

IRELAND

LINCOLN

Lincoln ·

Boston ·

NOTTINGHAM

DERBY

Darley ·

Derby ·

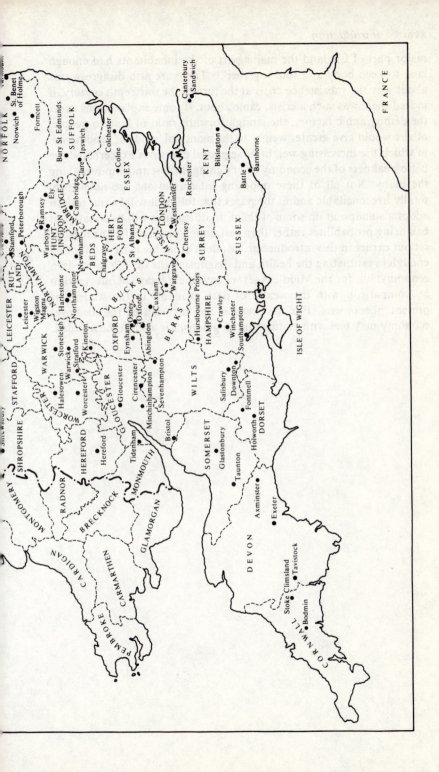

major part of England the major part of the inhabitants had enough
land to keep body and soul together'.[16] There are also disagreements
about why the subsistence crisis at the turn of the thirteenth century, if
indeed there was such a crisis, came about. If some explanations stress
the demographic factors, the straightforward ratio of land to people,
others would give greater weight to the manorial 'mode of production'
in which the increasing weight of seignoral exactions exacerbated the
basic weakness of the economy by enriching the few and impoverishing
the many. Not all of these opposing interpretations are necessarily
totally irreconcilable and in the pages that follow it will be our task to
adopt a standpoint on some of them. In doing so it will be a matter of
balancing probabilites rather than certainties, precisely for the reasons
set out earlier in this introduction. Modern economists have difficulty
enough in estimating the health and diagnosing the ills of our modern
economy: but for the Middle Ages we have mere scraps of information
by comparison with the wealth of data available to the student of
present phenomena. For that reason the historian of the medieval
economy may feel with justice that dogmatism is a sin to be avoided.

Chapter 1

King William's England

A study of England's medieval economic and social history which takes as its point of departure the coming of the Normans to this island begins with something like a false premise. It is true, of course, that the Normans made changes in the distribution and management of land and that the bridge King William built across the Channel furthered the integration of England into the emerging Western economy. On the other hand, one great act of the Conqueror's has over-emphasized the changes that conquest entailed. The Domesday survey William set in train in 1086 enables scholars to study the Norman tenurial revolution as they cannot study the effects of earlier invasions and conquests. For that reason they are easily persuaded to make too much of the transformation which followed 1066. Further, there had previously been nothing like Domesday Book. It was a *descriptio* of virtually all England, which can be compared directly with later surveys like those contained in the Hundred Rolls of 1279 and with the great mass of manorial extents. For that reason Domesday is apt to be treated as a point of departure because in practice investigation must begin with it; and the England which lies beyond Domesday is all too easily assumed to be in some way a very different England to that which was surveyed by King William's commissioners.

In truth, the 'catastrophic' view of the Norman Conquest has come under substantial criticism in recent years even in the fields of government, military arrangements and systems of land tenure. Similarly, if details are set aside in favour of essentials, the supposition of basic economic and social changes also withers away. Saxon and Norman England alike bore all the marks of an underdeveloped, pre-industrial economy: technical backwardness, the absence of manufacture as a significant specialized activity, the prominence of subsistence production. The economy was basically agrarian, markets were restricted, levels of real income per head were low, and there were extensive unused resources. Men who were powerful owed their power to the fact that they exploited a disproportionately large share of the cultivable land, or that they appropriated a share of what the great peasant majority produced, or that they did both. Before and after 1066

English society was rooted in the soil and dominated by territorial lords. Moreover, the great movement of economic expansion generated within this society, a movement which culminated in the thirteenth century, began neither in 1086 nor 1066. On the contrary, its commencement as a continuous and cumulative process probably goes back to the tenth century, the point at which England emerged from the worst tribulations of Viking raiding. To start this survey with King William's England, therefore, is a matter of convenience dictated by the fact that Domesday Book exists. That survey provides the evidential starting point for an investigation of English society and economy in the central Middle Ages just as it summarizes the social and economic outcome of the Anglo-Saxon centuries.[1]

The landscape of Norman England

Even Domesday, however, does not provide a portrait of King William's England that is easily deciphered. A *descriptio* Domesday may be, but one of rights, charges, customs, duties and titles; it is apt to be much more reticent about the landscape of eleventh-century England. Woodland described as so many leagues in length and breadth can be given a certain impressionistic concreteness on the map in the form of a cross drawn to the appropriate scale; but when we are told that there was wood for such a number of pigs or meadow for such a number of cattle, these measures may have been elastic and may have varied with the fatness or the leanness of the animals. Again, Domesday says little directly about the pattern of communications. In the nature of things overland communications were likely to have been poor and difficult, for the Roman roads were now centuries old and after the Romans left public authorities capable of supervising road maintenance and construction had commonly been lacking. This deficiency was probably mitigated by the facts that no part of England was far from the sea and that rivers were navigable far inland by shallow-draught boats. Consequently, Torksey on the Trent was a Domesday port; Cambridge had its hithe to which boats plied in the reign of Henry I; and in 1086 the king had four ways to York, three by land and the other by water.[2] None the less communications must have been slow, especially overland communications, making the carriage of bulky commodities both difficult and costly. This was one feature of the landscape which isolated localities, restricted the volume of exchanges and limited the extent of markets.

Defective communications were not alone in isolating communities from each other. Reginald Lennard has rightly pointed to the fact that the England King William conquered was an 'old country' which had 'passed beyond the colonial stage' and in which the colonizing efforts of Saxon pioneers had laid out 'the framework of rural England as we know it'. He has also demonstrated how Domesday sometimes conceals the extent of this achievement. Some apparently empty areas are surveyed as appendages to their manorial centres and subsidiary settlements known to have existed within them are simply ignored.[3] On the other hand, there remained substantial areas of unused land – both patches of 'waste' within settled territories and larger expanses of fen, woodland and high moor still imperfectly exploited by colonizing pioneers.[4] Marshland areas were still very extensive: around the Kent and Sussex coast, in the Somerset levels, along the Humber estuary and lower Ouse, in the hinterland of the Wash, in the Vale of Pickering and elsewhere. None of them, however, was quite untouched by colonists. Around the Wash, for example, the men of the parts of Holland had already won land from the sea before 1066 and defended it with banks; a belt of occupied territory across the silt fen joined the Norfolk and Lincolnshire uplands; and there were fields and villages on most of the islands of the peat fen interior.[5]

This partial occupation of less rewarding or more difficult terrain is paralleled in other contexts. In the highlands of Dartmoor spearheads of settlement were pushed up to 900 ft on the western edge and to 1,200 ft on the drier eastern side, but in most places the frontiers of cultivation lay lower than that. In the Yorkshire Pennines there were few settlements above 800 ft and in Lancashire above 500 ft; and in Shropshire the north-western uplands supported only a few small settlements, while much of the Wrekin district, the Clee hills and the south-west were sparsely occupied. Undoubtedly there were flocks and herds grazing these higher lands, but pastoral activities sustained relatively few people and they may well in some places have extended only to summer grazing. Relatively dense settlement in other words, was restricted to the lowland districts and here colonization had frequently progressed very far. Even in northern England much of the valleys and the plains were fully occupied: some five out of six of all the hamlets and villages there ever were in medieval Yorkshire, for example, were already established by 1066. On the other hand, of course, lowland settlements could be few and small where soils was poor or difficult, as on the boulder clays of western Leicestershire, on the limestone heaths of Lindsey and Kesteven, in the sandy Norfolk Breckland, or on the heaviest and least tractable clays.

These clay lands were often wooded and the great tracts of woodland clothing much of England also served as barriers to colonization. Many settlements surveyed by King William's commissioners are testimony of massive clearances long before 1066, but a great deal of wooded territory still remained. The *Andredesweald* forest divided the north of Kent and Sussex from the south. The forest of Dean, in the Midlands the forests of Arden, Charnwood and Rockingham, the woodlands stretching almost continuously across Cheshire from the Pennines to the Wirral, and the belt of wooded land extending from southern Northamptonshire through Huntingdonshire to Essex were, like the fens and moorlands, all areas of sparse settlement. So, too, was the tree-clad heathland radiating from Southampton Water which King William, that lover of the tall red deer, made into his New Forest. The contrast between wooded and non-wooded land is particularly striking in Warwickshire. In the open 'felden', south of the Avon, in 1086 there was an abundant population in large settlements; in woodland Arden to the north settlements were scattered, small and possessed of few ploughs.[6] From Norman times, moreover, efforts to colonize woodland were hampered by a special forest law designed to preserve whole areas of wood and heath for the king's hunting; this law not only punished poaching but made the colonist pay heavily for his enterprise. It did not prevent assarting, but it enhanced the cost.

Long centuries of internal colonization had, by 1066, substantially modified the natural landscape of England; but this modification was far from complete. There were substantial areas touched slightly, if at all; the intensity of colonization appears to diminish as the land rises from the plain to the moorland and towards the northern and western peripheries of the kingdom; and men's hold upon land already settled was sometimes precarious. It might be loosened in the interests of the king's hunting. In the making of the New Forest, for example, a considerable number of men were evidently displaced and Domesday speaks of Downton (Wilts) men who *ibi manentes fugati sunt propter forestam regis* (dwelling there, were driven out by reason of the King's forest).[7] War, too, temporarily pushed back the frontiers of cultivation. Welsh raids before 1066 and King William's campaigns left their mark in the west Midlands in 'waste' recorded in Domesday Book, though by 1086 recovery was already evident. Yorkshire was far harder hit by the ravaging of the north in 1069 and subsequent population movements, so that the value of land there fell by two-thirds between 1066 and 1086 and more than half the villages of the county were wholly or partially 'waste' in 1086.[8] Recovery soon set in on the more fertile lands, but on the poorer soils 'waste' sometimes persisted until, from the twelfth century onwards, monks and laymen combined to push forward the frontiers of cultivation once more. The domestication of the English countryside to the use of men was a process by no means without setbacks.

Settlements

King William's England, then, had progressed far beyond the colonial stage, but it was still a land somewhat less than completely settled. Much of the wet lands and the high lands remained empty spaces. It may be an exaggeration to describe Durham as a county where, in the Middle Ages, 'oases of agriculture' were set in 'vast deserts of moor and forests';[9] but the western parts of the county were undoubtedly sparsely settled. Even where settlement was much denser, moreover, most villages probably possessed their encircling 'waste', a no-man's-land of unimproved pasture which played a vital part in supporting the livestock which, as draught animals or producers of manure, provided an essential complement to the arable fields. These basic characteristics of the eleventh-century landscape are one explanation of the low density of people in King William's England. What the total population was is a question likely to be eternally debated, but a figure somewhere between 1¼ and 2¼ million is probably of the right order of magnitude with a probability that it ought to lie somewhere in the upper part of that band.[10] So few people meant, not only much empty ground, but also that inhabitants were spread very thinly over the settled area. The average density was about thirty per square mile. People, furthermore, were very unevenly distributed. Lincolnshire, Norfolk and Suffolk accommodated almost a quarter of the whole population; Essex, Oxfordshire, Berkshire and Wiltshire were probably more thickly peopled than the average; but the north had only about four or five people per square mile. The rest of England lay between the extremes.

England was not only sparsely settled: in all probability about nine out of every ten of its inhabitants were countrymen. The settlements in which they lived differed in size and coherence and some scholars have made much of the distinction between those parts of the country where men lived in compact 'nucleated' villages and those characterized by dispersed settlement in scattered hamlets. It has also been pointed out that, in general, the average size of rural communities decreases as we move from east to west, an observable fact which has been related to an increase of Celtic elements in the population and of Celtic influence on social institutions.[11] Too much must not be made of the contrast between east and west (and therefore of racial explanations of it). In many parts of the country larger and smaller settlements are found in close juxtaposition. In the Cambridgeshire hundred of Wetherley the largest village had eighty-two tenants and the smallest only twelve; and across the country in Herefordshire, Putley had only two recorded inhabitants while Ashperton had thirty-five. Normally large villages were found in the areas of old settlement on lands easily won and

worked. Hamlets, on the other hand, were characteristic of the bleak
and narrow valleys of upland Britain, of the forest lands where colonists
were at work, and sometimes of fens in the process of being drained.

Domesday seized on this colonizing enterprise at a point in time which
did not necessarily represent the final stage in a perennial endeavour.
Single homesteads, perhaps representing a first incursion into the
'waste', were not unknown – such as the one house at Eardisley in
Herefordshire, with two slaves and a rent-paying Welshman attached,
which *in medio cuiusdam silve est posita* (is planted in the midst of a
certain wood).[12] Pioneering establishments of this kind shaded off into
hamlets like those of Langendale in Derbyshire or of the Welsh border
hills; but pockets of small communities were also found in districts
where large nucleated villages were the rule. There were hamlets along
the fen margins of Lincolnshire, as there were in the colonizing
woodland areas of Essex and Hertfordshire and south-east Cambridgeshire. Devon, in particular, illustrates changing patterns of settlement
closely related to advances of the frontier of cultivation. Especially on
the lower lands there were villages 'as large and compact as any of the
Midland plain'; but these were ringed by hamlets representing colonies
thrown off by the older settlements, and yet other hamlets and single
homesteads lying deeper in the woods or higher on the moorland were
the homes of pioneers at work on the outer margins of cultivation.[13]
Many influences helped to shape patterns of settlement as Domesday
Book recorded them: but not least important was the stage which had
been reached in bringing land into productive use.

Villages and hamlets were agricultural communities, and above all
communities engaged in arable husbandry. The central formula of so
many manorial entries in Domesday Book is that there was, in such and
such a place, land for so many ploughs, so many ploughs on the
demesne and so many in the possession of tenants, and perhaps too that
there was meadow enough for the plough teams. Rural settlements have
the appearance in most places of being first and foremost groups of
ploughmen. They were not, of course, that and that alone. Domesday is
often niggardly in the information it gives on matters outside the basic
formulae of the survey. Just occasionally, however, we catch a glimpse
of men engaged in rural crafts: a few potters in Wiltshire and
Gloucestershire, saltworkers in Dorset and Devon, ironworkers in
Devon and the West Riding, smiths in a number of counties, and a
solitary carpenter in Herefordshire (assuredly not the only carpenter in
the English counties). There were also men engaged in auxiliary
occupations: beekeepers in four western counties and fishermen in
various places, but especially numerous in Cambridgeshire. Fairly
obviously this sort of information is sometimes given and sometimes

omitted, but there is enough of it to indicate some diversification of occupations in village society.

Information regarding men principally engaged in livestock farming was no less sporadically recorded. Domesday tells of a couple of cowmen, 10 shepherds and 555 swineherds (541 of them in Wiltshire, Somerset and Devon). That these figures owed more to the vagaries of the Domesday compilers than to the realities of the situation in 1086 is suggested by the figures available for demesne livestock provided by the Exon and Little Domesday.

Table 1 Demesne livestock in eastern and south-western England, 1066–86[14]

County	Sheep	Cattle (incl. cows but excl. ploughbeasts)	Pigs	Goats
Norfolk	46,354	2,130	8,074	3,020
Suffolk	37,522	3,092	9,843	4,343
Essex	46,095	3,928	13,171	3,576
Dorset (part)	22,977	604	1,567	780
Somerset	46,981	4,422	6,847	4,505
Devon	50,039	7,380	3,682	7,263
Cornwall	13,243	1,119	505	906
	263,211	22,675	43,689	24,393

These particulars make clear the relative importance of livestock husbandry even in areas where arable cultivation was the basic agricultural activity. Sheep, and to a secondary degree goats, were first and foremost the providers of milk (most of it probably consumed in the form of cheese), although the sheep's wool and manure were obviously also valued. Sheep numbers, where the evidence serves, were already high and, if tenant flocks could be added to those grazed by lords, may well have been as high in Norfolk and Essex (and likely enough in Somerset) as they were able to be in the 1930s.[15] Cattle, on the other hand, do not appear particularly numerous and breeding stock was in general limited to that required to provide replacements for plough teams. Only in a few places as yet are there signs of dairy cattle taking the place of sheep and goats: in the Cambridge fens at Doddington, for example, and probably also in north-west Devon.[16]

Finally, as a source of meat, pigs were probably the most important of all livestock and demesne holdings suggest that they were very numerous. A landscape with much woodland, and much waste land where swine could dig for sustenance, enabled pigs to be kept on a scale sufficient to justify the employment of the many swineherds recorded by Domesday in early Norman Devon.

Despite the arable bias of Domesday, therefore, there are indications that, even where cereal culture dominated most completely, the village economy was to some degree based on mixed farming. Some pastoral activities were demanded in most communities by the need for breeding stock to replace draught animals, by the need for manure, and by the need for protein elements in diet. Stock-farming was obviously of greater relative importance in higher, wetter or more wooded districts; and in some parts of the country there were already signs of incipient specialization within regions. In East Anglia, for example, there was considerable concentration on sheep-farming on the Norfolk and Essex salt-marshes and in the Suffolk Breckland; and on the Bury estates there was above the average number of breeding stock on a few particular manors. A case in point was Southery on the margins of the Norfolk fenland, a township still important for its cattle as well as its sheep at the end of the twelfth century.[17]

There was, then, much diversity in the Domesday countryside; but in addition to many thousands of villages and hamlets the Conqueror's surveyors also recorded the existence of other settlements, sometimes called boroughs, inhabited at least in part by burgesses. Unfortunately, the record here is seriously incomplete, for it lacks London and Winchester; but the evidence is sufficient to demonstrate that townsmen constituted a significant element in Anglo-Norman society and that urban settlements showed quite as much variation in type as country townships did. In Lincolnshire, for example, Domesday begins with the county borough which in 1086 contained about 900 inhabited messuages within the city and 36 more in its suburbs. Twenty years earlier there had been more still, for some had been destroyed in castle-building and others by fires. Possibly these particulars imply a total population of 4,000–5,000. Next, Stamford with 500 inhabited messuages (77 belonging to sokemen) may have had a population of around 2,000–3,000, and Torksey, with 102 burgesses, one of about 500. Grantham's inhabitants were more diversified: 111 burgesses, sokemen of thegns holding 77 tofts, and 72 bordars. Its total inhabitants were perhaps about 1,200. Louth, with 80 burgesses, 40 sokemen and 2 villeins, was about half the size of Grantham. There were, then, differences of scale, Lincoln being ten times as large as Torksey or Louth. There were also differences of structure: Stamford, Grantham and Louth with their sokemen, villeins and bordars being less exclusively urban than Lincoln.

The diversity of the Lincolnshire towns has parallels in other counties. Even after many tribulations York and Norwich in 1086 still had populations of 4,000–5,000, much the same as that of Lincoln. Lower in the scale Cambridge, Huntingdon, Warwick and Leicester probably had 1,000–2,000 inhabitants; Huntingdon and Warwick had each 100 bordars as well as burgesses; and at Leicester the Bishop of Lincoln and the Countess Judith had land with agricultural tenants upon it. At Cambridge, on the other hand, Domesday makes no mention of agricultural tenants although we know the town had its open fields, for Maitland has made them famous. There were also still smaller places; Stafford with perhaps 750 inhabitants (including 25 villeins); Yarmouth with about 400; and Tewkesbury with 13 burgesses, 16 bordars and 36 slaves, implying a total which can hardly be above 300.

The particulars of burghal communities furnished by Domesday make clear the fact that in the England of that time there was no sharp break between town and country. There were sokemen, villeins, bordars[18] and slaves in many burghal settlements; and even at York and Lincoln we have fields on our hands. At the same time, it is important to note that Lincoln had only 12½ carucates of agricultural land attached to it, about the same amount as was needed to sustain a fairly large village; but Lincoln was a community very much bigger than even the largest village. It is probable, therefore, that in 1086 as later the arable land of Lincoln was in the hands of a few only of the 900 burgesses just as, at Derby, the 12 carucates of land belonging to the town were held by 41 out of the 243 burgesses.[19] The land belonging to Torksey averaged only about one acre per head of its pre-conquest burgesses; Norwich had very little arable; Ipswich with 538 burgesses in 1066 had only 40 acres; and nearly half the recorded population of Colchester had no land. As Tait has put it, 'nothing but an abundance of urban employment will explain these figures'.[20] Even Cambridge, that classic town set in an agrarian mould, was no real exception. It had twice as much ploughland as a large village but, as Maitland points out, it paid to the crown 'ten times what the Cambridgeshire village would pay'.[21]

Certainly, then, there was an agricultural element in the life of most Domesday towns but its importance should not be exaggerated. It is another matter to determine what it was that distinguished burghal from village communities. A good number of towns had a mint or moneyers; there were fishermen at Yarmouth; the Queen had established a market at Tewkesbury; in 1086 there were five mills at Cambridge and ten at Derby, suggesting that these places were active centres of the corn trade. Again, the men of Torksey had ships in which they conveyed royal messengers to York; Irish skins were imported into Chester; Droitwich was a centre of salt production; iron was worked at Gloucester; and the men of Dover traded widely, for they were exempted from toll throughout England. In aggregate these various indications tell us something. The association of mints with towns, and the multiplication of mints in late Saxon England, suggest an urgent

need for local supplies of coin generated by expanding trade focused on
town markets.

A passing glimpse of this trade can be caught in York in *c.*1080 and
1106, when carts carried goods into the city from all points of the
compass and grain was provided for it by the East Riding countryside.[22]
Local trade is likely to have been the dominant concern of most towns.
They needed foodstuffs from their rural hinterlands in order to support
populations larger than those the town fields could sustain. In return
they doubtless offered processing facilities for raw materials supplied by
villages and industrial products made by town craftsmen. The earliest
survey of Winchester, drawn up *c.*1110, reveals some streets named
from concentrations of craftsmen (Tanner Street, Shield-maker Street,
Shoemaker Street), demonstrating the economic base for the growth of
that town from the tenth century onwards until, around the middle of
the twelfth century, its population may have been some 8,000.[23] From
another angle archaeologists have revealed the dependence of country
folk on town manufacturers. Stamford, Thetford, Ipswich and St Neots
potters, for example, were serving more or less extensive hinterlands
both before and after the Normans won at Hastings.[24]

Some towns were more than a focus of local exchanges. They were
collecting and distribution centres along the arteries of much longer-
range commerce. Eleventh-century England had active commercial
dealings with Scandinavia, the Low Countries, the Rhineland and
north-west France; and, if men from these regions were to be found in
the port of London and no doubt elsewhere, it was also assumed that
English traders might cross the open sea at their own expense. The
evidence about the commodities that traders carried is fitful. Certainly
cheese was exported to Flanders in 1036; Scandinavia imported wheat,
flour and cloth from England; and there are some pointers to growing
wool exports to Flanders. Then Aelfric tells us that, in return, England
received from overseas fine cloth, silks, gems, wine and oil: quality
consumption goods attractive to kings, noblemen and rich men.[25] The
commercial mechanisms of the time – how goods were gathered up for
export and how imports were dispersed among consumers – almost
totally escape us; but borough markets, to which kings tried to confine
commercial dealings, almost certainly played a crucial part.

The presumption must be, then, that many Domesday boroughs were
enabled by commercial and industrial activity to sustain many more
inhabitants than their fields would support. At least in the larger towns
the typical burgess must already have been a man mainly engaged in
trade or in a craft; and many of the essential lineaments of the medieval
town had already appeared by 1066. In that connection the urban
charters of the twelfth century, which often appear to record the

beginnings of urban institutions, are possibly misleading. York's first charter of 1154–58, for example, can be shown to be a confirmation of existing rights; and it may be significant that there was a gild of burgesses at Canterbury in 1066 which some forty years later was described as a *cepmannegilde*, a word it is tempting to render as a gild merchant. Indeed, once we cease to regard the borough charters of the Angevin age as constitutive many difficulties disappear. These charters come down from an age when the central government was increasing its powers of regulation, but what they regulated were social forms and institutions which very often had developed slowly over time. Long before Normans and Angevins issued borough charters, tenth-century kings had tried to fix trade within borough boundaries, and a consequent concentration of industrial production around borough market places was likely enough. At the same time the existence from the tenth century of special borough courts probably facilitated the elaboration of special borough customs and tenures, for later these often possessed archaic features which suggest that they were of considerable antiquity.

About the internal life of the boroughs we can say all too little. The fact that they had separate courts, the probability that they had developed certain distinctive customs, and the arrangement by which many of them rendered a fixed annual payment or farm to the king may all argue that they had already developed a degree of communal solidarity which provided foundations on which the later structure of urban liberties was erected. At the same time the separation of town from country was imperfect for reasons other than the existence of borough fields, borough meadows and borough agricultural tenants. Boroughs were also enmeshed in the tenurial pattern which constituted the organizing principle of Domesday society, even if to a far greater extent than rural villages towns were characterized by what Maitland called 'tenurial heterogeneity'.[26] In any given town, while many burgesses held of the king, others held of a variety of private lords and were often said to be 'annexed to' or to 'lie in' some manor of their lord's outside the town. Even Londoners 'pertained' to a whole array of rural manors in Essex, Middlesex and Surrey stretching from Waltham in the north to Bletchingley in the south. These Domesday entries have provided material for much learned speculation, but their essential implication is that town soil had a variety of landlords. They might find such property useful in enabling them to maintain a town house for occasional residence or for storing the surpluses of their estates preparatory to putting it on the market. Much of it, however, they simply let out to burgesses who paid their rents for it at the manor to which they were annexed.

The landlords of Domesday England, then, had urban as well as rural property, although that need not imply that they exercised any very great influence within the boroughs. A few communities, it is true, had fallen more or less completely into the control of private landowners: for example Sandwich, Hythe and Seasalter to Christ Church, Canterbury; Fordwich to St Augustine's; and the quasi-burghal community at Bury St Edmunds to the great abbey at whose gates it was growing even in the interval between 1066 and the making of Domesday. In Leicester, too, Hugh de Grantmesnil not only had custody of the castle, but was lord of more than half the 1,320 houses and of 37 burgesses besides, and he also shared lordship over 24 further houses with the king. Various other lay and ecclesiastical lords also owned houses or had dependent burgesses in the city, the king's share of lordship extending only to about one house in eight.[27] In aggregate, however, the king was probably the largest lord of Domesday burgesses and very commonly he also had a claim to burghal revenues from courts and mints and markets. For the good reason that he had a real stake in a high proportion of towns his representative – the sheriff of the county or a portreeve – was invested with power within the town to safeguard royal interests and exact royal dues. The towns already lay in the shadow of the monarchy and it was under this shadow that civic institutions developed in medieval England.

Techniques

The Domesday boroughs reflect a society already based on exchanges, but that does not imply that technical progress had as yet gone very far. On this matter little light is thrown either by Domesday Book or by any other contemporary record; and it is rather on the basis of later evidence that we may presume that yarn was spun with the age-old distaff and spindle, that cloth was woven on simple vertical looms, and that it was fulled by trampling it underfoot and beating it with sticks. Similarly, while the potter's wheel had long been known, some pottery was still made without it;[28] and right down to the eve of the conquest the standard of building was at a low ebb. Timber or wattle and daub were the main materials; masonry work was rare and crude; and surviving Saxon churches are small, even tiny in scale. Something of an architectural revival set in just before the conquest with the Confessor's abbey church at Westminster; and after 1066 the Normans brought to building a revolution in scale, posing and demanding a solution of new technical problems. Nevertheless building remained essentially a handicraft carried out with simple equipment.

Mills, on the other hand, did represent one sector where mechanical power was replacing the power of hand or foot. As yet, however, they were put to limited uses, for horse or water mills in 1086 were apparently exclusively employed for grinding grain. Domesday, indeed, records some 6,000 corn mills among the profitable appurtenances of manors and towns, an average of one for every fifty recorded households.[29] Some, like the mill at Saintbury (Glos) valued at 6*d* yearly, were of little worth; but two mills at King's Stanley rendered 35*s* a year, in Shropshire Little Ness mill produced yearly 20*s* as well as 600 eels from the pool, and two mills at Burford yielded twelve loads of grain. The notorious Cambridgeshire sheriff, Picot, erected three mills in Cambridge which encroached on the building space and pasture of the burgesses and on the rights of other lords with mills.

There is no sign that water-power was applied to any other process than corn-milling at this time and industrial processes in general made small calls upon capital. The same is true of the basic production of foodstuffs. Scythe and sickle doubtless served for hay and harvest, and flail and winnowing fan for threshing; while weeding, sowing, ditching and spreading manure were hand operations. The equipment used for ploughing is a more controversial matter. Domesday assumed virtually everywhere the use of a heavy plough drawn by a team of eight oxen, presumably wheeled and fitted with a coulter to cut through the soil and a mould-board to turn the sod. There is no reason to doubt that such ploughs were in use, particularly on seignorial demesnes and to break up new land; but it is unlikely that these were the only type of plough employed or that, when Domesday tells us that at Plumstead Hugh had always ploughed 8 acres with two oxen, we need to assume that his neighbours contributed the rest of an eight-ox team.[30] The Domesday *villanus*, who on average had slightly under three oxen per head, the Domesday sokeman who appears to have been only slightly better provided on average, and the Domesday bordar and cottar with few if any ploughbeasts in very many cases,[31] could seldom have provided an eight-ox team on their own account. Their few oxen make manuscript illuminations of the tenth and eleventh centuries which show ploughs drawn by two or four oxen all the more interesting;[32] and when English needlewomen stitched a plough into the frieze of the Bayeux tapestry, it was drawn by what looks like a solitary donkey.[33] A reasonable deduction might be that, while the peasantry might combine to provide teams for the lord's demesne and possibly for major works of reclamation, in very many places they cultivated their own acres with smaller ploughs and smaller teams.

Little can be said about the details of agricultural practice in King William's England, but certain general characteristics of the rural scene do emerge from the evidence available. First, if indeed heavy ploughs and large teams were scarcer than Domesday implies, the long generations required to domesticate the land of England become more explicable and, in particular, the tardiness with which the plough reached the heaviest clays is more easily understood. Secondly, a routine of cultivation only to the slightest degree mechanized meant that for cultivation on any scale many hands had to be mobilized. The development of labour rents and the whole labour organization of the medieval manor are a direct reflection of that situation. Thirdly, the fact that the superficial area of land under crops was relatively large and the population it sustained was relatively small have certain implications. Yields per acre must have been low, so that a disproportionate amount of land was devoted to producing the basic food grains. There were some districts of Norman England, north Oxfordshire for example, where the natural woodland had been largely eradicated and the arable boundary extended to the frontiers of parishes.[34] In these areas particularly, resources for feeding livestock may already have been stretched and the supplies of natural manure required by the arable may already have been running short. There are other indications (for example the habit of East Anglian lords of compelling tenants to fold their sheep on the lord's land) that manure was scarce and, since few other fertilizers were known or used, fallowing as a means of restoring fertility was an essential part of agricultural routine.

That practice, moreover, in at least some parts of the country was followed within a context of 'open fields' in which, as at Charlton by Wantage (Berks) in 956, one man's acres adjoined the acres of other men.[35] The intermixture of parcels, however that is to be explained, and the need to rest the land periodically if it was to do the best it could do, called for organization. One course was to segregate that part of the arable under particular crops in a particular year, and that part resting in fallow, so that a pattern of rotation generated a pattern of fields – two or three according to the sequence of crops and fallow. How far this had happened, to what extent, and where the exceptions were, Domesday will not tell us.

What is clear is that in most places cereal production was the dominant rural activity, and that given the primitive techniques of which men disposed, a heavy expenditure of human labour was necessary to make extensive arable acres yield their limited return. The Domesday commissioners displayed a sure grasp of realities when they gave the first place in their enquiry, once questions of tenure and fiscal assessment were settled, to the number of ploughs and then to number of men: 'how many villeins, how many cottars, how many slaves, how many freemen, how many sokemen'.[36] These subordinate members of village society also either had their own stake in the village arable, or contributed to the cultivation of the lord's acres as slave ploughmen did, or fall into both categories as holders of tenures owing predial services. To this degree the scheme of Domesday Book corresponds with the facts of life in King William's England.

Landlords and the land

It is time to turn from the land to the men who lived on it. About them Domesday provides much evidence, although unfortunately it will not always answer all our questions about such matters as status or tenure. On the other hand it does permit a calculation of how land was distributed in 1086, a calculation which takes us away from the basic unit of settlement, the vill, to the estate or fief on the one hand and to the manor on the other. The estate or fief was the unit of large-scale exploitation supporting the principal members of the ruling class of Norman England; the manor was at once the constituent cell of which fiefs were composed and the framework within which operated the small-scale exploitations of the peasantry which, in aggregate, dominated the rural landscape.

Power and wealth, however, were notably concentrated in the hands of the relatively small class of landlords and, thanks to W. J. Corbett's patient investigations,[37] the annual revenue from land (assessed by Domesday at about £73,000) can be apportioned among different groups of them. Certain small categories – minor officials and royal servants, together with a few surviving Old English lords and their dependants, who between them enjoyed some 8 per cent of the 'rental of England' – may be left out of the account. Of the remainder of the value of the land, as its value was assessed by the Domesday commissioners, the king and the royal family were major shareholders: their portion of it amounted to £12,600 or some 17 per cent of the total, a figure that might reasonably be explained by the supposition that it had to bear, over and above the material support of the king's household, a good part of the cost of governing England. True, it has been argued as part of a general argument that land revenues at all times played a minor part in financing medieval government, that Domesday values grossly over-state the returns received by the Conquerer from his estates.[38] Certainly there is a stark contrast between the values attributed to royal manors in Domesday and the much smaller sums actually received by kings from county farms only a very little later. In brief, a good deal of the profit from the royal demesne was seemingly intercepted by the sheriffs and others who managed royal resources in the localities.[39] This was perhaps an inevitable part of the cost of governing England, even if the effect of it was to transfer some part of nominally royal revenues to a few select families among the nobility or to a small band of men climbing into the nobility by reason of the profit that could be drawn from place and office.

No accurate computation can be made of the precise share of revenue from the royal estates which went to the royal family and to those who served it; but it is clear that some three-quarters of the total profits from land as the Domesday commissioners estimated them were received by two fairly restricted classes. About a hundred priories, abbeys and bishoprics, together with their dependants, received £19,200 (26 per cent) and some 170 lay barons and their men got £35,400 (49 per cent). Much wealth, therefore, was concentrated in the hands of a small circle of lay and ecclesiastical landowners, who were regarded as holding their estates as tenants-in-chief of the Crown and who found themselves, as Crown tenants, saddled for the most part with more or less identical obligations. This is not to say that tenants-in-chief constituted a class of equals in wealth. There were wealthy bishoprics like Canterbury (£1,750) and Winchester (over £1,000) and wealthy monasteries like Glaston-bury (£840) and Ely (£790); but at the other end of the scale there were much poorer religious houses and much poorer bishoprics. The bishop of Selsey, for example, had a revenue of only £138. The fortunes of lay barons were no less disparate. The giants were few: Robert of Mortain with manors worth £2,500, Roger of Montgomery with manors worth £1,750; but only ten barons enjoyed revenues of £750 or more. Below them were some seventy middling men with lands worth £100 to £750 and lower still about ninety with lands to support themselves and their followers worth less than £100. This last group included some men of very small estate, like Robert of Aumale whose fifteen Devon manors were valued at only £26, an income no greater than that enjoyed by some of the sub-tenants of the tenants-in-chief.

The majority of landlords in Norman England, however, were not the barons but their tenants, most of whom had relatively small estates. Whatever the steps may have been by which feudal obligations were fastened upon tenants-in-chief, it is evident that barons were enfeoffing 'knights' in portions of their property almost from the morrow of the conquest. About the time of the Domesday Inquest, for example, Abbot Gilbert Crispin of Westminster conceded to William Baynard 'a certain berewick of the vill of Westminster called Tottenham to accommodate him (*ad se hospitandum*) and to hold for his life for the service of one knight . . . on this condition that, after his death, it will remain free and quit to our church'.[40] The provision that land should revert to the lord on the death of its tenant may well have been not unusual at this time, especially on church estates;[41] but in fact knights very soon acquired a hereditary lien on their 'fees'. Indeed, a list of Canterbury knights of *c.*1172 shows Lanfranc and his successors accepting the principle of heredity without apparent protest, for time and time again the archbishop's tenants in the reign of Henry II can be traced back to a Norman ancestor.[42] The planting of knights on the land, therefore, involved in the event the permanent creation within the framework of great estates of a landowning middle class.

The process had already gone far by 1086. The abbot of Abingdon had created by 1084 more fees than were needed to fulfil a *servitium debitum* of thirty knights; Domesday tells us that Walter Giffard had granted away fifty-one manors worth £226 from a total of seventy-one manors worth £375; and Lanfranc's 'numerous enfeoffments' from the Canterbury lands absorbed a sixth or a seventh of the endowment of the archbishopric.[43] The great barony of William de Warenne exhibits the same tendencies at work; out of lands worth about £1,150 he had conceded to tenants holdings valued at some £540. These tenants were not necessarily all of them knights, for they included Osward and Levenot in Sussex and Wimer in Suffolk who had held the same land before 1066. Most of them, however, had patently Norman names and we may reasonably suppose that a high proportion of them were in fact enfeoffed knights.

Warenne's property is worth close scrutiny because it illustrates conveniently many features common to most of the great estates. It was not only large but also widely dispersed. Half of it lay in Sussex, with a single outlying manor in Hampshire; and more than a quarter was in Norfolk. There were smaller holdings in Cambridgeshire, Suffolk and Essex; a few manors in Oxfordshire, Buckinghamshire, Bedford-shire and Huntingdonshire; and a single manor in Lincolnshire. Finally, farther north, there was the great manor of Conisbrough in the West Riding, with many sokelands attached to it. In all these counties except Yorkshire and Bedfordshire Warenne had subinfeudated part of his land; in all except Hampshire, Lincolnshire and Suffolk he retained some of it in demesne. There were, however, differences between the different parts of the estate. In Sussex, apart from revenues derived from the borough of Lewes, William's income came from four large manors worth between them about £200 yearly. In Oxfordshire, Buckinghamshire, Huntingdonshire and Cambridgeshire he kept in hand only one or two manors of medium value (£6 – £16), while his eight demesne manors in Essex ranged from medium to very small. In Norfolk, on the other hand, he had a stake in over seventy villages but had demesne land in only seventeen of them; more than half his revenue in this county came from the renders of free men or sokemen. His Bedfordshire lands, likewise, were mainly in the hands of sokemen and at Conisbrough, attached to a central manor assessed at five carucates, there were eighty-six caracutes in twenty-eight vills almost exclusively in the possession of sokemen.

Warenne's estate, then, differed widely in its parts. The classical manor, with a more or less extensive home farm, provided only a proportion of his revenue; renders from small cultivators also contributed significantly, especially in Yorkshire, Norfolk and Bedfordshire. Large Anglo-Norman estates, in other words, accommodated themselves to varieties of social structure inherited from Saxon England and from the start they were heterogeneous in their internal organization. The same is true of the estates held by Warenne's military tenants. William de Wateville, for example, held of him at Hangleton (Sussex) land which could be cultivated by eight ploughs. Some of it Wateville kept in demesne, for he had two ploughs of his own; but he also had thirty-one villein tenants and thirteen bordars holding of him. This has the appearance of a manor organized on classical lines. In Norfolk, on the other hand, Warenne's tenants held estates very like that which he himself retained, consisting of small demesne manors which acted as receiving centres for the renders of scattered groups of free peasants. The Norman Conquest involved vast changes in the occupancy of land; but there was no question of imposing uniformity on the methods by which landlords derived an income from it.

Finally, it should also be noticed that the holdings of Warenne's 'knight's' varied considerably in value: thirty-two were worth £1–£5, sixteen £5–£10, twelve £10–£25, three £25–£50 and two £50–£100. The majority of his military tenants, in other words, were men of small substance with less than £10 of yearly revenue. In that respect they resemble those knights whom Archbishop Lanfranc had enfeoffed in Kent before 1087 with no more than *villulae* – hamlets or parts of villages rather than large manors. These holders of modest estates were likely enough the professional or fighting knights of the Norman army of occupation.[44] Above them in the social hierarchy were richer men who were likewise military tenants of barons – the men sometimes described as 'honorial barons' who played something of the same part in the counsels of their lords as the barons did in the counsels of the king, who themselves brought little platoons of knights to the king's army on their lord's behalf, and who were in some cases capable of exercising political weight in their own right. Men of this standing, in terms of their wealth and influence, shade off into the baronage (and not a few barons held land as the tenants of other barons); and their estates, even those held by tenants of less than baronial rank, were often as scattered as were baronial estates. William de Wateville, for example, held both in Sussex and in Essex; William fitzRainald had four manors in Sussex and two in Suffolk; and both had military sub-tenants of their own. They were in a different category from the run-of-the-mill knight with interests more narrowly localized, though even some of this might hold in adjacent counties. One Lambert, for example, held of Warenne at West Wratting and West Wickham in Cambridgeshire and at Rudham near King's Lynn in Norfolk.[45]

The main point is that the actual distribution of land in Norman England did not entirely correspond to a man's position on the ladder of tenure. There were great estates, held by the major barons and the wealthier churches, normally composed of manors widely scattered over the English counties. Then there were a number of middling estates, again made up of manors lying in more than one county, the holders of which included the lesser lay tenants-in-chief, the poorer churches and the more important tenants of the greater lords. Finally, the rank and file military tenants were one or two or three manor men at best, with interests which were generally strictly localized. This distribution of property served as a point of departure for the development of landownership in Norman and Angevin England.

Manors

It has been impossible to avoid the word 'manor' to describe the elements which made up a baron's barony or a knight's fee, and some attempt to bring clearer definition to this word can no longer be postponed. Etymologically the word signifies a house and there are times when one of the essential features of a Domesday manor seems to be the possession by its lord of a 'hall' (*aula*). At the same time the word had a territorial connotation, for sometimes *terra* and *manerium* were used alternatively and indifferently to describe the same sort of property, or even the same property. A manor, in brief, was a block of landed property managed as a single unit from a particular centre. The definition is simple enough, but it is also sufficiently general to subsume the almost infinite variety of manorial structure in Domesday England.

There was variety, in the first place, in the relations between manor and village. The simplest form of this relationship was one of coincidence, so that the lord of the manor was also the lord of the vill. In no part of the country, however, was coincidence anything like universal; and especially in eastern England manors which comprised only a part of a village were very common: Trumpington in Cambridgeshire, for example, accommodated manors belonging to Ernulf de Arda, William de Warenne, Robert Fafiton and a knight of Picot the sheriff (to say nothing of smaller holdings in the possession of one Gollam and a burgess of Cambridge).[46] Hardly less common were manors conjoining elements from more than one village – which were, so to speak, federations of diverse components sometimes stretching over a considerable area. In brief, the manorial framework was a landowning and land-management grid superimposed on the settlement pattern of villages and hamlets.

Manors also varied in their internal structure. Some, like the abbot of Ely's manor at Thriplow (Cambs), belonging to what may be called the 'classical' type. If its rating assessment for national taxation accurately reflects the division of the land, rather less than half the arable was reserved for the abbot's home farm and he had three ploughs for its cultivation. It is likely, however, that the twelve villeins and five bordars occupying the rest of the land owed ploughing and other labour services on the demesne, for they were relatively well equipped with ploughs (five compared to their lord's three, despite the fact that the land was divided roughly equally between the abbot and his tenants).[47] Manors like Thriplow have been described many times, but they were not ubiquitous. Others consisted solely of demesne located in a single village; in others, parcels of demesne were scattered over other villages or hamlets at some distance from the main manorial centre. Conversely, there were demesneless manors composed only of peasant tenements; and sometimes manorial centres of a more or less classical type were a focus for dependent peasant groups in satellite settlements.

Nowhere was uniformity absolute, but the differences between manorial types were in considerable measure regional. Manors of the 'classical' type, for example, were most prevalent in the broad belt of territory stretching across England from the Wash to the Severn estuary and the English Channel, although even in this region there were deviant types. There were small manors consisting only of demesne at Kington St Michael (Wilts) and at some twenty places in Berkshire. There were manors consisting only of peasant tenements at Ditchampton (Wilts) and in at least thirty places in Berkshire. There were also federal manors grouping together a number of interconnected settlements: Calne and Ramsbury in Wiltshire; Taunton in Somerset with land for 100 ploughteams and worth £154; and Leominster in Herefordshire where there were 238 *villani* and 85 *bordarii*.[48] None the less the classical manor was ubiquitous enough in this central belt to be regarded as something of a norm.

It is a very different matter in other parts of England. In the northern Danelaw (comprising much of Yorkshire, Lincolnshire, Nottinghamshire, Derbyshire, Leicestershire and Rutland) there were many manorial nuclei reminiscent of the classical manors farther south; but very often, as at Warenne's Conisborough, they were ringed by appendages. These might be described as 'berewicks', outlying portions of the lord's demesne; not less frequently they were described by the word 'soke' – land held more or less freely by peasant tenants subject to the jurisdiction of the lord of the manor and owing him dues which, if only because of the distance separating them from the manorial centre, must often have been payable in cash or kind rather than service. These 'territorial sokes', in fact, seem likely to have originated in the acquisition by a lord some time in the past of jurisdictional rights over the inhabitants of a whole group of villages in the neighbourhood of his territorial base.

The work of Sir Frank Stenton has made the idiosyncrasies of the northern Danelaw especially familiar, but there were other areas with their own peculiarities. Traces of a social structure similar to that of the Danelaw exist in East Anglia and Cambridgeshire; and here too dependent freemen and sokemen attached, often very loosely, to manorial centres are prominent, their dependence created not only by the acquisition by lords of jurisdictional powers but also by peasants commending themselves to a lord in a search for protection and succour in evil days. This was also an area where the subdivision of vills amongst manors reached something of an extreme point and, in Suffolk for example, the outcome was often *maneriola* of 30–60 acres cultivated by a single team or less and by the labour of one or two *bordarii*.[49] Again, the manor of Domesday Kent was often composed of scattered parcels of arable, pasture, marsh and woodland, some of them distant from the manorial centre; and in parts of the north there were groupings of settlements about a central vill where the lord's residence (and probably his demesne) were situated, to which the inhabitants of a circle of satellite hamlets were judicially subordinate, at which they might owe some services and to which they rendered tribute for their land in cash or kind.

Between 1066 and 1086, it is true, there are signs in some places of a work of simplification being carried out by the new lords of English land. As Maitland put it, 'the Frenchmen are consolidating their manors, creating demesne land where their English *antecessores* had none, . . . doing what in them lies to make every vill a manor'.[50] The process is especially evident in eastern England. At Bourn (Cambs), the *caput* of Picot's barony, only seven remained in 1086 out of its twenty-two pre-conquest sokemen; and at Whaddon Hardwin de Scalers had made a manor. His land there in 1066 had belonged to a man of the abbot of Ely and fifteen sokemen; in 1086 half of it was Hardwin's demesne and the rest was held by nine villeins and twenty cottars.[57] None the less, as Warenne's estates in Norfolk show, this process of manorial consolidation was not pushed to its logical conclusion anywhere, least of all in these areas peripheral to the Midland plain. Some progress was made in tidying up the structure of rural society, some advance in reducing its organization to a 'manorial' norm; but much diversity remained. Consequently, the sources from which lords derived their revenues were similarly diverse. Some income came from the produce of their own home farms, some from peasant renders and some from the profits of jurisdiction and lordship. The composition of seignorial incomes, in other words, was complex from the start and offered various alternative possibilities to a lord seeking to increase or maximize the return he got from his possession of land.

The peasantry

In most instances the manor housed a dependent peasantry bound in one way or another to its lord; for lords in aggregate cultivated only from a third to two-fifths of the arable land the Domesday Commissioners surveyed. The greater part of the land of England, therefore, was in peasant occupation. Domesday divides the rural population into various groups. Most numerous were the *villani* totalling around 109,000 or 41 per cent of the total. It has been calculated they held some 45 per cent of the land of England.[52] The next most numerous class, the 87,000 *bordarii* and cottars (32 per cent of the population), was very much a class of small holders, holding only some 5 per cent of the land. By contrast, the 37,000 *liberi homines* and sokemen, who were about 14 per cent of Domesday countrymen, held some 20 per cent of Domesday land. Leaving aside a few minor groups of small moment, the only other group of significance were the *servi*. There were some 28,000 of them (nearly 10 per cent of the rural population). They were very commonly (but not quite universally) landless, and were evidently full-time workers on the land of their lord.

These broad classifications, of course, are a very imperfect guide to the status of individuals. There are many indications that the commissioners were inconsistent, and their categories in any case often cut across distinctions which were held to be of some importance. There was a sense, for example, in which all except the *servi* were free; but it is also clear that, in the ranks above the slaves, there were degrees of freedom. Domesday often stresses the freedom of *liberi homines* and sokemen in implied contrast to the relative unfreedom of *villani*, bordars and cottars. The former could depart, could sell their land, could go with their land wherever they wished. In such terms a far less close tenurial tie is implied than that which bound *villanus* or cottar to his lord, and less involvement (perhaps no involvement at all) in the provision of labour for the lord's home farm. Yet there were *villani* and cottars where there was no demesne, villein saltmen along the Dorset coast and villein fishermen in seaside vills who were unlikely to have been called on for agricultural labour. Conversely, in Norfolk there were sokemen and even free men who owed agricultural services, and in Suffolk and the Isle of Ely the sokemen commonly could not 'depart'.

Lines of status waver and the words of Domesday do not everywhere mean the same thing. One explanation is that Domesday used a few simple terms to describe a very complex society and another is the fact that this society was in no way static. Lordship in it was a dynamic force, making manors, drawing men who were more free into a lesser freedom. When Hardwin de Scalers made a demesne at Whaddon the outcome may have been the imposition upon the villagers of new terms of tenure, involving them in doing labour where none had been done before. In other places, too, free men were 'added' to manors (though possibly merely for the purpose of paying dues which were not very burdensome); and many free men and sokemen disappeared between 1066 and 1086 (in Cambridgeshire the number of sokemen fell from 900 to 213 and in Bedfordshire they were reduced from 656 to 69).[53] Even where such catastrophes did not happen the hand of the landlord after the Conquest sometimes rested more heavily on the peasantry. In 1066 twenty-three of the demesne manors of the archbishop of Canterbury were worth £453; in 1086 they were worth £741; in fact they yielded £863. The figures perhaps point both to the rationalization of his estates by Archbishop Lanfranc and to a measure of real oppression of his tenantry; and what the archbishop did his knights did to a lesser degree, for fifteen Kentish manors in their possession worth £95 in 1066 were rendering £147 in 1086.[54]

The peasant community, however, was not only a community of tenants; it was also a group of small-scale producers. Looked at from this angle the village communities of the time were evidently no communities of equals. They included men with a fair amount of land, enough to live on or more; but they also included men with far smaller holdings, perhaps no more than a cottage and a croft, who must have relied on supplementary earnings for some part of their daily bread. Very roughly the line of division corresponds to that between *villani*, *liberi homines* and sokemen on the one hand and bordars and cottars on the other – but only very roughly. There were bordars with half a virgate (around 15 acres); there were sokemen and freemen with the tiniest holdings. Economic lines and lines of status did not completely coincide.

Even the sub-groups amongst the peasantry were notably heterogeneous. In this connection the numbers of ploughbeasts possessed by the Domesday *villani* are likely indications of the land in the possession of individuals.[55] A few had eight oxen or more and 20 per cent of those for whom this information is available had between four and eight oxen; on the other hand, nearly half the *villani* had only between two and four oxen, and 28 per cent of them had less than two. These figures suggest a considerable disparity of holdings and are supported by the details of tenements given in the Middlesex Domesday. There, nearly one third of the *villani* had between one and two virgates and about two-thirds of them had between a half and one virgate, although there were a few men with more than two virgates and a few also with less than half a virgate. Apart from these differences in economic resources within the class of *villani*, they also appear to be better off in some parts of the country than they were in others. Comparatively the villeins of Kent, Lincolnshire and Norfolk had fewer ploughbeasts than their peers in Gloucestershire, Hereford and Sussex; while the Lincolnshire sokeman was no better equipped with oxen than the Lincolnshire villein and was noticeably worse off in this respect than the sokeman of Nottinghamshire. These disparities correspond to population densities. In so far as the number of oxen per family reflects the land the family had, therefore, the average holdings of *villani* and sokemen alike were smaller in the more populous districts than they were in those parts of the country where land was still relatively plentiful. In parts of eastern England, indeed, there were signs already that growing population was reducing some family tenements to dimensions which made them less than adequate for the sustenance of families.

What can be inferred from Domesday about peasant tenements has other implications. The half-virgater and even the virgater[56] could probably cultivate his holding himself with the assistance of his family. Some of the peasantry, however, appear to have held more than a virgate and are likely to have been, at least seasonally, employers of labour. Because their demand for labour was seasonal it is likely to have been met, at least in part, by men who had some land of their own but in quantities insufficient to absorb all their energies or to sustain their families – smallholding *villani*, bordars and cottars. That is not to deny the existence of full-time labourers. Younger sons and younger brothers, where they were not allotted a share of the family holding, must have provided a pool of labour in many villages; and manorial lords also had their slaves. On the other hand, the *servi* dwindled in some places even between 1066 and 1086, while the number of bordars increased; and at least in the south-west they sometimes had land and oxen of their own. They seem, in fact to be merging into the class of smallholding, unfree tenants. This was, in itself, nothing new; for the slave planted out on the land figures frequently in Anglo-Saxon wills.

To this extent Domesday evidence of the decline of slavery reflects a late phase in the long process by which the growth of villein services, and of the number of 'free' labourers provided by an expanding population, offered acceptable alternatives to the labour of slaves.

The wealth of England

This introductory sketch of the English economy at the opening of the central Middle Ages may have given, from one angle, a false impression. Looked at through modern eyes late Saxon and Norman England was a backward and undeveloped land. The techniques of production were primitive; and much land and much labour were needed to sustain a population relatively tiny. The overwhelming majority of that population, too, satisfied their needs (and many of them, doubtless, none too well) directly from the land. There was trade and there were traders; there were craftsmen with workshops in urban communities; but trade and industry as yet absorbed only a small proportion of the productive efforts of society, with all that this meant for the range of commodities available and the standard of living possible for most men. Yet this was not the contemporary reaction to King William's England. To the Conqueror's chaplain it was a land 'fertile by virtue of its own fecundity, the wealth of which merchants have increased by bringing in riches. Treasures have been amassed there which are remarkable for their number, their quality and their workmanship'.[57] His judgement may be coloured by memory of the loot the victorious Normans acquired; but the Fleming Goscelin, who spent much of his life in England, was enthusiastic enough for the wealth of England to improve on the description of the country he found in Bede.[58] He, too, commented on its fertile fields and expatiated on its herds and fish and wildfowl, the skill of its jewellers and its veins of metal. For him it was a land of diversified riches.

Men like William of Poitiers and Goscelin judged England by the standards of the west in their own time; and by those standards, evidently, it was a richer land, a more advanced land than some others. There is substantial backing for their judgement. Eleventh-century England, both before and after the conquest, was well provided with a silver currency, even if any calculation of the volume of coin in circulation is hazardous.[59] Such a calculation may even be misleading, for it is possible that the amount of the circulating medium was inflated beyond the essential needs of the economy in order to provide reserves of coin from which royal taxes would be paid. None the less, elements of a money economy had penetrated deep into the society of the time.

Many peasants apparently paid dues in cash as well as in kind or labour; and this fact must carry the implication that they, as well as their lords, made use of those borough markets which the late Saxon lawmakers sought to foster. As for lords of the land, their dependence on monetary transactions is indicated by the fact that the cash revenues assigned by Lanfranc to Christ Church priory were twice as large as those received at about this same time by the great abbey of Cluny in Burgundy. England's economy might be underdeveloped in the absolute sense; but, by the standards of the time, it was precocious in its capacity for development.

The two views of King William's England, then, are not basically incompatible. The relative wealth of the country is merely one more pointer to the fact that, in economic evolution, the Norman Conquest involved no new departure. A phase of expansion had begun at the latest in the tenth century; with periodic set-backs this phase continued throughout the central Middle Ages. On the other hand expansion took place within the framework of an underdeveloped economy. That framework set limits to the capacity of the economy to expand and, in the end, expansion generated something like a crisis. This is the essential paradox which lies at the heart of the history of the medieval economy.

Chapter 2

Land and people

The feudal society of King William's England, like feudal societies elsewhere at this time, was marked by small-scale activities and limited objectives. There were, of course, great estates; there were merchants who prospered to thegn-right by thrice crossing the open sea at their own expense;[1] but most men were peasants, small traders or craftsmen, and most of the land was occupied by peasant farmers. Again, the groupings of men were, so to speak, turned in on themselves. Peasants then as always were in most things self-suppliers; many townsmen worked to satisfy the needs of their fellows as much as for a wider market; and the organization of manor or estate was in great measure orientated towards sustaining its lord's household from his own land. There are even traces of a 'natural economy of the state' – an economy based on food liveries to the king's household from the king's manors. The memory of it was preserved as late as Henry II's time in FitzNeal's tale that 'in the original constitution after the conquest no sums of gold or silver were paid to the king from the crown lands, but victuals only'. Cash revenues took the place of revenues in kind, according to this version, only in the reign of Henry I.[2]

FitzNeal almost certainly postdates the change in the character of royal revenues, but this hardly affects the fact that very much of production (and especially of agricultural production) was undertaken for direct consumption and this in turn made for a good deal of economic and social immobility. The tendencies of the two and a half centuries following the conquest, however, were for enhanced mobility and for the further extension of existing expansive endeavours to tame the wilderness and increase production. Economic expansion may well have been in tune with the spirit of an age in which men's horizons were widened by crusades and colonization, in which political organization acquired new forms and a new effectiveness, and in which men showed willingness to speculate and explore new modes of expression in art and letters. Be that as it may, an expanding economy was a prime feature of the central Middle Ages, and before looking in detail at its manifestations there is something to be said for a review of the phenomenon of expansion in general.

The growth of population

In this connection we may begin with people, for there was a massive increase in population between the eleventh century and the early fourteenth. It is clear that the increase began long before the Norman Conquest and that it was common to almost all parts of Europe. How to explain it is another matter, for if one argument makes it an outcome of technical progress increasing capacity to produce,[3] another would make population growth the dynamic force which stimulated and made necessary the expansion of output.[4] We can feel some confidence that the gradual establishment of more peaceful conditions played a part, and speculate that the waning of epidemic disease was also a contributory factor, but certainties remain elusive. How even to measure the growth raises immense difficulties, despite the fact that England is uniquely fortunate in having two sources which are ostensibly capable of yielding national population statistics: Domesday Book for 1086 and the poll tax returns for 1377. Even these promising collections of data, however, raise formidable problems of interpretation.

Domesday Book, as we have seen, is a list of tenants rather than a register of population, and the poll tax was levied only on persons over the age of fourteen, genuine indigents also being exempted. Moreover, neither source covers the whole of the country, consequently, their use to calculate population raises a host of questions. What 'multiplier' must we use to transform the recorded population into total population? What allowance must we make for sub-tenants and landless men in King William's England? What was the extent of evasion in 1377 and how large was the population of under-fourteens who were not liable to the tax? Even if we feel that these problems are soluble, how do we project the figure for 1377 backwards, making allowance for the mortality occasioned by the Black Death and subsequent plagues, to achieve some sort of idea of the medieval population at its height in the years before 1349? These matters have given rise to endless discussion without, in the nature of things, producing conclusions which are verifiable.[5] It is even possible to doubt the value of striving for national totals, on the grounds that the trend of the population and the rate of its increase relative to available resources are of greater importance. Nonetheless, absolute figures have always exercised a fascination for historians and, although the path is fraught with innumerable pitfalls and possibilities of error, many have devoted much effort to the quest for them.

The most crucial unknown factor in attempting to transform the 275,000 or so tenants listed in Domesday Book into an estimate of national population is the size of the average household. Professor Russell, taking what from later evidence would appear to be a very low estimate of 3·5 persons per household, and assuming that all households were recorded, calculated that England had a population of 1·1 million in 1086.[6] Most recent commentators believe that the average eleventh-century household was far more likely to have contained 4·5 to 5 persons, and a multiplier of this magnitude combined with ample allowances for unrecorded sub-tenants and landless men, and for other omissions by the commissioners, produces a range of from 1·75 to 2·25 million. In using the poll tax returns the most crucial unknown factors are the number of persons under the age of fourteen years and the extent of evasion and under-enumeration. Estimates of the former range from 33·3 to 50 per cent, and of the latter from 5 to at least 25 per cent. Russell once again supports the lowest of these estimates and consequently arrives at a national population of around 2·2 million. If one makes much more realistic allowances for evasion and fraud, for indigents who were legally exempt from taxation, and for the inevitable inefficiencies in the collection of a new form of taxation, then the 1,386,196 taxpayers can be convincingly transformed into a total population of between 2·5 and 3 million.

But our statistical legerdemain cannot stop here. One further feat has to be performed, for to achieve an estimate of medieval population at its maximum we need to set a figure on the decline of population during the thirty years after 1347. In the course of these years England experienced four major epidemics, namely in 1348–49, 1360–62, 1369, and 1375. We cannot simply aggregate the death-rates of these plagues, however, even if we were able to compute them with any precision, since allowance has to be made for a measure of demographic recovery in the years between outbreaks. Fortunately there is a measure of agreement among historians, although their estimates are based on differing premises, that the net decline was probably of the order of 40 to 50 per cent.[7] We can therefore postulate, on the basis of 2·5 to 3 million in 1377, that the England of 1347 may well have accommodated between 5 and 6 million people. Whether population had begun to decline before that date, and if so to what extent, is yet another source of doubt and controversy, but one which we may leave to a later chapter.

Clearly we cannot place much weight on the accuracy of these figures. Nevertheless it is reassuring to find that although the estimates at which historians have arrived differ widely in absolute terms, few would dispute that the population of England between the late eleventh century and the early fourteenth more than doubled and somewhat less than quadrupled.[8] Furthermore, even if overall figures must remain speculative, the support lent by local data suggests that the trends they imply are not exaggerated. Of all local sources the 'hundredpenny' fines exacted at the rate of one penny per annum from each male over the age of twelve years on the Bishop of Winchester's great manor of Taunton in north-west Somerset are the most revealing. The uniqueness of evidence furnished by these fines stems from the fact that they are both virtually continuous and non-tenurial in character. The series runs almost year-by-year for more than a century and indicates the actual number of males on the manor, not merely the heads of households renting land directly from its lord. Thus the recorded increase in the number of males over twelve years of age from 612 in 1209 to 1448 in 1311, a growth rate of 0·85 per cent per annum, must closely reflect the actual increase of the population of the manor. As people multiplied, moreover, the average amount of land per head contracted, despite some transfer of demesne to the peasantry. The figure stood at 3·3 acres of arable in 1248, but only at 2·5 acres in 1311.[9]

Much less reliable but much more plentiful indications of the growth of population are obtainable from comparisons of the numbers of manorial tenants over time. Domesday Book usually provides the base for such comparisons, and manorial surveys and extents from the later twelfth century onwards provide subsequent points of reference.[10] Lists of tenants are, however, imperfect substitutes for direct demographic data. Apart from the consideration that surviving records are unlikely to constitute a true sample of the experience of the region or county from which they are drawn, there are many reasons why rates of increase in the numbers of tenants are likely to be significantly lower than rates of increase in the population at large. The relationship of the recorded tenantry to the manorial population is impossible to ascertain; we do not know the size of the household, sub-tenants are rarely recorded and the landless never. The twelfth and thirteenth centuries experienced increasing land hunger and while average holdings became smaller the proportion of sub-tenants and landless almost certainly grew. It was also a period when many completely new settlements were established, a high proportion of which have left no lists of tenants. If we simply concentrate on settlements in existence at the time of Domesday we are certain to understate the true increase in population.

Despite the inevitable tendency towards understatement and doubts about how representative surviving documents are, the value of manorial extents and surveys lies in their large numbers and wide geographical spread. Indeed, perhaps their greatest value lies not so much in the absolute figures which they can be made to yield, but in the marked diversity they reveal in the rates of growth not only between the highland zone and the lowland zone, but also within regions and counties. In the Lincolnshire fenland, for example, the number of recorded households increased more than sixfold at Spalding and more than elevenfold at Pinchbeck between 1086 and 1287, and this upward trend seems to have continued during the ensuing decades. Even more dramatically the increase at Fleet between 1086 and 1315 was sixty-two times. These rates of growth created some of the largest villages in England, with a population density in places reaching almost 300 per square mile (nearly half as high again as that of the mid-twentieth century in the same region). By the early fourteenth century the Wash basin contained the greatest concentrations of rural wealth to be found in England, and more wealth was attributed in 1334 to almost every fenland township in Holland and the Norfolk marshland than to the great majority of boroughs in the west and south of the country. At the same time, however, here too the pressure of population had led to a decline in the average of arable, meadow and pasture per head (excluding demesnes and fenland wastes) to somewhere around 1–1·5 acres. Obviously special conditions help to explain this astonishing multiplication of people in the fenlands. It was an area of massive drainage and reclamation from the sea. It was an area where auxiliary occupations were available (in salt boiling, the Spalding tanneries, sea and inland fishing, bird-snaring, and goose-grazing). It was an area where lordship was unusually weak and the peasantry unusually free and, consequently, more able to seize opportunities. It was an area where partible inheritance was common, which probably led to earlier marriages, more children and a low rate of emigration.

Rates of growth on this scale were not to be found elsewhere in Lincolnshire, for Lincolnshire as a whole does not appear to have been among the fastest growing counties. Even in the fenland rapid expansion is not invariably revealed by surviving extents. For example, the number of tenants on the western edge of the fen, no more than ten miles from Spalding and Pinchbeck, seems on average to have less than doubled between 1086 and the late thirteenth century.[11]

A comparison of Domesday Book and the hundred rolls of 1279 suggests that the growth of population in Warwickshire was likewise very uneven. Stoneleigh hundred in the Arden region, heavily wooded in 1086, was the setting for a more than fourfold increase of the landholding population over the next two centuries; and there was a seven-and-a-half-fold increase on Kenilworth manor. In Kineton hundred, in the anciently settled open Felden district of south-east Warwickshire, however, landholding populations hardly grew at all, and on some manors they were actually smaller in 1279 than they had been in 1086.[12] Many further examples of widely divergent growth rates could be drawn from most parts of the country. Yet the abundance of local detail is beginning to form a discernible pattern.

We have already seen that people were most unevenly distributed throughout England in 1086, that the uplands were far less densely settled than the lowlands, and that wide areas of forest, woodland, moor, marsh and fen were scarcely inhabited at all. One of the sharpest spurs to population growth was the availability of land and, as in Lincolnshire and Warwickshire, there was a tendency for the highest rates of growth to take place in areas which had the greatest potential for development. Of all regions the north, with four or five inhabitants per square mile where Domesday permits population density to be computed, was the most thinly settled at the beginning of our period. This is partly explicable by the natural disposition for people to gravitate to the most fertile and easily farmed land, which goes a long way towards explaining the very high density of settlement at this date in East Anglia and the coastal parts of Kent and Sussex. But other factors were also at work, in particular the devastation caused in Yorkshire, Lancashire, Cheshire, Derbyshire, Shropshire and Stafford-shire by Norman armies in 1068–70, and by Welsh raiders and further north by Scottish raiders. Starting from some very low bases we find that these upland counties recorded the highest rates of growth in England. An abundance of extents indicates average rates of increase in landholding populations of the North Riding of Yorkshire of twelve- to thirteenfold between 1086 and the later thirteenth century, and nine- to tenfold in the East Riding. Although the rate of increase in the West Riding was probably significantly lower, there can be no doubt that the growth of the population in Yorkshire was among the fastest, if not the fastest, in England. Even after the depredations of the Scots in the early fourteenth century, and the appalling mortalities of the Black Death and subsequent epidemics, the population of Yorkshire in 1377 appears to have been around seven times larger than it had been in 1086. A similar calculation reveals that the population ratios of other northern counties were also well above average for England as a whole at more than three times larger than in 1086. At the other end of the demographic spectrum were counties which were comparatively densely settled in 1086, and which did not even at that date have significant reserves of colonizable land. Even counties which were growing slowly overall, however, often had areas of rapid expansion, such as the Weald, the North and South Downs, and the woodlands of Oxfordshire, Berkshire and Hampshire.

Thus manorial extents, for all their deficiences, enable some of the diversities of demographic change to be appreciated. Moreover, not only do they suggest that minimum county growth rates were at least 100 per cent, and maximum rates some ten times greater, but also that the fastest rates of growth were in counties and regions which were the most

thinly peopled in the eleventh century. All in all, therefore, they lend
support to the contention derived from other sources, that the
population of England probably tripled between 1086 and the first half
of the fourteenth century. This was the dominant feature of life during
the central Middle Ages. Inevitably it had repercussions which in turn
are also some of the most telling indirect indices of demographic
growth.

Colonization

In many respects the clearest indication of the pressure of population on
resources was the way in which spaces still empty in 1086 were being
brought into productive use. Although some significant advances in
agricultural techniques were accomplished in the central Middle Ages, it
is evident that most of the ever-increasing numbers of mouths were fed
by the exploitation of more and more acres rather than by
improvements in the yields from existing farmlands. In the two and a
half centuries after Domesday hundreds of thousands of acres of forest,
woodland, moorland, heath and marshland were brought under the
plough or into use as pasture, and even the difficult task of draining fens
and sea marshes, and of defending the land so won from subsequent
inundation, was tackled with energy, if not always with permanent
success. Among the more spectacular manifestations of this universal
process was the planting of religious houses in virgin or scarcely
inhabited territory, as William did in 1071 when, to atone for the blood
shed in his victory over Harold, he founded a Benedictine abbey at
Battle in the Sussex Weald, 'in a desert surrounded by swampy valleys
and by forest out of which only a few homesteads had yet been carved',
or as the monks of the Cistercian order did in the mid-twelfth century
when they founded the abbeys of Rievaulx, Byland, Fountains, and
Jervaulx in devastated Yorkshire.[13] Less spectacular, but certainly no
less significant, was the piecemeal nibbling at the edges of the waste
carried on by thousands of peasants on village boundaries all over
England.

The most important source of all new farmland was the natural
woodland that was still so abundant in 1086. Woodland could often be
turned into good arable and it was the effort of clearance, together with
legal and customary obstacles, rather than the quality of the soil which
explains why so much woodland was left untouched for so long. But
with the rising demand for land and food men were increasingly
encouraged to replace trees with grain. The tendency for woodland
areas all over England to experience very high rates of population

growth has already been noticed in connection with the forest of Arden in Warwickshire. What was happening there was happening elsewhere, from the far north-east of the country to the far south-west. In Cumberland assarts from Nicol forest represented half the value of the sprawling manor of Liddel in the late thirteenth century, arable was gaining ground on woodland south of Prudhoe on the Tyne, and Bishop Hugh of Durham at the end of the twelfth century allowed a servant of his butlery to assart 'as much as he will' of the wood between Bradley and Bushblades.[14]

Further south Ranulf Fitzherbert was alleged to have planted villages in the Earl of Chester's forest of Wensleydale; the enclosure of assart land in the West Midlands transformed the landscape of that region; and one tenant of the Bishop of Worcester's at Bishop's Cleeve added 170 acres to his holding by clearing woodland. An extent of Cranfield (Beds), taken in the midst of a colonizing drive in the second half of the twelfth century, records 350 acres of assarts held by about thirty tenants; and it has been estimated that the Bishop of Winchester's manors of Wargrave (Berks) and Witney (Oxon) each grew at the expense of the surrounding woodland by about 1,000 acres in the first half of the thirteenth century, and by almost 700 acres between 1256 and 1306.[15] Within fifty years of the foundation of Battle Abbey the arable in the hands of the monks and their tenants had grown to 1,400 acres, and close by some 6 square miles of woodland were assarted in the manor of Rotherfield alone between 1086 and 1346, one good reason for the increase of its recorded tenantry during the same period from 24 to 294. There are scores of examples from twelfth- and thirteenth-century Devon of landowners granting portions of land on the extremities of their manors to potential colonizers, who subsequently appear as free tenants; one of many such grants made by the Bishop of Exeter on his vast manor of Bishop's Tawton, led in the twelfth century to the founding in a woodland clearing of *Akkelane*, seat of the Acland family.[16] These instances could be almost indefinitely multiplied.

Sometimes these records have a certain ambiguity. Royal and private forests were vast tracts of land reserved for hunting, not all of which were woodland. They included much land that was sparsely timbered and even some land without trees at all. The royal forests, in particular, were subject to a forest law administered by special courts and special officials whose activities seriously hindered colonization over a very wide area. After the area subject to this special law had been extended to its maximum under Henry II the royal 'forests' possibly covered one-third of the realm. Yet, while new areas were being subjected to forest law, the right to reclaim them was being conceded at a price. Not later than 1179 the Exchequer had imposed 'a common and fixed penalty' on those who made assarts, 'to wit a perpetual rent of one shilling for each acre sown with wheat, and sixpence for each sown with oats'.[17] Already the King's need for money was prevailing over his obsession with hunting, and within a few years of the death of Henry II the steady flow of fines for assarts and 'waste of forest' became a veritable flood to the benefit of crown and people alike.

Enormous sums were also raised by associations of knights and freeholders and by religious houses to release stretches of land and even whole counties from restraints on assarting. In 1190 the knights of Surrey offered just 200 marks to Richard I for the disafforestation of large parts of their county; the price appears to have risen steeply thereafter and in 1204 the men of Cornwall paid 2,200 marks and 200 palfreys to John for the freeing of their county, the men of Devon paid no less than 5,000 marks for similar privileges extending 'up to the metes of the ancient regards of Dartmoor and Exmoor', and the men of Essex paid 500 marks and five palfreys for 'the forest of Essex which is beyond the causeway between Colchester and Bishop's Stortford'. Among the larger sums paid by ecclesiastical institutions were the £882 rendered by Waverley Abbey (Hants) in the decade after 1171 for 'pleas of the forest, assarts, waste and purpresture', and the £667 rendered by Stanley Abbey (Wilts) in 1203-4 for 'pleas of the forest'. Other ecclesiastics were similarly eating into forest land. Forest assarts on the Bishop of Lincoln's estates in the twelfth century extended into Lincolnshire, Huntingdonshire, Rutland and Oxfordshire; and Richard I pardoned the canons of Waltham for intakes from the forests of Essex and Berkshire totalling over 1100 acres.[18]

Obtaining the right to assart was merely the first stage of a long process. Trees had still to be felled, shrubs ripped up or burned, roots and stumps dug out; beyond that the land might need ditching and weeding, and possibly hedging or fencing to exclude animals, before it was ready for ploughing and sowing. This slow and ardous work, which can seldom be seen proceeding in detail, must have absorbed much time on the part of countless labourers and peasants. Their memorial is preserved in those numerous place-names throughout the country which include elements indicative of woodland clearance: from -*cut*, -*cot*, -*quite*, -*coose*, -*coys*, and -*kelly*, found in Celtic Cornwall, to -*leah*, -*stocc*, -*stub*, -*ge*(*haeh*), -*hyrst*, and -*holt* widely dispersed throughout England.

The extensive marshlands clearly discernible in Domesday Book were also the subject of widespread reclamation; potentially good farmland could no longer be ignored because it was waterlogged or subject to periodic flooding. In Kent, in the Walland marshes, some 23,000 acres of arable and pasture were 'inned', some apparently at the behest of Archbishop Becket himself; and a code of custom binding upon all grew up to regulate the management of the Romney and Walland reclamations.[19] There was similar activity in the Pevensey Levels in Sussex, in the Somerset Levels, in the estuarine marshes of the Clyst, Exe, Otter, and Taw in Devon, in Holderness and the Humberhead marshes of Yorkshire, and along both banks of the Tees estuary where, on the Durham side, a little group of new vills (Cowpen Bewley, Newton Bewley and Greatham) first appears in the records in the second half of the twelfth century.[20] Activity in all the districts bordering on the Wash was perhaps more intense. Pre-conquest expansion of settlement in the Norfolk marshland was continued; in the Isle of Ely some inroads were made into the more accessible parts of the peat fen and there were more substantial gains from the silt fen around Wisbech. Here, at the end of the twelfth century, Bishop Longchamp gave 2,000 acres of purprestures to his cathedral priory. It should come as no surprise, given the dramatic increases in population already noted, that the most spectacular gains of all were realized in the Lincolnshire parts of Holland. In Elloe Wapentake some fifty square miles were reclaimed from the fen alone between 1170 and 1240, and in the whole of Holland perhaps around 100 square miles. To this must be added a substantial area won from the sea. The sea defences then established continued to provide the basic protection of these new lands down to the eighteenth century.[21] A great deal of reclaimed marshland and fen was put to use as meadow and pasture rather than arable, and much of what was cultivable was suitable for oats rather than wheat, but it represented none the less an extension of productive resources, however precarious some of the gains proved to be.

The high moorlands as well as the marshy lowlands attracted colonists, and their ascent can be traced up even the most inhospitable of slopes. We can chart the settlement of the fells of Westmorland from the dates when place-names are first recorded, many as evocative as Southwaite ('damp sour clearing') which is first mentioned in 1324, Roundthwaite ('clearing of the mountain ash') in 1256, and Eller Gill ('elder tree ravine') and Gaisgill ('ravine of the wild geese') in 1310.[22] At the other end of England, Devon men were systematically attacking the edges of the moorland in the twelfth century and by the early fourteenth century settlements were multiplying on Dartmoor. Their Cornish neighbours, meantime, were colonizing Bodmin Moor and the granite outcrops of Penwith, Carnmenellis, and Hensbarrow.[23] Highland settlers often came as pastoralists rather than arable farmers. Sheep farmers put to use especially the lower hills like the Cotswolds and the Lincolnshire and Yorkshire wolds. The narrow valleys of the wilder and higher moorland, on the other hand, were more likely to be the sites of cattle farms and, occasionally, studs. The Earl of Lincoln at the end of the thirteenth century had extensive cattle ranches on the Pennine slopes of Blackburnshire, and also a stud at Ightenhill near Burnley; while over in Yorkshire cattle herds were the main source of profit in the sprawling manors of the Dales – Arkengarthdale, Healaugh in Swaledale, and Bainbridge in Wensleydale. Just before the Black Death well over 10,000 cattle spent each summer on Dartmoor. The same prominence of stock-farming is found in the Derbyshire Peak and Welsh March.[24]

Closer study reveals further developments in the uplands indicative of an increasingly intensive exploitation of resources. Particularly notable was the evolution of the 'shielings' of northern England, which began as summer pastoral encampments and subsequently became permanent settlements, sometimes with arable fields of their own. A case in point is Gosforth (Cumb), where the earliest shieling grounds, the Seascales, were in the coastal sand-dunes. In this coastal part of the parish there is evidence of permanent occupation as early as 1165. Thereafter, Gosforth's summer pastures were on the fells to the east, but there, too, a permanent settlement appears to have been established by the mid-fourteenth century and an early field system associated with it can still be discerned on the ground.[25] The colonization of the moorland, in brief, was frequently not merely pastoral but seasonal at first, but by the thirteenth century arable cultivation was creeping inexorably up the hillsides. In Northumberland, when Hugh Bolbec granted land rising from the Derwent Valley to the canons of Blanchland before 1214, he conceded they might cultivate it as seemed best to them, but he reserved for himself the right of enclosing forty acres either for arable or hay; and a survey of Shoreston in 1250 reveals that part of the common pasture had recently been converted to arable. In Durham, too, Sir Robert Lumley and his heirs were empowered to approve the common moor at Murton in 1307; in Yorkshire the monks of Fountains were entitled to break up land for cultivation *deversus montem* at Kettlewell in Upper Wharfedale; and in North Lancashire assarts from Ulverstone common in Furness were used for arable crops.[26] Although colonization of the moorlands of south-west England produced some exclusively pastoral hamlets, such as Trewortha uncovered 900 feet up on Bodmin Moor, perhaps more typical was the group of farmsteads not far away at Garrow Tor, 'one of the loneliest parts of Cornwall', which practised both arable and pastoral husbandry.[27] As some of these examples suggest, the laying down of permanent arable fields was accompanied by an increasing use of the moorland for temporary or shifting cultivation; after a few years of continuous cropping, and when the fertility of the soil declined, the intake would be abandoned and a new 'breach' would be made elsewhere.[28]

Much of the work of colonists, of course, was less dramatic than the wresting of vast acreages from fen and moor and forest. Some of it, indeed, represented a recovery of old arable that had reverted to waste. The most conspicuous example of such work was the recolonization of the Vale of York devastated by the Conqueror's armies; but even here the ancient nucleus of village territories, once recovered, continued to be extended piecemeal in succeeding generations. Thus the fields of thirteenth-century Yorkshire villages were the result of successive accretions of freshly cleared land which expanded with the expanding numbers of the village community.[29] The same process is visible in Herefordshire where in the Hindwell valley the arable consisted originally of 'islands of cultivated clearings which did not run into each other'; but 'cultivation was later extended up the sides of the valleys and from one settlement to the next until, wherever the lie of the land permitted, their cultivated lands became coterminous'.[30] This sort of enterprise went on everywhere, not least in the older settled parts of England. It was literally a 'journey to the margin',[31] the logical conclusion of which is to be read in two thirteenth-century charters about land at Boxworth (Cambs). One refers to a headland adjoining the field of Lolworth and the other to a selion abutting on Conington field. Here the arable land of three villages seems to be without intervening waste.[32]

The expansion of settlement and the more intensive exploitation of the land led to massive increases in agricultural production, but not without producing a number of harmful consequences. Wastes and woodlands might be under-utilized land, but they were far from valueless. They provided essential reserves of rough grazing, pannage for pigs, wood and turves for fuel and timber for building. Their loss often produced hardship and made the remaining reserves even more valuable. An early example of the tensions that could be created by the loss of commons occurred in 1189 when 'the men of Holland' invaded the precincts of Crowland Abbey desiring 'to have common of the marsh of Crowland. For since their own marshes have dried up, they have converted them into good and fertile ploughland. Whence it is that they lack common pasture more than most people.'[33] Colonization brought neighbours closer and close proximity could generate quarrels, especially where boundaries had been undefined and where groups of villages had exercised joint rights of common over undivided stretches of waste or woodland.[34] Consequently, there were many disputes over inter-commoning rights in Durham; boundary stones and walls were erected to mark off the pasturage rights of different communities and

owners in the Yorkshire moors; in Lincolnshire the division of Wild-
more fen, in which the villages of the sokes of Bolingbroke, Horncastle
and Scrivelsby had inter-commoned, was begun in the twelfth century;
and in due time, many of the southern fens in Lincolnshire, Norfolk,
Cambridgeshire and Huntingdonshire were similarly divided and sometimes even enclosed for individual use.[35]

These disputes and divisions are repeated many times in many other
parts of England; and here we touch on a problem which had become
acute by the thirteenth century. Landlords in search of profit and
peasants in search of sustenance had been taking in new land from the
'waste' and, in the process, curtailing the amount of pasture available.
Some places in consequence were beginning to experience a shortage of
the pasture necessary to maintain the traditional type of mixed farming.
This situation in turn seems to have generated something like a battle
for common rights between lords and tenants. In 1227, for example, the
men of Killinghall (Yorks) petitioned the King because William de
Stuteville had deprived them of their pasture *voluntate sua propria*; and
Henry III ordered that, if this were so, their rights should be restored to
them.[36] In 1235 the magnates of England raised this question of the
commons to a general plane. They complained that, having enfeoffed
knights and free tenants in small tenements on their great manors, they
were prevented by the latter from making a profit (doubtless by assarting and enclosing) from their wastes, woods and pastures even when
sufficient common land remained for their tenants.

The implication seems to be that before 1235 lords had been obliged
to secure the concurrence of their free tenants before extinguishing
common rights; if so, the rule was modified by the Statute of Merton
which answered the complaint of the magnates. In future free tenants
would have no grounds for action against their lord provided he could
show that he had left sufficient pasture for their needs. Unfree tenants,
of course, had no grounds for action in any event. In 1285 another
statute extended these provisions where a lord was hampered in his
desire to approve land by neighbours, presumably in a village where
there was more than one manor or where commons were shared
between more than one village. All that was required of him was to show
that he had left enough common for the needs of his free tenants and
neighbours.[37]

The thirteenth-century legislation conveys the impression that the
landlord was the chief agent of approvement, and of course there is
evidence enough of seignorial enterprise in this direction,[38] but we
should not underestimate the achievements of lesser men. When we
look at the rapidly expanding settlements of Lincolnshire it is evident
that, on the whole, assarting was 'a small man's enterprise' and that the

'real pioneers were the free peasants and the small landlords'. In the longer term, however, some of their gains passed into the hands of greater landlords who, like Gerard de Camville at Sutton (Lincs), were able as lords to appropriate a share in peasant reclamations or who had money to invest in the purchase of land.[39] The role of the small man is scarcely less marked in the work of reclaiming marsh and woodland in Kent. True, both Kent and Lincolnshire may be exceptional as the homes of a peasantry enjoying unusual freedom, yet peasant pioneers appear to be equally prominent among the colonists of the Norfolk and Cambridgeshire fenland, in the colonizing settlements of the west Midlands, with their rings of little enclosed fields standing in such marked contrast to the landscape of the older nucleated villages, and in the Surrey woods and heaths where small men were making little enclosures of a few acres, an acre or even less. The fact that so many of these latter intakes were made originally without the lord's licence points clearly to an initiative coming from below;[40] and on the rare occasions when small fines are not aggregated in the pipe rolls, we can see that sums ranging from a mark (6s 8d) down to twelve pence or even less were paid to the crown by peasants *pro vasto* and *pro proprestura*.[41] When the initiative came from above, moreover, it often consisted of the offering of incentives, such as low rents and free status, to encourage peasant colonization, rather than direct seignorial assarting using hired labour.[42]

There were, at the same time, wide variations in the pace and chronology of colonization. The expansion of agriculture, like the demographic expansion, was a dramatically cumulative process, but it was often fitful and in places inevitably small in scale. The influences which shaped the expansion of settlement were similarly diverse, but they may be grouped together under two main heads: the quest for profit and the quest for survival. Landlords, moved by a search for profit, developed an increased capacity to make more of the territories over which their lordship stretched; and there were elements among the peasantry which likewise sought to better themselves by grasping opportunities to add new acres to old land, take advantage of expanding markets and improve their economic standing. Even men whose arable endowment appears modest might use it as a platform to exploit the natural resources of forest or fen, of moor or minerals, of fish or fowl, to achieve a degree of prosperity belied by the paucity of their grain crops.

When all allowances have been made, however, the numerous smallholders in many villages, whose contribution to pioneering was restricted to tiny intakes on the margins of cultivation, or to taking up some modest plot which their lord no longer felt worth farming, strongly suggest that in a large number of districts rising numbers were pressing heavily on available supplies of land. That suggestion, in turn, carries the implication that a principal dynamic behind the expansion of colonization was the steady multiplication of people over the two centuries or so after Domesday. The process, moreover, was cumulative. If a growing population was a driving force behind reclamation, the land thus won enabled new families to establish themselves and provide the younger sons who in the future would similarly look for a stake in the soil. It is impossible to see this equation as anything but a central theme in the economic development of the central Middle Ages.

Mobility

The growth of population, then, helped to generate an expansion of land in agricultural use; it also contributed to an increased mobility of English villagers. New settlement necessitated migration, and we can be certain that there was much movement from the well-settled areas to the colonizing areas. In addition there was constant migration from the countryside to the towns, and men and women also moved, on a permanent or a temporary basis, to villages where fresh sources of land were available. When we add to this mobility the normal day-to-day economic and social intercourse between neighbouring settlements it becomes clear that medieval villages were anything but closed communities.

The personal names indicative of a place of origin, that are such a commonplace of extents and rentals, throw light upon immigration into some of the estates of the church of Ely. The holders of 'new land' in the colonizing manor of Elm (Cambs) in 1222, for example, included Giles from Wattisham in Suffolk, Nicholas from Tilney in the Norfolk marshland and William from Northwold in south-west Norfolk. At neighbouring Wisbech in 1251 there were men whose origins or that of their ancestors lay in the adjacent hamlet of Newton, in Tilney, East Dereham and Reymerstone (Norfolk) and in Caxton and Burwell (Cambs). Nor did agricultural opportunity alone beckon immigrants. Holders of butchers' stalls in Wisbech market included men from East Dereham, Docking, Grassenhall, Terrington and Walsoken in Norfolk, Tydd in Lincolnshire and Beccles and Hunston in Suffolk; while at the little market town growing up at Needham in Suffolk there were immigrants from Bures and Stonham and from neighbouring Barking.[43]

Nor was the immigration only a feature of market towns or of villages that were centres of extensive colonization. At Haddenham, in the south of the Isle of Ely, there were assarts indeed, but the scope for them was limited by the problems of drainage in the peat fen that surrounded the island on which the village was placed. Reclamation in any case was apt to produce new pasture or meadow rather than arable. Haddenham, therefore was a settlement in which the leading peasant families – Colevilles, Warloks, Redes, Kibbells, Huberts, Thorolts, Wrongs, Atwells, Frosts, Hogs, Trusses, Swetewines – displayed a remarkable continuity from the survey of 1222 down to the tax assessment of 1327. Even here there were also immigrant families in 1222 and 1251, among the free tenants and molmen if not among the villeins. Men or their ancestors had planted themselves in Haddenham from the adjacent vills of Wentworth and Little Thetford, but they had also come from Upwell or Outwell near Wisbech, from Lawshall in Suffolk and from Runhall in Norfolk.[44] On this estate, then,the incomer was common enough in the village and the partially urbanized community alike.

The central role of the immigrant in the making of medieval towns will concern us in due course, but everything suggests that his presence in the rural manors subject to the church of Ely was in no way unusual. The evidence from the neighbouring Ramsey estate indicates, from the earliest date at which court records became available, a 'continual movement' into the abbey's manors and, at the same time, no great effort to restrain a parallel movement out of them. Professor Raftis has revealed, from the court rolls, the presence in the manor of Warboys (Hunts) between 1290 and 1353 of persons from forty-three different places in nine different counties. Indeed, there is earlier evidence for these phenomena than that furnished by the court rolls. The Knapwell survey of *c.*1195 speaks of Thomas son of Walwin who dwells in Boxworth, having married a lady of that place, and of Herbert son of Hardwin who is living on William son of Andrew's land in Swavesey.[45] Similarly, in 1327 the Cambridgeshire village of Soham, a fair-sized and flourishing place with considerable reserves of fen, housed taxpayers whose families had originated not only in the neighbouring villages of Swaffham, Waterbeach or Landbeach, Barway and Chippenham; but also others deriving from Boyton and Mildenhall (Suffolk), Ringland (Norfolk), Thorney (Isle of Ely), Colne (Hunts), Pirton (Herts), Sleaford (Lincs) and Mackworth (Derbys).[46] A little earlier, too, the Suffolk village of Ashfield Parva had inhabitants coming from Radwell Ash, Tuddenham and Redgrave in the same county, and others from Upwell in Cambridgeshire and Banham and Walsingham in Norfolk.[47]

Nor were these particular features of eastern England. The free tenants of the Wiltshire manor of Sevenhampton in the 1270s included men whose roots were in Aylesbury and one or other of the Eastons of the county; and there was also a cottar whose ancestors had come from

South Marston;[48] while in the West Midlands, the 134 men who paid tallage in the nine townships of the manor of Stoneleigh in 1305 included at least fourteen who were immigrants (or the descendants of immigrants) from various Warwickshire villages, as well as others whose origins can be traced to Wroxton and Balscott (Oxon), Cannock (Staffs), and perhaps to Chevington and Halesowen in Worcestershire.[49] In the north, too, Tynemouth taxpayers in 1296 included men named from neighbouring Backworth and another priory manor, Wylam, further up the Tyne; Middle Chirton in 1294 housed another Wylam immigrant; and Preston had taxpayers originating in neighbouring Chirton and Murton. As for Wylam, a freeman there took his name from Chirton and a free woman born at High Rochester also acquired land there and passed it to her son, and on his death his widow took it in a second marriage to a man from Eltringham, near Prudhoe.[50]

Much can be learned about emigration from villages from the records of chevage payments made by the unfree for leave to live outside their native manors, which sometimes indicate a very high rate of emigration indeed. In the last quarter of the thirteenth century, for example, on average around 100 *nativi* each year paid to live away from the manor of Forncett (Norfolk), a figure all the more remarkable because there were no more than 135 servile tenements there. Similarly high rates of emigration are found on other Norfolk manors of Roger Bigod, for in 1273 there were thirty-two chevage payers from Ditchingham and ninety-three from Little Framlingham.[51] The exodus of *nativi* from the Somerset manors of Glastonbury abbey was on a comparable scale, for on each of its largest manors in the late thirteenth and early fourteenth centuries those licensed to live elsewhere totalled well over 100.[52] Further west, in Cornwall, mobility may have been even greater in the decade preceding the Black Death: on the Duchy manors the number of chevage payers usually approached and sometimes exceeded the number of unfree holdings. The records of this estate also reveal a very high turnover of tenants. Barely half of the 900 or so customary tenants of 1337 were still in possession of the same holdings ten years later and at Helston-in-Kerrier in the far west no less than 75 per cent of holdings changed hands over the same period.[53]

It is dangerous, of course, to generalize from the experience of individual manors. There were also manors on which chevage payers were very few; and in some regions circumstances may have specially encouraged mobility. In Cornwall, for example, the regional economy offered a wide range of alternative employments and the fact that leasehold was the predominant form of tenure was likely to favour a rapid turnover of holdings. At the same time, examples of manors where chevage was paid by twenty or more bondmen are by no means uncommon[54] and the record of these payments itself underrates the full degree of mobility. The movement of freemen, who were not liable to chevage, is not recorded by it; and many *nativi*, after paying for a time, subsequently default and disappear from the lists.[55] We would be ill-advised to exaggerate the immobility of the medieval peasant.

Some influences inevitably made for immobility. Many villagers had limited horizons and an imperfect knowledge of the prospects of land or employment in other places; and lords made some effort to restrain the movement at least of unfree tenants. Again, the peasant heir with a family holding to step into when his father died or determined on retirement, had an obvious incentive to stay where he was. At the same time the evidence suggests that the average family had in excess of two children. In the Lincolnshire manors of Weston and Moulton in 1270, for example, the average number of adult surviving sons alone in each family was 1·86 and 2·5 respectively.[56] Even where partible inheritance was practised, as at Moulton, the children's shares might ultimately become so small that heirs would be pushed into assarting in order to enlarge their portions or into emigrating in a search for better opportunities elsewhere. Where the family holding passed to a single heir, on the other hand, other surviving sons had to seek their fortunes as they could. We may suspect that many of them are to be found among the colonists pushing forward the frontiers of cultivation; and they are likely enough to have been no less prominent among the mobile elements in the English countryside. It is significant that chevage payers were sometimes called 'anlepimen', which implies that they were 'single and sole in the sense of being unmarried' and probably not householders.[57]

The motives behind mobility were diverse, and by no means all movement ended with permanent settlement in another place. It seems clear that, at least by the late thirteenth century, seasonal labour was an important element in the manorial economy and temporary residents were willingly accepted into village communities, especially at harvest time. When opportunities presented themselves villagers might also move in search of work in local industries on a seasonal basis. At the same time, as we have seen, many men did move permanently. Sometimes, like the Upwood man living married outside the lord's fee at Walton, they acquired a stake in another place by wedding a widow or heiress. Others, however, may have used savings to buy themselves land in another place; but many more migrated from old-settled areas to colonizing districts, as they almost certainly did from the Warwickshire *felden* to the land of opportunity in Arden. The cumulative impression from every source, direct and indirect, is of old villages filling up with more people and of new villages and hamlets taking some of the overflow that old villages could no longer sustain. In these respects population growth, colonization and peasant mobility are three aspects of a single phenomenon.

Competition for land

The evidence of a massive increase in both population and the acreage of agricultural land in the twelfth and thirteenth centuries is overwhelming, but this does not mean that we can assume that new land and new people were neatly balanced over these two centuries. It is probable that at certain times and in certain places colonization produced gains larger than those strictly warranted by the multiplication of people, and that sometimes output per head was increased simply by applying more labour to the same amount of land and capital. At the same time there can be no doubt whatsoever that overall neither the growth of agricultural production nor of agricultural acreage ultimately matched the growth in the numbers of people. The inevitable consequence was a fall in the average amount of land per head and, when for the majority of people land meant quite literally their daily bread, competition for it was inevitably heightened. Competition for land existed both between communities, like that between the men of Holland and the men of Crowland for pasturage in Crowland fen noted above, (p. 38) and within communities, where it was reflected in the price that men were willing to pay for holdings.

Rents paid for land rose despite the capacity of custom to endow traditional charges with an eternal immobility. In East Anglia and Kent in the eleventh century, for example, rents of around one penny per acre were relatively common. Charges ran much higher by the thirteenth century. At Pulham (Norfolk) in 1251, while the main body of *censuarii* paid on the average fourpence per acre, certain 'newly enfeoffed men' paid more like sixpence. Elsewhere in Norfolk at this time tenants-at-will paid up to 1s5d per acre and in the early fourteenth century demesne leaseholds at Somersham (Hunts) ranged from 8d to 2s4d per acre.[48] The same process is evident on the Kentish estates of the Archbishop of Canterbury, where by the late thirteenth century the ancient *gabulum* of 1d per acre was almost lost in new rents at higher rates. In Sussex 'new assart' in the mid-thirteenth century was let at twice the 1d per acre charged for 'old assart' of the early thirteenth century.[59] These assarts may have been poor land, but even poor land was going up in price. Rising rents were a universal phenomenon and it was not only in the south of England that some rents ran high. In the north in the early fourteenth century, on the Lancaster estate at Tanshelf in Yorkshire, land was leased at 2*s*9*d* an acre; and in Northumberland the constable of Bamburgh exacted 2*s*6*d* to 3*s* an acre from leasehold tenants there at the cost of bitter recrimination.[60]

Customary tenants commonly had obligations over and above their rents in the form of tallages, labour services, entry fines on taking up a tenancy, and sometimes food rents. Levels of entry fines paid on succeeding to or acquiring a servile tenement are especially significant, since they seem to have been far more sensitive to market forces than other charges. Evidence for the amounts paid before the mid-thirteenth century is scarce, but what there is suggests that entry fines rose even more steeply than rents. The Winchester rolls provide the earliest data and show that at Fonthill (Wilts), for example, fines at a rate of 1*s* to 1*s*8*d* per virgate in 1214 rose to 8*s* to 46*s*8*d* by the years 1277–1348. The ample evidence available from the mid-thirteenth century onwards confirms the steepness of the rising trend. On the Ramsey estates a son succeeding his father in a virgate holding around 1250 usually paid a fine of 13*s*4*d* or 20*s*; after 1300 he might have to pay over 60*s*. On the Peterborough Abbey estates and in the West Midlands, too, fines increased markedly between the later decades of the thirteenth century and the opening decades of the fourteenth.[61]

The most extreme manifestations of this rising trend are found in the fertile and densely peopled villages of the Vale of Taunton and Sedgemoor in Somerset, where fines reached £40, £60 and even £80 per virgate.[62] These figures, so often quoted, are however wholly exceptional: they are far in excess of the vast majority of fines anywhere else in England and, in this region itself, average fines are substantially lower. On the Bishop of Winchester's manor of Taunton the average fine during the years 1283–1348 was only £5.9*s*2*d* per virgate, and a relatively large virgate of around 40 acres at that. On the Bishop's Oxfordshire manor of Witney, on the other hand, where there was still land to be colonized, the average fine for a holding of comparable size was £1.18*s*10*d*.[63] In fact the levels of entry fines varied widely both between regions and within manors. On the Earl of Cornwall's estates in 1296–97, comprising over fifty manors in a score of counties, fines averaged 30*s* but ranged from 2*s* to £6. 13*s*4*d* per virgate. Doubtless the size of the virgates varied, but far less than the levels of fines.[64]

If fines ran high in parts of the south-west they were apt to be low in the north. On the manor of Wakefield in 1275, for example, a father paid only 8*s* to pass on a bovate to his two sons, although its acreage was probably only a third or less of the acreage of a Taunton virgate. A charge of 10*s* for nine acres of land at Wakefield, however, was unusually heavy. Fines on the Lancashire estates of the Earl of Lancaster in 1323–4, too, were usually assessed at a few pence per acre and only rarely reached 1*s* per acre.[65] The weight of this charge tends to increase as we move south, but nowhere approaches the levels on the Somerset estates of the bishopric of Winchester and Glastonbury Abbey. The highest fine per virgate on the Peterborough manors in Northamptonshire in the early fourteenth century was £5; fines of 66*s*8*d* were 'definitely high'; and the norm where a son succeeded his father was in the region of 20*s* to 30*s*. At Weedon Bec in the same county charges of £2. 13*s*4*d* for a half-virgate were considered oppressive.

How widely fines might vary within a single manor is illustrated by the court rolls of Chalgrave (Beds). In the years 1281–90 a son succeeding his father paid 13*s*4*d* for half a virgate, but a daughter taking up a similar holding from her father paid 10*s* and another following her mother paid only 6*s*8*d*. Men marrying heiresses with half virgates also paid very variously, for Simon son of Richard of Sharnbrook paid 16*s* (possibly including some element of marriage fine) and Walter son of Richard 2*s* only. (In this last instance there may have been some doubt about his wife's title to her land.) These were not nominal charges in a place where a virgate might be leased for as little as 5*s* a year, but neither do they reach the excessive heights found at Taunton.[66] On the Surrey manors of Chertsey abbey, too, fines on occasion exceeded £6 for a virgate, but most were 20*s* or less. Westward in Wiltshire they were substantially higher: Thomas de la Drove paid £14. 13*s*4*d* for entry to a virgate at Stratton in 1282, and two years later Henry Pipar paid £5.6*s*8*d* for half a virgate of demesne. At Sevenhampton in 1281 William son of Osbern le King even paid 6*s*8*d* for entry to his father's cottage.[67]

The wide disparities revealed by rents and fines in different places reflect many circumstances not all of which are fully explained by our sources. Differential fertility must account for some of the broad differences between regions: Lancashire, for example, simply lacked land as fertile as that of the Vale of Taunton. Again, nearness to markets, access to by-employments or ample availability of pasture might enhance the value of good and poor soils alike. There was also the factor of scarcity. Men would offer less even for good land in a colonizing manor like Witney, where there was still waste to be reclaimed, than at Taunton, where reserves available for assarting were virtually exhausted. In fixing the levels of fines the condition of a holding was often taken into account: they might be reduced or remitted if the holding had been neglected by its previous tenant. The circumstances of the prospective tenant might also be brought into the reckoning. Compassionate landlords relaxed fines on account of poverty while demanding high sums from those who were able to pay; and traditional presumptions in favour of preserving recognized lines of succession tended to result in widows or children being charged less than strangers.[68] Possibly the age of the incoming tenant (and therefore the interval before another fine would be payable) was borne in mind; and a high fine might compensate for a low rent and vice versa. On the Crowland estates a heavy fine might also entitle a tenant to quittance from tallage throughout his tenure. Finally, the force of custom and inefficient lordship sometimes nullified the tendency for the rising demand for land to push up charges. This is the most likely explanation for the static character of rents and farms on the earldom of Cornwall estates, until Queen Isabella introduced a less indulgent pattern of management after 1317 which produced increases of the order of 50 per cent over the next twenty years.[69]

Given the great variations in rents and fines, and the many influences they reflect, we must be cautious in framing general conclusions. Even so we are compelled to recognize that, over our period, increased demand for land pushed the rents and fines that men were willing to pay to progressively higher levels. This fact may have reflected two very different situations – that of land-hungry peasants striving for sufficient acres to provide subsistence for their families and that of men taking up land as a profitable investment, whether they intended to cultivate or sublet it. Since prices for agricultural produce rose over much of the later twelfth and the thirteenth centuries, and labour was either provided by peasant families themselves or obtainable at a cost which lagged behind prices, the profitability of a farm capable of yielding a sizeable surplus over and above the subsistence of its tenant was enhanced. The average virgate holding must certainly be regarded in this category in most years; consequently the fact that men paid high fines for virgates need not necessarily indicate an acute shortage of land. Indeed, many of the highest fines were paid by men taking up additional holdings, suggesting that their tenants were speculators or commercial farmers.

Recognition of that fact does not imply that we must ignore incontrovertible symptoms of economic stress elsewhere. For most villagers, with holdings less (and often very much less) than a virgate and paying charges that were heavy, farming was less a pursuit of profit than a struggle for survival. The smaller the holding the greater the proportion of its produce needed to sustain the tenant and his family, and the less there was over for sale; and the smallest holders must have needed to find additional sources of income or food supply. Entry fines and heriots weighed particularly heavily on smallholders and, unable to accumulate reserves, they must often have been compelled to resort to the moneylender to pay them. In many cases, too, their rents were relatively high: the 'newly enfeoffed men' at Bridgeham (Norfolk) in

1251, for example, owing 1*s* or even 2*s* (with tallage and other servile charges) for half-acre tofts, look like tenants paying very dearly for very little land.[70] The multiplication of tenants with exiguous holdings and the growth of what amounted to a rural proletariat are testimony to the progressive failure of productive capacity and employment opportunities to keep pace with the number of people. That failure was one clear sign that the great medieval age of expansion was reaching its term.

Competition for employment

The tendencies in the distribution of land carry the implication that growing numbers of countrymen were being compelled to seek part at least of their livelihood otherwise than from the cultivation of their own family farms. Many joined the stream of immigrants into towns, and others were absorbed, at least for a significant part of their time, into the ranks of country craftsmen – textile and leather workers, miners, manufacturers of metal goods and so forth. There remained very many villagers who had to depend to some degree on employment as agricultural labourers in order to supplement whatever living they could wrest from the land in their possession. As villages became more populous, as the number of men with holdings inadequate for subsistence increased, competition for employment as well as for land was intensified; and, if competition for land raised its cost to tenants, competition for employment tended to depress the rewards of labour.

The evidence for this tendency is harder to handle than the evidence for the movement of prices, for the data we have do not provide an adequate base for generalizations about national trends (see pp. 64–9). Manorial accounts often present information about wages in ways that are incomplete or difficult to use comparatively. At Sevenhampton in 1273–74, for example, when we are told that 10*s*3*d* was expended *in omnimodo blado sarclando*, or at Mere in 1296–97, 28*s in expensis autumpnalibus*, we have no indication of the rewards of individuals or the time spent in earning them. Even if we are given the rate at which casual labourers were paid for the task or the day, we cannot discover how many days an individual worked in a given period; we can establish wage rates but not earnings. The problems are even more daunting when we turn to the full-time employees. Again, at Sevenhampton, we are not told what each full-time employee was paid, merely that the annual total stipends of a hayward, seven ploughmen and two carters amounted to 47*s*. Even when information about the earnings of individuals is given, moreover, money wages were frequently not the end of the story. At Sevenhampton the hayward, ploughmen and carters were each paid, over and above their money wage, a quarter of barley every ten weeks, and oatmeal was ground for their pottage. At Mere, on the other hand, labourers got their quarter of barley only every twelve weeks; and on the Bec manor of Combe in 1307–8, while some workers got a quarter every ten weeks, the hog-herd received his livery only every twelve weeks, a cowherd-harrower a livery every fourteen weeks, and a dairymaid hers every sixteen weeks in winter only. Here, furthermore, these payments in kind were of barley mixed with oats and they were suspended during the harvest season when the estate labourers fed at the lord's table.[71]

Although the piece-rates paid to casual labourers might be said to present the fewest problems of interpretation, close examination reveals a number of disturbing discrepancies between the two major series. The longest, that of threshing and winnowing rates on eight of the Bishop of Winchester's manors, demonstrates that wages remained virtually stationary throughout the thirteenth century, and that even by 1310–20 they were scarcely a quarter higher than they had been a century before.[72] These wage rates, in other words, increased less than a quarter as much as grain prices over the same period. The other major series, drawn from two of the Abbot of Westminster's manors in the vicinity of London, reveals rewards that were not only substantially higher but also far more variable than those on the Winchester manors.[73] Moreover, from the beginning of the Westminster series in the 1250s they tended to keep pace with prices (at least with the best price series we have, which is heavily dependent on Winchester data).

There are good reasons for assuming that neither the Winchester nor the Westminster data are typical of wage rates in England as a whole. The Bishops of Winchester were conservative, even miserly employers, and on the majority of manors the rates they paid remained stable for long periods. At Ecchinswell (Hants), for example, the wages for threshing and winnowing a heaped quarter each of wheat, barley and oats, scarcely varied from 3*d* in the eighty years after 1220, while at West Wycombe (Bucks) it remained at just under 3½*d* from the 1250s to the 1300s. Such rigidity strongly suggests that wages were being fixed by custom rather than by market forces. All in all the Winchester data probably present too pessimistic a picture of the fortunes of the English labourer. On the other hand, there can be little doubt that the data from the Westminster Abbey manors of Knightsbridge and Ebury present too optimistic a picture. We know little of the precise workings of the London labour market, but we do know that wages in the vicinity of the capital were far higher than elsewhere: between the 1250s and the 1340s the rates for threshing and winnowing on these Westminster manors exceeded those on the Winchester manors by between 50 and 100 per cent. By contrast it is possible that London wheat prices were not substantially above the national average at this time.

The Westminster wages seem to be alone in their tendency to match price increases. On the manor of Hinderclay (Suffolk), for example, agricultural wage rates increased by less than 5 per cent in the five decades after 1270, compared with a 25 per cent increase in the 'national' price level.[74] Falling real wages is also implied by the evidence we have of building wages expressed in terms of the price of consumables. Once again the evidence is less than perfect, but the real wages of these craftsmen appear to have been lower than in the 1260s during the ensuing decades, and a tendency towards improvement in the opening decade of the fourteenth century was again reversed by the famine prices of 1315–17.[75] To put the matter another way, a labourer needed to work longer in order to earn enough to purchase a given quantity of foodstuffs; and, in villages that grew more overcrowded as the thirteenth century progressed, it cannot be assumed that he was in fact able to find additional work. This combination of falling real earnings per job done and the growing difficulty of securing jobs at all may help to explain the apparently disproportionate rise of mortality among the village poor in the famine years of the early fourteenth century.[76]

It is much more difficult to establish trends in the earnings of full-time manorial employees – the *famuli* who served throughout the year as ploughmen, carters, shepherds and the like. There may well have been a tendency for their money wages to settle down at a customary figure, at least for prolonged periods, and so to fall in real terms;[77] but money wages were not uncommonly a minor element in the rewards of the *famuli*. A quarter of barley, or of mixed barley and wheat, every ten weeks, together possibly with doles of food or meals provided by the lord, were worth a good deal more than the five shillings a year or so that the Sevenhampton ploughman or carter earned in cash. These payments in kind, moreover, were not devalued by the rising curve of prices: on the contrary, in principle they were the labourer's hedge against inflation. Even in this respect, however, we must not take too optimistic a view of the labourer's lot. His earnings in kind were not inevitably immutable. The Bishop of Winchester reduced food liveries and substituted cheaper for dearer grains in 1282, a year when the harvest was poor and prices were high; by 1300 the Abbot of Ramsey paid his *famuli* a slightly smaller amount of cheaper grains than their livery of wheat and barley in 1250; and at Oakington the Abbot of Crowland in 1322–3 apparently reduced the grain liveries to his ploughmen and shepherd during part of the year *propter caristiam bladi.*[78] Even the full-time labourer, with a substantial part of his earnings received in kind, was not entirely insulated against the tendency of real wages to fall.

At the same time the indications are that this trend of real wages, or at least of agricultural real wages, did not persist right down to the Black Death. The effect of the violent price rises in the second decade of the fourteenth century was to push up money wages, and the gains of the labourer were not thereafter lost, or not wholly so. Piece-rates for threshing and winnowing, indeed, continued to rise slowly down to the 1340s, and if by that time other wage rates had fallen back a little they were still better than those paid at the end of the thirteenth century. The fact, moreover, that the cost of consumables also fell slowly from the 1320s gave the labourer· some increase in the real value of his cash earnings. The full-time *famuli*, who received more of their wages in kind, may well have gained less in these years than casual labourers; but it is hard not to see some improvement, however marginal, in the conditions of labour during the generation before the Black Death.

In any event, the state of the labour market was an important influence on changes in agricultural organization and the fortunes of landlords in the period under review. When that period opens the problems of providing satisfactorily for the labour requirements of seignorial demesnes had not everywhere been solved. In so far as they had been solved, a good deal of compulsion went into the solution: slaves worked full-time because they were not free and villeins part-time if they wished to keep their land, for labour was a great part of the rent they paid for it. The need for compulsion may well indicate some shortage of available labour and the rapid decline of slavery after 1066 might make any such shortage worse. By the opening of the thirteenth century, however, the labour market was very much more favourable to employers and, since most men were countrymen, to agricultural employers in particular. A growing population provided reserves of almost every type of labourer lords might desire: men anxious to take up villein tenures for which they could be compelled to work part-time; men with small agricultural holdings who needed casual work to supplement the inadequate produce of their land; and landless men who sought full-time employment. Labour, moreover, was not only available, for when workers were paid in cash their real cost tended to fall. These were among the conditions which, throughout the century, made large-scale demense production both possible and profitable.

It seems likely, however, that these conditions, which had been so exceptionally favourable to lords of manors, had begun to worsen by the third decade of the fourteenth century. In particular, in the present context, the real wages of agricultural workers began to rise and the increase in costs entailed is likely to have been one influence cramping the scale of demesne enterprise a whole generation before the Black Death dramatically gave new strength to the bargaining position of labourers. The movement of wages after 1320 suggests that the long-term growth of population had been checked, or that it may have been reversed, by the famines of the second decade of the century. Those famines caused heavy mortality, and it seems likely that it was especially heavy among the poorer sections of the community (see pp. 57–8). Their vulnerability to dearth is likely to reflect, at least in part, the growing difficulties labourers had experienced in earning their daily bread. In 1310, indeed, the Abbot of Battle calculated that the value of the three meals a day he provided for tenants doing labour services was greater than the sum for which wage labourers would do the same work: the conclusion must be that labourers could not earn three square meals a day even for themselves, let alone something over for their families (see p. 58). The miserable rewards of labour were one foundation of the flourishing demesne economy of the thirteenth century; and the fact that its rewards were miserable also explains why, when that economy was at its most robust, wage labourers to an ever increasing extent took the places of older types of service.

The limits of expansion

In certain districts the expansion of the cultivated land, and even of the ranks of the tenantry, ended at an early date. We have already noted the virtual stagnation of the Felden of Warwickshire after 1086, and there are indications that the tenants of Glastonbury Abbey's Wiltshire manors, who multiplied with great rapidity in the century after Domesday, ceased after 1189 to increase significantly.[79] In other places, by contrast, the expansion of the cultivated area continued well into the fourteenth century, perhaps most dramatically in Cornwall and west Devon where, after a late start, colonization on a considerable scale continued to the eve of the Black Death. Somewhat less spectacular assarting was also taking place at this time in parts of neighbouring Somerset and Wiltshire, while in the west and north-west substantial additions were made to the agricultural acres of Cheshire, Lancashire, Shropshire and Herefordshire. Late assarting was also a feature of woodlands throughout the country: of the New Forest (Hants), the wooded parts of Essex, the Forest of Dean and the Peak Forest. When all due account has been taken of these areas, however, the great weight of the evidence clearly suggests that both an early cessation of assarting and its continuance on a large scale into the fourteenth century were exceptional. In most areas a progressive slowing down in the rate of new settlement began around the middle of the thirteenth century.

At Wigston Magna in Leicestershire there were already more people in 1086 than there were to be in the reign of Elizabeth, and while the expansion of agriculture towards the village frontier continued until around 1300, it no longer kept pace with the growth of population.[80] Here migration to Leicester and other towns relieved pressure on the land, just as elsewhere the availability of assartable land within reasonable reach may have provided a like relief. The growth of a country cloth industry, especially in the generation or two before the Black Death, and a development of mining for metals or coal in some districts, likewise mitigated the tendency for population to outrun available supplies of land. None the less there is much to suggest that over a good deal of England the opportunities open to the surplus people of the countryside were running out by the late thirteenth century. The foundation of new towns was ceasing and very many towns were reaching somewhere near the limits of their medieval growth.[81] The slowing down of urban growth, coinciding with the attainment by so many villages of something like the furthest frontiers of cultivable land available to them, imprisoned more and more men in overcrowded rural communities. Even the colonizing areas of the Lincolnshire marshlands, making all allowance for the ancillary sources of income furnished by the 'all-providing fen', appear at least as full of people as those old-settled communities in which the cultivated area had long ceased to grow. In the Sussex Weald, too, the twin pressures of population growth and landlords seeking to expand their demesne pastures created a large body of landless and near landless who were forced to migrate in search of seasonal work on coastal farms.[82]

Even in Yorkshire, cottars with less than 5 acres of land were in some places very thick upon the ground in the late thirteenth century. Sometimes, as at Kirkby Moorside where 60 out of 240 tenants were cottars or at Thoralby where the proportion was 51 out of around 80, the explanation may well be that the moorland offered scope for pastoral enterprise. At the same time there are comparable figures at Cottingham in the Hull Valley (137 cottars out of 365 tenants) and, in the Yorkshire plain, at Buttercrambe (62 out of 134), Riccall (45 out of 82) and Stillington (48 out of 87).[83] In these half dozen villages the overall proportion of cottars is around 40 per cent of the tenantry. A similar proportion appears to have prevailed generally in the county, for around 1300 on twenty-four manors where holdings are expressed in acres, 42 per cent of the tenantry had under 5 acres and 21 per cent had under one acre. In Northumberland at about the same time 30 per cent of tenants had under 5 acres and 19 per cent had under one acre, and in

Lancashire the figures were 32 per cent and 13 per cent respectively. The fact that these data derive from the northern shires, where there seems to have been more elbowroom than in many parts of the south, adds to their significance and underlines the very high proportion of villagers throughout the country with arable holdings inadequate for the support of a family. (See below, pp. 143–50 for further discussion of the size of holdings.)

Smallholders, and in particular men with at best a very modest share in the village arable, were not of course newcomers on the rural scene. Bordars and cottars were a substantial class in 1086 and there were also the Domesday *servi*, most of whom were totally landless. The impression from every quarter of the land, however, is that the number of landless or near landless men grew steadily in the ensuing generations, even though no small proportion of them are screened from our view. There is, for example, frequent mention in many parts of England of 'undersettles' who held some small plot sublet by a more prosperous neighbour;[85] and there were also, as the Littleport jurors testified, 'anilepymen' or even 'anilepywomen' who held no land but who might rent a house.[86] Countryfolk so inadequately endowed must have earned much of their living as labourers. The growth of this rural proletariat depending on wages which lamentably failed to keep pace with rising prices is one of the clearest indications of how severely population pressed on the supply of land by the end of the thirteenth century; and the size of this proletariat can easily be underrated. At Wotton Underwood (Bucks) early in the fourteenth century there were twenty-two tenants of land; but the village population also included thirty-one *valetti* who appear to be landless. Many of the latter, moreover, had the same family names as the villeins, suggesting that the landless class was recruited in part from younger sons excluded from inheritance of any part of the family patrimony. Some, of course, might in due course step into dead men's shoes; but the size of the landless group at Wotton Underwood points to the failure there of agricultural expansion to keep pace with a rising population.[87]

The limitations of expansion may be looked at from another angle, namely the productivity of the land. Reclaimed land was not infrequently marginal in one way or another. Fenland assarts, for example, were frequently precarious. The Bishop of Ely's tiny demesne at Elm in 1251, it was said, 'sometimes decreases and sometimes increases on account of the sea' (in other words, sometimes more of it and sometimes less was liable to flooding); and both here and in the Norfolk marshland a good deal of reclaimed land was once again inundated in the early fourteenth century. Much the same was true of the Sussex and Kentish marshes. Expenditure beyond the revenues of the manor was required to repair flood damage at Appledore in the 1290s, and at Ebony, despite heavy investment by Prior Henry of Eastry, there was little or no permanent increase in the demesne area under cultivation.[88] This makes it less surprising that landlords very often handed over responsibility for reclamation and marshland drainage to the peasantry; but while the latter built up communal organizations and customary codes to defend their gains, their horizons were almost inevitably limited. The lack of really comprehensive controls over drainage and embanking, although that lack was in part made good by commissions of sewers, contributed to the precarious character of medieval fen reclamations.

Apart from being precarious, assarts were frequently modestly fertile, a fact indicated by the prominence of oats as a crop on reclaimed land. Oats bulked large on the Bishop of Ely's demesne at Wisbech in the early fourteenth century and even larger on the neighbouring manor of Coldham in Elm, on land described as 'morose and marshy' of which only one acre in ten could be cultivated each year. Marsh intakes in Kent were very little better and wheat acreage was increased only by heavy and perhaps uneconomic applications of manure, marl and lime. Nor was marginal arable peculiar to the colonized fenland. Arable villages were established during the central Middle Ages on Domesday sheep pastures in the Norfolk and Suffolk Breckland, a district so sandy that it approximates to desert; at places like Aunby and Holywell on the heaths of west Lincolnshire; on the high and dry wolds of Yorkshire; and well up in the moors of Devon and Cornwall.[89] How very marginal some of this land was is strikingly illustrated by the records of the forest justices at Pickering in Yorkshire in 1334. The justices uncovered some 1400 acres of reclamations taken in over several generations. The cropping record they assembled is incomplete, but only 23 acres seem to have ever carried a normal sequence of winter- and spring-grown grains. Other assarts had been sown only with oats; others again were cropped successively with oats and hay; but most frequently of all, this new land was cropped intermittently or for a period of years and then permitted to revert to pasture.[90]

Land use in the Pickering forest assarts shows very clearly that reclamation might be literally a 'journey to the margin'. Even when villages merely made only modest additions to their arable they might well be putting under the plough land which had been left 'waste' precisely because it was of lower fertility. This was not, of course, inevitably true: much of the land won from standing woodland was good land for the grain farmer. On the other hand, the fact that much of the land pressed into arable service during the central Middle Ages was marginal in the qualitative as well as the locative sense is strongly suggested by what happened in the generations after 1349. As the pressure of population was relaxed villages on the poorer soils contracted their territories and in some instances disappeared altogether. These were lands that men ploughed in their necessity rather than from choice.

We are on much less certain ground when we consider the fertility of the old-settled land. The view that much old-settled land declined in fertility, and that new reclamations often merely replaced tired and worn-out land, has recently been resurrected.[91] The most substantial body of surviving yield data, deriving from the demesnes of the bishops of Winchester for the period 1208 to 1349,[92] lends some support to the thesis of declining grain yields. At the same time the data for wheat exhibit no clear trend, and we must be careful not to overstate the extent of falling yields. Even so, the performance of the Winchester demesnes is likely to have been superior to that of land in the hands of most peasant smallholders. The man with only enough land to feed a family, or less than enough, must have been tempted to overcrop and so deprive his land of the benefits of fallow; in times of dearth he might be forced to reduce sowing rates to the detriment of the next harvest; and at all times he was under pressure to expand arable onto pasture land and thus curtail manure supplies that more abundant livestock might have afforded.

The increasing numbers of landless, and the seemingly progressive decline in the size of the average holding as the thirteenth century wore on, had their inevitable consequences, particularly since a high proportion of the peasantry had resources too small to put anything to reserve for an evil day. Further, seignorial charges compelled most peasants to market everything they did not themselves consume; and even great lords took no particular care to carry forward in their barns the surplus of one year to the next. In these circumstances, especially for that large section of the population existing on or below the subsistence margin, a bad harvest spelled disaster. As Matthew Paris graphically recounts, the successive poor harvests of 1257 and 1258 drove prices up to four or five times their normal level. Even the rich depended on imports from Germany and the Low Countries for their salvation, and many of the poor died of hunger and pestilence, until in the end solemn fasts and processions were said to have effected a change for the better in the long spell of inclement weather.[93] The Dunstable annalist also noted the tribulations of these years, when the convent ale ran short for lack of malt, necessitating the purchase of wine instead.[94]

Most revealing of all, however, are the implications of the heriots paid when tenants died in the century after 1245 on five Winchester manors: Taunton (Soms), Fareham, Waltham and Meon (south

Hants), and Wargrave (Berks). They indicate a noticeable increase in mortality rates over this period, rising to periodic peaks coinciding with or following immediately upon years of high prices (years, in other words, of below average harvests). These peaks came not only in 1258, but also in 1248, 1253, 1272, 1289, 1297, and above all in 1308–19. Apparently, too, in these bad years mortality was especially heavy among those who paid their heriots in cash and not in the form of animals. These payers of money were usually the poorer villagers, men with few or no beasts and, by inference, with few or no acres of land. That the death-rate in years of dearth was especially high among the village poor has its obvious significance.[95] Although the precise orders of magnitude may be disputed, it is difficult to deny that at least in the areas represented by these manors, 'every appreciable failure of harvests could result in large increases in deaths', and that in them village society was 'balanced on the margin of subsistence'. The evidence also suggests that the situation was deteriorating progressively. Eight of the years between 1308 and 1319 were years of high, in some cases dramatically high, mortality; and, even after these exceptionally bad years, others between 1321 and 1345 were marked by death rates high compared with the bad years of the thirteenth century. Other evidence points in the same direction: in the early thirteenth century prices were pushed up when wheat failed to yield three and one third fold the seed sown, later in the century yields of three and one half fold were needed to avert a price rise, and by the early fourteenth century a rise of prices began when yields were nearer four fold.[96]

In some of the more populous and old-settled parts of the country, then, it looks as though famine conditions had become almost endemic by the early fourteenth century. This situation lends support to the contention that there was an appreciable fall in the average expectation of life between 1250 and 1349.[97] And sheer pressure of population generated the movement of wages and prices so unfavourable to the labourer, strikingly illustrated by an inquest jury at Barnhorn in Sussex in 1310: it reported that, in view of the cost of food with which the lord provided his tenants when they performed customary services, harrowing and mowing were costing more than they need do, for labourers could be hired to do this work for 4*d* each whereas the cost of feeding the tenants was 5*d*. Admittedly the latter were furnished with a generous three meals a day, but the implications are clear enough: a labourer's wage was scarcely enough to feed himself, let alone a family.[98] It cannot be assumed, of course, that the lot of the peasantry was everywhere as hard as on the Winchester manors and at Barnhorn. Economic expansion can still be discerned in some districts, especially those taking on a partially industrialized complexion; and pioneers were still at work in others, especially those which joined late in the movement of agricultural advance. Even the experiences of the five Winchester manors discussed above were not identical, for the rate at which the Taunton death rate increased between 1245 and 1348 was about double that on the other four manors.[99] Conditions at Taunton did not apply everywhere, but by the opening years of the fourteenth century the living conditions of the majority of Englishmen had worsened, sometimes drastically, compared with a century earlier. The precariousness of many people's existence, their sensitivity to catastrophe, was soon dramatically exposed in the agrarian crisis of 1315–22.

At the same time a simple equation of land and people is, by itself, an inadequate explanation of the economic problems of the early fourteenth century. There are indications from many quarters that, at the latest by the last quarter of the thirteenth century, the exuberantly profitable demesne economy of the previous generations was running out of steam. The late thirteenth-century manorial records of Ramsey abbey display a 'cutback from that bustling life of full employment on the demesne for market production, which had been realized at the mid-century'; and on Ely estates at the same time 'earlier expansive tendencies had begun to go into reverse, and leaseholds were carved out of the demesne in a few places'. The curtailment of seignorial enterprise was even more marked on the estates of the bishop of Winchester: his demesne, which had been over 13,000 acres in 1269, fell below 11,000 acres in 1284, below 10,000 acres in 1310, and below 9,000 acres after 1321.[100] Falling yields, as we have noted, may have played a part in bringing about this contraction, with the least productive acres being the first to be discarded. But perhaps more significant was the behaviour of rents and prices, which increasingly tempted estate managers to choose leasing rather than cultivation for the least productive or the more inconveniently sited areas of the demesne. The upward trend of grain prices was punctuated by a number of quite severe setbacks in the last quarter of the thirteenth century and the first decade of the fourteenth, while rents in the same period frequently rose with undiminished or even enhanced vigour.

By no means a universal phenomenon in its early years, this new mood of seignorial retrenchment gained momentum after about 1320. From about the same date there was also some slackening in the competition for land and a significant increase in the number of unwanted holdings in some parts, a downturn in wool exports, and the onset of a severe urban depression. With few exceptions the era of expansion was over well before the Black Death. How far this reverse can be explained in terms of a severe check to population growth, or even a downturn of the population curve following upon the heavy mortalities of the famine years of the second decade, is a question that at present cannot be answered with any certainty. That population growth was checked seems altogether likely, and that this check contributed to changing economic conditions during the pre-plague generation is a reasonable hypothesis; but that the population trend was the sole explanation of these changing conditions seems less probable.

A formidable case has been made for regarding the period of severe harvest failures and livestock epidemics between 1315 and 1322 as a dividing line in the history of the medieval countryside.[101] A succession of disasters made these eight years one of the most troubled periods in English agricultural history. The first signs of stress can be traced to the harvest of 1314, which was poor because of the wet conditions, and grain prices rose sharply in the summer months of 1315. Torrential rain throughout that summer turned the harvest of 1315 into a disaster. Grain, already in short supply, became extremely scarce, and the price of wheat, which had averaged between 5s and 6s per quarter in the first decade of the century, reached 26s8d in many parts of the country, and was as high as 40s on occasions in London and 44s in Leicester. Prices other than grain prices also rose and there is much evidence of a widespread scarcity of all foodstuffs. The dearth of food doubtless encouraged the spread of virulent epidemics of an enteric type, greatly increasing an already high death rate. The harvest of 1316 was, if anything, even more disastrous than that of the previous year and conditions almost certainly worsened. It was only with an improved harvest in 1317 that suffering was alleviated, but the end of the food scarcity did not come until the bountiful harvest of 1318. This harvest did not, however, by any means mark the end of the distress. Widespread sheep murrains had accompanied the harvest failures of the previous years and much other livestock must also have been slaughtered for food or perished from starvation and disease. In 1319 a terrible epidemic spread among cattle and oxen throughout the country, and between 1319 and 1321 cattle herds perished on an unprecedented scale. Yet again in 1320 and 1321 the harvests failed and grain prices were driven up to levels approaching those of 1315–17. The real end of the crises, therefore, came only after 1322.

Such a prolonged succession of severe crises would have gravely damaged the fortunes of even a well-balanced and prosperous society, so there can be little wonder that it wrought havoc in a society with so high a proportion of its members living so close to the margin of subsistence. Most directly and most sorely afflicted were undoubtedly poor families with little or no land and with scant reserves to draw upon; but heavy losses of sheep struck at all who owned them, and losses of oxen and breeding cows at the supply of draught animals essential for the cultivation of arable holdings, large or small. Landlords, therefore, had to face heavy costs in re-equipping their demesnes and perhaps were the more easily persuaded to jettison the less productive parts of them. They might also be influenced in this same direction by a tendency for profits to decline which seems to be implied by the movement of prices and wages during the twenty years before the Black Death. The average price of grain in the 1330s and the 1340s was 20 per cent lower than it had been in the 1280s, and agricultural wages were between 25 and 40 per cent higher (see p. 66). Profit margins were almost inevitably narrowed.

Not all the acres shed from the demesne were taken up by the peasantry, and in many places there were peasant holdings which could not be let, or not without compelling tenants to take them up against their will.[102] Some vacancies were shortlived, and were obviously the result of the sharply increased death rate and the widespread poverty caused by the famines and murrains; but others persisted or even became more numerous. By the 1340s, indeed, the amount of uncultivated land had reached serious dimensions in some counties: in Sussex, apart from flooded land, 5,600 acres were untilled, and at least 4,870 acres had gone out of cultivation in Cambridgeshire. These amounts are not dramatic, particularly when measured against the area which continued to be cultivated, but at least they show a significant trend away from the almost continuous increase of the area under crops during earlier generations. A cutback in the level of population may explain something and, of course, in some places special causes operated: Scottish raiding in the northern counties as far south as Lancashire and Yorkshire; and also the failure of drainage systems in sea marshes and fens, flooding land previously cultivated or grazed. Contemporaries, however, pointed to other reasons than these for land lying untilled: losses of beasts and crop failures in Lincolnshire in 1322, and the poverty of both land and tenants in Derbyshire about the same time. In 1342, too, the jurors of the *Nonarum Inquisitiones* frequently explained low assessments by reference to 'sterile', 'boggy', 'sandy', 'worn-out' soils, and to the poverty of tenants and their *impotencia*, their inability to cultivate land that had once been ploughed.[103]

The poverty of tenants is frequently traceable to the losses (especially of working animals) suffered in the bad years from 1315 to 1322. It was also implicit in their social situation. Large sections of the peasantry were liable to heavy seignorial exactions and, increasingly, to mounting government impositions as well.[104] The fact, moreover, that the long rise of the population curve had moved a progressively larger proportion of villagers towards the margin of subsistence or even below it meant that a principal manifestation of the 'calamity sensitiveness' of

English rural society was the calamity of the village poor, impotent to cultivate land that was there for the taking. At the same time, where the records speak of poverty or inability, a degree of unwillingness on the part of potential tenants to take over land may be concealed. The increasing number of tenants who had to be forced to take up holdings suggests that the lessening of population pressure was generating an increasing resistance to seeking a living from marginal holdings. To that extent abandoned acres may often indicate a new-found ability to discriminate between better and worse land rather than that formerly productive soils had become exhausted. Some men may even have migrated in search of better land; while the choice of others to refuse worse was made easier because they could be increasingly content as labourers, for in the 1330s and 1340s real wages were higher than at any time since wage data became available more than a century before.

These, then, were the limits beyond which economic expansion during the central Middle Ages failed to proceed. The situation revealed by the records of the early fourteenth century reflects the inability of the society of that time to create the supplies of capital and investment opportunities that would have provided outlet for a growing population. Individuals, of course, did save and invest: enterprising peasants, some among the rising gentry, and high-farming prelates and peers. Even among 'high-farmers', however, the rate of saving was apt to be relatively modest (see pp. 232–3), and most of those with the largest resources on the whole preferred consumption or hoarding to investment. As for the peasant, his potentiality for saving was narrowed by the tendency for the average amount of land per head to fall and was all too often extinguished by seignorial or public charges. The medieval countryside, therefore, lacked some of the capacities for self-improvement. Nor was salvation for the countryman to be found in the urban and industrial sectors of the economy. Those sectors absorbed many immigrants from the agricultural sector but, except perhaps in some textile and mining regions, they were proving less and less capable of doing so in the generations around 1300. The countryman's, and especially the smaller countryman's, dilemma was a real one: the scarcity of opportunities for him to break into craft or commerce on the one hand; and, on the other, poverty and *impotencia* in his village. These were the basic limits reached by the expanding agricultural society of the English Middle Ages.

In conclusion it must be mentioned that in seeking to present as clear lines of description and argument as possible we have avoided detailing the controversies which surround so many of the topics with which this chapter has been concerned. Our conclusions represent what seems to us the balance of probabilities so far as research has gone at present.

This is not to say that all problems, perhaps even that many problems have been settled, or that there is any consensus among historians about a number of key issues. As we have seen, estimates of population at different dates still vary widely; what precisely the population trend was in the generation or two before the Black Death remains a matter of debate; and differences on these matters are reflected in very different assessments of the living standards of English villagers at the end of the long period of economic expansion. In the face of these debates conclusions can only be provisional and reached in the knowledge that debates, and more important research, will continue.

Chapter 3

Markets

The deep-seated problems facing the medieval economy became evident enough in the generation before the plague came in 1349, but the existence of these problems in no way detracts from the fact that the period since Domesday, and in all likelihood since the tenth century, had been one of cumulative expansion. One impetus behind expansion was a growing population, and economic expansion in turn made it possible for more people to be supported, although apparently with increasing difficulty. The interrelationship of people and resources (resources of land in particular) is a part only, however, although an important part, of a more complex pattern. Economic expansion involved more than the taking in of new land and an increasingly intensive exploitation of soil and livestock. Other features of these same generations were the growth of production designed for the market, the increase in the volume and intensity of exchanges, and the increasing sophistication of the institutional framework facilitating exchanges.[1] The development of commercial opportunities, in turn, was likewise a stimulus to production; and, in the more developed economic organization which emerged, achievement was measured not only by the satisfaction of immediate consumption needs but also in terms of profits. In that organization, therefore, the price of commodities became a matter of increasing moment and the trend of prices became increasingly significant as an indicator of economic opportunity.

The trend of prices

It must immediately be admitted that the examination of medieval price trends is no easy undertaking. The amount of material surviving before the year 1208 is very small and that which survives for the rest of the period down to 1349 is dominated by the incomparable series of accounts from the lands of the Bishops of Winchester. The researcher is further hampered by a bewildering diversity of local measures, by price levels varying from district to district, and by the slightness of information about the conditions under which a particular bargain was struck. These were the good reasons why the remarkable pioneering work of Thorold Rogers[2] had few imitators until very recently. It was not until the 1920s that Lord Beveridge tried systematically to exploit the Winchester series of accounts, showing that by comparison with the period 1200–49 wheat prices in 1300–49 had increased by 58 per cent, wool by 63 per cent, oats by 64 per cent, oxen by 67 per cent, barley by 69 per cent and salt by 92 per cent. It was Beveridge's further contention that the upward trend of prices in the thirteenth and early fourteenth centuries was 'only the slackening end of a movement which other figures show beginning about the middle of the twelfth century'.[3] Subsequent investigators,[4] who have extended Beveridge's enquiry and refined the methods he applied to it, have basically reinforced his findings and in particular have endorsed his suggestion that a period of especially rapid price rises was on the point of ending when the Winchester accounts begin. In aggregate this work indicates that, during the central Middle Ages, England was submitted to the pressures of inflation as well as the pressures of a growing population.

The study of prices over this period, of course, shows a multiplicity of short-term fluctuations, some of them very violent. Prices responded most dramatically to harvests so that wheat which sold for 2s 5½d a quarter in 1244 sold for 3s 4d in 1245 and 6s 5d in 1246. Livestock epidemics similarly sent up the price of animals; the price of wool responded to government intervention in the export trade or to the weight of taxes on it; and all prices tended to rise when much clipped coin was circulating and to fall when the currency was restored. These short-run fluctuations, however, do not conceal the long-run trend. How to present the data in the most effective fashion is another matter, for the points of comparison we choose will affect the rates at which prices rose and may mask the different behaviour of the prices of different commodities. The broad comparison between half centuries which Beveridge made partially conceals the real increase of prices over the whole period, while a simple comparison of decennial averages in the 1160s and the 1340s obliterates many of the major fluctuations which occurred in the intervening years. For these reasons there is advantage in looking separately at the three sub-periods for which we have adequate evidence – roughly speaking the decades between 1160 and 1210, between 1210 and 1320, and between 1320 and 1347.

The middle and longest of these periods was a time of steady rather than spectacular inflation, although it culminated in the years of catastrophic harvest failures and recurrent livestock epidemics in the second and early part of the third decades of the fourteenth century. These were also years when prices soared, so that in 1310–20 the price of wheat was 120 per cent higher than in 1210–20, the price of cows 80 per cent higher, of ewes 90 per cent higher, of wool 150 per cent higher and of salt 200 per cent higher. After the effects of famine and disease had subsided, usually by the mid-1320s, prices fell back from these peaks; and by the 1340s most prices were 30–40 per cent lower than they had been three decades earlier. The existence of an inflationary trend is evident enough; but particularly if we stop short of the scarcity decade between 1310 and 1320 the weight of inflationary pressure does not seem to have been excessively severe.

Figure 1   Price movements 1160–1350 (decennial mean).

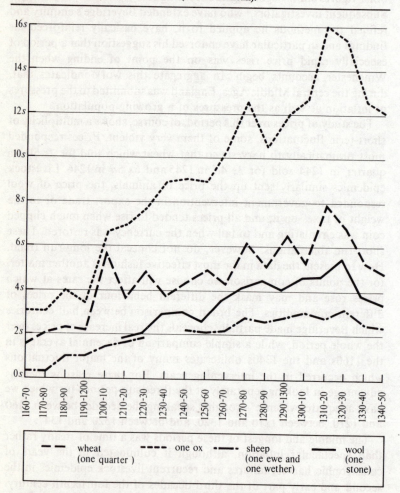

Constructed from data compiled by Farmer (1956, 1957, 1969) and Lloyd (1973)

It is another matter if we adopt as our baseline the 1160s rather than the second decade of the thirteenth century. Compared with prices in the 1160s oxen and ewes in the 1340s cost four times as much, cows three-and-a-half times as much, and wheat three times as much; while in the decade 1310–20 prices had been four and a half to five times as high as in the 1160s. These proportions indicate how severe inflation was in the late twelfth century. If we compare the 1160s with the opening decade of the thirteenth century, in the latter period the prices of oxen were 118 per cent higher, of ewes 132 per cent higher, of cows 155 per cent higher and of wheat 264 per cent higher than forty years earlier. The greater part of these increases, moreover, appears to have been concentrated in the years around 1200, suggesting a rate of inflation at that time which must have affected budgets severely. What evidence there is seems to indicate that this was was something new. Prices of livestock, at least, were apparently remarkably stable during the tenth, eleventh and much of the twelfth centuries. In the reign of Aethelstan oxen were valued at 30*d*; over 150 years later they were reckoned in Domesday Book to be worth 24*d* and 30*d*; and in the 1160s and 1170s the King seldom paid more than 3*s*. By 1200 he would pay double that amount.[5]

Table 2 Prices of Crown purchases, 1190–1210[6]

	Wheat (per summa)	Oats (per summa)	Oxen	Sheep	Pigs
	s. d.	*s. d.*	*s. d.*	*s. d.*	*s. d.*
1190	1 7½	10½	—	—	—
1191	1 6	—	—	—	—
1192	1 10	1 0	3 0	5	1 0
1193	—	2 0	3 0	5	1 0
1194	—	—	3 10	6	8½
1195	—	—	3 10¾	6	—
1196	—	—	3 3	4	—
1197	—	—	3 10	6	—
1198	—	—	3 0	1 0	1 0
1199	4 0	—	—	4	—
1200	—	11	5 11	—	—
1201	6 4	3 8	6 4	6	—
1202	7 8¾	—	6 6	1 0	—
1203	7 7	—	6 4½	—	2 7¼
1204	—	—	9 0	1 1¾	—
1205	—	1 8½	7 6	—	—
1206	3 11¼	3 4	5 2¼	8	1 8
1207	—	—	5 10	—	2 6½
1208	—	—	6 6	10	1 6¾
1209	—	—	6 6½	—	2 8¼
1210	—	—	5 11½	—	2 3½

The evidence, then, points to a period of very rapid inflation for a short period around 1200 and a steady inflationary trend from the 1160s to the 1320s. At the latter point it first tailed off and then was decisively reversed; but even so, on the eve of the Black Death, prices were running at three to four times their levels of two hundred years earlier. It is another matter to explain this phenomenon, and how to explain the violent upsurge of prices around 1200 is most difficult of all. A contributory influence on the long-term inflationary trend may have been the direction of bullion flow and the supply of currency within the country. There are some indications that bullion was flowing into the country during much of the thirteenth century and in the early fourteenth, a movement closely connected with England's flourishing export trade in wool and metals. From the 1320s, on the other hand, there are many signs of bullion shortage and mint output virtually ceased until the mid-1340s.[7] These may be part causes of the downward turn of prices in the decades preceding the Black Death. If that was so, then conversely the inflow of bullion earlier may have contributed to the rise of prices which is so marked a feature of the times.

At the same time it must be doubted whether monetary influences were the only ones at work. It is also unlikely that the cost of labour contributed significantly to increased prices, for until well into the fourteenth century the real wages at least of agricultural workers were, if anything, falling (see pp. 49–53). It is more probable that the steady upward trend of prices down to the 1320s mainly reflected two other characteristics of the period. First, the growth of a market economy is likely to have entailed some increase in the velocity with which money circulated; it also exposed producers to a diversification of demand for their products – an urban, even an international demand for foodstuffs and certainly an international demand for English wool. Secondly, always in the background was the tendency for population to outgrow the means of subsistence. These influences appear to be the most likely cause of the evolutionary inflationary trend during the period as a whole. It is the violence of inflation around 1200, however, when the price of wheat, oats and barley quadrupled and the price of oxen, pigs and sheep doubled in a decade or two, that demands additional explanation.

In terms of the analysis we have just used, price stability before the late twelfth century seems to imply both monetary stability and, most important of all, that population growth was matched or even exceeded by gains in agricultural production, the fruit of the long history of rural colonization. The abrupt changes in price levels at the end of the twelfth century have been attributed to the fact that 'England was suddenly flooded with silver', a flood occasioned by a massive increase in her exports, especially of wool to Flanders[8]. This may well have been a contributory factor to the sudden surge of inflation, but it may also be doubted whether it stood alone. The ratio of exports to total agricultural production was probably too small to account for such an explosion of prices over so short a period. Other influences, in brief, must certainly have played a part in so dramatic an episode. One possibility is that, for some time before 1200, custom had imposed restraints on price increases and that these restraints were reinforced by the unwillingness of royal purveyors to pay higher prices.[9] Consequently when the dam finally burst, inflationary pressures contained perhaps for quarter of a century were released in little more than a decade. It may be, too, that this period around 1200 was one of particularly rapid population growth, raising pressure on land and its products to a critical level; and that the crisis of subsistence was exacerbated by adverse weather conditions which ruined harvests on a scale that might bear comparison with the disasters of 1315–17.[10] The fact that the grain prices of 1203 and 1204 were not surpassed for half a century or more lends support to this possibility. The explanation of the trend of prices in these years remains uncertain; all that is certain is that the first phase of the inflationary movement that dominated the central Middle Ages was violent indeed.

The inflationary leap of prices at the opening of the thirteenth century and the longer term upward movement continuing into the first quarter of the fourteenth century had far-reaching consequences. The steep fall in the real value of customary payments for land, particularly those in cash, at a time when the prices of agricultural produce were soaring was probably a principal reason turning landlords away from leasing to the direct exploitation of their demesnes around 1200 (see pp. 210–13). Thereafter, the fact that prices continued to be buoyant during a period when labour became more abundant and cheaper, encouraged many landlords to go on producing for the market on a grand scale in some cases well into the fourteenth century. At the same time the peasant with a larger than average holding, or lower than average outgoings, or greater than average initiative, was likewise in a position to seize the chances that the market offered. Market opportunities at every level – for the peasant to deal in penny packets at one end of the scale, and at the other for the great landholders selling their own produce and that which they bulked for smaller producers – were in many respects revolutionized. The intensification of exchanges is as characteristic a feature of the central Middle Ages as were the increase of people and the expansion of land under cultivation.

The growth of towns

The intensification of exchanges had many aspects. There was trading between arable and pastoral districts, between fishing ports on the coast and inland villages, between village craftsmen and their farming neighbours, and between foreign merchants and Englishmen. At the same time one of the clearest signs of the expansion of exchanges was the growth of towns. Towns were above all markets – markets for the sale of country produce, for the sale of town manufactures, for the sale of goods that merchants brought or merchants sought. They were relatively densely populated centres that could not be self-sufficient in foodstuffs: they depended, therefore, for their existence on supplies from their rural hinterlands. As manufacturing centres, moreover, they needed raw materials from the countryside (wool, hides, timber, metals); and the sale of their manufactures was the obvious way for the towns to pay for the foodstuffs and materials the countryside provided. Further, because towns were established centres of trade able to offer the appropriate facilities to traders, they were natural points of call for long-range merchants with goods to sell in the provinces or seeking to buy up local surpluses for sale elsewhere.

Towns, of course, were no novelties of the twelfth and thirteenth centuries: the character and economic role of the Domesday boroughs make this a matter calling for no elaboration (see pp. 8–12). Most of the towns that existed in 1086, however, expanded in the ensuing generations and a very substantial number of new towns were added to them by the opening of the fourteenth century. What the rate of growth of urban population was, is even more difficult to establish than a figure for the growth in the population of the country as a whole. The evidence we possess (lists of householders, taxpayers, entrants to the freedom of a town and the like) is fragmentary and in any case very difficult to manipulate statistically in order to turn taxpayers, householders or freemen into heads of population. It is possible to offer some justification for estimates that the population of York doubled between between 1086 and 1334 or that Leicester was half as populous again in 1300 than it had been in 1086, but such calculations are of the roughest possible sort. Perhaps a more convincing sign of the growth of urban populations is the physical growth of urban areas and the evidence for a high density of housing within them. The crowded character of town sites is vividly brought home by an enactment of the London authorities at the end of the thirteenth century. Buildings, we are told,

'are so close together that in many places there is no vacant land and some occupy a neighbour's walls where they have no right at all; and occupy them maliciously, as by putting into the said walls beams and

*corbels or chests or cupboards; and . . . such purprestures are made in
cellars and rooms where no-one can enter and know the same, except
the occupier's household, and . . . are concealed during many years and
not perceived.'*[11]

One reason for this congestion is suggested by the plentiful evidence
for an inflow of population into towns from the countryside, even if
some immigration was required to compensate for the failure of town
populations to reproduce themselves. In the Leicester tallage rolls of
1336, for example, only 294 out of 460 taxpayers were identical with, or
had the same surnames as, the taxpayers of 1318. The remaining third
were new names, some of them doubtless men who had prospered
sufficiently between 1318 and 1336 to move into the ranks of the
taxpayers. Many of them, however, had names suggesting that either
they or their ancestors had been immigrants from elsewhere: some from
places overseas (including Dublin and Lille), some from English towns
as far apart as Tiverton and Chester, but the majority from the English
countryside. Of this last group most came from villages in Leicestershire
and Rutland, some from the other Midland counties and a few from
remoter places in Lancashire and even Northumberland.[12] Immigrants
were equally prominent in other English towns; and in London it has
been maintained that the influx from East Anglia and the East Midlands in the later thirteenth century and the early fourteenth was on a
sufficient scale, and that immigrants from these districts were
sufficiently influential in the city, to ensure that by the fourteenth
century their dialect had pushed out the old southern speech current in
London in earlier days.[13]

The movement of people from village to town, which augmented as
well as maintained urban populations, illustrates once more both the
overpopulation of the countryside and the growing mobility of people.
Villages had bodies to spare and villagers were attracted to towns by the
opportunities they offered to the enterprising. At the same time the
surviving evidence relating to towns in the thirteenth and early
fourteenth centuries carries an implication that men were drawn into
them by hope even more than sober calculation. There may be an
element of overstatement in the contention that 'thirteenth-century
towns were not so much populated as swollen and choked with people,
all hoping for the living that the countryside could no longer give them,
and all but a few hoping in vain';[14] but the exaggeration is not all that
great. Town populations grew to such an extent that, side by side with
merchants and craftsmen, there developed a submerged proletariat,
including many men whose productive capacities were less than fully
employed.

London, Leicester and York were old towns, already the centres of urban life before the Normans came to England, but the emergence of new towns or proto-towns was just as much a feature of the central Middle Ages as was the expansion of the Domesday boroughs. Clare in Suffolk, for example, was said in 1086 'always' to have had a market, but apparently its forty-three burgesses were then a new group appended to what was essentially a rural manor. By the mid-thirteenth century, however, burgage rents and tolls from the market and fair were the principal revenues drawn from Clare by its lord. It never became a fully fledged borough, but it clearly developed some essentially urban characteristics even if it remained of modest size.[15] How much the earls of Clare contributed to its development is not clear; but the abbots of Ramsey certainly played a part in creating in St Ives an urban appendage to the Huntingdonshire manor of Slepe. This vill was conveniently situated to provide a meeting place for denizen merchants from the East Midlands and foreign merchants coming down the Ouse; and the abbey exploited the advantages of the site by building a bridge over the river, obtaining the grant of a fair in 1110 and encouraging the building and repair of houses and shops. Even so, agriculture was never pushed entirely into the background at St Ives, for its commercial life was centred on its fair, which lasted only a week each year. It was, so to speak, almost a temporary or periodic town which never achieved municipal standing.[16] Chipping Campden, on the other hand, was made into a borough by Hugh de Gonneville in 1173 and became one of the main marketing centres for Cotswold wool; but it, too, never entirely outgrew its agricultural characteristics. The Bishops of Worcester were more successful in imposing an urban character upon Stratford-upon-Avon. There were no burgesses here in 1182, when Bishop John de Coutances obtained a market for Stratford and conceded certain burghal privileges. By 1252 there were about 300 tenants of burgage holdings and some of them had surnames indicating that they pursued industrial crafts. [17]

Places like Clare or even Stratford were towns of no great size, but some of the urban centres created during the central Middle Ages came to play a more prominent part in the economy of medieval England. Newcastle developed rapidly into a port of some importance at the gates of the fortress which William Rufus established on the banks of the Tyne; and Boston, not mentioned in Domesday Book, emerged almost equally rapidly within the confines of the earl of Richmond's manor of Skirbeck. Its famous fair was established before 1135 and by 1183 contributed up to £105 yearly to the revenues of the honour. The commercial activity of the port of Boston very soon threatened the pre-eminence of the merchants of Lincoln in the trade of the county.[18] The story of Bishop's (later King's) Lynn, at a crossing point on an inlet of the Wash between Norfolk and Lincolnshire, is very similar. The nucleus of the town was established when a few traders settled on reclaimed marshland in the Bishop of Norwich's manor of Gaywood. The rapid growth of this settlement encouraged the Bishop in the mid-twelfth century to grant to settlers the 'new land' north of the original site on which a distinct settlement grew up; and probably in the second half of the century South Lynn developed as the third component of what had become, by the end of the thirteenth century, one of the major ports of eastern England.[19]

Boston and Lynn owed their growth to the fact that their sites offered opportunities of participation in an expanding maritime commerce. At the same time urban development on a comparable scale was not impossible inland. The town of Salisbury had its beginnings when the Bishop and his clergy migrated in 1219 from the irksome shadow of the royal garrison in Old Sarum castle. They were followed by the townsfolk from the old centre and, while Old Sarum gradually degenerated into the ideal type of the rotten borough, New Salisbury was laid out and its streets gradually filled with citizens. By 1377 it ranked eighth amongst the towns of England.[20]

The founding of towns was an enterprise which attracted many medieval landlords. The Bishops of Winchester alone established six between 1200 and 1255; out of twenty boroughs in Hampshire and the Isle of Wight in 1295 only three (Winchester, Southampton and Christchurch) are so described in Domesday; and by the mid-thirteenth century thirteen new towns had been added in Devon to the four which existed in 1086. Altogether, Professor Beresford has calculated that some 140 new towns came into existence between 1100 and 1300. These details, together with the very rapid growth of places like Boston and Salisbury, are a clear indication of the substantial growth in the urban sector of medieval society. At the same time this growth should not be exaggerated. There were success stories in the history of medieval town foundation, but there were also catastrophes. Every incipient port did not necessarily thrive into a Boston. Somewhere about 1250, for example, the island of Ravenserodd was formed in the Humber estuary and became a centre of fishing and a resort of merchants. By the end of the century it was flourishing sufficiently to alarm neighbouring ports, and in 1299 Edward I charged it £300 for a borough charter. In 1304 it even sent representatives to parliament. By the 1340s, however, Ravenserodd was in full decline, for the sea had eroded most of it and by the 1360s its destruction was complete.[21]

Here, seemingly, the forces of nature permitted only a brief career to a new foundation, but in other instances the patrons of new towns seem to have been excessively optimistic. The Northumbrian village of Warkworth was called a borough in the thirteenth century. It was inhabited by a mixed group of craftsmen and agriculturalists living in the shadow of the castle, with an attached settlement of fishermen across the river in Newtown; in 1293 it also had a weekly market and an annual fair. These incipient urban characteristics, however, did not endure; and Warkworth remained a mere village. Warenmouth not far away had even less success. This place was newly built about 1247 by William Heron, constable of Bamburgh, as a port for the castle. He got a royal charter for it conferring the liberties of Newcastle and Winchester; but despite the éclat of its foundation Warenmouth was never anything larger than a small fishing community. There were said to be some twenty burgage tenements in 1330, but only three inhabitants were rich enough to pay the king's taxes in 1296. Very quickly the borough faded away and the only trace of it on the modern map is Newtown farm in the parish of Budle.[22]

One question remains: how do we strike a balance between the success of Boston and Salisbury and the failure of Warkworth and Warenmouth? What was the rate of urban growth between Domesday and the Black Death? No answer, in the light of present knowledge, can be given to these questions. The expansion of old towns, the establishment of new towns,and the acquisition by a good number of villages of certain urban features must surely imply that men engaged in properly urban activities increased absolutely. On the other hand, in the light of the fact that the total population of England increased between 1086 and 1349, and that there were many signs of serious rural overpopulation before the thirteenth century was over, we may well wonder to what extent urban populations increased relatively to the population of the country as a whole. There is a good deal to be said for the supposition that this relative increase was not very great, since if that were so the incipiently critical situation in the countryside around 1300 would be the more comprehensible. Future research may enable a firmer answer to be given to this crucial question; as things stand any resolution of it can only take the form of a hypothesis.

Markets

Whatever the rate at which towns grew, their growth is a pointer to the growing volume of exchanges. The little town of Clare, Domesday tells us, had always had a market; the Bishop of Norwich set up a separate market place for the secondary settlement he established on the 'new land' at Lynn; and the acquisition of a market by Stratford-on-Avon was the starting point of its urban development. The character of the trade that engaged a town of no great importance is indicated by a list of tolls charged at Carlisle in 1300 to raise funds for repairing the bridge there. They were imposed on many commodities: grain and malt; horses, cattle, sheep, goats and pigs; fish of divers sorts; wool, hides and skins, including those of rabbits and squirrels; cloth, linen and leather; iron and copper; woad for the city's clothworkers and wax for its chandlers; charcoal, turves and wood.[23] At Ipswich about the same time there was an elaborate arrangement of separate markets. Imported cloth as well as cloth made in the town itself and at inland centres like Coggeshall and Sudbury, together with linen, canvas and made-up garments, were sold in the cloth market. There was also a fishmarket, a wool market (where hides were also sold), a cheese market (where potters also disposed of their wares), a wood market for timber, domestic utensils made of wood, baskets, spades and cartwheels, a bread market, a fleshmarket for the retail sale of meat, and a market for livestock.[24]

These urban markets of the thirteenth century were evidently links in a complex chain of exchanges. They enabled, in the first place, the townsfolk to procure essential foodstuffs. The oldest Leicester market was probably that held on Wednesdays in the town-centre where the four main streets joined. Originally it seems to have been a general market for provisions, although by the fourteenth century it was mainly a place where country folk sold butter and eggs (corn and livestock being sold in the south-east corner of the town close to the secondary markets where butchers, bakers and fishmongers plied their trades).[25] These Leicester markets, like some of those at Ipswich, illustrate the dependence of towns on the surrounding countryside for their food supplies, although fish, for example, might have a more distant origin; and provision markets were of particular concern to townsmen because densely populated urban areas were especially susceptible to shortages. On the other hand, the town markets of Ipswich accommodated rural as well as urban customers for goods made in the town (cloth perhaps, made-up garments, earthen pots and wooden dishes, spades and cartwheels, ladders and baskets) and also for imported goods including foreign cloth, fish, wine, oil, canvas, millstones, Spanish and Normandy iron, perhaps even sea coal. Some of the goods sold in the Ipswich markets, on the other hand, were sent elsewhere by sea: wool, hides and skins, herrings both to London and to France, Essex and Suffolk cloth, and butter and cheese for which Essex and Suffolk had some medieval fame. Some buyers in the markets, however, might be town craftsmen, who needed wool or hides or imported woad to carry on their crafts. Ipswich, in brief, was a centre of exchanges between town and country, between regions, and even between nations. Its markets provided the institutional framework within which these various currents of exchange operated.

Ipswich, of course, was a port of some size, but even smaller inland towns were market centres for a region large or small, and some were of inter-regional or even international importance. In the fourteenth century, Stourbridge fair, just outside Cambridge, was attracting buyers other than Cambridge townsfolk. It was attended each year by a party of monks from Crowland Abbey, who stayed at their manor of Oakington, rode down daily to Chesterton ferry and so crossed to the fair; the nunnery of St Mary de Prés, near St Albans, bought there large supplies of dried fish, together with tar, nails, horseshoes, mats, baskets and cloth; and in 1351 sufficient textiles were on sale there for thirty-eight cloths to be seized as not conforming to the proper measure. By the fifteenth century Londoners were coming to Stourbridge and the fair was one at which an Oxfordshire priory might expect to buy silks and Eastland boards and Spanish iron.[26] Much earlier, in 1224, Winchester fair had been attracting merchants from Spain, Toulouse, Normandy, Germany and the towns of Flanders;[27] Boston fair in the thirteenth century was a mart for wine and wool and cloth; Northampton and Stamford fairs were scarcely, if at all, less important; and if the monks of Crowland went to Stourbridge the Abbot of Westminster sent his agents to Winchester fair.[28] These commercial gatherings, essentially interregional and even international in character, supplemented the network of exchanges centred in the more routine assemblies of sellers and buyers that met in town market-places.

Markets and fairs, however, were by no means exclusively located in towns. In thirteenth-century Cambridgeshire, for example, there were markets at Abington Piggots, Caxton and Gamlingay and both markets and fairs at Great Abington, Bergham, Burwell, Brinkley, Eltisley, Hildersham, Linton, Swavesey, Whittlesford and Wilbraham.[29] Most of these were largish villages, Swavesey having ninety-five taxpayers in 1327; but almost all of them, with the partial exception of Linton where there were some burgesses in 1279, were basically rural communities. A few were very small: Abington Piggots mustered only thirteen taxpayers in 1327; and Bergham was a mere hamlet, its population being taxed along with the larger settlement at Linton. In this matter of rural markets Cambridgeshire was in no way peculiar. Henry III, in the early months of 1227, granted or confirmed a number of fairs and markets. A few were for boroughs (Coventry, Peterborough, Hereford) or for places like Baldock which were developing urban features; others were for rural centres including Kineton, Beaudesert and Southam (Warwickshire), Denham (Bucks), and Knaith (Lincs), Halesworth, Newmarket and Hacheston (Suffolk) and Creake and

Runham (Norfolk).[30] Derbyshire, again, closely resembled Cambridgeshire in this regard. Derby and Chesterfield had markets and fairs long
before the grant of their first charters in 1204; but in total twenty-eight
places had markets in the county and twenty-four of them also had a
fair. The distance between markets ranged from about a mile up to
about seven miles – just over the $6\frac{2}{3}$ miles which Bracton regarded as a
reasonable distance for a man to travel there and back in a day and have
an interval between his journeys in which to do business.[31] In brief, the
village markets of Derbyshire and Cambridgeshire put most men within
the reach of opportunities for buying and selling, and the multiplication
of markets and fairs achieved the same result throughout the land.
Between 1227 and 1350 kings granted to some 1,200 places in England
and Wales the right to have markets. They were an essential part of the
equipment of a developing economy.

Grants of markets and fairs, of course, like the grant of burghal
status, often proved nugatory. In Derbyshire in 1330 the right to hold a
market and fair at Sandiacre had not been exercised since it was
conceded in 1252; and the markets at Aston-on-Trent and Ilkeston
attracted few participants. In general, by the early fourteenth century,
there seem to have been too many markets and fairs (just as there were
perhaps too many towns) to serve the needs of society. None the less
markets and fairs contributed to the economic expansion of the twelfth
and thirteenth centuries. In particular the right to hold a market or fair
often generated urban development or even the formation of new
towns. In a great variety of places in the earldom of Cornwall estate in
1296 urban features are found in close association with the right to have
markets and fairs: at Berkhamstead, Wilton, Wallingford and
Knaresborough; at Lostwithiel and Saltash in Cornwall; in Devon at
Bradninch, chartered by King John, and Lydford, an Alfredian
borough which was decaying in face of competition from Tavistock and
Okehampton; at Oakham, Rockingham and Boroughbridge; even at
Newport (Essex) where there was a 'borough' as well as a manor, or at
Holme in Huntingdonshire where a 'new borough' had been tacked on
to a manorial core.[32] The same association is evident in the
Hertfordshire liberty of St Albans. Codicote with its market and fair
had tenants *in foro et burgagio*; Winslow had burgesses in 1279;
Watford had tenants with shops in its market; Barnet had a weekly
market and was growing into a small town.[33] None of these places was
to enjoy the destinies of Boston, but their development forms part of the
spectrum of urban development during the central Middle Ages.

An increasingly dense network of markets and fairs, both in towns
and villages, contributed to economic development in another way.
Sometimes medieval townsmen seem to be pursuing the ideal of a land

consisting of a honeycomb of rural islands with, at the centre of each, a town in which industry and exchanges were concentrated. If this autarchic notion ever corresponded to reality, however, it very soon ceased to correspond to facts. The international trader broke through the barrier because he had desirable commodities for sale; and townsmen themselves reached out beyond their own 'natural' hinterland in a search for supplies and markets. The greater fairs, too, attracted both merchants from other towns and merchants who were 'foreigners' in the modern sense of the word. What this meant can be glimpsed in the records of Leicester in the thirteenth and early fourteenth centuries. Its merchants, being the inhabitants of an inland town, were not especially prominent in overseas commerce, but in inland trade their horizons were rapidly expanding. They sought timber not only from Leicester forest but from Arden, Cannock Chase and Needwood. They travelled to Chester, Shrewsbury, Derby and Coventry, buying in this last place mailed gloves for the contingent the town sent to the Scottish wars in 1318. In 1207 it was assumed they would frequent Winchester fair, but above all they were found at the great fairs of the East Midlands – Boston, Lynn, Northampton, St Ives and Stamford – selling wool, hides and cloth and, at least at Boston, buying wine.[34]

The dealings of Leicester merchants illustrate the extent to whch by the thirteenth century exchanges were integrating the English economy and linking it through ports and fairs with the international economic system of Western Europe. This integration was less than perfect. Towns did not relinquish easily, and preserved if they could do so, a most-favoured position in trade with their immediate hinterland. Local market areas, in this sense, continued to exist if only because they corresponded to the mutual interdependence of towns and their immediate environs. On a larger plane the difficulty of communications limited the degree of integration. It seems clear, for example, that different levels of grain prices prevailed in the different regions of England. The fertile lands of the upper Severn and the Cambridge region were relatively low priced areas; the Lower Thames, on the other hand, was a district of relatively high prices, mainly presumably because of demand from London.[35] At the same time, while differential price levels for cereals were symptomatic of the imperfect integration of the economy, they also stimulated exchanges. The fact that grain was relatively cheap in the districts bordering on the Wash encouraged export to the higher price region dominated by London. The Cambridge region, therefore, became one of the granaries of the capital and the coastal grain trade helped to make the fortune of the new town which the Bishops of Norwich fostered at King's Lynn. The regional economies of the twelfth and thirteenth centuries were one condition for the intensification of exchanges.

International trade

Exchanges were not limited to dealings between townsmen and countrymen in local markets or between the merchants of different towns in regional fairs. Alien and native traders bought English goods to ship them overseas and goods from foreign places were brought to England for sale. A western European economy was emerging, in fact, of which England was an essential part. The beginnings of these international aspects of the medieval economy long antedate the Norman Conquest. There was trade between England and Gaul in the time of Charlemagne; one fruit of Viking raids and Cnut's conquests was a commercial nexus between England and the Baltic; and in the year 1000 tolls levied in the port of London show trade contacts with the Low Countries, Normandy, Northern France and the German Empire (especially the Rhineland region dominated by Cologne).[36]

In the years that followed the trade links existing in 1000 were strengthened and diversified. Direct Anglo-Scandinavian trade remained important well into the thirteenth century. In the early twelfth century the Lincolnshire merchant, Godric, frequented Danish harbours before he abandoned commerce for meditation and sanctity at Finchale by the Wear. Later in the century Danes and Norwegians had a privileged position in London trade; sagas suggest that Danish merchants were familiar figures in Grimsby; and in 1217 and 1237 Norwegians and Swedes made trade treaties with England at a time when the merchants of these countries appeared regularly at King's Lynn.[37] True, Anglo-Scandinavian trade passed thereafter increasingly into the hands of German merchants, but as the German Hanse established its economic control over the whole Baltic area and the region of German colonization in the Slav lands east of the Elbe, this northern commerce waxed rather than waned in importance.

In the meantime there had also been development in the other trade connexions existing under King Aethelred. Anglo-Cologne trade continued to be important in the reign of Henry I, and William of Malmesbury gave pride of place to goods from the Cologne region when he described the merchandise which packed the wharves of London.[38] True, the Cologners in the thirteenth century lost ground relatively to merchants from the Baltic ports, but they remained influential among the various interests that came together in the German Hanse. This is one example only of the strengthening and diversification of old trading links. Throughout the twelfth and thirteenth centuries Flanders became progressively more dependent upon supplies from England, especially of wool, and closer commercial contacts were established, particularly through the east coast ports from Hull to Ipswich, with Holland and Brabant. Naturally, too, the Norman Conquest strengthened commercial links with Normandy and northern France, and these were broken neither by the severance of Normandy from England in 1204 nor by periodic Anglo-French conflict thereafter. Cross-Channel and North Sea traffic, in other words was a growing traffic; and it gave England access to the goods and markets of all north-western Europe, and at the same time to desirable commodities from even further afield that were available at the growing international markets of the day, in particular the fairs of Champagne and the entrepôt of Bruges.

The development of trade with southern Europe had a greater novelty. It was undoubtedly facilitated by Henry II's marriage to Eleanor of Aquitaine, which made Gascony part of the dominion of the King of England from 1154 to the fifteenth century. For that reason the Anglo-Bordeaux trade was the main axis of this southern commerce; but by the thirteenth century it was expanding to take in the whole of south-western Europe – Spain, Portugal, Toulouse, Provence – and the points of access these lands afforded to the wider Mediterranean world beyond. Towards the end of the century, moreover, Italian merchants established direct contacts by sea with England and, by the mid-fourteenth century, Venetian and Genoese galleys were making regular voyages to Southampton, Sandwich and London. True, as yet, the value of their cargoes was normally modest: in the period 1322–36 the average annual value of all alien imports to and exports from London excepting wool, wine and cloth was only just over £8,300. The cargo of a single Italian galley in the fifteenth century was often worth nearly as much.[39] None the less the sea way between England and the Mediterranean was fully open well before 1349.

The increasingly dense network of trade routes is easy enough to discern, but of even greater importance is the character of the goods that moved along those routes. For the greater part of our period, until the customs accounts throw some light upon it, the pattern of English trade is sadly lacking in accurately determined dimensions. Even so, its basic features appear clearly enough.[40] Imports included some raw materials: iron from Spain and the Baltic, dyestuffs from Picardy and southern France and the Mediterranean, and timber especially from the Baltic which appears to have been more easily transported by sea than for any distance by land. Far more characteristic of imports, however, particularly if reckoned by value, were consumption goods (either fully or partially prepared) and luxuries or semi-luxuries. Textiles probably ranked first in terms of value. They included silks and cloths of gold, often of Italian manufacture, but above all cloth from Flanders, the high quality of which is attested by Chaucer's compliment to the Wife of Bath – that her cloth surpassed even that of Ypres and Ghent.[41] In the opening years of the fourteenth century foreign merchants alone were bringing into the country from Flanders and the adjacent regions some 12,000 cloths yearly; and incidental scraps of evidence show English merchants, from London and Gloucester and Sandwich,[42] similarly engaged. True, by the 1330s these imports were falling away and in the 1340s, admittedly in exceptional wartime conditions, foreign textiles were virtually ousted from the English market; but for most of the preceding two centuries, at the least, cloth had been a major import into England.

By the thirteenth century imports of wine probably did not lag far behind textiles, in particular imports of wine from Bordeaux once La Rochelle (previously of importance in supplying England) passed to the French crown in 1224. In the opening years of the fourteenth century one fifth to a quarter of the wines exported from Gascony came to England, to a total amount of some 20,000 tuns yearly[43] worth wholesale some £60,000. Of growing importance, too, with the growth of the Hanseatic interest in England, was the import of Baltic furs and especially of vair or miniver, the red squirrel skins of which nearly 120,000 were bought annually for Edward I's household alone in the 1280s.[44] These main import lines apart, Hanseatic and sometimes Dutch merchants brought in fish and, at the latest from the 1320s, grain from the new lands east of the Elbe in years of scarcity in England. Far more characteristic was an almost infinite variety of goods: arms and armour from Mainz and Milan, metalware from towns of the Meuse valley, lace from Cambrai, and ultimately from the Mediterranean or farther east (even if immediately, more likely, from Bruges or the Champagne fairs) spices and rare fruits (figs, raisins, almonds, dates, pomegranates) as well as sugar and rice. The tastes for which the Italian galleys of the later Middle Ages catered were already being whetted.

The character of exports is in marked contrast to that of imports: they were virtually all primary and most of them agricultural products. Certainly by the thirteenth century the staple export was wool, most of it going to Flanders, which the barons alleged in 1297 to be 'almost half the value of the whole land each year'.[45] If that estimate was an exaggeration, wool exports certainly reached a peak in the first decade of the fourteenth century, when they averaged nearly 36,000 sacks yearly; and they were still running at over 30,000 sacks a year in the 1350s after a period of vicissitudes during the early phases of the

Hundred Years War.[46] Wool, however, was by no means the only product of the English countryside to be shipped overseas. Flemish concentration on textile manufacture and the specialization of Gascony in viticulture were in part made possible by English food exports, as well as by the export to Flanders of English wool. Already in the reign of Henry II East Anglia and some southern counties shipped grain to Flanders, and Bruges around 1200 imported cheese from England; in the first decade of the fourteenth century exports of grain from Hull, King's Lynn and Sandwich alone totalled around 10,000 quarters in some years;[47] and in the same period Boston, Southampton, Ipswich[48] and Bristol[49] were also exporting grain and dairy produce. The export of grain was possibly checked by the famine of 1315–17, when desperate attempts were made to secure supplies from overseas: from the Channel Islands, France, even through the good offices of Spanish and Italian merchants.[50] None the less, for much of the twelfth and thirteenth centuries, when many at home knew what hunger was, a significant amount of foodstuffs grown in England was sent overseas.

Wool, grain and dairy produce were not the only primary exports. Hides and Yarmouth herrings[51] again were principally exported to the Low Countries. At the same time, mining as well as farming contributed to the export trade. A little iron, doubtless from the Wealden industry, was exported from Sandwich; lead from Derbyshire and probably Richmondshire went out from Boston and Hull; and tin from the south-west sometimes reached very distant markets. As early as 1195 Richard I sent 100 tons of tin to La Rochelle and three years later two merchants of Bayonne in Gascony bought a similar quantity in Cornwall;[52] later exports from the south-western ports, Southampton and London not only reached the metal-working towns of the Low Countries and France, but, in Italian vessels, the major trading centres of the Mediterranean, Asia Minor and the Black Sea.

The basic pattern of English trade for most of the central Middle Ages, then, is clear enough. The chief imports were quality consumer goods, reflecting the tastes and the purchasing power of those landowning classes that were the principal beneficiaries of economic expansion. The availability of these imports enabled them to gratify their instincts for conspicuous consumption, even at the expense of saving and investment. At the same time England exported wool, metals and hides during a period when industrial development was failing to achieve the momentum required if rural overpopulation was to be relieved; and also grain and other foodstuffs at a time when dearths were becoming increasingly frequent and causing rising mortality. This contrast between the character of imports and of exports is not, of course, absolute. Manufactured goods, for example, were not quite absent in export cargoes: in early days England supplied Scandinavia with cauldrons and other goods; in the early fourteenth century Bristol shipped horse-shoes, nails and bronze jars to Gascony; and a century earlier cloth made in the towns of eastern England enjoyed an international market extending even to the Mediterranean lands. This early textile industry collapsed during the thirteenth century in the face of Flemish competition; and the contribution other branches of manufacturing industry made to exports was minimal. The great suppliers remained miners and, above all, agricultural producers.

True, in the generation preceding the Black Death, there were signs of change.[53] Less grain was going overseas (and some occasionally came in); a smaller proportion of England's wool was being exported; conversely, English textiles – first low-priced kerseys and worsteds, but before 1350 West Country broadcloths too – were once more finding international markets. It is unlikely that the character of imports changed very much, with the salient exception that imported cloth provided for a significantly smaller proportion of English consumption. The economic balance between this country and the other western lands was shifting perceptibly, however modestly as yet.

For immediate purposes we must return to the commodity prices with which this chapter commenced. These prices were market prices and they were of general concern: to lords of manors who produced for the market on a very large scale, but also to a very high percentage of the peasantry, since they were compelled to sell some of their produce if only to meet their rents and other charges. Thus development of commercial facilities (towns, fairs, markets) directly concerned a large part of the population, the activities of merchants influenced the fortunes of very many people, and the situation of landlord and peasant alike was governed by markets as well as by lordship and soil and weather. The development of markets in the twelfth and thirteenth centuries was a consequence of the intensification of economic activity during that period, but it was also one of the conditions which made possible the economic expansion of these generations. That is why, here, it has been given a logical place as a prologue to the story of rural enterprise.

Chapter 4

Villages

In discussing the background of change in the medieval English economy it has been necessary to say a good deal about merchants and markets, about the growth of towns and the fortunes of craftsmen. There is little doubt, moreover, that the volume of goods coming on to the market, the extent of the market those goods reached, and the number of men involved in market transactions increased notably in the two centuries after Domesday. None the less the economy of these centuries was a profoundly rural one. The overwhelming majority of men lived on the land and got their living from it; indeed, the proportion of the population doing so may have fallen very little, if at all, during these centuries of expansion. A survey of the medieval economic and social scene may, therefore, very properly begin in the countryside. This scene was often envisaged by contemporaries in terms of a hierarchy of 'communities'. Sometimes attention was concentrated on territorial groupings: the network of villages; the larger communities, the hundreds (or wapentakes) and the shires; and the totality of hundreds and shires (together with privileged cities and boroughs) constituting what was coming to be called in the thirteenth century the 'community of the realm'. Society, however, could be pictured in another fashion, a tenurial or feudal fashion. Here the baseline was occupied by manors, which were grouped into lordships or baronies or honours, the sum of which Henry I called 'my honour',[1] the honour of all England, the feudal equivalent of the territorial notion of a community of the realm.

Obviously these two hierarchies intersected, overlapped and were superimposed one on the other; and in the real world they were inseparable from each other. For purposes of analysis, however, they can be distinguished; and convenience and historical priority justify us in starting with the countryman as a *villanus* in the eleventh-century sense of that word. Literally it meant a man who lived in a *villa*, a *tun*, a village. The description, in other words, reflects the reality of how most men lived their lives. To that extent there is good reason for looking at the countryman first of all as a villager and at the countryside in which he lived as a land clothed in a network of villages.

Village forms

As soon as we ask what a village is we run into difficulties. To begin with, settlements varied greatly in size. Isolated homesteads were by no means unknown, especially on the margins of cultivation in moorland, forest and fen. They were, on the other hand, anything but characteristic of the medieval landscape, for most men lived in groups ranging from tiny hamlets of a few families up to settlements of considerable size, often with certain urban characteristics (a market, a few craftsmen, a few *mercatores*). Size varied considerably even within the same district: cheek by jowl in Cambridgeshire in 1327 were Gamlingay with fifty-seven taxpayers who paid almost £5 in tax and Hungry Hatley (the name is perhaps significant) with only fourteen taxpayers paying under 33s. Not far away were even smaller places, for East Hatley and Clopton (the latter, it is interesting to note, became one of the deserted villages of Cambridgeshire in the late Middle Ages) mustered only twenty-one taxpayers between them.[2]

Judged by the criterion of the number of taxpayers, even the smaller Cambridgeshire villages appear less small when they are looked at in comparison with settlements in certain other parts of England. Small communities were the rule, for example, in the Northumberland plain, to say nothing of the hill country. In Warkworth parish in 1296, before Scottish raids had affected prosperity, all the townships resembled Hungry Hatley rather than Gamlingay. High Buston and Birling combined had ten taxpayers, Low Buston eleven, Brotherwick three, Amble nine and Hauxley twelve. The picture from Hexhamshire is much the same: fifteen townships had from three to seventeen taxpayers and averaged between eight and nine.[3] These comparisons are rough and ready: different taxes were differently assessed in different places at different times, and a similar number of taxpayers may well be compatible with markedly different populations.[4] None the less the disparity between the tax rolls for Cambridgeshire and for many of the northern and western counties indicates that in much of the latter regions the hamlet rather than the village was the most common settlement form. A similar conclusion may be drawn from records of landholding in the Duchy of Cornwall during the generation before the Black Death. These records suggest that in Cornwall as a whole 75 per cent of settlements were hamlets in which the land was held by no more than five families and that in the more rugged reaches of the far west of the county over half the settlements consisted of a single tenancy.[5]

Although the proportion of hamlets increases as one advances towards the uplands of the north and the west, a sharp geographical dividing line between village and hamlet is no more valid in 1300 than it was in 1086. The size and type of settlements were determined by topography rather than the racial origins of their inhabitants, and therefore hamlets and villages co-existed in many parts of England. On chalk and limestone, for example, compact villages are found at the points where scarce water supplies were available; where springs were plentiful, as in Devon, settlements were apt to be much more dispersed. But Devon had its nucleated villages as well as many hamlets and isolated farms: the latter largely in the colonizing uplands and the former in the older-settled and more fertile coastal districts. Great Beare, a thirteenth-century settlement consisting merely of two houses and corn-drying ovens was perhaps not untypical of the pioneering establishments on the margins of cultivation,[6] while Axminster in east Devon was a nucleated village with many 'classical' features and more than sixty tenants in 1260.[7] The juxtaposition of village and hamlet, moreover, is no peculiarity of the south-west. The Archbishop of Canterbury's colossal manor of South Malling in Sussex, surveyed as a single unit in 1086, was divided by 1285 into two groups of 'borghs'. Those 'without the wood', lying on the coastal plain and on the downlands around South Malling, had a typical village structure. The 'borghs within the wood' (in the great Wealden forest), on the other hand, were made up of hamlets each endowed with about 100 acres of land held only by a few tenants at most and occasionally only by one.[8] The same diversity of settlement types is evident in the woodland landscape of Hertfordshire; and, in the very different environment of the Lincolnshire fen, the large elongated parishes accommodated a mother village and also a number of hamlets both on the fen side and towards the sea, the latter being the creation of the great work of reclamation undertaken in the twelfth and thirteenth centuries.[9]

Hamlets, in brief, were often simply pioneering settlements established in the course of agricultural expansion during the central Middle Ages. Precisely because expansion occurred to varying degrees in most parts of the country, some examples of hamlet settlement are found almost everywhere. At the same time the dividing line between village and hamlet was by no means immutable. If the terrain was favourable hamlets could grow into villages; but their development tended to be limited by the very fact that they were so frequently established on marginal land, one reason why hamlets are so typical of the poorer upland regions. On the other hand, hamlets were groups of men jointly engaged in the exploitation of their territories: their organization may have been simpler and more embryonic than that found in the larger villages, but it was still essentially of the same nature.

Communities varied not only in size but in their relationships with each other. At one end of the scale were completely independent villages:

self-contained settlements with definite boundaries and exclusive rights over their territories. At the other extreme were groupings of villages and hamlets bound together by a variety of ties. The composite manor of South Malling, comprising a chain of settlements stretching from Lewes to the Kent border, was linked together by the obligation imposed on the 'borghs within the wood' to provide services at South Malling, Stonham and Southerham, the 'borghs without the wood'. Cornish hamlets were usually grouped together in manors; suit of court and the payment of customary dues were the cement of the territorial 'sokes' of the northern Danelaw; in the north and in the fenland, villages with independent arable were often linked together by intercommoning rights on some large moor or waste; and whole groups of villages were united by mutual responsibility for drainage works or sea defence in the marshlands of Lincolnshire, Cambridgeshire and Kent.

If villages differed in their external relationships, so they did in their internal arrangements. As Beresford has so aptly put it, the cluster of dwelling places which constituted a village or hamlet was as variously arranged as the cloud with which Hamlet teased Polonius.[10] Sometimes the houses were strung out along a single street; sometimes they were placed upon the arms of a cross-roads; sometimes they were grouped about a village green; and very often they had no discernible shape at all. Very few, in fact, conformed to a pure type, for as might be expected in an age of expansion an existing nucleus might by added to in a random sort of way. The classification of villages into types, therefore, is apt to be an exercise in oversimplification. It is perhaps best to leave them in their infinite variety and their natural lack of order.

Messuages

At the same time villages or hamlets had this in common: they were clusters of buildings. They might be grouped around one or more capital messuages: each a dwelling place for a manorial lord (although in Gloucestershire in 1327 only a third of the villages had a resident lord),[11] or at least a centre for the administration of the lord's demesne, together with the necessary farmyard and farm buildings. Most of the buildings in the village would be the farmsteads of the peasant community and normally they would be smaller and poorer, often very much smaller and poorer, than the buildings of the *curia* (see pp. 156–8). For the most part, medieval records tell us less about houses than about messuages, *mansurae* or tofts and crofts. Simon de Kyme, for example, gave Bullington priory a three-acre toft along with a bovate in Burgh-le-Marsh; the prior of Bullington granted to William fitzIvo a toft in Cotes

(Leics) measuring 10 by 8 perches (possibly over 4 acres); and Gervase Paynel gave the nuns of Eaton a *mansura* measuring 19 by 6 perches (possibly over 7 acres) at Waltham on the Wolds.[12] Tofts and crofts, of course, were not always of this ample size. At Holworth in Dorset,[13] there were at least seven tofts in which the houses of the villagers were sited, and stretching away to the north of each of them were long narrow crofts enclosed by banks (or banks and ditches) measuring 280–300 by 70–100 feet, that is closes of more like half an acre in area. Whatever the size of the toft and croft, the centre of the peasant's holding was a plot of land on which his house was built (and which might leave room for other cottages to accommodate aged parents or 'undersettles') and a further plot of enclosed land subject to his individual exploitation. The layout is still clearly evident at Braunston (Northants)[14] where the houses lie along a single street and the crofts stretch away from this frontage to the back lane, the line of demarcation between them and the open fields beyond.

Precisely because they were not subject to communal regulation, it is not easy to discover what use was made of the crofts. They might provide grazing or hay for livestock; or they might, as Piers Plowman tells us, enable a poor cottar to improve his 'livelihood' with a harvest of grain. Doubtless they were differently used by the different classes of villager. The man with little or no stake in the village arable would be the more likely to use them for corn-growing. A man more adequately provided with ploughland would be better placed to use his croft for more diverse purposes: to provide feed for stock, to produce garden crops, even to grow industrial crops such as hemp or flax. However they were used the crofts were a distinctive element in the agricultural fabric of most villages. In them individual discretion was far less fettered by communal rules and routine than elsewhere in the village territory; they were probably more intensively manured than the rest of the village land; and it is most likely that, when they were used as arable, they were more intensively exploited than the village fields. Perhaps, indeed, they were like the two acres (in English called Garbradakers) lying apparently in a croft at Potterne in c.1176, *quae excoluntur singulis annis* (which are cultivated every year).[15]

The fields

Beyond the back lane or the perimeter of the crofts in open-field England lay the village arable. Here the individual's power of decision was normally limited by communal routine. His tenement, moreover, was usually scattered and dispersed, intermingled and interlocked with the parcels of other tenements. The most familiar manifestation of these arrangements is that which Seebohm described in 1883, taking as his example the township of Hitchin in Hertfordshire.[16] It is no longer possible, of course, to assume as Seebohm did that Hitchin's fields were typical of all medieval English villages; but at least it has been assumed that the open field system he found in Hertfordshire was characteristic of a great wedge of the country: its base rests on the south coast between Beachy Head and the Devon border, and it stretches northwards as far as Durham.[17] There were enclaves within this area where other systems prevailed and there were sporadic examples of the open field system outside it (in the Devon coastlands, for example);[18] but only in the 'Midland' region did this system approach the typical. It is in this region, therefore, that we must look for its characteristics.

Cuxham in Oxfordshire, because it has been investigated in detail, may serve as an example. There, in the later Middle Ages, the arable lay in three large fields containing respectively 121, 126 and 127 acres. This division into fields was related to a scheme of crop rotation: each field in turn was under a winter crop such as wheat, and then a spring crop, such as oats or barley; each was finally fallowed for a year to recover fertility, so that one-third of the village arable was rested each year. Each of the fields, moreover, was divided into furlongs and each of the furlongs into strips. The holdings of individual tenants consisted of scattered strips intermixed with those of their neighbours, although the demesne land had been partially consolidated by purchases and exchanges in the thirteenth century. The meadowland was similarly divided and ownership was similarly dispersed. Finally lord and tenants had rights of common pasture on the moor and, almost certainly, on the arable fields when fallowed or after harvest.[19] Here we have the classical open-field system in all its simplicity; and Cuxham, too, was a 'common field' village in the sense that the villagers enjoyed common rights on the arable after harvest, on the fallow, and on the uncultivated 'waste'.[20]

For the present, however, we are concerned with arable fields rather than common pasture, and even within the heart of the Midlands very many villages had more or less than than three open fields. There is evidence of a four-field system: in south Warwickshire and Worcestershire, for example, possibly associated with a four-course rotation of fallow, barley, legumes, and wheat. Some villages can be found which had five or more open fields, often the result of adding to an original nucleus of fields by assarting; and woodland districts were characterized by patchworks of small open fields and enclosures. Perhaps the most common of all were villages with two fields; they predominated over much of Gloucestershire, Oxfordshire, South Warwickshire and South Worcestershire.[21] H. L. Gray associated this regime with a two-course rotation (half the land being fallowed each year) and therefore with settlements on the poorer soils.[22] This association has been contested, for it has been demonstrated that field patterns did not necessarily correspond to patterns of rotation.[23] By subdividing fields a three-course rotation could be practised in a two-field township, and some three-field villages, from a comparatively early date, adopted cropping schemes much more complex than a simple three-course rotation. In some cases, the correlation noted by Gray between field systems and fertility is still not entirely without foundation. In Berkshire, Woolstone at the foot of White Horse hill, Harwell on the edge of the Downs and downland Ashbury were two-field villages, but Beenham in the more fertile Kennett Valley had three fields; and in Wiltshire, overwhelmingly a 'two-field' county, three-field villages are found on the richer lowlands in the north and west.[24]

Field systems were not static, and there is increasing evidence that many two-field villages adopted a three-field system as the thirteenth century wore on. In Wiltshire, for example, two fields were converted into three at Poulton and Heytesbury during the century after 1250; and even earlier, at South Stoke in Oxfordshire, the Abbot of Eynsham 'partitioned into three parts his lands which previously were partitioned into two parts'.[25] There are a fair number of other instances of the conversion of two fields into three in the Midland region. Sometimes the object may have been to adjust the layout of the village arable to a pre-existing three-course rotation; sometimes, to increase the amount of land under crops by decreasing from one-half to one-third the arable area fallowed each year; and sometimes it was simply to accommodate land which had been assarted. The fact that most of the examples come from the period when population pressure was reaching its maximum suggests that increased output was the aim. At the same time, while this object might be successfully achieved in some cases, attempts to increase the annual acreage under crops in this way might, especially on poorer soils, eventually result in declining yields.

For the time being, however, we must come back to the two or three great fields characteristic of the Midland region. As at Cuxham[26] each was a patchwork of 'furlongs', blocks of land of varying shapes determined essentially by the lay of the land. Furlongs were no less variable in their dimensions: in Cambridgeshire most of them were in the 5–15 acre range, but some were smaller and others were as much as 100 acres.[27] Each furlong in turn was a bundle of selions, long narrow strips again varying considerably in area. On Osney Abbey's manor at Addington, for example, we hear of three strips making an acre,[28] but quarter acre strips seem even commoner. The strips were sometimes separated from each other by an unploughed band of turf called a 'balk', although the term was also used for unploughed areas demarcating the boundaries of fields and furlongs and serving as means of communication to the various parts of the field.[29]

It was a further characteristic of these fields that a given man's holding was not at all in one place. Some of it, in any given year, might be sown land and some fallow: thus, at Quarrendon (Bucks) we hear of a (presumably 30-acre) virgate of which 15 acres could be sown each year. Again, at Upton, two half-virgates were equally divided between South Field and North Field, and at Water Stratford a 20-acre virgate, perhaps somewhat deformed by exchanges, lay 10½ acres in one field and 9½ acres in another.[30] Holdings were not merely more or less equally divided between fields, however, for they were also dispersed within particular fields. Coming back to the Osney manor at Addington, a virgate consisted of 13 acres in West Field and 13 acres in East Field; the 13-acre portions lay respectively in nine and eleven furlongs; and in each furlong the tenant possessed a number of selions, like the three selions which made up one of the acres in one of the furlongs in East Field.[31]

This pattern of the open fields was anything but static. Quite apart from changes wrought by the operations of the landmarket, fields were in many cases growing organisms during the twelfth and thirteenth centuries, for if Cuxham had virtually reached the limits of its growth by 1086 the fields of Wigston Magna only attained the frontiers of the parish around 1300.[32] Very often, therefore, the furlongs making up the fields look like 'successive increments of land' brought into them as growing population demanded augmentation of the arable.[33] Assarting could also result in open fields being 'encircled' by enclosures farmed in severalty. In places, too, the change from a two-field to a three-field pattern called for a revision in the layout of the village ploughland; and, in the years around 1300, when some land was lapsing from cultivation as its fertility declined, there might well be a need to alter the disposition of what remained. The great open fields of the Midland plain were no unmoving expanses of farmland: on the contrary, they were full of change and movement. They, too, were as varying in appearance as Polonius's cloud.

At the same time, as every schoolboy knows, an 'open-field system' of the sort described above was far from universal in the medieval countryside. Gray observed that, 'had Seebohm gone ten miles to the south or to the east, he would have found no field arrangements like those of Hitchin'.[34] Such arrangements, in fact, did not prevail everywhere even in the Midlands and elsewhere very different arrangements were the rule. These other regimes are not easily classified, for they display an almost infinite local variety: but, even at the expense of oversimplification, three broad patterns may be distinguished. First, there was a regime of irregular fields; second, a regime of enclosures; finally, and of lesser importance, the infield-outfield regime. An irregular field system is very common in northern England. Here the terminology is often confusing: furlongs were sometimes described as fields, while at the same time all or the greater part of the village arable was also described as a field or 'the townfield', a term already current at Whitworth (Lancs) in the thirteenth century.[35] In one sense we have here a 'one-field system', and crop rotations and fallow must have been organized according to the field's constituent furlongs.

These northern fields had their irregularities. Not infrequently they comprehended furlongs divided into strips, blocks of assarted land (sometimes enclosed), and intervening patches of meadow and pasture. This field pattern, if pattern is an appropriate description, was more or less the rule in much of Lancashire and the West Riding and common enough, too, in Northumberland and Durham; but it also appears in varying other guises in various other places. It is characteristic of many of the areas in which assarting continued actively until a relatively late date. In south-east Cambridgeshire, for example, or the Chilterns, or parts of Kent and Surrey, villages were endowed with multiple fields created out of piecemeal assarts which, for cropping purposes, had to be flexibly combined. The East Anglian system, too, belongs to the same order of things. The field pattern and its subdivision into strips and parcels was markedly irregular, and individual holdings tended to be concentrated in one part only of the village territory; but here again a flexible combination of furlongs under a particular crop enabled regular rotations to be followed despite the complications of the territorial and tenurial schemes.

Despite some dissimilarities, the open-field and the irregular field systems had much in common: they tended to create an 'open' landscape, the fields were divided into strips which were shared among a number of cultivators, and a communally approved rotation of crops was practised on them. On the Bishop of Chichester's manor at Aldingbourne on the Sussex coastal plain, for example, land dispersed in a variety of fields was combined into three roughly equal 'seasons' for cropping purposes: the first of 118 acres in four fields and crofts, the second of 140 acres in five fields, and the third of 124½ acres in three.[36] In East Anglia, too, furlongs were grouped into 'shifts' as a basis for three-course husbandry, as were assarts and embryonic fields at West Wratting in Cambridgeshire and multiple small fields and closes in wooded Hertfordshire. Irregular field systems, in other words, did not preclude more or less regular rotation; while conversely a regular three-field system did not prevent rotational flexibility. At Wigston Magna, while one field was sown only with barley, the other accommodated winter-sown wheat and rye as well as spring-sown peas and oats. In this latter field cropping must surely have been organized by the furlong.[37]

The regime of enclosures was another matter. It produced a landscape of small fields which were often cultivated by a single family according to that family's own wishes. Enclosures were prominent in those districts where land was being filched from the woodland: in Essex and Hertfordshire; in the wooded uplands of the West Midlands; in Sherwood, Charnwood and Rockingham forests in the East Midlands; and in the Kent and Sussex Weald. The prevalence of enclosures in Kent outside the Weald may be explained in part by their derivation from individual intakes from the woodland subsequently modified by the custom of partible inheritance and the play of an active landmarket. Enclosures also appear in other colonizing contexts: on the moorland frontier as well as in the lowlands of Cornwall and Devon, and in a very different form in the fenlands of eastern England. In Lincolnshire much of the land which sustained a burgeoning population took the form of intakes from the fen, often cultivated in severalty, which needed to be dyked to preserve them from inundation. Where it existed, indeed, this landscape of closes was one in which the individual pioneer was prominent, even to the extent of having escaped from the confines of hamlet or village. In Devon and Cornwall, in Kent and Sussex, on the Chiltern hills and in the Hertfordshire woodland the isolated farmstead was becoming a more familiar part of the rural scene. In these regions, and wherever closes were an important part of the village arable, the villagers must have enjoyed a larger measure of self-determination and a greater opportunity to substitute flexibility for routine.[38]

It would appear that enclosures were often cultivated more intensively than open fields. In Devon and Cornwall, and probably elsewhere, a system of convertible husbandry was pursued in which the closes were subjected to a rotation of crops followed by a number of years under grass; there was no clean fallow. The length of the arable and grass cycles could be altered to suit the needs of the farmer and the quality of his soil, and the rotations helped to improve both crop yields and the quality of the pasture.

The so-called 'infield–outfield' system has perhaps been given too much prominence by historians. In essence it involved the simple expedient of supplementing the yields of the more fertile and intensively exploited lands (the infields) by cultivating portions of the less fertile 'waste' (the outfields) on a temporary basis. The terms infield and outfield may also be misleading, for the intensively farmed lands did not necessarily form a core or nucleus and the areas of waste were not necessarily on the peripheries of the settlement. The temporary cultivation of the waste was a logical response to the increasing demand for food, and it appears in various forms in places where soils were poor: the Norfolk and Suffolk Breckland, some places in the Yorkshire wolds, the heaths of Nottinghamshire and Staffordshire, in parts of north Kent and the Kentish marshes. It was perhaps most widespread in the high lands of northern and western England (and in Wales and Ireland), where land suitable for arable cultivation was relatively scarce and where 'waste' available for temporary reclamation was plentiful. Yet even in the south-west the cultivation of wastes never provided more than a small fraction of the total arable. The high cost of preparing rough pasture for cultivation, coupled with the inevitable brevity of the cropping cycles, rendered it a marginal exercise even in times of high and rising grain prices.[39]

The origins of the variant field patterns of the medieval countryside cannot be discussed in detail here, for they involve problems transcending the time-scale of the present study. At the same time the diversity of field arrangements lends support to the hypothesis that open and common field systems evolved slowly.[40] Some of the stages of evolution can be observed in a foreshortened fashion in many of the colonizing areas and particularly in those parts of the plain of York that had to be recolonized after the Conqueror devastated them. Here the fields were built up again from successive assarts from the waste.[41] A not dissimilar process of reclamation took place over a longer term at Wheldrake, though it stopped short of creating fully-fledged open fields. When the story begins there was already an 'old-field' occupying the best land around the village and shared out amongst its inhabitants. In the century or so before 1235 the extent of the village arable was more or less doubled, mainly through the work of individual pioneers in making intakes from the waste. These reclamations, however, tended to be assimilated with the 'old-field' into a single common field area because, when they were not under crops, all the villagers enjoyed common rights over them. After 1235, on the other hand, the Statute of Merton gave lords much greater freedom to reclaim or authorize reclamations without reserving to commoners grazing rights in the assarts so made. Reclamation went on at Wheldrake, but it was now more usual for the colonist to preserve the land he had won for his sole use in a permanently fenced enclosure, so that in the event the common field of Wheldrake came to be ringed with closes.[42]

In brief, individual colonists often appear at the beginning of the story of the village fields. They won land from the waste for their own use, and very often what they won perpetuated their names long after they were dead: their assarts continued to be known as Gamelridding, Swainsrode and the like. At least while they were under crops, moreover, these plots of reclaimed land were likely originally to have been held in severalty, but ultimately very many of them were partitioned into parcels and absorbed into regular or irregular open fields. The process of absorption and partitioning almost always eludes us, but in bringing it about a number of influences were probably at work. The fact that colonists might have to allow common rights over their closes to their neighbours in the 'open time' after the harvest may be one; so may the custom of partible inheritance, said to be *quasi veteri more Anglicano* (according to the old English custom) at Malham in Craven in the twelfth century;[43] and so may the sales of small plots of land as the land market became more active. At the same time, it is doubtful whether this is the whole story. The intermixture of parcels found to one degree or another in most field systems often suggests an origin in communal assarting, in which the members of the colonizing group shared the proceeds with each other. Sometimes, however, there appears to have been a greater element of seignorial direction. In those Yorkshire and Durham villages where the parcels of holdings lie in a uniform order throughout the village fields we seem to have the results of the organized recovery of land in which a lord systematically parcelled out the gains amongst his dependants. In many of the medieval field systems a good deal of individualism remained, particularly where the regime of enclosures was the dominant one; but in most systems a complex pattern of land sharing in scattered parcels was a norm.

A variety of influences imposed a collaborative scheme on the elements which composed the village arable. In order to provide for a regular cropping sequence furlongs and closes were grouped into 'seasons'; and 'seasons' in turn, especially as assarting filled up the interstices between them, were consolidated into fields. When that point arrived, the regulation of grazing rights characteristic of the 'common fields' became a necessity; but grazing rights, especially as reclamation reduced the availability of pasture, might themselves be a motive for reducing an irregular disposition of arable to regularity. Late in the Middle Ages the Abbot of Fountains and his tenants at Marton in Dishforth divided the arable there into three fields 'so that one part each year would be fallow', and therefore subject to common pasturage.[44] The grazing rights of commoners were best served by a regular disposition of the village arable.

The growth of the open fields, therefore, is closely associated with assarting. The circumstances which favoured the emergence of the 'Midland' field systems were principally the prevalence of an agriculture in which winter and spring crops alternated with fallow, a growing population pressure demanding the fullest use of resources, and an increasing shortage of pasture which called for a field layout permitting grazing of the fallow and of the cornland after harvest. There were likewise conditions which inhibited the full development of anything like the 'Midland' systems. They were less likely to appear where population densities were low and where pasture was abundant; where terrain made the reclamation of continuous tracts of arable a practical impossibility; and where something approaching an oats monoculture made unnecessary the more elaborate rotations developed elsewhere. In very many parts of the country the prevalence of these conditions, or of some of them, explains systems that stop some way short of developed open-field. At the same time, social institutions also helped to preserve less developed forms of arable layout. In East Anglia and Kent, for example, a large body of free peasants, as well as the terrain, helps to explain the irregular field systems that are a feature of these regions. A corollary might be that the force of lordship also helped to impose regularity upon the fields of the Midland plain and that there is a close relationship between the Midland open-field systems and the strength of seignorial power.

As to the time-scale of the developments which produced the open and common field systems of lowland England, there can be little doubt that the time of definition in many places did lie in the twelfth and thirteenth centuries.[45] These were times when the level of medieval population was reaching its maximum, when the pressure on land resources was most intense, and when inroads into the waste were depleting supplies of pasture. On the other hand, there were some parts of England that already show many signs of being so densely peopled even in 1086 that it is difficult to believe they were not subjected already to precisely those pressures which elsewhere made for the full evolution of open and common fields in the following generations.[46] The time-scale of economic evolution in a society in which colonizing endeavours extended over centuries is almost certain to be long.

Before leaving the village fields it must be added that not all lines of evolution led in the direction of open fields. As we have seen there were whole regions where colonization issued in closes and isolated farms, creating a landscape of enclosures long before any recognized enclosure movement had begun.[47] At the same time some influences were at work even in the open champion country leading in the same direction. We have already seen how, at Cuxham, the Merton College demesnes had in the thirteenth century been gathered up into a limited number of blocks of land by purchase and exchange. The object, doubtless, was easier management and more economical cultivation than a regime of scattered strips permitted. It is likely, too, that the same motives underlay the small purchases and exchanges which enabled many an enterprising peasant to acquire strips adjoining those already in his possession. Here again we see the open fields full of movement. The existence of common rights over the arable tended to prevent this type of consolidation extending to enclosure; but individualism had some footholds in the open fields as well as on the colonizing frontiers of arable England.

Meadows and commons

There were some places on the colonizing frontiers of medieval England where fields were of minor importance and where enterprise was basically pastoral. This was true of the upper reaches of the Devon and Cornish moors, of the Pennines, of the Lake District; it was partially true even of some of the sheep-rearing districts like the Yorkshire wolds. It seems truest of all, however, of the cattle country. On the Pennine slopes of Lancashire, for example, around 1300, Henry Lacy had a series of vaccaries in Blackburnshire stocked with some 1,200 breeding cows. By contrast at Ightenhill, one of the centres of his estate, the demesne amounted only to 8 acres of arable and 1 acre of meadow and tenant holdings to a mere 151¼ acres.[48] In Northumberland, too, the great sprawling manor of Tarset in the thirteenth century included 38 acres of demesne and 280 acres of tenant land worth some £16 yearly; but an array of hopes and sheilings and grazings in the moorland valleys and pastures was worth nearly £192.[49] Here there is no doubt where the emphasis lay.

Specialization as extreme as this did not prevail in many places. For the majority of men arable land had a clear primacy, implied in the formulae of charters like that by which the prior of Bullington gave Henry son of Osbert a bovate of land in Hackthorn (Lincs) 'with the meadow pertaining to that land and with common pasture and with all other appurtenances and with one perch of meadow in Westmoor'.[50] Meadow and pasture pertain to arable land; they were ancillary to it – but that did not mean that they were any less indispensable to the village economy. A high proportion of the peasantry had some livestock: many, but not all, plough-beasts and probably rather more a cow or pigs or poultry or sheep (see pp. 152–5). Medieval farming was always mixed farming in most regions and in some there was a nice balance between arable and stock-rearing. In Norfolk the obligation of many tenants to fold their sheep on the lord's arable points to that association between corn and sheep which has endured in the agriculture of the county; and in the west the husbandry of the Cotswolds and the vales was complementary. Livestock, whether belonging to lords or peasants, posed problems of pasturage and winter feed. These problems gave importance to the pastoral appurtenances of arable tenements.

So far as meadow went there are many signs of how indispensable it was. At a time when modern root crops and manufactured feeding stuffs were unknown, and when grain was hardly to be spared for stock except for plough beasts, hay was almost the only winter fodder. Hayfields, therefore, tended to be scarce and precious. At Laughton in Sussex, for example, 213½ acres of arable were valued in 1292 at 65s2½d, but 78½ acres of meadow were worth £8.11s6d.[41] In most places, moreover, meadow was much scarcer than at Laughton and each man had a limited apportionment of it, like the virgater at Quarrendon (Bucks) who was granted meadow *quantum pertinet ad unam virgatam eiusdem ville* (as much as belongs to one of the virgates of that village). Shares of meadow, like shares in the arable, often consisted of dispersed parcels (the portion of a virgater at Addington being held in plots of 2 acres, 1 acre, ½ acre and 2 acres).[52] Finally, shares of meadow were sometimes less permanent than arable shares and were redistributed by lot from time to time. This practice was carried out annually at Chertsey and Thorpe in Surrey even in the fourteenth century. It looks like an attempt to deal out fairly a scarce commodity.[53]

The scarcity of meadow made pasturage rights all the more important to the villager, whose needs in this respect were met by a variety of rights of 'common'. These rights are illustrated by a charter of 1270 concerning the Buckinghamshire village of Hartwell. Common pasturage there was of two sorts. It extended over '500 acres of arable land and meadow lying in divers places in the fields and meadows of Hartwell', pastured during 'open time' (i.e. when fallowed or between crops); and also over 'other foreign pastures outside the arable lands and hay meadows' (i.e. the uncultivated waste, in the medieval sense of that word).[54] To a greater or less extent these two types of common were available in most villages. Where a regime of enclosed fields prevailed, common rights over the arable might be restricted or even non-existent, but by no means infrequently in these circumstances the grazing rights of neighbours were reserved. Elsewhere it was of the essence of the common fields that they were 'open' for grazing whenever they grew no crops and that individually held selions within the fields were thrown into common pasturage available to the whole community. Conversely, once crops were sown again, the arable selions (strips of arable land) passed back to the individual landholder and the field concerned literally ceased to be open. Permanent fences, if they existed, had to be repaired or temporary ones erected by each landowner to keep out stock from the growing corn. Failure to do so was to the damage of a man's lord and of his other neighbours.[55] Possibly in many places this right of common enjoyed by all neighbours on the common arable fields was a relatively late development, and it may have been preceded by a more restricted right of joint grazing in a particular part of the village territory shared only by those who held land in that particular tract.[56] It was a mark of the full development of the common field regime at Dishley in Leicestershire that *in seysona quando campi aperti sunt . . . . vicini cum vicinis comunicare debent* (in the season when the fields are open neighbours should enjoy common rights with neighbours).[57]

Common rights in the open fields and associated rights in the village waste were accorded to the body of neigbours which made up the village. A man who 'was not a member of their community' was not entitled to common pasture, nor was a man who did not 'have any tenement or ground there',[58] Common rights, indeed, were very frequently related to the size of a man's holding. The Glastonbury surveys of 1243, under the rubric *de admensuratione pasture*, (concerning the allotment of pasture) lay down that a virgater should have pasture for four oxen, two cows, a horse, three pigs and twelve sheep, the amount of stock considered adequate *ad tantam terram colendam et sustinendam* (to cultivate and keep in good heart that much land). Again, a grant of three bovates at Spaldington in Yorkshire in the late twelfth century carried with it 'common pasture pertaining to the said three bovates' for forty cows and their calves and ten mares and their foals.[59]

Common rights did not apply only to the open fields and waste grassland, as two other Yorkshire charters clearly show. One refers to common pasture *in bosco et plano* at Holme on Spalding Moor, 'and timber in the wood to make their houses and fences and to burn', together with the right to feed pigs in the wood. Another relating to the same place specifies the amount of timber to be taken yearly from the woods, the number of pigs to be fed there and the number of oxen to be run in the common pasture. Turf to burn and thatch for houses might also be taken in the marsh belonging to Holme.[60] Fenland and woodland, in other words, offered valuable adjuncts to a villager's holding. Cattle and geese could be grazed on the fen and pigs in the woodland; and, while woods provided indispensable timber, fens provided opportunities for fishing and fowling. Both, moreover, were reserves of pasture: livestock-farming bulked large on marshland that might be marginal for arable purposes and cattle as well as pigs were grazed in the woodlands, possibly a preliminary step to their reclamation.

In most medieval villages, then, tofts and crofts, arable selions, meadow and common pasture were coordinated elements of the agrarian scheme. Obviously the composition of village territories varied according to terrain; but arable cultivation was seldom entirely absent even on the high and bleak lands, and the lowland arable farmer could hardly manage without hay and pasture even if, as at Cuxham, he had to rely in part on the surplus endowment of neighbouring villages.[61] The composition of village territories also varied over time. The expansion of cultivation between the Conquest and the Black Death altered substantially the balance between arable and pasture. Often this development was a healthy one, bringing into use new productive land; but it was not always so. Reclamation also brought marginal land into arable cultivation and, especially in some of the older settled parts of the country in which population pressure was most intense, there are signs that pasture became genuinely scarce. The results were the thirteenth-century competition for pasture already noticed (see pp. 38–9), seemingly more stringent definitions of common rights enjoyed by holders of arable tenements as time goes on, and the apparently small numbers of livestock owned by most peasants even in such naturally pastoral areas as the Wiltshire downlands (see pp. 152–5). At the same time, expanding arable and contracting pasture, even when there was compensation in the more systematic grazing of arable fields in 'open' times, evidently tended to restrict the scale of stock-farming, and consequently supplies of natural manure, in arable villages. The inadequacy of manure supplies, combined with the reclamation of land that was marginal for arable purposes, may have occasioned some deterioration of the average productivity of land under cereals at the same time as supplies of animal products were failing to increase in most places to match a growing population. In combination these trends may have accentuated the prevalance of malnutrition and the vulnerability of no small part of the population to diseases and epidemics, so that there is justification for the conclusion that by the thirteenth century 'the frontier between corn and hoof had moved very far, indeed too far, cornwards'.[62]

The community of the village

The tofts and crofts of villages and hamlets could be used by their holders with a good deal of individual self-determination; but it was a different matter once the back lane was crossed, certainly in the 'classical' open-field area and frequently even in areas of more irregular field patterns. The character of the arable fields is underlined by charters dealing with land in villages divided between more than one manor: it is said to lie 'in the territory of Hackthorn', 'in the field of Hackthorn', 'in the territory of the field of Hackthorn'.[63] Fields are village fields; individual tenements, even the tenements of lords of manors, were commonly dispersed in them, intermingled with parcels of the tenements of others. Agricultural routine, therefore, had to some degree to be communally rather than individually determined. Meadow was so much a communal asset that in some places the shares in it were periodically re-allotted and the individual's right to common pasture was regulated by general rules which became stricter as grazing land was filched for corn. The territorial organization of medieval villages therefore made it necessary for the individual to be subordinated in certain respects to the generality. In consequence medieval Latin knew of the *villa*, the group of houses and tract of land, the village in its geographical aspect; but it also knew of the *villata*, the body of villagers who lived in and from the village territory, the human community of the village. However limited their sense of solidarity, the existence of village communities was a contemporary assumption which must not be ignored.

In this connection Henry III's order of 1242 about the keeping of peace throughout the land is not untypical. It ordered watches to be mounted each night *in singulis villis integris* (in each whole village) by either four or six men according to the number of the inhabitants. To ensure men were properly equipped for this purpose each sheriff, accompanied by two knights, was to go round his county hundred by hundred, calling before him all men between the ages of fifteen and sixty, whether free or villein, and swearing them to procure arms appropriate to the amount of land or the value of chattels in their possession. In each village, too, he was to see to the appointment of one or two constables, and in each hundred of a chief constable, who would be responsible 'for carrying out what pertains to keeping the peace'.[64]

In this order we have an expression of the contemporary view of England as a community of the realm composed of a hierarchy of subordinate territorial communities. The base of the whole structure was the 'whole village', treated as an entity even though its soil might well be divided between a number of landlords. How it came by this unity is a matter which calls for some discussion. Maitland sometimes stresses the determining role of extrinsic forces. Speaking of villages among the other communities, he tells us that 'the community is a community, not because it is a self-sufficient organism, but because it is a subordinate member of a greater community, of a nation. . . . The communities are far more often the bearers of duties than of rights.' Men, in fact, 'were drilled and regimented into communities'.[65] In this sense village and other communities were artificial creations. The royal government of medieval England seized on them for its own purposes, imposed on them corporate duties and responsibilities, and in the process fused them into communities.

Up to a point the truth of this contention is undeniable, and so is the fact that the forces making for communalism appeared very early. The taxation and military systems which the Normans inherited from the Old English kings started from a presupposition that counties and hundreds were composed of corporately contributory townships; and the Domesday commissioners, too, regarded villages as communities which could be 'represented' before them by their priest, reeve and six *villani*.[66] The same assumptions underlay the organization of courts in Norman and Angevin England. Suit to the shire and hundred courts in the early twelfth century was owed by the vill; and Henry II's Assize of Clarendon ordered the justices to enquire regarding malefactors by the oath of twelve of the more lawful men of each hundred and four of the more lawful men of each *villata*. Soon afterwards vills were required to testify regarding mysterious deaths before the coroners and under Henry III the village communities might sue by their representatives in the king's courts. At about this same time they were made units in the system of watch and ward for keeping the peace, and the pool of men suitably armed for this purpose became one which could also be tapped for the recruitment of armies. Simon de Montfort in 1264 planned to levy four or five men from each vill; in 1295 each northern village was to send two men to the king's commissioners to receive instructions regarding the defence of the Border; on a number of occasions under Edward II each village was to provide one man for the army and pay him his wages for a specified period.[68]

In this fashion the duties of village communities accumulated, and others continued to be added. The village had the task of maintaining roads and bridges within its territory; the village was the basic unit for raising lay subsidies; lands forfeited by felons for a year and a day were often handed over to village communities with the injunction to answer to the king for their issues.[69] Corresponding to corporate duties was a liability to corporate punishment, beginning with the murder fines the Conqueror exacted from villages or hundreds in which a man was murdered whom it was impossible to prove to be no Norman. 'Common fines' were the natural concomitant of common obligations. The scope of village obligations makes it all the more remarkable that they had so little equipment to fulfil them. The constables of the peace, whose office developed from the arrangements of 1242, were almost the only officials responsible for 'public' duties.[70] Manorial officers might often be used for these purposes and in the long run much of the burden came to rest on the shoulders of parish officials; but in the thirteenth century *ad hoc* conscription was more characteristic. When Edward I was granted a subsidy of one-ninth in October 1297, for example, the chief taxors in each county were directed, 'in good faith and by good examination', to

choose two or four men according to the size of each vill to assess their
fellow villagers. Only if a vill could not supply sufficient responsible
men was the choice to be extended to men of neighbouring villages.[71]

This absence of organization in vills to carry out public duties is
significant. It may lead us to place less emphasis than Maitland did on
the constitutive force of governments drilling and regimenting men into
communities. Action from above probably reinforced the communal
aspects of the vill, but it did not create them; on the contrary, the devices
of government bear witness to a communal potentiality in villages, an
outcome of intrinsic forces which kings, ill-equipped with administrative resources, seized on for their own purposes. The roots of this
solidarity are to be found in the character of the *villata* as a group of
agricultural shareholders, with interlocking interests in fields and
meadows and commons. Even in this regard villages have little in the
way of organization. Very often communal routine and joint interests
were supported not so much by organization as by custom; but in the
circumstances of the thirteenth century, when the struggle for existence
was sharp and profit could be made by stealing a march upon custom,
some sanction was needed to give it backing. Most commonly this was
provided by the manorial court. Important as that tribunal was as an
instrument for prosecuting the lord's interest (see pp. 194–5), it also enabled
the villagers to have their say. Even in the manor of Hales, the lord of
which was less than tender to manifestations of peasant insub-
ordination, the suitors could lay down what custom was and have it
registered on the rolls of the court for better security in the future.[72]
Custom here might be manorial rather than villar, but wherever village
and manor coincided the distinction is a fine one.

Statements of immemorial custom in the manor court were not the
only way in which villagers showed a capacity for joint action. Much is
heard in the records of 'common' officers – swineherds, cowherds,
shepherds, gooseherds and so forth – who were sometimes chosen by
their fellow villagers.[73] Neither their titles nor the fact of their election
proves them to be villar rather than manorial officials, for reeves (whose
principal duty was to safeguard the interests of their lords) were also
chosen or elected. On the other hand, the thirteenth-century custumal
of Bleadon in Somerset seems to draw a distinction between the lord's
shepherd and the village shepherd and, in a case before the forest
justices in 1251, there is mention of the lord's cowherd and the
herdsman of the cattle of the vill of Sudborough in Nottinghamshire.[74]
Common herdsmen chosen by the villagers to look after the cattle of the
village look very like the servants of the village community.

The role of the community may well have been the stronger in villages
under divided and absentee lordship, like Wigston Magna in

Leicestershire. At the beginning of the seventeenth century it was alleged that its inhabitants met yearly to order their fields and commons and that this was 'an ancient custom and order'.[75] The custom cannot be traced back to the twelfth and thirteenth centuries at Wigston, but traces of communal action on the part of villagers are not altogether absent. Those traces, moreover, are likely to underrate the vitality of the village community because villages did not keep records, their customs being recorded in the memories of men. If they were written down it was because lords were persuaded or found it desirable to do so. When that happened lords no doubt also played a part in shaping customs to suit their own ends, but that did not preclude villagers from making their own contributions to them.

The capacity of villagers to play a positive role side by side with their lords is illustrated by an episode which Vinogradoff made familiar. When in the twelfth century the village of Segenhoe in Bedfordshire was divided between two lords, some redistribution of lands was entailed; and subsequently men encroached on each other's lands, apparently during the rebellion of 1173–74. All this left a legacy of disputes and a general uncertainty about what lands belonged to particular tenants. So, the record tells us, 'all, by common consent' and in the presence of the two lords of the vill, handed over their tenements which were measured as though they were new land being apportioned, so that they could be redistributed *rationabiliter* (in a reasonable manner).[76] The circumstances at Segenhoe were doubtless very exceptional and a more commonplace matter concerned the inhabitants of the much divided village of Cottenham (Cambs) in 1344: the right to dig turf in the common fen for 'housebote' (i.e. to build or repair houses). Here, 'it was ordained in the church of Cottenham' by the councils of the various lords of the vill and 'by the assent of the freemen and villeins of the said vill' (subject only to the subsequent concurrence of the manorial lords) what rules should govern the exercise of this right in the future.[77]

If village communities often collaborated with their lords they could also combine against them. Whether or not Marc Bloch was right to maintain that agrarian revolt was as common in the seignorial regime as strikes are in modern industrial society, it was inevitable that conflicts of interest arose between lords and peasants. The majority of these conflicts seem to have concerned the actions of individuals, and they span the whole gamut of human emotions from the amusing, as when Hugh Walter's son of Shillington (Beds) 'lay at the head of a ridge in harvest and impeded the work of the lord' and Robert Crane of Broughton (Hunts) 'played alpenypricke during the lord's work',[78] to the tragic, as when a tenant of the Earl of Gloucester was reported to have drowned himself in the River Severn rather than take land on servile conditions.[79] On occasion, however, large numbers of villagers joined together and took collective action in defence of their interests, thereby displaying another aspect of the potential cohesiveness of the village community. One such example, which seems to have been a hasty response to a reduction in fringe benefits, occurred when 'all the villeins of the township of Broughton went away from the great harvest boon, leaving their work from noon till night . . . giving the malicious and false cause that they did not have their loaves as large as they were accustomed formerly and ought to have them'.[80] The size of loaves is scarcely the stuff of which rural revolts are made, but there are some instances of more serious disputes between lords and villages, or large sections of villages, which arose from matters of great importance and principle and which persisted in an atmosphere of bitterness, and sometimes violence, over many years.[81] Notable among the causes of such disputes were the claims of tenants to the privileged status of villein sokemen of the ancient demesne, and notable among the disputes themselves was the remarkably protracted conflict between the Abbey of Halesowen (Worcs) and the tenants of its great manor of the same name. This conflict lasted intermittently from 1243 until all labour services were commuted into money rents in 1327, and involved many proceedings in the court of King's Bench, royal inquests, even a petition to the king and his council, as well as the desertion of their holdings by a number of villeins.[82]

Corporate action by villages, however, was normally less dramatic and concerned with more everyday matters. A charter of 1308, for example, records a grant of certain lands at Harleston (Northants) including 'all that portion of the heath when, by the agreement of the community of the vill, it will be broken up'.[83] Characteristic products of this capacity of villages to take common decisions, often of course jointly with their lords, were village by-laws regulating such things as gleaning after harvest, exercises of rights of common, and the grazing of village paths and ways. Such rules at Staines (Middlesex) were 'provided and ordained by the community of the whole vill' in 1276; at Newton Longville (Bucks) in 1290 they were 'granted and ordained by the community of the vill' and in 1291 'by the lord and the community of the vill'; at Great Horwood in 1314 they were 'granted and agreed by the whole *villata*'[84] At Littleport (Cambs) in 1325 there were 'keepers of the by-law' who presented offenders against it in the manorial court; and both there and at Wilburton in 1251 only half the penalties imposed on those convicted went to the lord. The other half at Littleport went to the men of the vill *pro opere ecclesie* (for work on the church). Here the men of the vill were not only capable of acting corporately in receiving money; they also appear to have had some corporate responsibility for the upkeep of the village church.[85]

There is, then, a good deal of evidence for the corporate action of village communities, especially where the interests of its members interlocked in the communal routines of open-field agriculture and common pastures. This in turn makes it a good deal less surprising to find villagers leasing whole territories from their lords. In the years around 1200 royal manors were occasionally farmed to their inhabitants, although the practice was commonest in the case of manors with quasi-burghal characteristics; but as early as 1086 some manors were leased to their peasant inhabitants, for the *villani* held the St Paul's estate at Willesden and the Chertsey Abbey manor at East Clandon.[86] At a much later date, in 1280, the Abbot of Ramsey granted Hemingford Abbots (Hunts) to the men of the place for seven years at an annual farm of £40. They were to have not only the demesne and other issues but even the proceeds of all actions in the manor court excepting those which could only be determined before the abbot or his bailiff.[87] In such arrangements some sort of capacity for the men of a village to act corporately is assumed as a matter of course – an assumption not infrequently made on the Ramsey estates. At Graveley the whole *villata* paid the abbot 8d; at Elsworth the abbot owed the *villata* 12d for mowing his meadow; at Hemingford the *villata* held a certain meadow from the abbot for 30s.[88] The communal potentiality of the village was not the only influence which shaped medieval rural society, but neither should its force be underrated.

Village and parish

Villages also sometimes displayed this potentiality in the endowment of churches. Churches were most frequently founded and endowed by lords but on occasion the villagers participated in this pious work. Clearly documented cases are rare but there is one at Hutthorpe (Northants), apparently originally a part of the parish of Thedingworth (Leics). Sometime in the mid-twelfth century the men of Hutthorpe gave an acre from each virgate in each of the two fields of their village to establish a chapel there. A similar donation of a portion of his tenement by each member of a community to the village church is apparently implied in a slightly later charter relating to Kedington (Lincs); and in the same county 8 acres of arable were given by the *rustici* of Great Sturton to the chapel of that village.[89] These proceedings may be untypical, but at least they suggest that a village church was an important element in the life of a village. More than that, it is also clear that the action of the church as well as the policy of the state helped to make villages into communities.

There was, in fact, a tendency in the Middle Ages for the territorial vill to coincide with the ecclasiastical parish. That coincidence was never perfect. If we take the road from Cambridge out to Soham, we pass on the right the two large churches of St Mary and St Cyriac in Swaffham Prior, both in the one churchyard and both dramatically raised above the existing village street. Such duplication usually means that the lords of two manors within a village had each secured the right to establish a church. At Wigston Magna, for instance, St Wistan's church served the Champayne manor although it had to acknowledge dependence upon the mother church of All Saints at the other end of the village.[90] Much commoner was the grouping of villages into very extensive parishes served by a central 'minster'. This arrangement was characteristic of the missionary phase of the Anglo-Saxon church and still leaves its mark in many places in 1086 – at Taunton in Somerset, Hartland in Devon, Bosham in Sussex, Morville in Shropshire, and Leominster in Herefordshire to name only a few of them.[91] By 1086, however, these large parishes of southern England were already breaking up where they still existed; and even in the remote south-west the modern parish boundaries of Devon had mostly been drawn by the end of the twelfth century.[92]

The same tendencies were at work in the extensive parishes, comprehending many townships and hamlets, characteristic of the north, although here the pace was often much slower. St Andrews church at Corbridge in Northumberland, for instance, was an ancient Anglian foundation that had originally been the ecclesiastical centre for a vast royal estate embracing the whole of middle Tynedale. Three townships were detached, however, probably in the eleventh century to constitute the thegnage of Halton and they became a separate chapelry. Three more townships by 1162 had been alienated to the barony of Bolam and likewise came to constitute the separate chapelry of Little Whittington. Northern parishes and chapelries, however, commonly continued to contain more than one township or hamlet (it was not until the nineteenth century that Acklington, which had thirty-six tenants in 1248, and the little port of Amble were detached from the ancient parish of Warkworth); but even in the north the general tendency was for the area of parishes to contract through the formation of dependent chapelries and for the number of churches to multiply.[93]

In most of England, even in 1086, the village church was already a familiar feature of the rural scene; and thereafter, the village and parish communities were identical in many places, making the village an ecclesiastical as well as a secular community. Here again the communal aspect of the village was reflected in communal obligations. The parishioners were called on to keep the nave in repair and the churchyard in good order, to provide many items of equipment including, according to Archbishop Winchelsey, bells for the steeple, a pyx, a Lenten veil, a font, a bier for the dead, a vessel for holy water and certain other items of equipment.[94] They were also taxed for the support of the church and its incumbent, for they paid tithes of their corn and other crops, of the increase of their livestock, and even of their garden produce. Further, at least the villeins had to render up their second best beast to the rector when they died in recompense for the tithes they could safely be assumed to have concealed; and all made oblations at mass on the great feast days and on such family occasions as baptisms, weddings and funerals.

The church had its own weapons to compel the villagers to fulfil these obligations. It was a positive duty of parish priests to excommunicate those who failed to pay their tithes, however reluctant Chaucer's good parson was to do so. None the less defaults continued to occur, and the periodic visitations of churches by officials of dioceses or religious houses frequently revealed buildings that were in disrepair and ecclesiastical equipment and ornaments that were 'broken', 'old', 'worn-out', or simply 'missing'.[95] The burden of ecclesiastical dues and their exaction by 'cursing' could turn the parochial community into a community of resentment, especially where rectorial revenues were impropriated by a monastery or an absentee pluralist. There are many examples, especially from the late thirteenth century, of organized resistance on the part of the parishioners, involving the withholding of offerings and sometimes even assaults upon priests.[96] Moreover, the attempts of ecclesiastical courts to regulate the morals of the laity, particularly with regard to sexual matters, must have provoked some resentment. Punishment usually took the form of beatings, with excommunication for those who refused to submit or who were guilty of especially offensive behaviour.[97] At times, therefore, undertones of anticlericalism appear in the relationships of villagers and church.

At the same time this was far from being the sole relationship between church and parishioners, as William Berner's gift of two acres in alms to the church of Habrough (Lincs) testifies. The grant was made 'in honour of the altar of St Katherine in that church'; it was witnessed by 'the whole parish of Habrough', 'on a certain Sunday when the abbot of Barling celebrated mass at the said altar'.[98] Such small donations to their church by donors evidently of peasant status are common enough wherever free peasants were numerous. The motives inspiring them escape us since the medieval peasant was not articulate about his religious beliefs: he was in any case illiterate, and the church did not make it an easy thing for him to grasp its doctrines. Services were in

Latin and sermons rare; so that what the peasant learned of doctrine was more likely to come from wall-paintings and images (with their stress on the pains of Hell, the anguish of the crucifixion, and the mediatory compassion of the Virgin and the saints), and from the music, miming and imagery of the services culminating in the 'one great mimetic rite' of the mass.[99] Men learned by eye and ear rather than through rational apprehension and lessons so learned issued principally in emotions, whether fear of hell, hope of salvation, thankfulness or humility. The emotions were important in persuading many villagers to be generous to their village churches.

At the same time, the church's relationships with the agricultural community were more complex than this, for it identified itself with the whole routine of agrarian life.[100] The cycle of ecclesiastical feasts was roughly coincident with the cycle of traditional popular celebrations marking turning points in the farming year. All Saints (1 November) was the start of the winter, when cattle were brought in to the byre, as well as the time when the evil spirits abroad on Hallowe'en had to be propitiated. The twelve days of Christmas were the first great holiday after the autumn ploughing and the sowing of the winter grain – a holiday ending with Candlemas and Plough Monday, when the spring ploughing began. The latter task, if luck and weather held, was over by Easter which began another holiday lasting to Hockday, two Tuesdays later. Fallow ploughing, weeding the corn and sheep-shearing filled the time to midsummer (the feast of the Nativity of St John the Baptist) which was the traditional beginning of haytime just as the feast of St Peter ad Vincula (1 August) was the beginning of harvest. The latter was more popularly known as Lammas day, possibly pointing to a custom of bringing loaves made from the new wheat to the church to be blessed. By Michaelmas (29 September), again given luck and good weather, the harvest was done and St Michael's feast could coincide with harvest home, the end and crown of the farming year. It was also the time when the autumn work in the fields began all over again, making Michaelmas the start as well as the end of the eternal agricultural cycle.

Parish and village, therefore, were more than territories which tended to coincide geographically. By absorbing into its calendar many of the traditional festivals of the agricultural community, the church gave those festivals new meaning and helped to fuse the community of parishioners with the community of the village. Moreover the bonds between the church and the village extended beyond religious festivals to customs, habits, observances and uses which were by no means entirely religious. Churches were often the largest and most impressive buildings in villages, so it is not surprising that they were used for a variety of secular purposes, some of which appear very strange to us.

Courts and other meetings might be held there; it was not uncommon for the belt of knighthood to be conferred in a parish church. Goods might be stored there, and in the face of Scottish raiders north-countrymen and even their livestock took refuge in the village church. We also learn that churches were often the venues of games, of secular and even pagan plays, of banquets, and on occasion of unrestrained drinking; the latter, called scot-ales, were sometimes sponsored by the clergy. The churchyard, too, could be a place for gossip, a place where village girls danced and carolled and, despite the fate of the moneychangers in the Temple, a village market-place.

This interpenetration of village and parish strengthened the fabric of the village community in a way which was astonishingly enduring. During the later medieval and early modern centuries, when the manor decayed, the village retained and developed its communal capacity and exercised it through parochial rather than village officers. Villages, as we have seen, had many duties, but relatively little in the way of organization; yet parishes had to have some organization. The initial focus was the resident rector or vicar or stipendiary priest who gradually acquired helpers drawn from the ranks of the ordinary villagers. As early as 1300 we hear of churchwardens at Woodhurst in Huntingdonshire[101] and ultimately these officers took on many duties over and above the keeping of the village church. The selection by the Tudors of the parish as a basic unit for local administration had its distant roots in the relationship forged during the Middle Ages between the village and the parish.

If we return to the twelfth and thirteenth centuries, however, the church's contribution to the many-textured quality of English rural life is evident enough. It added to the cohesion of the honeycomb of communities that made up the English countryside. The coincidence of village and parish, admittedly, was by no means universal; but it became commoner and it was most prevalent in the oldest and most densely settled parts of the land. These were also the regions where manorialism was at its most robust and, between them, the church and the manorial lordship reinforced the ties which bound together land-sharing communities. Those ties were evidently slacker in the colonizing peripheries of the old-settled land. The north, with its far-ranging parishes embracing many townships, was merely one of the regions where social bonds (including ecclesiastical bonds) were weaker than they were in Midland England, where communities were less coherent, where society was more diffuse, and where peasant individualism had an ampler scope. Once again the variety of the medieval scene is its dominant characteristic.

Chapter 5

Villagers:
I. Status and tenure

In the preceding discussion much stress has been laid on the communal aspects of the medieval village. There is good reason for that stress for the way in which men shared arable and meadow, collaborated in the expansion of the village territory and enjoyed common rights in waste and pasture forced community upon them. These aggregating forces, too, were not infrequently reinforced by the influences of lordship and the church. That is not to say that communalism was the sole characteristic of village society. In the first place, communalism was conjoined even in the most coherent village community with a strand of individualism. Individuals were subjected to common rules and routines, but the produce of a man's holding and the yield of his stock (subject to appropriations by the church for tithe and by the lord in recognition of lordship) were for the most part his own. That was true however servile the terms were under which he held land. Secondly, communalism in no sense implied equality. Men were unequal in their personal status and unequal in their economic standing, and inequalities between sub-groups easily cut across the solidarity of the *villata*. Finally, every villager was a member of a group more intimate than the village community – of a family or kindred, the interests of which did not necessarily coincide with the common interest of neighbours.

All villagers, of course, had certain characteristics in common. From the economic point of view they were engaged in small-scale agricultural enterprise compared with the larger-scale enterprise of manorial lords. All of them, moreover, were tenants paying to their lords 'rents' of some sort or another. When we look closely, however, these similarities dissolve into dissimilarities. Not only were holdings unequal but there were also differences in the levels of charges paid for them. Further, there were disparities of legal status which might or might not coincide with disparities of economic standing but which, none the less, could influence prospects of poverty or prosperity significantly. The bewildering variety of terminology used to described villagers, therefore, is hardly surprising. Within the limited territory of Cambridgeshire in a single year (1279) they were recorded as *liberi*,

liberi tenentes, liberi homines, sokemanni, liberi sokemanni, bondi sokemanni, custumarii, custumarii tenentes mollond, tenentes in villenagio, villani, bondi, servi, cotagii, cotarii, liberi cotarii, croftarii, coterelli, liberi coterelli, croftmanni, cotmanni.[1] And if we move but a few miles northwards into the south Lincolnshire fens we can add *consuetudinarii, pleni villani, molemen, monedaymen, bordarii, bordi, werkmen*, and *operarii*.[2] We are very far here from the simple division of the peasantry into free tenants, villeins and cottars that has sometimes been thought sufficient.

In certain respects these lengthy lists of archaic words merely reflect a lack of precision and consistency on the part of those who drew up the documents in which we find them. Men of similar status in different places were described by different words. At the same time differing terminology also reflected real differences of status in a society with many degrees of freedom and servility. Freedom might be more or less complete, and the burdens incident on those deemed to be unfree varied between regions, within regions and over time. This was the lesson the pre-Conquest author of the *Rectitudines Singularum Personarum* endeavoured to bring home to his readers: 'The estate-law is fixed on each estate; at some places . . . it is heavier, at some places . . . lighter, because not all customs about estates are alike.'[3] This verdict is no less applicable to the late twelfth and thirteenth centuries when the surviving evidence, for the first time, enables us to scrutinize medieval villages in detail. That evidence, however, faces the historian with the task of rationalizing a positive jungle of rules governing social relationships. The Angevin lawyers, faced with the same task, drew a line between men who were and men who were not free. In so doing they undoubtedly oversimplified and, as R. H. Hilton has argued, they may also have dug a trap for a large section of the peasantry.[4] There is also a trap for the historian in that his main sources of evidence – the legal treatises, the records of proceedings in the king's courts, and the day-to-day information afforded by innumerable manorial documents – not only differ in their testimony but are frequently in direct conflict with each other. The conflict may be principally one between theory and practice, between the letter of the law and the actual relations of people; but it is one that needs to be faced and, if possible, resolved.

Villein status and tenure

At the same time the increasingly varied sources of the Angevin age are unanimous on one point: that no small proportion of English villagers were to one degree or another 'unfree'. In attempting to distinguish the free from the unfree lawyers used a variety of criteria, none of which proved altogether satisfactory; but one line of approach revolved around the question of personal status rather than the tenure of land. The distinction was a legitimate one, for the condition of villeinage did not necessarily depend on the holding of land even though it was commonly associated with it. In Bracton's view *omnes homines aut liberi sunt aut servi* (all men are either free or serfs) and for many commentators men were either *liberi homines* or *nativi*, the latter word carrying the clear implication that 'native' men were born to unfreedom. One way of determining whether or not a man was a villein, therefore, was to scrutinize his genealogy: as one strange law book put it 'serfage . . . is a subjection issuing from so high an antiquity that no free stock can be found within human memory'.[5] Time and time again, willingly or unwillingly, litigants in the courts had to demonstrate into what sort of stock they were born. When in 1202 a Berkshire man laid claim to land it was alleged against him that he was *villanus . . . ex nativitate* (a villein by birth);[6] and in Lincolnshire that same year Hawise de Kyme, in order to prove that Robert Drop *origine est villanus* (is a villein by origin), produced various of his villein kin in court – a brother, a cousin and the grandson of his father's sister. Robert's answer was that they had taken bribes to testify to their villein status and that, if 'they for hire or any other reason want to make villeins of themselves, he for his part does not want to be a villein'.[7] A more normal defence was that of a Suffolk man claimed as a serf by William Faithless in 1206. William produced four kinsfolk of the alleged serf, claiming them to be villeins, but unfortunately for him one of them turned out to be a freeman. When the defendant produced three more freemen belonging to his kindred the court proceeded to a statistical judgement of Solomon: because he 'has produced enough suit that he is free and of free birth, it is considered that he should depart free'.[8]

The determination of status was frequently complicated by marriages between partners of different legal status; for it was not at all uncommon for serfs and free to wed. Since the child inherited its status from its parents, mixed marriages necessitated rules to determine whether the paternal or the maternal line was to be dominant. In the course of the thirteenth century it seems that the courts most frequently decided that legitimate offspring took their father's status. Bastards, on the other hand, more often took that of their mother, although by the second quarter of the fourteenth century all bastards were deemed free in common law.[9]

People, then, were born free or unfree and their personal status might be quite independent of landholding. Walter Aylbern of Sutton in 1292 had to acknowledge he was 'a serf of the lord prior (of Ely) and of servile condition. . . . He holds no tenement of the lord but is under the lord prior's lordship (*advocacio*) in the same condition as other villeins.'[10]

This personal quality of serfdom is attested in a variety of ways. We find a man granting an assart to a certain lady with the note that she was not his *nativa* but the *nativa* of the overlord, the prior and convent of Winchester.[11] Again, men remained *nativi* of the Abbot of Ramsey even though they had moved from the abbot's manor of Knapwell to dwell outside his domain in Boxworth and Swavesey, of from Graveley to Godmanchester and Potton, or from Warboys to Stewkley, Huntingdon and Somersham.[12] The exaction from such emigrants of chevage (a small annual payment to the lord) was a token of his continuing lordship over them (see pp. 43–4); and from early Norman times lords enjoyed the assistance of the royal administration and the royal courts to recover their 'fugitive' villeins.[13]

One result of this personal character of serfdom was that unfree men were bought and sold. Most commonly, perhaps, villeins were sold or given away with the tenements they held: thus *c.*1184, a benefactor gave to Osney Abbey a virgate at Draycot held by Syred *cum ipso homine et filiis suis sicut nativis et omni progenie sua* (with that man himself, and his children as villeins born, and all his progeny).[14] Clearly the man, and not only the man but all his issue for ever, were granted away with the holding. At the same time, equally evidently there was a market in villeins quite distinct from a market in villein tenements. An agreement in 1230 regarding certain lands in Warwickshire and Leicestershire included the provision that one of the parties should have the body and chattels of John Kinebaut, a villein, while the other party was to have the tenement which John had held.[15] References to the sale of villeins where no land is stated to have passed are numerous. Hubert de Mountchesney sold a serf, his wife and children to Colne Priory for a mark of silver; William de Pinkeny sold the sister of a villein (who held land freely by charter) for 4*s*; William Coleville sold Maud de Biham for 5 marks: Osney Abbey bought *nativi* for 26*s*, 40*s*, and 2 besants respectively; the canons of St Paul's were not infrequent purchasers of serfs; and Geoffrey Clinton gave to Eynsham Abbey a man, his wife, their sons and daughters and all their possessions for the redemption of his sins, for the souls of his father and mother and ancestors, and in recompense for a silk cope he had borrowed from the abbey and lost.[16] The operations of the market in serfs even partitioned families. When the church of Lincoln acquired two bovates at Burgh-on-Bain in 1251 it also acquired the villein tenant of the land with all his chattels and progeny – except his two sons, Gilbert and Richard.[17]

These instances have been drawn from the older settled regions of England where, it might be supposed, serfdom was at its most stringent. Yet the sale of serfs is not restricted to such regions. As late as 1276 Glastonbury Abbey was granted a man at Shepton Mallet in Somerset, with his chattels and his progeny, *ut servum et nativum* (as a serf and a villein born).[18] If Somerset is still considered too old an area of settlement, this traffic was at least as prominent in northern England. Furness Abbey bought serfs in the north-west, Guisborough Priory bought serfs in Durham, and the Archbishop of York bought serfs in Northumberland. Cockersand Priory even had copied into its chartulary a list of the *nativi* it acquired in Lancashire: the total was 290, although by no means all of them came without land. Some of them, however, did come to the priory severed from any tenement.[19] The personality of serfdom applied in all regions.

There were other consequences of the personality of villeinage. Lords claimed powers of discipline over their villeins beyond those normally regarded as within the routine competence of manor courts. If they were rebellious the Abbot of Hales thought it proper to pursue them with axes and staves; others held that they might be set in the stocks, but that to put them in irons or pour water over them was an abuse.[20] Further a villein might be arrested and cast into prison – a particularly useful right when the villein was the lord's reeve who had failed to pay what he owed.[21] The Abbot of Kirkstall even thought he was entitled to whip a recalcitrant villein after putting him in the stocks.[22]

It was also held in law that a villein's goods and chattels were his lord's. For that reason Glanville argued that it was impossible for a villein to purchase his freedom with his own goods since in fact they belonged to his lord. Enfranchisement, therefore, had to come circuitously, the lord selling his villein to a third party, who then freed the serf and doubtless got recompense from him for the costs incurred.[23] This notion that a villein's goods were his lord's had other consequences. Early in the thirteenth century a Lincolnshire lord appropriated the goods of one deceased villein *sicut suam propriam* (as his very own);[24] on the estates of Vale Royal Abbey the abbot claimed 'all the pigs of the deceased, all his goats, all his mares at grass, and his horse also, . . . all his bees, all his uncut bacons, all his cloth of wool and flax, and whatever can be found of gold and silver. The lord shall also have his brass pots or pot. . . . Also the lord shall have the best ox.' There were similar charges levied on the peasantry of the Bishop of Lichfield's and the Earl of Lancaster's Staffordshire manors, and on the Duchy manors in Cornwall all the goods of villeins were liable to forfeiture after their deaths.[25] Not surprisingly, villeins as villeins were accorded a certain value, and it was an infringement of the proprietary rights of heirs to 'waste' them. It was possible, therefore, to have recourse to the law when a guardian 'destroyed the villeins by tallages and other . . . exactions', or when a Surrey widow exiled and impoverished the villeins as well as destroying a heronry, or when a widow in Norfolk 'destroyed two rich villeins so that they were made poor men and mendicants'.[26] Conversely, it was equally reprehensible for villeins themselves to waste their substance either by incurring fines from Holy Church for committing adultery or spending too much of their time in the ale house.[27]

The notion of the personality of villeinage was important, both in theory and practice, during the twelfth and thirteenth centuries; but it does violence to the facts of medieval rural life to divorce the peasant from the land. Another possible consequence of villein status, indeed, was that of being compulsorily settled on villein land. Abbot Roger of St Albans ordered diligent enquiry to be made about the whereabouts of sons of *nativi*, so that they could be sought out and planted on vacant holdings.[28] On the Chertsey Abbey manors, too, even in the fourteenth century men not already holding land were chosen in the manor court to take up derelict tenements, and placed in the stocks and fined if they refused them; while at Chalgrave (Beds) a man who showed a similar unwillingness had his chattels seized, and later paid a heavy fine when he took a wife.[29] For most men, however, the tenure of land was a matter of necessity rather than compulsion, for the possession of land was the sole guarantee of their daily bread. They appear in the records, therefore, as *liberi tenentes* as well as *liberi homines*, as *homines in villenagio* as well as *nativi*. The distinctions in tenure were as various as the distinctions of status; but just as a large proportion of villagers were held to be personally unfree, so were very many of them deemed to hold their land unfreely. The unfree tenant bulked as large in the village as the unfree man, and very many of the peasantry were held to be unfree both in their persons and their tenure.

Here again, by the opening of the thirteenth century, the lawyers were trying to bring rationalization into the jungle of day-to-day relationships. So far as tenure went they drew a line on one side of which lay certainty and on the other uncertainty. They argued, in other words, that the tenant who was free held on fixed and certain terms with the right freely to dispose of his land and to transmit it to his heirs under the protection of the king's courts. The unfree tenant, on the other hand, enjoyed a possession regulated by a private manorial court and held his land, as a Gloucestershire villein had to acknowledge in 1231, *nisi in villenagio et ad voluntatem . . . domini sui* (merely in villeinage and at the will of his lord).[30] To the extent that the villein in fact held at his lord's will, uncertainty did lie at the heart of villeinage – an uncertainty extending both to the security of his tenure and the terms on which he held his land. The king's courts would neither afford him protection against eviction nor award him damages against his lord; the villein had no standing in the public courts against his lord unless the latter's actions went beyond all reason (e.g. maiming or killing);[31] and as for services, Bracton argued that it was the characteristic of the villein tenant that he did not know in the evening what he would be called upon to do the following morning. The logical conclusion is that lords could regard the custom that governed villein tenures 'as but a revocable expression of their own wills'.[33]

Examples of lords exercising the arbitrary powers over their villeins conferred by the letter of the law are not lacking. We are told that, before the time of Abbot Faritius (1100–17), villeins on the manors of Abingdon Abbey were liable to be expelled from their tenements and their sons denied the right of inheritance; at the end of the twelfth century the Abbot of Cirencester considered himself entitled, when a villein tenant died, to seize his holding, grub up his garden and pull down his house; and a Lincolnshire tenant in 1202 conceded that, since he held in villeinage, 'the said (lord) could remove him at will'.[33] Here the uncertainty of villein tenure reaches its extreme point.

At the same time, both villein status and villein tenure involved other disabilities and other uncertainties. Fathers paid fines to marry off their daughters (*merchet*) or if the latter were detected in immorality (*leyrwite*); unfree tenants might be taxed under the name of tallage, in principle whenever and at whatever rate their lord determined; their sons might not be sent to school or enter the Church without the lord's leave, and his leave had to be bought. Liability to these restrictions and their attendant charges, in fact, were in many cases recognized by the courts as an indication that a man was a villein;[34] but the commonest test of all was liability to labour services. This obligation, too, had as the courts treated it a penumbra of uncertainties. One Hampshire lord claimed he could commute services for money and then reimpose them irrespective of the wishes of his villeins; and the villeins of a Northamptonshire manor acknowledged their duty to work whenever their lady commanded them to do so.[35] Bracton's view about the uncertainty of villein obligations finds a periodic basis in the court rolls.

Diversities of standing

The energy that the lawyers deployed in hammering out a doctrine of villeinage must not mislead us into peopling English villages around 1200 solely with villeins or, necessarily, into accepting their doctrine as a total description of contemporary realities. The criteria of unfreedom they adduced still left very many villagers on the free side of the line. Their rights were the converse of the villein's disabilities. Their goods were their own to do with as they would; their persons could neither be sold nor bought; they had the freedom of movement theoretically denied to the villein; they could buy and sell free land at will and the charges they paid for it were immutable and fixed; above all they had access to the royal courts which protected their rights and their properties. The free tenant's person and holding and goods were safeguarded in a way the villein's were not.

At the same time a simple dichotomy of free and unfree is a less than adequate description of the facts revealed by the records of the thirteenth century. On very many manors they chronicle between the free tenants and the villeins intermediate grades described as *consuetudinarii, censuarii, molmen* and so forth. At Great Shelford (Cambs) in 1251, for example, Adam son of Richard held 9 acres amongst a group of such tenants. He owed certain villein incidents: labour in harvest-time, tallage, a fine to marry his daughter, the obligation of folding his sheep on his lord's land. On the other hand he did not owe regular work for the lord outside the harvest season as the villeins on this manor did; and the main charge he paid for his holding was a rent of 4s6d, which was seemingly immutable.[36] Again, at Foxton, not far away, the Abbess of Chatteris granted half a virgate to a man, his son and their heirs for a money rent, a few seasonal works and some servile incidents; once again substantial labour service was missing, the grant was in perpetuity, and like a grant to a free tenant it was made by charter.[37] The lawyers found such men hard to deal with. If tallage and merchet might, on one view, make a man a villein, a few boon services and customary payments did not.[38] These semi-free categories did not fit the sharp lines of legal differentiation, for no amount of sophisticated rationalization could make simple a reality that was essentially complex.

There were other categories of tenants that accommodated ill to the legal straitjacket. They include the 'villein sokemen', tenants of 'ancient demesne' manors in many parts of the country – manors which had been in royal hands in 1066 but which, thereafter, had passed in many cases into the possession of private lords. As the name of these tenants implies their status combined an unusual mixture of servile obligation and free privileges. At Stoneleigh in Warwickshire, for example, the thirteenth-century villein sokemen owed some seasonal labour services and other characteristic villein incidents; on the other hand their heirs had an undisputed right to succeed to the family holding and the amount they could be charged on succession was fixed.[39] These favourable conditions may help to explain why the Stoneleigh villein sokemen were great dealers in land; and why the Abbots of Stoneleigh were anxious in the late thirteenth century to buy them out and either add their land to their demesnes or relet it on more precarious terms.

The conditions of tenure on ancient demesne manors, however, were no more uniform than condition on other estates. At King's Ripton in Huntingdonshire, the tenants admitted that since Henry I's day they had been paying arbitrary reliefs and arbitrary merchet; they needed the lord's licence to have their sons ordained or to leave the manor; and they owed one day's work a week throughout the year and three days a week during August and September.[40] The tenants of Havering in Essex, which had remained in the king's hand, were at the other end of the spectrum. They owed only light works; they could marry their children, leave the manor, and enter Holy Orders without the lord's permission; and they could demise their land for a fine fixed at one year's rent.[41] Despite the differences, however, there were, or should have been according to the law, certain inalienable rights which all villein sokemen enjoyed: they could be tallaged only when the king tallaged his demesne lands and the sum taken was not to exceed in amount one-tenth of the value of their chattels; the services their lord could demand were not to be greater than those owed when the manor was in the king's hands; and these conditions of tenure were protected by the public courts. The coveted status of tenants of the ancient demesne, and the proclivity of lords to undermine it in the centuries after Domesday, were to be sources of many disputes.

Villein sokemen were not the only nonconformist groups: there were others equally notable even if they were less widely distributed. It may be sufficient to cite two examples from the far south-east and the far south-west. The custom of Kent, in the first place, was wholly exceptional and the so-called gavelkind tenants of that county held on unusually privileged terms (indeed, it was often sufficient for a man to plead Kentish origin for his freedom to be admitted).[42] This custom (*Lex Kantiae*) as it was codified in the late thirteenth century contains the following resounding statement:

All the persons of Kentishmen should be free, as much as the other free persons of England . . . they should be able to give and sell their lands and their tenements without asking leave of their lords, saving to the lords the rents and services of the same tenements. And each one should be able by the King's courts, or by plaint, to plead and pursue his right, as well against his lord as against other men. . . . And they claim also that if any tenant of Gavelkind be attainted of felony by which he suffers judgement of death, the King shall have his chattels, and his heir immediately after his death should have by inheritance all the lands and tenements which he holds by Gavelkind in fee and in inheritance. Whereof it is said in Kentish
'The father to the bough

The son to the plough'

. . . And they claim that if a tenant of Gavelkind dies, who holds by inheritance lands and tenements in Gavelkind, all his sons should divide the inheritance by equal portion.

It may further be added that labour services in Kent were invariably extremely light and that by the time the *Lex Kantiae* was compiled gavelkinders had established their exemption from tallage.[43]

If Kentish gavelkinders bear some resemblance to villein sokemen, the Cornish *conventionarii* have an entirely different appearance. When the Duchy of Cornwall was established in 1337, the 800 or so conventionaries on its Cornish manors outnumbered the free tenants by three to one and the villeins (*nativi de stipite*) by no less than ten to one. The conventionaries, who could be either free or unfree, were in essence leaseholders. They held their lands on seven-year leases at freely negotiable rents and had no automatic right of renewal of their leases when their term ended. The labour services owed by conventionaries were extremely light and rarely exacted, although the unfree amongst them were burdened with most of the other common incidents of serfdom such as *merchet, leyrwite, chevage*, and the need to pay a fine if a son were sent to school or to take Holy Orders. Documentation for other south-western estates at this date is scarce; but it is sufficient to indicate that conventionaries were not restricted to Duchy manors, and that tenure by contract or lease was becoming increasingly popular in the later part of our period.[44]

The standing and numbers of villagers who were neither conventionally villein or free varied markedly from one part of England to another, but so did the proportion of them whose freedom or unfreedom conformed to the criteria that the lawyers were determining. The precise ratio of villeins to freemen in thirteenth-century England cannot be calculated; but on the basis of a sample of some 10,000 tenants in parts of Cambridgeshire, Huntingdonshire, Bedfordshire, Buckinghamshire and Oxfordshire surveyed in the 1279 Hundred Rolls the proportion in these counties was three villeins to two freemen.[45] Even here the ratio fluctuated sharply from hundred to hundred, and once we move outside these counties fluctuations become even more pronounced. In the Northern Danelaw (Yorkshire, Derbyshire, Nottinghamshire, Leicestershire, Lincolnshire and Rutland), for example, free tenants sometimes exceeded 60 per cent of village populations. Sir Frank Stenton made familiar the men of this region, many of them quite small men, who were 'as fully free as anyone could be under the conditions which prevailed in early medieval England'. They could grant their land freely, they had a standing in the public courts, they were subject to a minimum of seignorial control.[46]

How tenaciously they clung to this freedom is brought out in a memorandum which gives a little history of two bovates which Richard Broyer held of Darley Abbey for a rent of 5s yearly. To begin with, *quia non fuit securus de statu suo* (because in regard to his standing he was not free from danger), be surrendered half a bovate to the abbey in order that he might hold the rest more freely and peacefully. His only child was a daughter, whose son, William, went off to the Holy Land and stayed so long he was assumed to be dead. Richard now made William's sister, his grand-daughter Juliana, his heir. In due course she succeeded to the holding, having in the meantime married a villein. At this point William returned, but played the gallant brother and surrendered his right in the holding in return for 1s8d annual rent. Juliana was followed in the tenement by her son Geoffrey and then by her grandson John. Over the years, it is true, a little land was lost and a small new rent-charge was created; but despite some initial doubt about the family's status, a protracted pilgrimage, successive female heirs and a villein marriage, the lien of Richard Broyer's family upon most of the holding was preserved. They made their own arrangements for its devolution, their rent was not drastically increased, and heir followed heir in as direct a line as circumstances allowed.[47]

If free men were prominent in the Danelaw, so they were in other regions. There were villeins owing heavy services in East Anglia, but 'large numbers of freemen and socmen' were also found there both in 1086 and subsequently. Indeed, it was their habit of treating their holdings as joint family inheritances or of partitioning them between heirs that largely explains the disintegration of many standard tenements in these counties.[48] On the other hand even the east of Sussex, which marches with free Kent, was a district in which *nativi* were prominent and villeinage with all its familiar incidents was well developed.[49] The districts of England had their own individualities which were one of the influences governing the incidence of freedom and unfreedom.

Distribution of labour services

The diversity of medieval England may be further illustrated by the differing extent to which bondmen's labour, a central attribute of villein obligations in the eyes both of modern scholars and medieval lawyers, contributed to the cultivation of manorial demesnes. On manor after manor there is a basic similarity in villein services. Unfree tenants generally owed modest money rents and frequently some rents in kind (especially fowls at Christmas and eggs at Easter); they owed seasonal works, often described as 'boons' – a few days ploughing, harrowing, threshing, haymaking and, commonly with some extra hands or even with their whole family, harvesting. They might have to do carting service, or fencing, or cutting thatch, or ditching. Their heaviest obligation in many places, however, was 'week-work', a regular obligation to work their lord's land rather than their own for a certain number of days during each week[50] throughout the year save for brief holidays around the principal festivals of the Church.

The burden of week work in some Cambridgeshire villages in 1279 was not untypical of a broad belt of Midland England. On Ramsey Abbey's manor at Graveley villeins holding virgates worked for two days each week for most of the year and for four days, not counting additional boon works, in the harvest season. The half-virgaters holding 15 acres on Robert de Ho's manor at Eversden worked harder: three days each week (including one day ploughing during ploughing times) for most of the year, and in harvest two days together with reaping works amounting at least to a further two days a week.[51] This sort of burden we find in many places. On the St Paul's estates, half-virgaters at Caddington (Herts) owed works for two days each week, and virgaters for three days for most of the year and six days in harvest; while at Sandon (Essex) the holders of 10-acre tenements owed two days work weekly from Michaelmas to Whitsuntide, four days from Whitsun to Lammastide, and five during harvest. In southern England, on the Bec manors, virgaters at Ogbourne St George (Wilts) and half-virgaters at Combe (Hants) alike worked three days a week for most of the year, but the former worked for six days weekly during harvest; while in the west, on the lands of Worcester Priory, virgaters at Boraston (Salop) and Broadwas (Worcs) worked normally for three days a week and for four days in harvest.[52]

There were places where services were heavier than on the manors instanced above, and places where they were lighter, perhaps much lighter, even for men undoubtedly reckoned unfree; and these diversities may depend not only upon where we look, but also upon when we do so. In any given manor the tendency was for the weight of services to be related to the size of the villein's holding, so that a virgater worked more than a half-virgater, though not necessarily in strict proportion to his additional acres. As between manors, too, heavier services might also point in part to larger holdings, so that one reason for the fact that the villeins of Walpole owed six works a week and those of Fen Ditton only two may have been that the villein tenement at Walpole was twice as large as the tenement at Ditton.[53]

At the same time this was merely one element in a much more complex equation. Services, to begin with, varied between different types of estate. They were apt to be heavier on large estates, and heaviest of all on large estates of ancient formation. It is perhaps no accident that, on the Glastonbury lands in 1189, the holder of a half-hide at Nettleton (Wilts) found a man every day *ad opus domini*; 5-acre holders worked every day at Ashbury (Berks); and half-virgaters at Shapwick (Somerset) also worked daily during harvest.[54] On the other hand there was no uniformity throughout large estates. On the Crowland manors the villeins of Dry Drayton (Cambs) owed only thirty-nine works a year, but those of Gedney (Lincs) owed 255; and, while the Bec villeins at Ogbourne and Combe owed heavy services, there was no week-work at all at East Wretham (Norfolk) and labour dues were light on the other East Anglian manors belonging to the abbey.[55] Once again, in developing the labour organization of their manors, landlords had in a measure to accommodate themselves to the differing institutions of the English regions, so that regional characteristics were yet another influence on the distribution and weight of labour services in the English counties.

It is not easy to map this diversity, but studies of the decline of labour services in the generation before the Black Death,[56] supplemented by E. A. Kosminsky's analysis of the hundred rolls of 1279,[57] permit an approximate picture to be drawn. The area of heavy villein labour dues – say two or more days each week – was relatively small, extending only over the East Anglian counties, Essex, Cambridgeshire, Huntingdonshire and parts of Lincolnshire, Hertfordshire, Sussex and Northamptonshire. Outside this area, although on particular manors the weight of services might be heavy, the average level of villein obligations tends to drop; and there is a large minority of counties (Northumberland, the north-west, Cheshire, Herefordshire, Yorkshire, Derbyshire, Nottinghamshire, Leicestershire, Cornwall and Kent) in which services were normally light (a few days each year) or even non-existent.

Even within counties, moreover, there were marked disparities. In Warwickshire, for example, week-work was owed in only two out of the forty-five villages and hamlets of Stoneleigh hundred, and in eighteen of those settlements no services at all were owed. In the Felden country, by contrast, services were noticeably heavier without being excessively heavy in most places: in Kineton hundred in only ten out of forty-eight villages and hamlets were there no services due at all, while in eight week-work was owed. In both districts the remaining vills were liable to light or seasonal services. In the very different circumstances of Northumberland labour services in any way comparable in weight to those owed in Cambridgeshire and Huntingdonshire, for example, are found almost exclusively in the townships around Tynemouth. Here the lordship of Tynemouth priory was undoubtedly the major influence, and possibly the fact that the priory was a cell of the abbey of St Albans, a connection which brought southern influences to bear upon this corner of the northern countryside.[58]

The way in which the policies of landlords might influence the nature and the weight of the services owed by villein holdings is illustrated by these Tynemouth manors; and the policies of landlords not only varied in response to the different circumstances of different regions, but were also modified over time. The practice of lords (or some of them) to exact labour from their dependent tenantry was a very old one: for the laws of Ine of Wessex in the late seventh century regulate the situation in which lords demanded work as well as rent from those who hold of them. By the tenth and eleventh centuries, indeed, the surviving evidence suggest that quite onerous services were owed in very many places: the *ceorls* of Hurstbourne Priors (Hants) had 'to work as they are bidden every week but three'; from the *geburs* of Tidenham (Glos) 'much labour is due' (including week-work); the *geburs* of the *Rectitudines Singularum Personarum* were required to work from two to three days a week according to the season, and the cottars every Monday save in harvest when they worked three days each week.[59] In brief labour obligations in every way comparable to those owed in the thirteenth century were well established long before the Normans came.

The picture presented by the late Anglo-Saxon surveys had been substantially modified before 1349. First, the services owed by many tenants (and not infrequently by all the unfree tenants of a manor) had in a good number of places been definitively commuted into money rents. At Little Weighton (Yorks), for example, in 1328, the works of the customers had been so converted *ab antiquo*; and where that happened the tenurial position of the villein became much more like that of the free and semi-free tenants. Secondly, even where the villein's theoretical duty to provide labour remained, it was mitigated by the lord's willingness in practice to 'sell' some of the services owed to him year by year. On the Bishop of Ely's manor at Little Downham in 1319–20, for instance, he excused thirteen winter works for a payment of $\frac{1}{2}d$ per work and, out of $720\frac{1}{2}$ hay and harvest works, he sold $110\frac{3}{4}$ at $1d$ each.[60] Both practices grew as many lords relinquished parts of their demesnes in the century after 1250 and as, for some purposes, villein labour was replaced by that of full-time and casual labourers. In these ways, by the later thirteenth and early fourteenth centuries and even in the minority of counties in which most villeins had been burdened by heavy services, this particular characteristic of villeinage was on the wane.

It had, of course, not disappeared everywhere: in 1319–20 the villeins and cottars of Little Downham, even when account is taken of works excused gratis to manorial officials, still performed 88 per cent of the 3,698 winter works due from them (the proportion in hay and harvest was smaller at 76 per cent). Furthermore, even where works were going or gone, that fact cannot be represented as the outcome of a steady and continuous progression. The lines of development may have been relatively straight down to the early twelfth century, when two or three days of week-works together with various seasonal boons were exacted in very many places. In the absence of accounts we cannot be sure that all the works due were actually performed, but what does seem certain is that in the course of the twelfth century labour services were in retreat on manors as far apart as those of the Durham estates in the north-east and the Glastonbury and Shaftesbury estates of the south-west. Tenements *ad opus* almost everywhere were being replaced by tenements *ad censum*, a tendency closely associated with the leasing of manors as a device of estate management. (The trend is more fully discussed below, p. 209). Examples of this widespread phenomenon may be drawn from the manors of Minchinhampton (Glos) and Fontmell (Dorset). Minchinhampton was surveyed three times between the early years of Henry I's reign and the closing years of Henry II's. In the first survey twenty-six virgates were held by services and nine by rents; in the second, nine were held by services, eleven were held by rents, and eleven with the option of performing work or paying rent; in the third all were held by rent alone. At Fontmell, in 1130–35 the villein tenants owed a small money rent, three days week-works, and various ploughing and harrowing services; but forty years later they no longer performed week-works and paid instead much heavier rents, amounting to between 30*d* and 50*d* per tenant.[61]

These twelfth-century trends were reversed on many estates before the century was out as inflation raised the costs of servicing seignorial households and enhanced the potential profit of large-scale cultivation. Manors were taken into direct management, the scale of demesne cultivation was in many cases expanded, and amounts of labour required sharply increased (see pp. 213–24). One method of securing the labour needed was the withdrawal of the concessions of the twelfth century which had permitted villeins to render money in lieu of services; and another was to augment the aggregate supply of villein labour by increasing services. The latter course may well have been rarer than has sometimes been supposed[62] and both provoked a measure of resistance; but landlords achieved a degree of success. The Burton Abbey villeins, most of whom were holding by rent alone in the mid-twelfth century, were once more performing services in the thirteenth century; and the Bishops of Ely increased the total week-work due to them by some 10 per cent between 1222 and 1251.[63]

Thus the story of labour services is one of ebbs and flows. The imposition of heavy obligations on a large section of the peasantry appears to have gone very far by the tenth and eleventh centuries, and to have proceeded somewhat further in certain districts in the immediate aftermath of the Conquest. At least in the middle decades of the twelfth century, however, there was a pronounced tendency towards relaxation, only for old services to be reimposed and for attempts to be made to exact new ones in the later twelfth and much of the thirteenth centuries. By the latter part of the thirteenth century, on the other hand, relaxation was again in full swing; and eventually, in the era after the coming of bubonic plague in 1349, the movement away from labour services was decisive and ultimately complete.

The development and decline of labour rents, therefore, did not run a smooth course, and this fact makes more controversial the view that the closing decades of the twelfth century 'were the crucial period for the depression of the majority of the rural population'.[64] In the first place, however we interpret the course of Anglo-Saxon social history, all the indications (with due allowance made for the paucity of the sources) are that most Englishmen by the tenth and eleventh centuries were of dependent status. They were free in the sense that they were not slaves, a class distinguished from the most dependent of the landholding peasantry; but they were not free in the sense that would be attributed to that word in the thirteenth century. The *gebur* of the *Rectitudines* was 'trembling on the verge of serfdom',[65] and his heavy labour services and liability at death to cede all his possessions to his lord would, at a later time, have consigned him to the villeinage. The opening of our period, in fact, witnessed on many other estates than the lands of Peterborough Abbey, as they are described in the *Black Book* in the 1120s, 'manorial economy at its more robust'.[66] The implication of that robustness was that, apart from extra ploughing and harvest works, along with rents in cash and kind, the *villani* on this estate did a mere day's work a week at Collingham, but two days at Tinwell, Cottingham, Great Easton, Thurlby, Fiskerton and Scotter, and three days at Kettering, Oundle, Warmington, Pytchley, Pilsgate, Elton, Longthorpe, Glinton and Castor.[67]

Undoubtedly, in many places, the twelfth century witnessed a modification of these burdens and the conversion of works into cash rents; equally undoubtedly, as the century closed, there was a 'manorial reaction' as landlords sought to mobilize labour for directly managed demesne enterprise. To that end lords like Abbot Henry de Sully of Glastonbury sought to discover 'if any land which ought to tender work had been made free . . . and to what extent it is free'. The answer was not always clearcut. One Glastonbury peasant held 'more freely than his predecessors were accustomed to hold'; while conversely some of the tenants of Cirencester abbey were 'not so free' that they were exempt from ploughing and carrying services'.[68]

There is an imprecision about these verdicts reflecting the complexity of the social ties with which landlords had to grapple in their efforts to revise the whole pattern of estate management. Men were variously free and variously unfree: and it was these degrees of unfreedom that the Angevin lawyers sought to simplify. The peasantry, or no inconsiderable part of the peasantry, lost in the process; for villeinage became a disability more clearly defined, particularly in terms of the criteria distinguishing villein from free and the exclusion of the villeins for many purposes from the protection of the public courts that were becoming the common law courts of the land. At the same time not all the gains of all the peasantry during the twelfth century were cancelled, for some of the semi-free *censuarii*, and perhaps some of the free tenantry, were classes of twelfth-century creation which survived at least in part into the high-farming age which followed. Further, if labour services were revived or reimposed on many manors, those services very often bear a close relationship to the services described, however laconically, in older surveys dating from before and immediately after the Conquest. The latter tell us little or nothing, it is true, about the other charges that fell especially on villeins (*merchet, heriot,* tallage); but tallage (and possibly a synonym, *gersuma*) is mentioned in 1086 and *heriot* in the form of a dead man's best beast might seem a lighter charge than that to which the *gebur* of the *Rectitudines* was submitted – 'when death befalls him let the lord take charge of what he leaves'.[69] An argument from the silence of early and imperfect records is not one that can be taken as conclusive.

The fact remains that, alike in the eleventh century and the thirteenth, an obligation to provide labour on their lord's land rested on no small proportion of the English peasantry, and rested heavily on a good number of them. It is another matter to assess with any accuracy at all just how onerous this obligation was. It has often been discussed in emotive terms inspired by revulsion against the forced labour of slavery or by the liberal movements for the enfranchisement of serfs in more recent times: but these sentiments provide no yardstick for measuring the peasant's burden. In very general terms it was evidently of no great weight when all that was due were a few seasonal works; but where it entailed two or three days work each week, and perhaps like the villeins of Boldon in Durham, extra ploughing and four boon-days in harvest 'with his entire household except the housewife',[70] it was a very different matter. To the extent that these services were exacted and not 'sold', and even if in many cases a day's work meant in fact only working for half the day, the villein was diverted from the cultivation of his own holding for a very substantial part of the farming year. Given the English weather he might well miss chances that were vital to the success of his crops. At the same time other considerations may enter into the equation. The man with grown sons at home, or the man with a holding large enough to provide the resources to hire labourers to perform his services for him, was better placed than the man without a family or with a smaller holding. How to allow for the different conditions of peasant cultivators is a question at present insoluble and one that may never be resolved. There might even be circumstances in which a move towards 'freedom' in the sense that money rents replaced labour rents, particularly for the tenant with a holding barely sufficient for subsistence, could entail positive disadvantage, for the extra cash he had to find could come only at the expense of consumption.

Tenure, status and peasant fortunes

To determine the influences acting favourably and unfavourably on peasant fortunes, therefore, is no simple matter, and it is none the simpler because the doctrines the lawyers elaborated cannot always be taken at their face value. Above all there is no absolute correlation between freedom, however that is defined, and prosperity. That is not to say that freedom entailed no advantage. Men with holdings of a reasonable size, with reasonably stable obligations, and with the protection of the royal courts if they needed it, were favourably placed to prosper, especially as producer prices rose from the late twelfth century onwards. There are many examples in the records of free tenants who in fact had prospered, including Warin the Hayward of Littlebury (Essex) as he appears in a survey of that manor in 1251.[71] The nucleus of his holding was 2½ virgates (some 75 acres) for which he paid 26s8d, not an excessive rent when others in the same village paid 1s or 1s6d an acre. He had also added to this nucleus: he held a meadow as a tenant at will for 2s; 10 acres, once the widow Gunnilda's for 4s a year; and 7½ acres, once Robert the son of Brian's for 1s3d yearly. The fact that, as a free tenant, many of his outgoings were fixed must have assisted Warin in his climb into what might almost be called the yeomanry.

At the same time, the logic of law and custom, which seems to give all the advantages to the free man and none to the villein, must not be pressed too far. Freedom had temptations as well as advantages. The man who could do what he liked with his land could alienate it in whole or in part, and sometimes his tenement was divisible between his heirs. Partible inheritance was not entirely unknown in the villeinage, but in certain parts of England (especially in Kent and East Anglia) it was very common among the free tenantry. Its consequences were set out succinctly in a Kentish charter of 1276: 'It often happens that lands and tenements, which . . . undivided were accustomed decently to suffice for the subsistence of many men, . . . afterwards are separated and divided into so many . . . parcels amongst coheirs that to none of them does his part then suffice for his subsistence.'[72] In other words, freedom to alienate, particularly in combination with partible inheritance, created miniscule free tenements as well as opportunities for the enterprising to engross scattered parcels which, by themselves, were inadequate to support a family. Freedom was apt to be accompanied, therefore, by increasing social inequalities. It generated quasi-yeomen but also a fringe of impoverishment. The ranks of the free peasantry in most manors show signs of this polarization, and it is most conspicuously evident in traditionally free areas like Kent, East Anglia and Lincolnshire.

One must not, because some freemen were impoverished, minimize the villein's disadvantages – the restrictions placed on his freedom of action, the weight and in some degree the arbitrariness of the charges to which he was subjected, and his rightlessness in important respects in the eyes of the law and lawyers. As men deemed to hold at will villein tenants could be at a disadvantage, particularly in the generations that began in the late twelfth century, during which lords sought new sources of revenue and labour and lawyers reinterpreted notions of liberty and servility. On many manors the burden of labour services increased over time; it was for the lord to decide whether he exacted those services or took cash in lieu; money rents and entry fines generally tended upwards; and tallages and heriots were often heavy burdens. The lessee of one Essex manor so tallaged a certain villein that he fled; and on the manor of Hales one heriot paid on a villein's death consisted of two good oxen, a foal and two sheep, which looks like a serious inroad into that family's livestock.[73] Even freemen who took up unfree land did so at their peril. When William le Deghere did so at Egham in 1331 he was dragged before the king's justices and compelled to acknowledge that thenceforth he was the *nativus* of the Abbot of Chertsey.[74] At the very least the villein's servility, the precariousness of his tenure, the combined weight of the charges he paid for land, and the opportunity offered to lords by mounting competition for land to augment these charges imposed on the least secure of their dependents, put his prospects of prosperity in peril.

When these facts of life in the late twelfth and thirteenth centuries are admitted, however, it may also in a sense be misleading to dwell too much on examples of the extreme manifestation of the power of landlords and the extreme statements of those powers contained in the law books and the pronouncements of lawyers. Once again we must return to the gap that often existed between theory and practice. The doctrine that a villein's goods and chattels were his lord's, as those of the eleventh-century *gebur* had been, was much modified in many places: the family of a dead villein commonly fulfilled their obligation by delivering his best beast to the lord as heriot and the second best to the church as mortuary. Sometimes even these obligations could be commuted to a cash payment and the poorer families almost always met it by a modest money render. Sometimes, too, as on the Prior of Ely's manor of Melbourne (Cambs) or the Abbot of Battle's manor of Barnhorn (Kent), villeins with no beast were spared heriot altogether, as were many others to whom the charge was pardoned in the light of their poverty.[75] There were lords who exacted all that law and custom allowed, but there were others who exacted a good deal less: and in the end these lesser exactions became the custom that governed their proceedings.

What was true of heriot was true of other things. Tallage, theoretically arbitrary in incidence and amount, often became a customary levy even though, in the process, it also became a regular (even an annual) impost. This was already happening on a Norfolk manor in 1233 when the lord agreed that two villeins should pay 'aid' only at Michaelmas, each of them at the rate of 12*d*, *et hoc nomine tallagii* (and this in respect of tallage).[76] The same applied to labour services. The villein might indeed not know what precise task the reeve or bailiff would assign him on his work days, or indeed whether or not his work would be required at all, but increasingly detailed surveys and custumals narrowed the area of uncertainty to smaller and smaller proportions. They not only recorded the number of days of work villeins owed, but often the days of the week on which they fell, how many hours constituted a day's work, whether or not the lord provided food (and if so what that food was to be), how many miles constituted a carrying service, how many bundles of brushwood a gathering service. The list might be almost indefinitely extended, indicating the extent to which custom had prevailed over caprice. Villein tenure, too, was far less uncertain than theoretically it was supposed to be: evidence of evictions is rare and of arbitrary evictions rarer still. Indeed the villein who defaulted on his services, or allowed his house or holding to deteriorate through his neglect, was usually subjected to a small fine and allowed time to mend his ways before the ultimate sanction of eviction was applied. This is why, perhaps to an increasing extent, villeins were able to look on their holdings as a family heritage (see pp. 138–9).

In other respects the theory of villeinage was frequently belied by the facts. First, to an increasing extent, lords were willing that villeins should buy themselves out of their disabilities: for a cash payment they were allowed to alienate land, send a son to school or into Holy Orders, above all to move away in search of new opportunities. They moved to other agricultural villages; but we also find a man from Broughton (Hunts) who had taken the monastic habit at Merton (Surrey) and another was 'living in service' at Barnwell (Northants). Others again had betaken themselves to towns, like the man from Amesbury (Wilts) who went first to Wilton, where he was a 'travelling merchant', and then to Andover where he married a wife.[77] Secondly, in a paradoxical way, the villein might be afforded some protection by his very unfreedom. So long as villein tenements were regarded as units on which labour services were assessed, lords had an interest in maintaining their integrity. That interest may help to explain why, at Wilburton (Cambs), 'the manor seems to have kept with wonderful conservatism . . . its external shape' in that, from 1222 right down to the end of the Middle Ages, the distribution of customary tenements was preserved almost unchanged.[78] In part this may be an illusion, for villein tenements were often far less stable than manorial records make them out to be (see pp. 140–3); but the very dependence of the villeins enabled lords to insist that their holdings were kept intact or nearly so in order that they would be capable of sustaining families that would provide the reservoir of labour lords might need.

The compensations of villeinage must not be overstated. Areas of great uncertainty remained: in the thirteenth century, particularly, services were increased on many manors, rents tended upwards, and the levels of entry fines paid by villeins on taking up a holding by succession or otherwise often rose most sharply of all. At the same time the force of custom, both written and unwritten but gaining precision as more of it was written down in custumals and manor court rolls, mitigated these additions to the villein's burden. Despite the inflationary trend of the time and the growing land hunger of the villagers, many lords found it difficult or even impossible to increase the rents and services from their villein holdings to a degree that matched the increase in the value of land. To that extent the thirteenth-century villein enjoyed a measure of protection against the play of market forces that many a sixteenth-century countryman might have envied.

On the other side, of course, it has to be admitted that at a time when the underlying economic forces were working to the disadvantage of the mass of the peasantry, on the whole the burdens sustained by the villeins were apt to be heavier than those that freemen bore, and the occasions when lords could extract a profit from the former were more frequent than those which enabled them to exploit the latter. At the same time there is no simple formula equating freedom with prosperity and villeinage with poverty, just as the lines the lawyers drew between bond and free lose their sharpness when we subject them to scrutiny. It is not merely that there are many gradations between the fully bond and the fully free: everyday behaviour in the villages appears neglectful of these lines.

A curious marriage at Castle Hedingham in the early thirteenth century is indicative. Ralf de Hodeng, seemingly one of the lords of the place, came back to find that a kinswoman of his had married one of his villein tenants. Ralf was 'angered at this marriage' and took away some of the land he had given to the lady until her villein husband found security to live on it and had built a little house there. Only when the villein built a large house in another fee and went to live there, however, did Ralf confiscate the land definitively.[79] What is interesting here is the misalliance between a free-born lady and a villein. It is by no means a unique instance in the opening years of the thirteenth century. In Dorset the sister of a tenant by knight service was said to have married first a villein and then a knight; in Norfolk a man was allowed to be free despite the fact that his father had married a villein woman; in Cambridgeshire no less than three members of a free stock married into villein families; in Bedfordshire the son of a villein mother, who had married a free man, claimed himself to be free.[80] On a number of occasions, it is true, a free woman married to a villein was denied any share in the family inheritance,[81] a disability which might be expected to discourage marriages between bond and free; that it did not prevent such alliances is equally self-evident.

The implications are clear enough: in day-to-day village life there was often no very significant class-barrier 'along the line of legal freedom and legal serfdom'.[82] Other evidence reinforces that view. When villagers litigate with each other, 'status seems of no importance'. Villeins and freemen enter into bargains with each other; freemen hold bond land and unfree men hold free land; and when a manorial aristocracy emerged, it might well be an aristocracy of villeins.[83] The stories of individuals illustrate these generalities. Stephen Puttock, of Sutton in the Isle of Ely, was probably a villein virgater of the Prior of Ely, but he greatly enlarged the amount of land he held in the course of his lifetime (sometimes by purchase from free tenants). In his village, moreover, he was a man of weight. Doubtless, it was in fulfilment of his obligations as a villein that he served as the prior's reeve in 1310; but he was also a chief pledge for quarter of a century, the village ale-taster from time to time, and a frequent juror in the manor court.[84] In brief, in the village a man's enterprise and economic standing might matter more than his status. The notions of status devised by the lawyers have about them a measure of artificiality. In part this arose from the fact that the new common law rules imposed distinctions not previously recognized;[85] in part it reflected the failure of status and standing to coincide. Perhaps most important of all, however, a doctrine imposed from outside was not easily accommodated to the relationships of men living together in villages that had their own coherence and solidarity.

Chapter 6

Villagers:
II. Family and fortunes

It is natural to look at villagers first in terms of status and tenure, as has been done in Chapter 5, for our records more or less dictate such an approach. Until a much later time what we know of them derives from manorial surveys listing holdings, rents, services and other obligations or from court records in which the enforcement of obligations bulks large. These sources provide only oblique information about the other relationships into which villagers entered – with relatives or neighbours. These other relationships, however, were important and not least the villager's relationship to his family group and the customary rules which governed it. This represented an important segment of the ties,which bound the peasant to others and it also had its influence on the fortunes of individuals. If we are to endeavour to estimate how the villager fared in the central Middle Ages we must move from the tenurial network to the domestic circle of his family.

The family

The extent of the family group and the strength of its cohesion are far from easy to gauge. It is probable that extended kinship ties had weakened since Saxon times, but that they should not be under-estimated is a possible implication of a case that came before the Wiltshire eyre in 1249 in which the kinsmen of a man who had been hanged were suspected of murdering the man responsible for the case being brought against the deceased.[1] Those kinsmen may have included remoter relatives than the felon's sons and this may be an instance in which family solidarity stretched as far as the pursuit of a vendetta. This is an area of much obscurity, but some light on family structure is thrown by a common custom regarding the descent of a dead man's chattels. It takes as the norm the stem family consisting of a husband, his wife and their children. When the husband died, at least if he was a villein, his best beast probably went to his lord as heriot and his second best to the parish church as mortuary fee; but, those dues paid, only the family was afterwards concerned. Certain tools and utensils, essential for husbandry and housekeeping, remained on the holding for the heir (the heirloom in the original sense of the word, for loom meant any sort of tool and not solely a machine for weaving). What goods and chattels remained were divided into three shares: one for the widow, one divided equally between the surviving children, and one which the dying man could dispose of as he liked by his last will and testament.[2]

In these arrangements the villager is seen in relation to those who were nearest to him. He had special obligations to his wife and his heir, but he also had a duty to all his children. In the disposition of the chattels belonging to a peasant household the family was a coherent group, each member of which had specific rights. That coherence extended in various ways to the relationship between the family and the land. In some places (especially in Kent and East Anglia), though normally this was no more than a temporary expedient by the thirteenth century, holdings were held jointly by the heirs of a common ancestor. It was far commoner, however, both in these districts and sporadically elsewhere, for free and occasionally even villein tenements to be partible among all the sons of a landholder. This practice may have its origin in the tribal customs of particular peoples – Celts or Jutes or Frisians; alternatively, it may have been a custom common to most parts of the Anglo-Saxon England.[3] Whatever its origin it represents the lien of the family on the land in its most positive form.

More usually, a dead man's land went to a single heir. The latter might be the eldest son, primogeniture probably being the commonest rule of succession amongst both villeins and freeholders. Not infrequently, however, the youngest son inherited under the custom known as borough English. This custom had some advantages: it allowed the older children to make their way in the world as they grew up, leaving behind the youngest to take over the family holding when his father died. Its disadvantage was that, at a time when expectations of life were short, the heir was likely to be a minor when the time came for him to succeed, and minorities were always times of danger for patrimonies. This may explain why the tenants of certain Chertsey abbey manors in 1339 paid good money to have primogeniture substituted for borough English, since the latter custom was 'to the grave damage and detriment of the whole homage'.[4]

Either primogeniture or borough English tended to keep the family holding intact, though this is a statement needing immediate qualification. First, even where the rule was that the eldest or youngest son stepped into the father's holding, free tenements were divided between a man's daughters if there were no sons to succeed. Secondly, even when there was a son and heir, his right did not always prevail immediately against the claims of his mother. These varied widely from place to place. It was very common for the widow of a free tenant to have a right to one third of her dead husband's holding for her life. Sometimes the same rule applied to villein holdings, but sometimes a widow's rights were much greater. Some customs allowed her to keep the whole tenement for her life provided she did not remarry; while on the Prior of Ely's manor at Sutton or the Bishop of Winchester's manor at Taunton, the widow could take the holding to a second husband who might in turn hold for life, pass it on to a second wife, and so defer the heir's expectations almost indefinitely.[5] Occasionally the widow's title was strengthened still further, as often happened on the manors of Ramsey and Chertsey abbeys, if she had shared the tenancy with her husband before his death.[6]

The determination of the respective rights of widows and children in family inheritances has always presented difficulties in peasant societies. From the lord's point of view it was in his interest to ensure that at all times the holding was provided with an adult male capable of fulfilling the obligations incident upon it. This interest doubtless explains the curt command issued in the manor court at Wistow (Hunts) in 1294: 'Sarah Byssop is a young widow and order is given that she marry before the next court.' It may also explain why two men in 1279 were instructed to take Agatha of Hales to wife; but perhaps she was ill-favoured, for one of them preferred to fine to avoid matrimony and the other refused either to marry or to fine.[7] At the same time the lord's interest was not the only one at work. On colonizing manors, where land was still being added to the village territory and opportunities existed for landless men to secure a stake in the soil, the chances of the heir succeeding to the family holding were relatively high. By contrast on manors where the arable had ceased to grow, particularly when the pressure of population reached its extreme point in the generation around 1300, the best opportunity of getting a holding might well be to marry a widow.[8] In other words, there was pressure within the village populations themselves which made the heir's rights more precarious.[9]

Sometimes, it is true, the heir did not have to await the death of his parents to step into his own. Here again more than one interest might be at work. Obviously it was to the lord's disadvantage if a villein holding owing heavy labour services was in the hands of a man who was 'impotent' – old or sick or merely incapable. The lord might then insist that he should 'retire', as at Chalgrave in 1287 when Robert Gaylon's land was taken into the lord's hand 'because of his impotence to serve', or at Epsom in 1342 when Robert Walshe's lands were taken from him 'because he is impotent to amend them and they lie waste'.[10] These were cases where no heir could be found for the holdings, but in other instances the peasant family itself took the initiative to ward off the possibility of confiscation. At Bookham Matthew de Baggedene surrendered his land to his son, who was to provide his father and mother with eight quarters of grain yearly; at Chalgrave a widowed mother surrendered her dower to her son in return for an annual pension of half a quarter each of wheat, beans and summer corn; while at Sutton a father who handed over his holding to his son stipulated that he should be accommodated in the son's messuage.[11] Nor were such arrangements peculiar to eastern and southern England. We also find them in the north, for William Johnson took up the family holding at Monkton (Durham) after engaging himself to sustain his parents honourably to the best of his ability for the rest of their lives;[12] and one of the most elaborate bargains of this sort comes from the West Midlands. A widow surrendered her late husband's lands at Halesowen to her eldest son in return for his finding all necessaries for her – specified amounts of wheat, oats and peas to be delivered at Michaelmas, Christmas, Good Friday and Midsummer, five loads of sea-coal at All Saints, and 5*s* in cash at Whitsundtide. In addition he was to build her a competent house, the dimensions of which were carefully specified.[13] The lady was leaving nothing to chance.

These arrangements meant that for the time being the peasant inheritance was burdened with extra mouths to be fed; but they are by no means the only indications that the holding was regarded as in some sense the support of a more extended family group than inheritance customs suggest. A variety of arrangements show brother caring for brother. When an elder brother became 'impotent' a younger brother provided a 'pension' for him consisting of a garment, two pieces of linen cloth, a pair of shoes, a pair of woollen hose, 4 bushels of fine wheat flour and 4 bushels of barley each year. Conversely, at Wakefield, it was assumed to be the duty of older brothers to provide maintenance for a younger brother who was under age; while at Sevenhampton Reginald Dameolde, on inheriting the family virgate, provided a house and a quarter of wheat each Michaelmas for his younger brother so long as he remained unmarried and in the manor.[14] There were other beneficiaries of family solidarity. A father at Sutton (Cambs) detached a portion of his toft to accommodate his daughter and her husband; and in Wiltshire it was said to be a father's duty to keep a grown-up son if he had forbidden him to enter the service of another.[15] Another Surrey man gave his sister half an acre of his land, although she had to pay 1*d* rent for it and cut half an acre of corn on the lord's demesne for service; and a man from Barford (Wilts) employed his sister's son looking after his sheep, but when the latter was careless he was so angry that the boy ran away.[16] These, for the most part, appear to have been individual arrangements within families; but on the Cambridgeshire manors of Crowland Abbey it was a customary rule that the heir of a villein holding must give his brothers and sisters half an acre in each of the fields in which the holding lay. This land they held collectively until they married or moved away, the heir in the meantime remaining responsible for the rents and services due from the whole tenement.[17]

The forces brought to bear on the peasant tenement, therefore, did not all tend in the same direction. Some made for the integrity and stability of holdings, in the lord's interest in particular. Services were most conveniently assessed on standard tenements and most effectively exacted where each was kept intact in the hands of a single tenant. Consequently, lords were mainly concerned to preserve the intergrity of villein holdings, although they may well have found that object less compelling as labour rents were replaced by money rents. At the same time seignorial interests do not appear to have been the sole influences keeping tenements intact, for the patrmonial principle seems to have been almost as much an element in peasant psychology as it was in the psychology of their lords. The idea of the tenement as an indivisible inheritance was deeply implanted in the villeinage. One Reginald in 1279 'demanded the land of his father in the name of inheritance as eldest son according to the custom of the manor'. The manor court found that he was the son of Herbert and that he was the eldest son and nearest heir to Herbert's land; therefore he was received as tenant and had possession of the land, doing for it the service due and accustomed. This, as Maitland said, 'is just the formula a man would use in the king's court were he claiming a freehold inheritance, save that at every turn reference is made to the custom of the manor'.[18]

The legal theory that a tenant in villeinage could have no heir but his lord, and that he held only at the lord's will, did not prevent a villein from regarding his holding as an inheritance. This assumption went very far. At Wakefield, for example, a sample of some seventy-five instances of succession[19] shows that there, most commonly, a single son followed his father (forty-seven cases), but a daughter or daughters sometimes succeeded, presumably because there was no son (nine cases). A son or daughter might also follow a mother (three cases); but a brother or sisters succeeded a brother (eight cases), a sister a brother (one case), an uncle a nephew or niece (four cases), a cousin a cousin (two cases) or, in one solitary instance, a (presumably second) husband a wife. The net of kinship covering succession to land was stretched very wide. Nor were the rights of heirs easily set aside. When one heir died before succeeding to the family holding, his son followed the grandfather even though he was only three years old;[20] and at Rastrick (Yorks), when the land of a dead villein was handed over to another man for a sum that would acquit the debts to the lord the villein had accumulated as reeve, it was carefully provided that at the end of the term the villein's heirs would recover the holding provided they could pay the costs the lessee had incurred.[21] By the fourteenth century, moreover, villeins were aping their freer contemporaries in making arrangements in the manor court that safeguarded the expectations of the heir. In 1336 Hugh and Margaret le Hunte surrendered their villein half virgate at Thorpe (Surrey) and received it back to hold in bondage for their lives with the remainder to their son Walter and his heirs.[22] Once again the formulae are those applicable to dealings in free inheritances protected by the king's courts.

Of course there were influences pulling in other directions. The rights of widows diverted at least part of the holding from the heir for his mother's lifetime and sometimes virtually meant his disinheritance; while in some places partible inheritance prevailed over the principle that patrimonies should descend intact. Customary rules, or a sense of family solidarity, commonly moved heirs to make some provision for cadet branches of the family. Fathers naturally were concerned that younger sons should not be left completely landless, nor daughters without a dowry, even if it was only half an acre of land.[23] These influences might contribute to some fragmentation of holdings, even to the extent of creating uneconomic tenements which drove their holders either to sell them or to buy more land. At the same time, the mounting pressure of population upon resources enlarged the class of men seeking a stake in the soil and the class whose allotments of land were very small. This pressure, therefore, intensified the instability and movement in the material foundations of rural society. Individual and human factors abetted these fundamental economic and social tendencies. There are among medieval villagers feckless men who wasted their inheritances. There were ruthless and enterprising men like Stephen Puttock, who knew how to take advantage of the misfortune or incapacity of their neighbours. It is against this background that we must consider the economic standing of the medieval villager.

The fortunes of the peasantry

Any attempt to tackle this problem is fraught with obstacles. The evidence available normally provides information about the amount of land a peasant family held of a lord and a statement of the terms on which the land was held. On the other hand, we are seldom in a position to make an estimate of the aggregate outgoings of the peasant. His rents and labour services may be laid down in great detail; but it is almost impossible to put a figure on what such things as tallage, heriot, merchet, entry fines and judicial penalties cost the individual. Holdings, too, were often described in terms of customary virgates and customary acres which make comparisons difficult: after all, on the Gloucester Abbey estates a virgate might be as little as 28 acres or as much as 64 acres and a customary acre in the Isle of Ely might be either 1½ or even 2 'measured' acres.[24] Moreover, even when we know the precise measurements, we usually remain ignorant of the quality of the soil. As soon as we begin to compare the standing of men in different places we are all too often dealing with the incomparable.

There is yet a further difficulty; that of knowing just what was the population of a peasant holding. Occasionally we catch glimpses of the complexity and variety of this rural world. At Wootton in Bedfordshire in the mid-thirteenth century John Hunter had a small free tenement of about 36 acres of arable and 4½ acres of meadow. Of this, however, he retained only the messuage, a croft, 18 acres of arable and 4 acres of meadow in his own hand. He had devolved 6 acres on his three sisters, and 12¾ acres of arable and ½ acre of meadow were held of him by seven subtenants.[25] Again, in the later twelfth century, Eynsham Abbey obtained a villein virgate at Histon (Cambs) and the deed of gift lists the 'men dwelling therein'. These were William Bighe with his wife and sons and daughters, and also Nicholas son of Ailbert Bighe with his mother and his brother and his sister.[26] This tenement was the base for an extended family group; and at Wootton John Hunter not only provided for his sisters but may well have sold off portions of his inheritance for rents which were relatively nominal.

Fragments of information of this sort warn us against accepting at their face value the description of peasant holdings found in the manorial extents. Gloucester Abbey's manor at Littleton (Hants) in 1265 had the usual neat arrangement: there were six virgaters, nine half-virgaters, eight men each with 10 acres and five with small-holdings. Similarly, at Linkenholt, there were five virgaters, eleven half-virgaters and a cottar (though one half-virgater had added a cotland to his holding).[27] How closely this apparent neatness corresponded to the real distribution of land is another matter. It can be questioned on general grounds. The peasant family, after all, was not a constant unit. Some families had more mouths to feed and others fewer, and families at different times had more or fewer members to sustain. Consequently, where land was distributed in standard holdings, there would be moments when one family had need of more land and another had land to spare. Thus, quite apart from the facts that some men were more ambitious and enterprising than others and that the growth of population gave a sharper edge to peasant land hunger, there was a need for some 'mechanism whereby the rigorous system of customary virgates could be fitted to the unstable fortunes of peasant families'.[28] This was an important part of the background of the active peasant landmarket of the central Middle Ages.

In areas where peasants had freedom to deal with their land as they would the evidence for this market takes us right back to the beginning of our period: in the Danelaw, for instance, peasant charters of the twelfth century reveal a distribution of land originally based on the bovate but greatly modified by division amongst coheirs and by the purchase and sale of tenements or parts of tenements.[29] Everywhere, in fact, free holdings show a greater and a more precocious instability than villein holdings; but from the mid-thirteenth century onwards court rolls document a mobility of customary land which casts grave doubt on the apparent immobility recorded by the extents. One device which bulked particularly large was the villein lease. Precisely because it was a short-term contract it could reflect the temporary situation of the parties, the need of the one for land and the fact that the other had land to spare, without permanent commitment for the future when circumstances might change. The land market in this sense provided the solution of a permanent problem in villages where much of the land was distributed in standard tenements. This fact may further imply that in some form its existence must precede any point in time when there is record of it. At the same time, the need for some mechanism to meet the short-term requirements of families is likely to have increased as the availability of gains from assarting decreased. For that reason the level of activity in the peasant land market was probably intensified over the twelfth and thirteenth centuries.[30]

Whatever the chronology of this development, when the records of the land market do become available they make clear that inter-peasant leases frequently involved relatively small parcels demised for relatively short periods: on the Ramsey manor at Houghton in 1311, for example, 3 roods were leased for seven years and one rood in a croft for five years.[31] They might none the less presage the dissolution of a tenement. William Attetouneshend of Dry Drayton (Cambs) leased parcels of his half virgate on three occasions and eventually, through 'impotence', gave up his holding in favour of his son. Under William the younger the rake's progress continued, for in twelve years he appeared as a lessor no less than thirty-four times. In the outcome he had to surrender the holding.[32] Leases, in fact, shade off into more definitive alienations. Hugh Russell of King's Ripton, for example, sold various parcels of his 12-acre tenement in return for rents which more or less fully covered what he owed for the holding to the Abbot of Ramsey.[33] The numerous 'sales' of customary land could involve a whole variety of arrangements.

Some of them were precisely what they professed to be, a definitive alienation for a lump sum in cash; in others the purchase price was in effect a loan and the sale had the character of taking out a mortgage on the land in question; and in others, again, a more or less permanent subtenancy was created. The man at Epsom who alienated 5 acres for 12*s* a year obviously looked to the rent as the main consideration involved in his concession.[34]

Lords often set their faces against the villein land market, as Abbot Roger of St Albans did when he enacted that villeins should not be allowed in future to sell their lands even to other villeins, *quia plurima destructio est* (for this is most damaging).[35] The fact is, these transactions correspond to the needs of peasant families, to the play of individual capacity and enterprise, and to the insistent demand for land in overpopulated villages. To one degree or another lords were compelled or persuaded to give way. In villages with more than one lord their concessions might be limited to permitting alienation between tenants of a given manor while forbidding dealings with men of other lords: thus, at Chatteris, the Ramsey tenants were barred by manorial 'statute' from leasing lands to the men of Chatteris Abbey or of the Bishop of Ely. Sometimes, on the other hand, lords followed the path laid down by the statute *Quia emptores*, allowing alienation but insisting that the purchaser of land should hold directly of them. Thus, at Weston in 1294, a man was ordered 'that he should correct his charter regarding 3 acres of land which he bought ... so that he should hold it of the chief lord'. Most commonly of all, however, they capitulated to alienation on condition that the transaction should be registered in their courts, enabling them to charge a fee for their concurrence. When the land Walter de Dene bought from Richard of Alconbury at King's Ripton in 1294 was taken into the lord's hand, it was not because the Abbot of Ramsey refused to countenance the villein land market, but because that land 'was never delivered into the hand of the lord in court or fined for according to the custom of the manor'.[36]

The consequence was that the tenurial pattern of medieval villages, in the villeinage as well as in the free tenures, was in constant flux. Some tenements were in process of dissolution. When John Watts succeeded his father at Petersham in 1336 half the family holding of 20 acres had been alienated by his father to a variety of tenants; and Robert Blake's holding at Epsom in 1334 had fallen apart into at least eight parcels ranging in size from one to six acres. He gave up the struggle to hold the dismembered fragments together and attorned the rents of his subtenants to his lord, the Abbot of Chertsey.[37] Conversely, thrusting and acquisitive men like Stephen Puttock built up considerable agglomerations in a variety of ways, not infrequently as the charters tell by taking advantage of the necessities or the poverty of neighbours. When they had done so, moreover, they might find takers for some of what they had accumulated among land-hungry men who lacked the acres required to sustain a family. The existence of men eager to take up plots of customary land, even on a share-cropping basis, was assumed in the customs of Bradford on Tone: all that was prescribed was that such land should not be demised to 'strangers'.[38]

The manner in which transactions between peasants are recorded makes accurate calculations of the way in which land was distributed virtually out of the question. On the other hand survey material yields useful approximate data. At Stoneleigh (Warwicks) in 1280, for example, about 60 per cent of the tenants were listed as holding less than 7 acres of land and only 10 per cent had more than 30 acres. 'Middling' men were fewer than one-third of the tenants and men with 15–30 acres fewer than one-fifth. At about the same time, on the Crowland manors of Oakington and Cottenham, half the 106 tenants had 10 acres each, two only had more than 10 acres and the rest had 5 acres or less.[39] Isolated instances of this sort, however, cannot be assumed to be typical. Indeed, a different impression of Warwickshire might be created by choosing instead of Stoneleigh some village in the Felden, where holdings 'tended to be substantial . . . and one or even two virgates were not uncommon'; and likewise in Cambridgeshire there were some manors on which middling tenants predominated, like Elm and Leverington where more than half the tenantry in 1251 had over 10 acres.[40] Though this approach, too, has its dangers, it is necessary to deal in large samples and strike averages.

The most comprehensive exercise of this sort has been that undertaken by E. A. Kosminsky using the material for Huntingdonshire, Cambridgeshire, Bedfordshire, Buckinghamshire, Oxfordshire and Warwickshire contained in the 1279 hundred rolls for some 22,000 peasant holdings, both bond and free.[41] His results, in the first place, make it difficult to envisage the peasantry as any more a single economic class in 1279 than it had been in 1086. A high proportion had relatively small allotments, for 29 per cent of villeins and 47 per cent of free tenants had less than 5 acres. Only in Oxfordshire were these small-holding tenants less than one-third of the peasant population; and in all the counties covered by the hundred rolls taken together, holders of under 10 acres accounted for 46 per cent of the total. By contrast, men with over a virgate (say 40 acres) were rare, for only one per cent of the villeins, 8 per cent of the free holders and 4 per cent of the tenantry as a whole fell into this category. Even the virgater, the 20–40 acre man, was a rarer bird than has sometimes been supposed, for only about one-fifth of the peasantry had that much land. More than one-third of the villeins, in fact, were half-virgaters, making this the next most numerous group after the smallholders.

These conclusions refer, of course, only to a limited range of Midland counties; but, although there is no other source that compares in scope with the hundred rolls, they can be extended by aggregating data provided by the rentals and the surveys of individual manors. These records confirm that the land hunger revealed by the hundred rolls in much of central England was a feature of a much larger part of the country. The picture drawn by M. M. Postan from over 100 manors scattered through the home and southern counties, the West Midlands, Dorset and Somerset illustrates that fact.[42] Only 22 per cent of the 7,000 or so tenancies were a virgate or more, 33 per cent were between a quarter and a whole virgate, and 45 per cent were a quarter virgate or less. A number of the records used for these computations, moreover, date from the late twelfth century or first half of the thirteenth, so that these figures probably present a rosier view of the pattern of peasant landholding on these estates than that prevailing in the generation around 1300.

Everything suggests that there is nothing unusual about this prominence of smallholders in English villages. In eastern England about 30 per cent of the tenants of the Bishop of Ely's manors in Essex in 1251 had under 5 acres, and the signs are that the proportion of men with similarly modest endowments on his Norfolk and Suffolk manors was significantly higher. When it is remembered that in the Lincolnshire fen the amount of land per head was as low as 1½ acres, and that in Cambridgeshire in 1279 41 per cent of villeins and 68 per cent of freeholders had less than a quarter virgate, these eastern districts appear to be among the most crowded in the country. As we move towards the peripheries, on the other hand, tenants seem rather better endowed. On the Cornish estates of the Duchy of Cornwall, although the average size of holdings varied greatly from manor to manor, very small holdings were far rarer than further east: three-quarters of the conventionary and villein tenants held more than 10 acres and only 5 per cent held less than 5 acres. In the north, on the other hand, 60 per cent of tenants on Yorkshire and Lancashire manors for which evidence is available had less than 10 acres, and more than half the tenants in Yorkshire and a third of the tenants in Lancashire had under 5 acres. Even in Northumberland, where there was more elbow room, 35 per cent of tenants had less than 10 acres and 30 per cent less than 5 acres.[43]

General averages, of course, conceal significant variations. First there were contrasts between villeins and free men. In the districts covered by the 1279 hundred rolls 61 per cent of the villeins, but only 33 per cent of the free tenants, were in the middling range of tenantry with a half to a whole virgate. Free tenants, in other words, were more likely than villeins to be found at the two poles of the economic scale. Taken at their face value, the hundred rolls suggest that lords had enjoyed some success in their endeavours to preserve the integrity of villein tenements. They further imply that, if favourable conditions of tenure had enabled some thriving freemen to add to their holdings, freedom to alienate and partition had multiplied the number of miniscule free properties. Freedom bred peasant poverty as well as a sort of yeomanry.

Secondly, there are indications that the distribution of peasant property changed over time. The Bishop of Ely's manor at Great Shelford (Cambs) affords an example the more significant because changes were not dramatic. Three thirteenth-century surveys[44] show a slight erosion of half-virgate free tenements between 1222 and 1279. Nonetheless, in 1279 two freemen, compared with one in 1222, had holdings larger than an 18 acre half-virgate; and over the same period the number of unfree smallholders increased from fourteen to eighteen. By 1279 there were two tenants with more than half a virgate, eighteen half-virgaters, eighteen quarter virgaters and twenty-six men with smaller holdings – a total of sixty-four. Change during the thirteenth century seems to have been slight (suggesting that Shelford was already a fully settled territory in 1222).[45] By contrast, the difference between the extents of that century and the entry for Shelford in Domesday, provided the latter can be taken at its face value, is striking. In 1086 there were only twenty-eight tenants – twenty *villani* and eight smallholding bordars. Not only had the total number of tenants more than doubled by the thirteenth century: the average holding of the middling peasant landholders had fallen by about half and the number of very smallholders had increased more than threefold.[46] This tendency for smallholdings to multiply during the twelfth and thirteenth centuries is found in most places and so, apparently, were fissiparous tendencies in the holdings of the middling peasantry. At Shelford the process had nearly reached its term by 1222; but at Wilburton Maitland noted how some 'full lands' were divided into 'half-lands' subsequent to 1222.[47] At a somewhat later date, at Acklington in Northumberland, twenty-one bond tenants each with 30 acres in 1248 were replaced by thirty-five with 16 acres before the Black Death, when mortality cast some of the holdings back into the hands of the lord.[48]

Finally, there were marked differences in the distribution of holdings between regions. Cambridgeshire outside the fens, for example, had a high proportion of free and villein smallholders with under 5 acres of land (68 per cent and 41 per cent respectively), while only about 5 or 6 per cent of the peasantry were full virgaters. In Oxfordshire, on the other hand, only about 20 per cent of the peasantry had smallholdings while 46 per cent of the villeins and 29 per cent of the free tenants were virgaters. The contrast may be partly explained by the fact that Cambridgeshire was an old-settled and populous district in which a growing population caused the fragmentation of holdings, whereas in Oxfordshire opportunities for colonization in the woodlands and in the Chiltern uplands relieved pressure on the older settled parts of the county; but there are difficulties in accepting this as the sole reason for the differences between the two counties. In Warwickshire, too, there is the marked contrast already mentioned between the largish holdings characteristic of the old and densely settled Kineton hundred and the smaller tenements of the colonizing Stoneleigh hundred north of the Avon. Here opportunities for pastoral and industrial pursuits in the latter area possibly made smaller arable holdings viable there; possibly, too, the prevalence of large manors with extensive demesnes and villeinage in Kineton hundred helped to preserve there the tenemental arrangements on which manorial production was based. This contrast may also shed light on the differences between Oxfordshire and Cambridgeshire. The former was a county, on the whole, of largish manors and demesnes and fairly extensive villeinage; in Cambridgeshire, on the whole, the small estate and the small manor were predominant, and lordship may have been less capable of controlling the disruptive potentialities of the peasant land market.

In seeking explanations for regional discrepancies the possibility must also be faced that we are merely explaining away illusions induced by our records. In a county like Cambridgeshire, where the manorial structure sat loosely on the villages, the record of the landholding population may be closer to reality than it is in more manorialized Oxfordshire. Even in Cambridgeshire a villein heir had sometimes to make at least temporary provision on the family holding for his younger brothers and sisters (see p. 138); in Oxfordshire, therefore, apparently intact virgates and half-virgates may well have had to accommodate a population well in excess of the titular holder and his family. At Wotton Underwood in neighbouring Buckinghamshire, as we have seen (p. 55), landless men (*valletti*) were almost half as numerous again as tenants in villeinage and at least some of them were members of established villein families. Again, particularly in areas where there were few opportunities for colonization, peasant 'sales' and leases resulted in a substantial, but often concealed, disintegration of holdings. How far this could go is indicated by the fact that one tenant of the Bishop of Winchester at Meon presented himself for harvest works with no less than twenty-five sub-tenants.[49]

It is, therefore, impossible to calculate with any pretence of accuracy how the land was distributed among the medieval peasantry. It can be said, however, that a great diversity of records point to a high proportion of tenants with very little land; and the probability is that the records underrate rather than overrate their numbers. To some extent the larger average holdings of the north and west served to compensate for the greater proportion of poorer soils to be found in the remoter and higher regions. Even within regions it is unwise to take differences in acreage solely at their face value. In 1345 more than 90 per cent of holdings on Dartmoor were 10 acres or larger while at Axminster in 1260 almost 80 per cent of holdings were less than 10 acres.[50] Yet it is manifest that an acre of rough Dartmoor moorland was not so productive as an acre of fertile lowland in east Devon, and it cannot be proven that the smallholders of Axminster were more wretched than the assarters of larger holdings on the moors. By the early fourteenth century, moreover, the long era of colonizing endeavour had resulted in the planting of many holdings on the poorer margins of rural settlements, and for this reason they must have been less productive than those situated upon more rewarding soils.

What a man and his family could live on depended not only on the fertility of the soil, of course, but also on the size of his croft and the availability of meadow and pasture to supplement his arable, and of auxiliary resources like those provided by the sea or the fen or the woodland. Apart from these factors what a family could live on must have depended on what had to be paid for the land. These charges by the thirteenth century were often very high, especially for the villeins: one calculation of their relationship to the product of the holding puts them in some places 'near or above the 50 per cent mark'. Apart from customary rents, they included payments for additional pieces of land and for pasture, entry fines, heriots, merchet, penalties imposed by manorial courts, tallages often exacted annually, payments for labour services 'sold' or commuted, and tithes levied by the church.[51] For this reason an 'economic' villein holding might need to be larger than the tenement required to support a free tenant's family, simply because the latter's outgoings were smaller. This cautionary note is important for any attempt to evaluate what the medieval distribution of land meant in bread-and-butter terms.

Scholars have tried to compute how much arable land an average peasant family needed for its sustenance, and most modern attempts show a modest measure of agreement. H. S. Bennett argued that the virgater in a good year could grow enough for his family's needs and have a sizeable surplus for sale or exchange, but that the minimum requirement for a normal family lay between 5 and 10 acres, and probably nearer 10. Kosminsky, stressing the charges borne by villeins, came to the conclusion that the living standards of many peasants with even more than 10 acres of land were precarious. Most recent estimates have tended to push the area of land required for subsistence still higher: R. H. Hilton sees the half virgater 'living on the very edge of subsistence', and J. Z. Titow would set the minimum requirement at 10 acres under a three-field and 13 ½ acres under a two-field regime.[52]

Other considerations suggest that the economic condition of the medieval villager should not be viewed in too optimistic a light. First, full-time manorial servants (ploughmen, carters and the like) commonly received much of their stipend in kind, often at the rate of 36 bushels yearly and sometimes more than that.[53] To produce that much corn (together with the tithe corn due, seed for the following year and the miller's fee) might require in the region of 4 acres of land (6 acres in all where a three-course rotation was followed). Furthermore, manorial servants had other emoluments: food at the lord's table in certain seasons, and cash wages running at about $1d$–$1\frac{1}{2}d$ per week in many places in the late thirteenth century. Even if paid at the lower rate, the money wage received by a *famulus* needed the equivalent of the produce of a further acre of land (or 1 ½ acres when fallow is taken into account). Manorial servants, of course, did not live by bread and ale alone, but then neither did the peasant, and the peasant had also to pay his rent and other seignorial dues. It is impossible to determine how many of these estate labourers were unmarried, but the fact that some of them lived in the *curia*[54] suggests that sometimes they were single; and the way in which landholding widows and heiresses were snapped up implies a large reserve of bachelors without land in most villages. If the wages and liveries in kind paid to the *famuli* were what was needed to support a bachelor, we will not set at too low a figure the acreage needed to sustain a peasant family.

Second, as we have seen, formal maintenance agreements were often made between parents and children on the surrender of the family holdings from one to another. Clearly the amount of sustenance depended on the size of the holding that changed hands, and possibly also on other sources of income open to the parents, but overall the conclusion to be drawn from these agreements is similar to that to be drawn from the wages and liveries paid to *famuli*. The 8 quarters of grain annually which John de Baggedene and his wife Matilda agreed to give John's parents would have taken the produce of at least 8 acres (12 in all under a three-course rotation) of the 'whole holding' which John received; while the 7 quarters of grain which John de Bretedon agreed to give to his parents each year, if 'they are unable to live together', would have absorbed the produce of the greater part of the half virgate, woods and 3 acres of assart which he took over from them.[55] Not all such agreements specified such large deliveries, and the average was certainly somewhat lower; but account must be taken of the fact that they related to the sustenance of old people without dependents, not to working peasants with families to support.

As far as arable holdings are a measure, the evidence suggests a village society divided into three main categories. In the bottom category were families with holdings too small to support them. At the very bottom of the scale were families with landholdings that were miniscule or non-existent. Many of this group are lost to our view, since the records often conceal sub-tenancies and almost invariably ignore the landless. Even if we leave this group aside and deal only with tenants holding directly from a lord, it is likely that in many counties a fifth or more of the peasantry held less than a single acre, and that in the country at large a quarter may have held less than 3 acres. To families such as these the produce from their holdings could have provided only a meagre supplement to income obtained from other sources. Where to draw the line delimiting an acreage sufficient to support an average family is a difficult matter. If we set it at 5 acres, which is almost certainly too low, then we consign at least a third of the peasantry to a very precarious existence. If we set it at around 10 acres, which may be a little too high, then almost half of all tenants, and more than half of all tenants in villeinage, had insufficient arable to support their families; and we must repeat that these proportions take no account of the numerous undersettles, sub-tenants and landless who seldom appear directly in our records. Many of these small-holders clearly supplemented the income drawn from their holdings in a variety of ways; but there seems no escaping the conclusion that a very large area of genuine poverty existed in many English villages, as well as a deep pool of labour that makes more comprehensible many thirteenth-century developments in the labour organization of manors.

At the very top of the scale were men with more than 40 acres. These men were the village aristocrats and some were climbing towards yeoman status and shading into the lesser knightly class. Yet this was a very small group indeed. Not many more than one in thirty of the tenantry recorded in the hundred rolls of 1279 or on the estates analysed by Postan held more than one virgate, and possibly not more than one per cent of all tenants in the country as a whole held more than 60 acres. Freeholders were more numerous than villeins amongst these incipient yeomen (8 per cent compared with only one per cent of villeins according to the hundred rolls). The difference can presumably in part be explained by the working of the advantage represented by the free tenant's low and relatively stable outgoings. On the other hand villeins were not excluded from the village aristocracy. In the Cambridgeshire fen John Tepito of Littleport was interested, solely or jointly with others, in seven tenements of varying sizes; John Albin of Littleport and Reginald Beringhale of Sutton each held a full land and two half-lands (perhaps some 50 acres in all); Stephen Puttock of Sutton added about 30 additional acres to his full land in a busy life dealing in land. On the St Albans estate some customary tenants amassed holdings of a fair size by inter-peasant transactions and by taking up leases of small portions of demesne; and on Chertsey Abbey's manor at Egham a virgater, John Morcok, over a period of nearly thirty years acquired by some thirteen transactions a further 8½ acres, four other parcels of land and a moor.[56] Far away in the north, John de Hedworth succeeded to his father's 40-acre holding in 1315; but before 1345 he had added to it 31 acres of customary and 170 acres of free land. Not content with these gains he had also 'usurped' a considerable amount of land and bought up 120 acres of moorland assarts. A good deal of his holding was probably fairly marginal, but evidently John's enterprise is not something to be discounted.[57]

Yet small as the numbers of truly substantial tenants were, we should not assume that they were all peasants. Some were free tenants who held large amounts of land for slight services of a knightly character such as riding duties or attendance at the hundred court on behalf of their lord, and clearly belonged to a distinct social group. Some were estate officials who had taken advantage of their position to invest in land. Such men were Ralph of Thorney, the bailiff of the western estates of Peterborough Abbey, who by his death in 1333 had accumulated by piecemeal acquisition nearly 300 acres, and Richard of Crowland, bailiff of the same abbey's property in the Soke of Peterborough, who on his death in 1346 held properties in the town of Peterborough, portions of a number of knights' fees, and two customary virgates.[58] Lawyers too invested their fees in land, as did burgesses and merchants their profits. On the Cornish manors of the Duchy of Cornwall true peasants did not feature among the tenants of the most substantial conventionary landholdings; in the first half of the fourteenth century the most extensive and valuable holdings were, without exception, amassed by estate officials, townsmen, tin dealers and mining entrepreneurs.[59]

Beneath this tiny elite lay a far larger group of substantial tenants, whose holdings tended to cluster around the virgate level. The records suggest that one in five of the peasantry fell into this category, although the proportion varied widely from county to county. In the West Midlands the proportion of virgaters was generally high, and in Oxfordshire it reached 40 per cent; in the East Anglian counties, by contrast, it was usually well below 10 per cent. These men had a sufficiency of land for subsistence, even in poor harvest years. But simple self-sufficiency was not their goal; in average and good years they could market sizeable surpluses and they often needed to supplement family labour with hired help. As we shall also see, their greater wealth enabled them to adopt consumption patterns which also differed from those of the peasantry in the lower echelons of village society.

Between the two poles of the social spectrum lay the men with less than a virgate but something more than a smallholding, a broad middling band of men who are, in some sense, the typical peasants. If so, it is precisely because smallholders were so numerous that these men in most places were 'no more than a large minority' constituting between a quarter and two fifths of village society. If they were the typical peasants it was because they were essentially the subsistence agriculturalists of medieval England; that is they had holdings capable of providing incomes sufficient to support a family without recourse to regular employment for wages, but insufficient to enable the family to live off rents or work its holding mainly by hired labour.[60]

Subsistence, however, was a knife edge. Men like Stephen Puttock or John de Hedworth, by the exercise of enterprise and a good deal of ruthlessness, could rise well above it. Others were favoured (as on some Durham manors) by customary rents fixed at a moderate level at a relatively early date or by formidable traditions of freedom, like those prevailing in Kent and the Danelaw, which circumscribed the power of the landlords to trench upon it. In some places, too, even in the fourteenth century there was still new land available to colonists. In much of 'the anciently settled core of medieval England',[61] on the other hand, the trend seems to have been for the outgoings of the customary tenant to rise. It was not only that seignorial charges were augmented: from the late thirteenth century onwards governments were also reaching into the peasant's pocket for taxes, soldiers' pay, military supplies and other contributions. In combination with the demands of lords the exigencies of the state placed 'the peasant's resources in a new and more precarious position'.[62] Bad harvests, (perhaps even more) disease that robbed him of his ploughbeasts, in these circumstances easily led to catastrophe. Perhaps the shortest route of all was by borrowing to meet present emergencies, such as a bad harvest or a heavy fine. Since usury was a sin it leaves few overt traces, but we catch glimpses of village usurers at work in Yorkshire. At Holme, in the famine year of 1316, Henry Wade was lending at the relatively modest rate of about 50 per cent per annum; but William Richardson lent money to a woman at over 200 per cent.[63] In this world the man who had just enough might easily find himself with too little.

It is possible, of course, that by concentrating attention on arable holdings the picture of peasant circumstances is made darker than in fact it was. There were non-agricultural occupations open to countrymen: as village smiths or carpenters, as charcoal burners in the woodlands, as smelters and metal workers in the forests of Dean, Arden or the Weald, as cloth-workers in many places, as part-time miners of tin in Devon and Cornwall or of lead in Derbyshire. Nature, too, provided bounty in some places. Men in wooded country, if they could circumvent seignorial restraints, might collect and sell timber. Fenlanders sold peat, sedge, wildfowl and astronomical numbers of eels. The seaside, too, offered special opportunities. Roger Barri had only a cotland at Cowpen in Durham and there is little doubt that his main livelihood came from the salt-pan he rented from his lord; and at Newton-by-the-Sea in Northumberland fishing was an occupation sufficiently profitable for the lord of the manor to levy £3 a year from the three boats there.[64]

Supplementary earnings of this sort cannot be ignored in assessing the peasant's economic standing. In some places they were clearly of considerable importance; but it may be doubted whether, over England as a whole, they raised the earnings of the rural population more than marginally, and in most places they must have taken second place to the profits of animal husbandry. In certain regions these were clearly a principal source of subsistence – on the northern moors, the high lands of the Derbyshire Peak or the Welsh marshes, the south-western moors, some of the marshlands of Kent and eastern England, in parts of the Lincolnshire Wolds and the Cotswolds. Even in the arable heart of England livestock was important. It has been suggested that at Crawley (Hants) nearly half the earnings of a 16-acre virgater in a good year, and more in a bad year, came from stock.[65] This calculation probably exaggerates and in any case the Crawley virgater had unusually generous common rights; but all the same the contribution of animal husbandry to peasant incomes must not be underrated. The fact that many paid rents in hens and eggs implies that most of them could be assumed to have poultry; the fact that many paid pannage for pasturing their pigs suggests that swine were also ubiquitous. Legal formularies envisaged a peasant's sheep straying into the lord's corn or meadow and both peasant husbandry and villein labour services called for draught animals. At Chalgrave in 1279 we even hear of a bondman who was a 'vagrant without a tenement or a dwelling place', and yet he had a cow to leave to his sister, a leper, though 'more animals he did not have'.[66]

It is far more difficult to proceed from such general impressions to precise estimates of how livestock was distributed among the peasantry. One possible source of information is the detailed assessments of the goods and chattels of villagers for purposes of taxation which have occasionally survived. Table 3 summarizes the evidence provided by some of these assessments for a number of different districts at different points of time. The evidence is not without its difficulties. We cannot be sure how complete the inventories of taxable goods were, to what extent the practice of the taxers varied from tax to tax and between districts, or whether evasion was sometimes less and sometimes more. Again, these records tell us nothing of those villagers who fell below the exemption line for taxation. On the other hand no other source provides this sort of broad picture of peasant livestock in whole districts: we can hardly afford to ignore it, whatever its imperfections.

Table 3   Livestock per taxpayer, 1225–97[67]

	Draught animals	Cows and calves	Sheep	Pigs
South Wiltshire, 1225	1·8	2·8	15·6	0·3
Blackbourne Hundred (Suffolk), 1283	1·0	3·2	10·5	1·4
Liberty of Ramsey manors (Hunts), 1291	2·4	4·5	6·2	3·8
Three Bedfordshire hundreds, 1297	0·8	0·9	2·6	0·1
Liberty of Ripon (Yorks, West Riding), 1297	2·4	1·5	4·0	—

If we can take it more or less at face value, it offers little encouragement to exaggerate the place of pastoral husbandry in the peasant economy. Most surprising, perhaps, is the paucity of peasant pigs: they are modestly ubiquitous only in Suffolk and relatively numerous only in wooded Huntingdonshire. At the same time Huntingdonshire had its fen pastures, helping to explain the high figure there for cows and calves; elsewhere relatively few peasants lacked cows (only about one-fifth of the taxpayers of Bedfordshire and Suffolk), but there is considerable variation between the regions. In Bedfordshire few had more than a single cow, the Yorkshire peasant was a little better off, but the average taxpayer in Suffolk and Wiltshire had around three cows and calves. While a high proportion of taxpayers had cows, it was otherwise with sheep: nearly one-third of the taxpayers in Suffolk, two fifths of them in Huntingdonshire and Wiltshire, over half the Ripon taxpayers and more than two thirds of those in Bedfordshire had no sheep at all. The average figure per taxpayer, moreover, only rises above a very modest level in the markedly pastoral 'Fielding' district of north-west Suffolk and the traditional sheep country in southern Wiltshire. In brief, in heavily arable areas (Huntingdonshire, Bedfordshire, even parts of the liberty of Ripon) the essentially cereal basis of peasant agriculture was diversified only to a very limited extent by sheep-farming. Even in districts with a stronger pastoral bias, moreover, many who were rich enough to be taxpayers had few or no sheep, so that 'a disproportionate share of the village flocks' was owned by a limited circle of comparatively wealthy peasants.[68] Large peasant sheep-farmers were no more typical of the peasantry as a whole than were men with large arable holdings.

The tax assessments carry a further implication: while almost all taxpayers were mixed farmers to one degree or another, arable husbandry was the main concern of most of them. The evidence the returns afford about draught animals is therefore especially important. Once again they suggest that Bedfordshire men were worst off: in Barford hundred 33 per cent of taxpayers had none at all, 54 per cent had one only and only 13 per cent had two or more. Not surprisingly the average falls below one per taxpayer, and the Suffolk figure is only marginally better. Here the indications are that there was an evident deficiency of peasant draught animals, and even in the counties where taxpayers appear to be better provided draught animals were hardly excessively numerous. Particularly is this the case when we remember that there was also a tail of villagers (how long a tail we cannot measure) who were excused taxation altogether: if their numbers could be taken into account they would inevitably lower the average of livestock per head because they must have had little stock themselves to bring into the reckoning. In Suffolk in 1283 men were exempt if the total value of their goods were under 6s8d: that sum would buy only a single cow or ox, or a poor specimen of a horse.

There is other evidence, some of it from a relatively early date, for the peasant's shortage of plough beasts. In 1183 a virgater of Buckland Abbas (Dorset) was expected to have a complete team, but provision was made for the contingency that he might have only half a team and even no more than two oxen. Similarly the holders of half a hide at Nettleton (Wilts) and of 3 acres at Meare (Somerset) were envisaged as having only two oxen or perhaps merely one.[69] A century or more later, in Huntingdonshire, a Ramsey tenant at King's Ripton was much worse off: he had 'no beasts of his own wherewith to plough and has only borrowed beasts'; while in neighbouring Somersham in 1222 a virgater, if he had 'no beast in his plough on account of his poverty . . . will be obliged to plough 9 acres each year with his pennies'. At Banstead in Surrey a yardlander without beasts had to dig four day-works with a spade; and at Newington in Oxfordshire in 1278 there were men who stole ploughbeasts in order to plough.[70]

Tax assessments, then, have their difficulties as evidence; but there is some corroboration of the data they contain. To that already quoted may be added the list of tallagable goods owned by the customers of Minety, once in Gloucestershire but now in Wiltshire, in 1313.[71] A domestic seignorial assessment is perhaps likely to be even nearer the facts of the situation than a tax levied by a remoter authority. Minety lay in sheep country: not surprisingly the number of sheep per head (14) approached the figure for Wiltshire, but here again nearly one-third of the tenants had none at all. On the other hand, pigs averaged only one per head and cows 1·4; most tenants had a horse, but only half had oxen although the average was 1·4 per head. The basic picture is very much the same as elsewhere. Cows were ubiquitous; and pigs were fewer than the obligation to pay pannage, so carefully recorded in the extents, would suggest. Even in sheep-raising country many of the peasantry had few sheep, if any at all, and still more was this true in districts where sheep-raising was less prevalent. Many villagers were chronically short of draught animals, so that they must often have been compelled to plough with their cows to the detriment of milk yields.[72]

Furthermore, if cornlands periodically yielded bad harvests, livestock were no less susceptible to acts of God. The visitations of murrain destroyed peasant capital as well as curtailing current profits. At Sevenhampton in 1273 the customary tenants paid to keep 652 sheep outside the lord's fold; but in the next year a great murrain reduced this flock to 320 and by 1276 it had fallen lower to 233. Slow recovery was punctuated by further epidemics in 1280, 1282 and 1284 and even in 1288 the peasant flock numbered only 409, less than two-thirds of what it had been fifteen years before.[73] The inroads of disease were even more serious when they affected draught animals, and the ravages of the epidemics among cattle in the years 1315 to 1322 may make this a period in which the destruction of the peasant's scarce capital deepened his impoverishment.[74] To the effects of disease, moreover, must be added the habit of lords and the church to take livestock from family holdings for heriots and mortuaries each time a villein tenant died.

These influences also contributed to that move cornwards of the frontier between corn and hoof; but the principal reasons for that move lay in the increasing scarcity of land and the sharpened struggle of ordinary men for subsistence. In this situation there was an inevitable bias towards cereal husbandry, for land under grain produced more calories for human consumption than land under grass. If this guaranteed the expansion of cornland, the fact that the larger animals might need to be fed scarce corn during winter was a disincentive to keeping up their numbers. At the same time, the relative scarcity of peasant livestock, which all influences conspired to create, reacted in turn on the productivity of peasant farming generally. Peasant holdings in particular may have been starved of manure to the detriment of the grain yields upon which the villager's sustenance depended.

There is, then, an overall compatibility between the different indices for measuring the fortunes of the medieval peasantry. There were among villagers some men with considerable arable holdings, an adequate equipment of ploughbeasts (even ploughbeasts they could hire out to others), and very considerable sheep flocks. Such men, however, were never more than a minority. Men with only marginally

sufficient arable lands for their subsistence and, at best, a small number
of animals were much more numerous. Possibly most numerous of all
by the opening of the fourteenth century were men with arable holdings
inadequate to sustain a family and very little livestock. A list of the
nativi of Coney Weston (Suffolk) gives details of their animals in 1302.
Some had four oxen or four horses; some had up to five cows or forty
sheep or nine pigs; but there was also a man with one sheep and one pig,
two with only a pig and two with only a cow apiece, one who had half a
cow and half a calf, and one who had no more than half a calf. More
than that, out of seventy-six tenants, twenty-two were credited with no
stock at all. True, three were *mercatores*, one was a carpenter and a few
seem to be widows; but this still leaves a balance of the plain poor and
one was explicitly said to be *mendicus*.[75] It is hard to escape the
conclusion that, around 1300, many villagers stood upon or had fallen
below the poverty line. All in all, despite the emergence of a few men of
enterprise as a peasant aristocracy, in many respects the tale of the
villager's fortunes in this period is one of the progress of poverty.

Daily living

When acres have been counted and livestock enumerated we are still left
with a generalized and external view of the life lived by the medieval
villager; and any closer view is restricted by the tantalizing paucity of
surviving direct evidence. Medieval villages must have borne scant
resemblance to the idyllic 'historic' villages of our own times; such
villages are largely the products of major improvements in the standard
of housing achieved in the building booms of the sixteenth and seventeenth centuries, and of the survival of the finest and most solid
medieval dwellings. Medieval villages are better described in the terms
used of Witham (Soms) in 1175 – 'old hovels, decayed beams and
half-destroyed walls'.[76] Nor did most of them before the fourteenth
century consist of houses neatly grouped around a green or laid out
along a road. On the contrary, most of the village sites that have been
excavated attest the haphazard and temporary nature of their development. Peasant houses seem constantly to have been rebuilt, often in
different parts of the croft, and the houses of even the richer villagers
seem neither to have been very substantial nor permanent. They correspond well enough to a time when material standards of comfort were
uniformly low.

The surviving evidence on the ground of medieval peasant housing is
inevitably biased towards the dwellings of the richer villagers rather than
the poorer, but the former were a minority and the majority lived a
precarious existence. It is only to be expected that their homes reflected

the poverty of their occupants. It seems likely that the commonest houses were crude and flimsy structures, generally errected by the inhabitants themselves from the cheapest of local materials – mud, wood and thatch. Normally they consisted of one room only, for returns from Colchester and the surrounding villages around 1300 show that even among taxpayers only a minority of families had more.[77] Most of them, too, were exceedingly small. One cottage excavated at Seacourt (Berks) had internal dimensions of 10 by 12 feet and another at Wharram Percy (Yorks) measured 10 by 20 feet.[78] Each cottage had a minimum of unglazed window area; the room or rooms were usually open to the roof; and there was a central hearth but no chimney, the smoke escaping as best it could through a hole in the roof. It was doubtless cottages of this quality that Henry de Bray had built on his estate in 1295–1306 at a cost of 10s–30s each.[79]

There were, of course, ampler dwellings and some that have been investigated are up to 100 feet long. Additional size, however, did not always mean additional living space: for, in the medieval 'long house', a considerable amount of space was normally devoted to the provision of storage space and quarters for animals. This character of village dwelling places can be illustrated from excavations at Joyden's Wood (Kent) and Holworth (Dorset).[80] At the former place rectangular buildings of 29 by 16 feet and 32 by 15½ feet were each a single-roomed cottage with a byre at one end; at Holworth a somewhat larger long house combined a living room, a byre and a grain store. There is other evidence, moreover, that men and animals often lived in close proximity. In 1340, at Hallow (Worcs), William de Hampton surrendered his holding, curtilage and long house to his daughter and son-in-law. They were to pay a rent of 6s yearly and perform some small services on William's behalf; but William reserved a right for his oxen to have their stalls in the house whenever he wished.[81]

It is reasonable supposition that long houses were, for the most part, the dwellings of the middle stratum of peasants: the sort of families that had the resources to build them and the livestock to house in their byres. There were, in addition, peasant houses on a somewhat larger scale and of a somewhat higher quality which doubtless served the needs of that small number of villagers who approached yeoman standing. The remains of an unusually large stone house in the deserted hamlet of Upton (Glos) may be a case in point. Built on the site of what was probably an earlier timber structure, it began as a simple dwelling of some 38 by 20 feet, but after successive extensions it reached almost 100 feet in length and, before its abandonment, it comprised two living rooms, a byre and a yard or storage area.[82] Houses which evolved through the rebuilding of lesser dwellings, in all likelihood as the fortunes of the families that occupied them rose, are to be found elsewhere: at Gomeldon (Wilts), for example, where a twelfth-century long house was replaced in the early thirteenth century by a larger one which was succeeded in turn in the next century by a cluster of farm buildings arranged around a courtyard; or at Wythemail (Northants) where an early thirteenth-century timber building was replaced first by a stone long house of 37 by 16 feet and then, in the fourteenth century, by a similar dwelling of 57 by 13 feet.[83]

There is some evidence for improvements in the construction of houses over our period. At Goltho (Lincs), for example, the earliest peasant houses (dating probably from the eleventh or early twelfth centuries) were made of clay without timber frames. By the later twelfth and early thirteenth centuries they had timber frames, and a century later, apart from more elaborate timber frames, they had clay walls built on stone bases to prevent damage from damp.[84] By the close of the period, for somewhat more prosperous families, building in stone had become common in areas where it was easily available, in the south-west replacing turf reinforced with hurdles. In the Cotswolds even humbler dwellings were often built of stone by 1300, but the local limestone slates were too costly to be used on peasant roofs.[85] Stone building required a greater initial outlay, but it was more durable and cheaper to maintain: walls of cob (mud or clay mixed with straw or dung as a binding material), by contrast, had a far shorter life. At the same time the higher initial cost must have put such improved dwellings beyond the reach of a large section of the peasantry. Their poverty condemned them to the poor and flimsy structures that St Hugh encountered at Witham: and because these structures were so poor and flimsy they have left few vestiges that we can recover seven hundred years later.

If many of the houses of a village were cramped and almost improvised, what little we know of their contents suggests that they were few. To modern eyes even the richest peasants had a very narrow range of possessions.[86] The most essential and most costly items in peasant houses were bronze cooking pots and pans: well-used pots of one or two gallons capacity were often valued at 2s or more. Iron hearth equipment – tripods for holding pots over the fire, andirons, gridirons, trivets and the like – were likewise essential and expensive. They were frequently valued at from 6d to 1s each. There is less information about furnishings, but we can assume that most cottages had a bed, a bench or chair or stool or two, and perhaps a trestle table, generally home-made like the cottages in which they found a place. Chests are sometimes recorded in peasant inventories, especially if they had locks; commoner, but seldom mentioned because no value could be placed on them, were dishes, mugs, platters and bowls made of wood or earthenware. The poorer peasantry probably made their own wood utensils, but tableware made of wood or clay fit even for the king's household could be bought for a shilling or less per hundred pieces. Clothing is mentioned only where it was unusually plentiful or fine; but most peasants appear to have possessed no more than a single outfit and little or no cloth or bedlinen or window curtains in their houses. The reason is simple: cloth, like metalware, was relatively very expensive.

This meagre list exhausts the items that might be found in the cottages of the poorer peasants, and not everyone possessed all of them. Some families, indeed, were too poor to own a metal cooking pot. The better-off among the villagers, on the other hand, not only had a comprehensive range of these basic items – two or three metal cooking utensils, sheets and coverlets, a fine coat – but also additional items purchased as much for the social prestige they conferred as for their utilitarian function. The subsidy assessments for Colchester and its district in 1301[87] reveal that the household goods of the great mass of the poorer taxpayers, if they are mentioned at all, were mainly restricted to cooking pots and hearth equipment. In some households, however, we also find metal ewers and basins for the washing of hands before and after meals, cups and drinking bowls of carved wood, some of them decorated with metal (mazers), and a silver spoon or two. These things, like jewellery (silver buckles, silver and gold rings, and decorated belts), were the symbols of rising social status. In the village, as in other medieval contexts, the marks of social promotion were a measure of display.

The details of peasant diet are even more difficult to discover than the details of his possessions, but once again the indications are that it was marked by limited variety and a contrast between the poorer and richer of the villages. The character of medieval agriculture, in the first place, determined that except in a few mainly pastoral regions rural diet was predominantly farinaceous. The average villager fed on large quantities of coarse dark bread, occasional dishes of pottage made primarily from oatmeal with a few vegetables or pieces of meat added to the pot when they were available, and copious draughts of weak ale made from the malt of wheat or more likely barley or oats. Families with a cow or ewes or goats would have a supply of milk, cheese and butter, and perhaps occasionally meat; but like the peasant's wheat crop, part of these animal products might have to be sold. Eggs were probably more plentiful, even though lords were apt to take a share of them at Easter; salted and dried fish were available in most parts of the country; and families living near sea and inland fisheries would have access to cheaper supplies. All in all, however, a very large proportion of countrymen had a diet that must have been deficient in protein.

In order to obtain sufficient calories, therefore, the peasant was compelled to consume very large quantities of carbohydrates. How large these quantities were is suggested by the information available about the food provided for manorial servants and the corrodies purchased by humble persons entering retirement. A main part of the pay of full-time male labourers, as we have seen, took the form of liveries of grain often of the order of 36 bushels a year, sufficient to provide them with about 5 lb of bread daily.[88] This figure is not beyond belief when we take account of the fact that the average consumption per head of the members of the household of Bolton Priory together with their guests, better provided as they were with meat and animal products than all but the tiniest minority of peasants, was of the order of 1000 lb of grain in bread and pottage and the equivalent in ale of 1600 lb of malt each year.[89] The basic character of peasant diet is also endorsed by John Gower's wistful reminiscences of the times before the Black Death when labourers knew their place:

Labourers of olden time were not wont to eat wheaten bread; their bread was of beans or other common corn, and their drink was of the spring. Then cheese and milk were as a feast to them; rarely had they other feast than this. Their garment was of sober grey: then was the world of such folk well ordered in its estate.[90]

The diet of those fortunate enough to be in a position to purchase generous corrodies included significant quantities of fish, meat and cheese; but, like the canons of Bolton, they too consumed large quantities of carbohydrate in the form of bread and ale.[91] The bread for which they convenanted might be of better quality, made of wheat rather than maslin, and their ale 'convent ale' rather than 'third ale', but the prominence of grain in their diet remains very striking. In all probability the food consumed by these better-off pensioners closely resembled that enjoyed by the richer peasantry: it cannot be better described than by the phrase 'coarse plenty' which Thorold Rogers applied to the condition of the medieval English peasantry.[92] It must be emphasized, however, that at least in the thirteenth and early fourteenth centuries that description was apt only for the upper stratum of English villagers; and also that it was only in a few overwhelmingly pastoral regions, like Wales, that people could 'live upon the produce of their herds, with oats, milk, cheese and butter, eating flesh in larger proportions than bread'.[93]

These indications provide a reasonable degree of assurance about the types of foodstuffs consumed by the peasantry, but it is more difficult to be certain how regularly peasant families were able to eat the quantities of the basic foods that were provided for estate workers. Lords had an obvious interest in supplying their servants with sufficient calories to enable them to work efficiently, but they sometimes responded to poor harvests by cutting back on payments in kind to manorial labourers. In 1316–17 grain liveries were even suspended altogether by the Bishop of Winchester 'on account of the dearness of corn'.[94] The quality and quantity of the peasant farmer's diet were no less dependent on harvests, as well as the size of his holding and the availability to him of other sources of income and foodstuffs. The indications are that, in times of really acute famine like the years 1315–17, some of the peasantry starved or were so weakened by hunger that they fell victim to diseases they might otherwise have resisted. More important, however, practice of the 'peasant art of starvation' in the not infrequent seasons of shortage might have the effect of so reducing calorific intake that working efficiency was impaired. In a world in which the machine as yet was applied only to a limited range of tasks, and in which physical labour was the main instrument of production, the result must have been to limit, and limit severely, potential *per capita* output.

The peasant in the medieval economy

Some indications of how the peasantry was housed are being provided by the spade of the archaeologist and some suggestions about their diet can be made by inference from the provision made from labourers, but the motives and pressures that governed the peasant's economic behaviour are far harder to discern. We can hazard a guess that the peasant's prime endeavour was, if not to achieve self-sufficiency, at least to supply himself with the main necessities of life from his own land. Competition for small plots of land by landless or semi-landless men may perhaps be interpreted as a reaching out towards this self-supplying position; equally symptomatic is the clustering of holdings about the point at which they would just sustain a man and his family. A barely conscious economic ideal, as well as the dynastic sentiments of families and the interests of landlords, helped to preserve the integrity of many tenements at just about this economic level despite all the pressure in the direction of fragmentation which arose from an expanding population.

This economic ideal finds expression in some of those peasant family arrangements already discussed. At Cranfield (Beds) a son was to provide his old father and mother with house-room and with 'honourable sustenance in food and drink so long as they live'; at Dunmow (Essex) Parnel de Teye's son was to find her a room together with 'reasonable victuals in food and drink as befit such a woman . . .

and a cow, four sheep and a pig going and feeding on the said half virgate . . . for her clothing and footwear'.[95]

In the peasant's eyes, then, the holding should provide the family with 'reasonable victuals in food and drink', seemingly primarily in the form of cereal products. At the same time, as Parnel's bargain with her son shows, this was not quite the end of the affair. The cow and the sheep might provide a little milk, butter and cheese, but their place in the scheme for her retirement was to secure her footwear and clothing. We can hardly suppose that cowhide, pigskin and wool were to be made up in the household for Parnel's shoes and gowns; more likely wool and dairy produce would be sold to obtain the means to buy what she wanted. The fact is that a peasant tenement could not supply directly all a family needed, for apart from shoes and clothing it required salt, pots for the kitchen and iron work for implements and tools, and perhaps some fish to supplement a farinaceous diet. To obtain money for such things peasants had to market some of their produce. Consequently we find them haunting markets both as sellers and purchasers: the men of Chatteris dealt in Swavesey market, which was ten miles away or more.[96] The multiplication of local markets during the twelfth and thirteenth centuries in part responded to the commercial needs of small men. So did the growth of a class of village *mercatores* – not so much merchants as petty dealers, like Peter *mercator* to whom two men from Houghton (Hunts) engaged themselves in 1309 for the sale of a single sack of wool.[97]

It is impossible to calculate the dimensions of peasant trading or even to describe the various articles which entered into it. Clearly there was nothing which might not be sold – fish by part-time fishermen, salt by part-time salt boilers, eels and reeds and turf by fenmen, and wood and charcoal by forest dwellers; but obviously the main contribution of peasants to the market must have been the produce of animal and arable husbandry. They presumably provided some of the meat, poultry and dairy produce bought by townsmen; certainly their wool helped to feed the looms of England and Flanders, for there was complaint that the Lincolnshire Cistercians in the thirteenth century bought up wool in small quantities in divers places and sold it with their own to merchant strangers.[98] Again, the hides which provided the raw material for an important branch of urban industry and a far from insignificant export commodity probably came in part from the backs of peasant stock. Given the character of peasant farming, however, we must presume that the most important cash crops were provided by arable holdings. The money the peasant needed came first and foremost from the sale of grain and, where it was grown and because it was relatively of good price, perhaps mainly from the sale of wheat. The family arrangements discussed above show that some wheat was consumed as food, at least by the more prosperous households; but for many it may have been regarded principally as a cash crop rather than an element in household food supplies.

Peasants sold, of course, in part to purchase what their own land did not provide and, as buyers in the market they suffered many disadvantages. As in all pre-industrial economies a relatively primitive technology and difficult communications added to the costs of production and distribution. How these affected the peasant cannot be determined by scrutinizing the budgets of villagers, for we have none; but some indication may be provided by setting the prices of consumer goods against wages. In the generations around 1300, as we have seen, an unskilled labourer (provided he could find work) might earn $1d$–$1\frac{1}{2}d$ per day. Salt may have been relatively cheap and plentiful, and shoes could be got at around $2d$ a pair; but the cheapest cloth on the market (russet and blanket) cost $1s$–$1s\ 6d$ a yard. A simple smock, therefore, could involve the expenditure of from two to four months earnings and it is not surprising that, in the inventories of the richer peasants, even 'worn' robes are given a value which may be $3s$ or more. Candles, too, were dear at $1\frac{1}{2}d$–$2d$ a pound; and the fact that pepper cost $1s$ a pound must have encouraged the peasantry to use wild herbs to add savour to their dull and sometimes unwholesome fare. High prices, too, were asked for some domestic utensils (see p. 158), high enough in many cases to discourage purchases by men concerned for their daily bread until the next harvest came round. This situation in market-places not only explains the meagre possessions of so many of the peasantry, but also a demand for manufactures that was inevitably restricted both by their cost to the poorer countryman particularly and, therefore, by his willingness to do without or to make for himself substitutes that would serve his turn.

At the same time, the peasant's incentive to market was not solely provided by his need for a few articles he could not himself produce. His rents and charges might be heavy; for the customary tenant they might grow heavier over time; and the commutation and 'sale' of services, especially in the twelfth century and during the century before 1349, meant that lords were taking a larger proportion of peasant dues in the form of cash. In brief, if the peasant had to produce a marketable surplus to procure those goods his land would not afford him, he had also to produce a further 'contrived surplus' to obtain the wherewithal to meet his outgoings to his lord. The tendency for those charges to increase was offset, at least in part, by the contemporary rise of commodity prices; but whether the latter fully compensated for increased outgoings is another matter. There is, at the least, a strong possibility that over the generations the peasantry made a progressively larger contribution to the marketable surplus of agricultural produce available in England. If they did so, however, they responded as much to the compulsion of rent as they did to the widening of commercial opportunities. In many cases they must have done so at the cost of saving and even at the expense of consumption. The result may have been some deterioration of the land of peasant holdings and a more pervasive malnutrition among the country population. By this route, too, we come back to that worsening of the economic position of considerable sections of the peasantry during the central Middle Ages. The measure of it is seen in the later Middle Ages when, after the plagues, people were fewer and land in relatively good supply. Rents fell and the peasant was under less obligation to divert land from crops for consumption to the production of cash crops. In these circumstances many of them became less, and not more, commercial farmers; they became more, and not less, subsistence farmers. In doing so they revealed, once again, the primary motive of peasant farming as an enterprise directed towards the self-supply of the family group.

These trends in the peasant economy are important, not only for their own sake, at a time when the peasant villager was the typical Englishman; precisely because the peasantry constituted the bulk of the population what was happening to the peasant basically influenced the direction of economic development as a whole. The many signs of overpopulation make it hard to suppose that production per head in agriculture can have increased during the central Middle Ages. Much new land was gained for production, but not apparently enough. At the same time the creaming off by manorial lords of a large share of the profits of peasant agriculture helped to stimulate certain lines of industrial and commercial development. Those lines, however, were often of a somewhat special sort: the trade in and the manufacture of more or less luxury consumer goods. The declining fortunes of important sections of the peasantry, and the raids made by their lords on their small margins, restricted not only their capacity to save but also their capacity to provide a rapidly expanding mass market for non-agricultural products. To that extent the failure of the agricultural economy to grow also stunted the potentialities of growth in other branches of the medieval economy.

Chapter 7

Lords

The ordinary countryman was a villager, a member of a territorial community; but he was also a tenant, for the Norman Conquest turned into a rule a situation already existing *de facto* in most places – that there should be no land without a lord. The villager, therefore, was also a member of one of those groupings of men subjected to a lord commonly described by the word 'manor'. This word raises problems of definition; but, before facing them, it is perhaps best to say something about the men who were the lords of manors. The history of lordship and its exercise will in due course bring us back to the ordinary countryman, but this time the approach to him will be downwards, through landlords, their bailiffs, their estates and their manors, rather than upwards through the family, the village and the parish.

Landlords

In King William's England the principal element in the fabric of Anglo-Norman society was a set of relationships designed to achieve certain political ends. At the same time, from the first, these political relationships had economic and social implications. The soldiers who, at the start, preserved the Norman hold on England were often landless, but every page of Domesday Book shows that by 1086 very many of them had already been paid in land for doing so. The thinking of the time takes for granted a social pyramid with the king at its apex, the mass of the peasantry at its base, and between them two classes of lords, one consisting of the king's 'men' and the other of 'men' of the king's men. Approximately the two classes can be called barons and knights, and also approximately they were related in a hierarchy of obligations centred on military service. The baron owed service to the king, not only in person but with a following; the knight owed service to the baron, his lord, thus enabling the latter to make up a following with which to serve the king, whether in the field or in the garrisons of castles.

The military relationship at the heart of the feudal arrangement was, at the same time, based on the personal relationship of vassalage which bound a man to his lord. Very frequently, moreover, it came to have a tenurial aspect, for service deserved a reward, a fee; the fee commonly took the form of land; and increasingly men spoke of the service as something that was owed by or in consideration of the land. The replies of two Lincolnshire barons to Henry II's enquiry about feudal service in 1166 were very characteristic. Lambert de Scoteny began: 'Know that I hold of you, by your grace, 16 carucates and 2 bovates of land by the service of 10 knights'; and Hugh Wake, after listing the men who 'hold of the barony which I hold of you', concluded: 'This is the service with which my predecessors in their time served King Henry (I), who gave them the land; and I owe you the service of my body, as to a lord who gave that land to me, whenever you will want to take it'.[1] The obligations of lesser military tenants are similarly expressed. In the mid-twelfth century, for example, William, Earl of Gloucester, gave land at Great Gransden (Hunts) worth £12 yearly to Ranulf fitzGerold to supplement land worth £8 yearly that Ranulf already held at Toppesfield (Essex). The charter continued, 'for these twelve librates of land in Gransden and for the eight librates in Toppesfield Ranulf will do me the service of one knight'.[2] Henry I's confirmation of a grant by the Abbot of Ramsey to Simon de Beauchamp of land at Holywell (Beds) continued, with admirable brevity, 'on this condition that Simon ought to do for it the service of one knight, fully and in everything'.[3]

What 'fully and in everything' implied is seldom specifically defined. The knight's service would naturally be military: serving in his lord's retinue and doing castle guard, either in a royal castle (the knights of the Abbot of Abingdon owed garrison duties in Windsor castle)[4] or at a castle belonging to his own lord. Guard at Richmond castle, for example, was due from the knights of the honour of Richmond enfeoffed in Cambridgeshire, Norfolk, Lincolnshire and Nottinghamshire as well as in Richmondshire and other parts of Yorkshire; on the other hand, guard duty at Chester castle was owed only by the military tenants of the earldom with fees outside the palatine county except when invasion was threatened.[5] Over and above, knights were required to give counsel and aid to their lord, a compendious phrase which might extend to financial subventions in certain circumstances. In some respects, too, they were subject to their lord's jurisdiction for, as a twelfth-century law tract puts it, 'every lord may summon his man to stand to right in his court; and if he dwells on a very distant manor of the honour, yet he will come to the plea if his lord summons him'.[6] More generally still a man owed to his lord a loyalty which, in Glanville's phrase, amounted to reverence and which was thus described a generation earlier: 'every man owes good faith to his lord in so far as his lord's life and limb are concerned and his earthly honour and for keeping his lord's counsel honestly and profitably – saving only the fealty which he owes to God and to the prince of his country'.[7]

These basic characteristics of the feudal order are familiar enough and need no labouring; but they bequeathed to the following centuries a social system in which lordship provided the principle of organization. A good deal that was older than the conquest was fitted into it. Bishops and the greater monasteries were assimilated as quasi-baronial landowners, and both barons and knights frequently stepped directly into the places of Saxon *antecessores*. The process introduced complications into the tenurial structure, and in the event neither barons nor knights emerged as homogeneous classes. The inequalities between the tenants-in-chief of the crown appear starkly in the Norfolk returns to Henry II's enquiry regarding knights' fees in 1166. They begin with that of Earl Hugh Bigod, whose possessions stretched into many counties and included 125 knights' fees created before 1135 and $35\frac{1}{2}$ created after that date. They end with the reply of Odo de Dammartin: 'Know that my father held of your grandfather and of you for the service of one knight, and so much I hold of you.'[8] The contrast is one between giants and pygmies. The contrast is almost equally marked between the knights enfeoffed soon after the conquest by the Abbot of Abingdon. Gueres de Palence owed the service of four knights for seventeen hides in six villages; Gilbert owed the service of one knight for five hides in three villages; Baldwin de Columbers likewise owed the service of one knight for part of the single vill of Sparsholt; and there were others *qui tenent minutas partes* (who hold tiny portions) and owed as little as the service of one sixth of a knight.[9] The important thing is, however, that whatever the reality of the military arrangements behind these records, they had come to determine the structure of landownership. As their military significance declined their territorial implications remained.

Partly because men were so diversely endowed the words used to describe them were anything but precise. From the very start, it is true, the word baron was sometimes used to carry 'implications of wealth and power'. Thus there was 'an early tendency towards the restriction of the term to lords who held important fees of the king',[10] the great 'honours' which were the endowment of the principal lay potentates. On the other hand, precisely because their landed possessions were comparable, prelates who held their possessions *sicut baroniam* (as a barony) shouldered obligations *sicut barones ceteri* (like other barons);[11] and, for a time at least, tenants-in-chief of modest substance were described as barons, while tenants-in-chief also continued to give the same title to some of their own principal tenants. The Cambridgeshire family of Scalers of Whaddon clung to their baronial status at least to the end of the twelfth century, but in the thirteenth they seemed happier in the ranks of the knighthood;[12] and in Norman England there were many 'honorial barons' like those holding in 1086 of William of Warenne (see pp. 17–19). At that date Wimar, steward of the Earl of Richmond held at Aske, Harmby and Leyburn in Yorkshire, at Hickling and West Somerton in Norfolk, and at Exning, Fordham and Carlton in Cambridgeshire; and before long he added to this initial endowment holdings in some twenty-eight other Yorkshire villages. For this fee he owed the service of fifteen knights and he sub-enfeoffed military tenants of his own to provide it.[13] There were king's barons who held and owed less.

The word 'knight' was no less variably used. From one point of view it described any member of the feudal military class, baron or tenant of a baron; and it was a personal label which carried no implications of landowning. The Abbot of Abingdon at first defended his abbey with a force of stipendiary knights and the knights quartered by the Conqueror on Ely Abbey received their daily rations at the hand of the cellarer. Robert of Belesme, too, had his stipendiaries who defended Bridgenorth bravely against Henry I in 1102[14] and landless knights were regularly found in baronial households in the twelfth and thirteenth centuries alike. On the other hand, the Abbot of Ely very quickly allowed the knights King William thrust on him 'to hold certain of the lands of St Etheldreda', and a territorial fief, held conditionally on performing a knight's service fully and in everything, was the natural ambition and the normal reward of the vassal knight. Some fiefs were considerable, quasi-baronial in dimensions; others were miniscule. The outcome was a three-class rather than a two-class hierarchy of landlords. At one extreme were the holders, both lay and ecclesiastical, of really great estates; at the other were the holders of, at best, a few hundred acres which gave them lordship over a few dozen peasants. Between lay a middling class of landowners of middling substance. They included the less well endowed churches; they included men holding modest estates in chief; and they included tenants of the greater barons whose lords had rewarded them well. As always social realities were somewhat more complex than the ideal scheme of tenure.

The situation created by the conquest did not, of course, endure in a fossilized state. Many things contributed to keep the distribution of property in constant flux. A knight who failed to serve might legitimately be dispossessed of his fee, although as time went on this danger receded as knightly obligations evaporated and the royal courts gave more and more protection to the possessors of land. On the other hand, confiscation of their land was not infrequently the penalty the king imposed on rebellious barons. By the first decade of the twelfth century a good number of the principal Domesday families had disappeared and much later, after 1265, Henry III removed the 'viper's brood' of the Montforts from the ranks of English landlords.

At the same time, if royal *malevolentia* destroyed the fortunes of some old dynasties, royal favour made the fortunes of new ones. Richard Bassett was one of Henry I's 'new men' and he was raised from the dust by the gift of much of the Domesday barony of Robert de Buci; his descendants still held this property in the fourteenth century. Robert Tiptoft, too, moved up from the ranks of the knighthood into those of the baronage as the friend and servant of Edward I, establishing a line which ultimately attained an earldom; and Border service as well as hard cash won Northumbrian lands for the Percy family to add to their patrimony in Yorkshire and Lincolnshire.[15] What happened in these exalted regions also happened lower in the social scale. The ancestor of the Lisles, future barons of Rougemont, was Ralf FitzOlaf, probably of Anglo-Scandinavian stock, whose service as chamberlain and steward of Bishop Nigel of Ely was rewarded by knight's fees in Norfolk, Suffolk and Cambridgeshire. This endowment established him in the knighthood and was the springboard from which his descendants advanced into the nobility.[16]

The subsequent advance of the Lisles, however, was the product of another sort of enterprise: successful dealings in the marriage market. Generation after generation the successor to the family estate added to it by marrying at least one heiress. Here we touch on another determinant of the flux of property. Given the rule of primogeniture, and with a certain amount of good fortune, a family might keep its inheritance more or less intact, provided in each generation it produced at least one male heir. If, on the contrary, a man left no children at all his land reverted to his lord – a baron's to the king and a knight's to the baron or other superior. If a man left no male heir but did have a daughter or daughters, his estate either went intact to a single heiress or was divided between the coheiresses if there were more than one. Heiresses in turn took the land with them to whatever man they married and to their heirs by those men. Not surprisingly, therefore, heiresses were much in demand and their matrimonial adventures did much to shift the frontiers of property, all the more effectively because failure of male heirs was very common. Only about 36 out of 210 English baronies during the period 1066–1327 remained for more than two centuries in the same male line.[17]

The operations of the marriage market could aggrandize a family. It did so with the Lisles, and even more conspicuously the Domesday lords of Tonbridge and Clare drew advantage from it. It was by marriage that they added to their patrimony much of the honour of Giffard (1189), the barony of St Hilary (1195), the honour of Gloucester

(1217) and part of the vast estates of the Earls Marshal (1247). Conversely, dynastic misfortune might dismember a barony. The Cambridgeshire barony of Bourn, was divided into thirds on the death of William Peverel in 1147; one of the thirds was subsequently partitioned into sixths, one of the sixths fell apart into eighteenths and one of the eighteenths was in the end subdivided into thirty-sixths. Here a succession of heiresses reduced a Domesday barony to dissolution.[18]

Circumstances other than dynastic ones might disperse property. The decision to go crusading moved Hugh Tirel to sell Langham to Gervase of Cornhill about 1146; and probably a need for cash for the same purpose lay behind the enfeoffment in Askham Richard of a York merchant, William of Tickhill, by Roger Mowbray later in the century.[19] Mortgages, too, were a means of raising crusading funds or funds for building and for high living; they might be the recourse of the feckless man or the man who lost in the political lottery, like the numerous supporters of Montfort who were saddled with heavy 'ransoms' under the Dictum of Kenilworth. Mortgages in turn often led to outright sale of land. A twelfth-century charter tells how Roger de Wanci borrowed from a London Jew and secured the debt on his manor of Stansted. By the time he died interest had greatly augmented the debt, so his heir Michael came to the king and begged him for the love of God to pay it off. In return Michael promised to give half Stansted to whatever religious house the king nominated lest he should lose the whole of it 'by reason of the usuries increasing day by day'. The canons of Waltham were the ultimate beneficiaries of his embarrassment.[20]

The successes and failures of individuals, however, do not of necessity point to general trends in the distribution of property: families rose and fell as families always do. What the general trends were over time is a problem still awaiting systematic study, but some rough calculations relating to about sixty Cambridgeshire villages suggest that important changes in the distribution of property did take place between 1086 and 1279. The royal demesne, about 16 per cent of these villages in 1086, had virtually all passed into other hands by 1279; lands held by the baronage in demesne had likewise been drastically reduced; on the other hand church land had greatly increased and land in the hands of men of knightly standing may have more than doubled. Little weight can be placed on the precise quantities deriving from these calculations but the direction of change is by no means incompatible with a good deal of impressionistic evidence from elsewhere.

The rapid dispersal of the Norman royal demesne is well enough known; and great lay and ecclesiastical tenants-in-chief were under a variety of pressures to devolve property on the class of middling landholders. They had to create fees to meet their feudal commitments;

their social importance was sometimes measured by the numbers of their vassals; and they were under constant pressure from relatives, household knights and servants for whom a fief represented social advancement as well as a livelihood. In the case of the church, there was a countervailing current. Both old religious centres and perhaps even more the new monastic establishments of the twelfth century (with the Cistercians pre-eminent amongst them) attracted vast endowments through their appeal to the lay piety of the age. When piety had done its work, moreover, ecclesiastical business acumen took over. Churches were great buyers of land and by no means averse to taking advantage of a layman's embarrassment. Paying the debts of William Fossard and William of Redburn to their Jewish creditors enabled Meaux abbey and Malton priory to step into portions of their patrimonies.[21] Beneficence and business enterprise permitted the aggregate gains of the church during the twelfth and thirteenth centuries almost certainly to more than balance its losses through subinfeudation in the Norman epoch.

If lands occupied by churches increased, so seemingly did lands in the occupation of the middling class of knights and gentry. That at least appears to be the long term tendency, though some recent investigators have asked whether it was not reversed in the course of the thirteenth century.[22] There are signs enough in the records that men of this class might fall into difficulties: the trail of their debts in the rolls of the Jewish exchequer, the purchases of land from both knights and free tenants by prelates like the Abbots of Peterborough and Glastonbury, the buying back of knight's fees by Bishop Hugh of Ely, the exploitation of usury by Bishop Burnell of Bath to get his hands on land, the acquisition of whole manors and of smaller parcels by the Earls of Gloucester by purchase or exchange, and even Edward I's unscrupulous dealings with subjects who had fallen into debt.[23]

One of the most poignant examples is furnished by the decline of the Northamptonshire family of Southorpe, which in 1100 held eight hides for the service of three knights. Over the next 175 years we can trace how the main line of the family lost significant portions of this patrimony to younger sons and to Peterborough Abbey (part no doubt as pious gifts to the abbey, but part in order to procure the wherewithal to pay off debts). Still, however, it successfully retained the central core of the estate consisting of two knights fees. Between 1276 and 1280, on the other hand, the family's fortunes plummeted: first Geoffrey of Southorpe sold Gunthorpe manor to Peterborough Abbey for 550 marks, then he disposed of various holdings for 300 marks, and by 1280 his last demesne manor, Southorpe, was in the hands of Stephen of Cornhill, a London merchant. After a spirited but abortive attempt to revive the family fortunes, by leasing lands and borrowing money from

Queen Eleanor, Geoffrey was hauled off to a debtor's prison. Some time after his release in 1289 he abandoned his fruitless struggle for worldly fortune and, 'stroke with admiration at the holy lives of several White Friars then living', entered a Carmelite monastery at Stamford.[24]

Some of the reasons why numbers of lesser and middling landlords lost ground in the thirteenth century may be surmised. As prices rose many may have been hit by the rising cost of keeping up a gentleman's way of life, especially if their incomes were derived mainly from rents which were either fixed or subject to strong customary restraints, and if their modest endowments of land precluded them from taking the fullest advantage even of a booming market for agricultural produce. The increasing charge of royal taxation, and possibly in some cases the expense of local office, may also have contributed to their embarrassment. Finally in this age, as in any other, profligacy combined with borrowing at high rates of interest was a short and certain path to ruin. A check to the advance of the gentry, therefore, is possible enough.

At the same time that possibility must not be pressed too hard. Smaller landowners who flourished were by no means unknown in the thirteenth century,[25] and because the archives of the larger landowners have far more often survived than those of small landowners the evidence at our disposal has a built-in bias. Indeed, the bias is magnified because the archives of small landowners which have survived are very often those of the failures, which passed with their property into the hands of greater men or the great ecclesiastical corporations. For this reason there is a risk in making too much of thirteenth-century evidence for a crisis of the gentry. It may be admitted that many greater landlords added to their lands, but hardly to an extent which reduced significantly the major shift of land towards the 'knights' which had taken place since 1086.

Nor should we neglect the evidence for the burgeoning fortunes of numerous officials, functionaries and lawyers, who throve as estate management became more professional, as the law became more complex and as the common law courts became more comprehensive in their competence. Their services were often very well rewarded, both with land and money, and many rose to gentry status, some even to knighthood. Robert of Madingley, who was the son of a family with a stake in the city of Cambridge and in the village from which he took his name, was the Bishop of Ely's steward from 1304 to 1310; he later went on to become a royal judge and attained the honour of knighthood by 1317.[26] Similarly, Geoffrey Russell was among the most notable of the many Peterborough Abbey officials who prospered greatly. Nothing is known of his origins, which hardly suggests that they were distinguished; but between 1250 and 1263 he was steward of the abbey, and then went on to be steward to Isabella de Fortibus, steward of the palatinate of Durham, and steward of Wallingford (1278–81). By the end of his life he, too, became a royal justice; and at every stage of his career he had profited from his positions of power, accumulating as he did so extensive holdings in land.[27] The way in which lawyers and officials gathered up property was a common theme in contemporary writings. An early fourteenth-century poem on the venality of judges dwells on the ways in which indigent men acquire office and at once become arrogant: 'their teeth grow', they hasten to buy lands and houses and pleasing rents, they amass money and despise the poor, and they make new laws and oppress their neighbours.[28]

Each generation, then, had its 'new men' and its new rich, and probably its share of established landholders who took advantage of economic opportunities as well as those who failed to do so. Indeed, one consequence of the active land market of the thirteenth century may have been a polarization of the class of middling landowners.[29] Some elements of that class fell on evil days, and some fell out of it altogether; but others learned to seize their chances, becoming the restricted class of knights of the late thirteenth century and the entrenched *busones* whose continuous activity in local government is attested by the administrative records.[30] Indeed the political 'rise of the gentry' of which the activity of the *busones* is evidence cannot solely be explained by the long-term increase of the share of land in the possession of middling landowners; it seems also to be related to the reduction in the numbers of the knightly class, probably associated with some concentration of property in the hands of the surviving members of that class. If twelfth-century arrangements envisaged some 6,500 knights, in the reign of Edward I there appear to have been only 1,500 or so men who had actually assumed that title and perhaps a similar number with sufficient substance to enable them to bear the cost of knightly status.[31] Of course the comparison here is not of like with like, but it is none the less significant for the changing character of knighthood. The twelfth-century knighthood includes a very large element of fighting knights whose landed endowment was very meagre (see p. 18). The knights and potential knights of Edward I's time were a body of landowners, on average substantially better endowed than the Norman knights, and bearing the description of knight (when they did so) not as an indication of their function but as a title of honour.

The important fact, however, is the existence below the great magnates of a broad range of lesser landlords that had crystallized out of the military and tenurial arrangements made in the first century of English feudalism. In the process other developments during the twelfth and thirteenth centuries dissolved the original tight-knit feudal groupings. To begin with, the growing complication of tenurial relationships made the old feudalism unworkable and drained the feudal connection of real meaning. When John de Burdeleys died in 1283, the king's escheator surveyed the modest properties the family had accumulated over the generations by inheritance, purchase and marriage. John held Sculton in Norfolk by serjeanty of being the king's larderer. In Cambridgeshire he held at Madingley, Rampton and Cottenham of Gilbert Pecche, who held in turn of the Bishop of Ely; and also in Comberton where he held of Saer of St Andrew who held of the Earl of Winchester and he of the Earl of Gloucester, and in Oakington where he held of Robert Bruce of the honour of Huntingdon. Finally, in Bedfordshire he held Stagsden of the Abbot of Wardon, Sir William de Montchesney and the Prior of Newnham, and some of the lands he held of Wardon were held by the abbey from the Beauchamps.[32] We may well ask, after this catalogue, who was the lord of John de Burdeleys, member of a modestly prosperous knightly family which provided Cambridgeshire with its representative in parliament in 1301 and 1309?

There is a good deal to be learned from the case of John de Burdeleys. First, the multiplicity of his lords was hardly compatible with the primitive force of the vassalic relationship. The loyalty and reverence a vassal owed to his lord were not sentiments infinitely divisible. Again, the long chain of intermediaries between tenant-in-chief and occupying tenant destroyed the hold of the former over the latter. The service the occupant of the land owed was to an intermediary, who might in turn owe service to another intermediary and so on up the ladder of tenure. It would be fortunate if service did not evaporate altogether somewhere along that way. Many of these complications were an outcome of the vagaries of inheritance, the marriages of heiresses and the active market in land held by feudal service. New tenurial links were continually being established, often in a lengthening chain; fees were acquired by tenants of other lords, and holdings were divided and sometimes divided again. In the event, lords acquired some strange tenants of military holdings. Osney Abbey, for example, bought Upton-next-Stone from Henry Huse in 1219. Part of the bargain was that the abbey would acquit Henry of the service of one knight owed to the chief lord of the manor; but since abbot and monks were no fighting men they doubtless expected that their obligation would be acquitted by the payment of scutage.[33] It was, after all, some years earlier than 1219 that a satirical writ had been entered on the rolls of the king's court ordering that no plea be entertained against a certain man 'so long as his money is in the service of the king beyond the sea'.[34]

A situation in which money served instead of men had developed at an early date, for the payment of scutage in lieu of service goes back at least to the end of the eleventh century. The plain fact is that the principal purpose of the feudal arrangements the Normans made – the policing of a conquered England – was obsolete almost as soon as those arrangements were made. It may well be that 'no king of this period would have doubted his right to demand service beyond the channel',[35] where a great part of the fighting in which the Norman kings were engaged took place. How consistently they exercised that right is another matter, but there are many indications that Rufus and Henry I were great hirers of mercenaries and that they exploited every possible source of revenue (doubtless including scutage) to provide their wages.[36] Henry II adopted a similar policy for his expedition to Toulouse in 1159. He professed himself 'unwilling to trouble the rustic knights'. He took with him only his chief barons with a few followers together with innumerable mercenary knights. From the rest of the military tenants both of England and Normandy he took such money as seemed right to him.[37] From that time forward scutages, raised by John at levels which were a matter of grievance for which Magna Carta sought to provide a remedy, were a normal accompaniment of overseas expeditions.

Royal tenderness to rustic knights was accompanied by some unwillingness on their part to participate in distant expeditions. Abbot Samson of Bury St Edmunds in 1197 found that his knights denied liability for service outside England and their argument was supported in that same year by the Bishops of Salisbury and Lincoln.[38] To the knight's unwillingness to serve must be added many a baron's incapacity to make his men do so as the tenurial pattern became more complicated. William of Kentwell, a small Suffolk baron owing the service of ten knights, had to confess in 1230 that he had lost control of seven of his fees and did not even know who held them.[39] One result was that Richard I and John asked their barons for only a fraction of the services they owed and in the course of the thirteenth century quotas were scaled down until they could, at best, produce only a few hundred knights. In this way the military heart went out of feudalism and kings had to find armies in other ways. The details have no place here, but most of the lay nobility continued to be regarded as 'natural' soldiers. They served, however, not as leaders of feudal contingents but, increasingly from Edward I's reign onwards, as military entrepreneurs recruiting companies of horse and foot under contract to the king in return for carefully defined cash considerations. In these companies knights also played an essential part, but they too served under contract and for wages and not as an incident of tenure. The social pyramid remained, but gained in flexibility as it was emancipated from its tenurial base.[40]

Everywhere, in fact, the nexus between lord and vassal was assuming a monetary form. Where money flowed from man to lord, however, it did so occasionally and intermittently. The lord had a right to guardianship (or the privilege of selling that right) when a tenant left an heir under age; a right to arrange or sell the marriages of his tenants' heiresses; and a right to take scutage from his military tenants when the king summoned the feudal host. The value of these rights is easily overestimated: a survey of the lands of John de Freville, Baron of Little Shelford, in 1312 records almost plaintively that the knight's fees held of the barony 'could be assigned no value since they do no service save scutage when it runs'.[41] Demands for occasional cash payments, moreover, were as apt to be solvents as the cement of the social order.

The attenuation of the basic links between lords and vassals had many other symptoms. The decline of feudal service and the complications of tenure removed the *raison d'être* of the honour courts and destroyed their effectiveness in action, so that royal courts by the thirteenth century had largely taken over the field of jurisdiction in which they had once been active. At least as early, and perhaps earlier, the hold of lords over their vassals was weakened as the vassal's land came to be regarded as a patrimony rather than a 'fee' held for service that would be rendered 'fully and in everything'. In 1100 Henry I promised that heirs would succeed their fathers on payment of no more than a 'just and legitimate relief'; and a decade later Robert Earl of Ferrers saw himself *nutu divino succedens in hereditatem bone memorie videlicet Henrici patris mei* (succeeding by divine decree to the heritage of Henry my father of noble memory).[42] What God had ordained it was not for a king or any other lord to set aside. Increasingly the tenant became the *verus dominus* (true lord) of the fee, with much freedom to dispose of it and with the protection of the royal courts for a possession which was verging upon property.[43] Such a tenant had gone far to emancipating himself from the dependence of vassalage.

These changes in the relationship between members of the landowning class ultimately led to a redefinition of the criteria distinguishing the grades composing it. By the thirteenth century, in practice, what made a man a baron was less tenancy-in-chief than the fact that he was the lord of much land, and barons were politically influential because relatively they were wealthy men. Political power, in turn, might be used to reinforce their wealth, but however it was won they were deeply concerned to perpetuate their family's hold on it. Like other landowners, both large and small, they made provision for all sorts of family contingencies;[44] but 'the justice of the inheritance was unshakably rooted in the ideas of noble society', and the magnate's first concern was to preserve it for the family.[45] Some families, of course, were wrecked on political reefs and some inheritances (or portions of them) were taken to other families by heiresses; but lay society continued to be dominated by great families whose power was rooted in wide acres and whose numbers, never more than 200 or so,[46] seems to have changed little from the time King William distributed the land of England among his followers on the morrow of the Conquest. This fact, in the early fourteenth century, helped to generate the notion of peerage: the notion, that is, that under the king there was a body of men more or less equal in rank, but standing higher than any other group in the land. The distinctiveness of the group was buttressed by the fact that its members (together with the bishops and some abbots) received individual summonses to the king's parliaments. In these various ways the social and political, as well as the military, significance of the great territorial nobility was preserved, even when the tenurial base upon which it had originally rested had lost its ancient meaning.

In the meantime the character of the feudal knighthood had also changed. In origin a high proportion of the knights were fighting men, most of whom held land in return for military service. By 1273, on the other hand, Simon Daubeny held one of his manors for 'the service of half a knight when scutage runs'.[47] Personal service, in other words, had dropped out of the picture, with the result that tenure by knight service (in fact an obligation to scutage) could be pushed down the social scale and knight's fees allowed to disintegrate into smaller and smaller fractions. In the process the line between military and non-military tenure became increasingly blurred. A tenement at Trumpington in 1228 was deemed a 'military' holding because the charter granting it stated that the land owed 'foreign' service and because the tenant collected scutage from the dependent peasantry, using the proceeds towards the rent he owed his lord.[48] This is hardly meaningful in military terms and implies an increasing lack of correspondence between knighthood and tenure by knight service.

So a man came to be regarded as a knight only when he was *made* a knight. Knighthood remained the natural destiny of a man of birth and property, as William d'Oilli implied in 1157 when he granted away the wardship of William de Bray 'until the said William is of an age when he may be a knight, or ought to become one and is able to do so'.[49] Henry III and Edward I imposed, or sought to impose, knighthood on all men with incomes from land amounting at different times to £20, £30 or £40; and Edward also tried to conscript them into his armies in order to meet his need for cavalry. He was treating them, however, not so much as vassals of lords, as the earlier knights had been, but as subjects of the crown, reflecting once more the decline of baronial control over the class of lesser landlords. These selected knights of Edward I's reign, moreover, were also a more restricted body than the class of military tenants of the Norman epoch. They represent only one section of the intermediary class between the peasantry and the great lords of the land (see pp. 172–3).

At the same time, the fact that Edward I could conscript them, and that both knights and other 'lawful men' were called upon to play an expanding role in local 'self-government at the king's command' from the mid-twelfth century onwards, is in itself significant. They had, to a large extent, emancipated themselves from their old feudal dependence, moved from the honour court to the county court and, in local rather than feudal communities, now served the king as sheriffs, coroners, commissioners and jurors; and, from Edward I's reign onwards, knights and lawful men represented their local communities in the king's high court of parliament. The middling landowners were taking on the appearance of a separate 'estate'. Some of them, in time of war, still served as 'fighting knights', but to an increasing extent they also had civil responsibilities. A fourteenth-century preacher summed things up succinctly: 'Knights and other gentles with them should set their business about the good governance in the temporality in the time of peace.'[50]

One thing remains to be said. However important the shifts of property between the different groups of landowners had been, the basic stratification of landowning society was much the same in King Edward's England as it had been in King William's. It was a three-fold structure. At the top there was a relatively small group of great lay and ecclesiastical landowners with extensive and often widely scattered possessions. These men of baronial standing shaded off into a group of lesser but still substantial landowners, whose possessions also frequently extended into a number of counties; and that group in turn merged into a larger body of smaller landowners whose interests were often, but not invariably, more strictly localized. There were no sharp lines of division and no insuperable barriers which prevented a man from moving, either upwards or downwards, from one group to another. At the same time, while the old tenurial and vassalic bonds, which in early days had joined the members of these various grades into vertical groupings, had largely lost their force, the tendency of landowning society to split up into 'estates' was countered by other influences. The cement might be subtly different in the society which emerged, but its hierarchical structure had strong affinities with that created by Norman feudalism.

From one point of view, the connections which replaced the feudal communities of the earlier age were a by-product of a royal device. When, to some small extent under Edward I and on a major scale under Edward III, kings used members of the nobility as entrepreneurs to raise complete contingents for their armies under contract, they were restoring to that class an essential ingredient of earlier lordship, the role of military leadership. At the same time, these soldier-noblemen were great landowners; their broad acres gave them influence; and they continued to attract into their orbit lesser landowners seeking patronage. As great landowners, moreover, the noblemen of the thirteenth and fourteenth centuries continued to need service of precisely the sort that 'knights and lawful men' could provide – as stewards, bailiffs, counsellors equipped with a knowledge of land management and an administrative expertise which had already made this class useful to kings in the government of the shires. As landowners as well as military entrepreneurs the great nobility were seekers after clients to serve them, and they attracted household and estate servants by pay just as they attracted soldiers into their military retinues in time of war. To this extent the vertical links between lords and men were perpetuated, even though the newer lordship which had emerged by the early fourteenth century was more flexible in operation and more regularly based upon cash contracts than the older, land-based feudal lordship had been. On the other hand, the coherence of what is sometimes called 'bastard feudalism' owed a good deal to traditional assumptions about the relationships of lords and their men. Perhaps it can be said that the survival of feudal ways of thought and of a feudal distribution of the basic sources of wealth, together with the capacity of the medieval nobility to adapt its modes of operation to changing circumstances, did much to modify the impact on society and politics of the medieval rise of the gentry.

Estates in land

Whatever part the payment of wages played in sustaining the superstructure of medieval society, that society continued to be rooted in the soil. Barons, knights and other lawful men depended first and last for their sustenance and their influence on the produce and the profits they drew from agricultural estates. The main heads of those profits at an early date may be illustrated from the revenues of the lands in the king's custody outside Cheshire belonging to the Lacy constables of Chester in the year 1211–12. All in all the issues amounted to £1,271. Of this total £366 came from various forms of rent; £245 from the sale of agricultural produce; £336 from tallage; £79 from mills and £345 from court profits and the like.[51] The precise proportions are, for present purposes, of little moment; what the record shows is that an estate was in the first place an agglomeration of land which yielded both a profit from agricultural operations undertaken directly for its lord and an income from rents paid by peasant landholders. In addition, *qua* lord, its possessor had other rights which were eminently profitable. Unfree tenants owed tallage, either regularly or intermittently, and King John squeezed the Lacy tenants particularly hard on this account. Like all medieval justice, that dispensed by lords in their private courts could be made to yield great emolument; so could a lord's right to compel his tenants to make use of a manorial mill. Rents, agricultural profits and seignorial profits – these were the issues of agricultural estates, though different estates might combine them in very different ways.

This difference arises in part from the fact that estates themselves were very different, both in their size and in their internal structure. To cite examples will not necessarily produce a catalogue of types, but it may provide an indication of how various they were. One may begin with two little estates in Cambridgeshire in 1279 where the small landowner shades off into the peasant. At Eversden William Jake held 100 acres or so, though he cultivated only some 30 acres himself; at Westwick, on the other hand, Richard Belebuche kept about three-quarters of a similar holding in demesne.[52] Only a little superior to William and Richard, and almost as localized in his interests, was Roger Tristram. At his death in 1289 he held at Babraham and three miles away at Hinxton, and let out to tenants only a very small part of his land: rents contributed only 15*s* to the total value of about £6 attributed to his estate.[53] Quite small landowners, however, had much more dispersed estates than Roger Tristram. Henry de Colne, whose lands were worth only about £8, held at Caxton (Cambs) as well as at Colne (Hunts), but once again his land was mainly kept in demesne; Henry de Clerbek, with an estate worth less than £14, had lands in Dorset, Suffolk and Cambridgeshire; and Nicholas Cheyney's £26 estate was situated in Hertfordshire, Cambridgeshire, Somerset and Devon. These latter two were also much better provided with tenants than Roger Tristram and Henry de Colne, for rents constituted 40 and 70 per cent respectively of the value of their estates.[54]

Moving further up the scale, towards that shifting line which divides the knighthood from the baronage, we find Edmund Kemesek in 1288 holding five demesne manors in Essex, Suffolk and Cambridgeshire. In all he had about 850 acres in demesne, although nearly half of this total lay in Great Sampford (Essex). His demesnes, however, were valued at only one third of his assets; money rents from tenants were worth rather more; and Tilbury ferry contributed a seventh of his income.[55] Ralf Cameys's estate in Northamptonshire and Cambridgeshire, with outliers in Norfolk, Surrey and Huntingdonshire, was both larger (it was valued at £184) and differently constituted. He had well over 2,000 acres of arable in demesne and his home farms represented 55 per cent of his total assets. Free rents were relatively insignificant except at Torpel in Northamptonshire; on the other hand the services of villeins and cottars were a prominent element in the valuation of most of his manors.[56]

This upward progression through lay society logically ends in the ranks of the magnates and the conglomeration of territories built up by a great lord like the Earl of Cornwall at the end of the thirteenth century (see p. 203). This can be grouped into five great masses: extensive lands in Cornwall and Devon, with outliers in Somerset, Dorset and Wiltshire; a Thames valley estate stretching from Oxfordshire to Middlesex, comprising the honours of Wallingford and St Valery and the bailiwick of Berkhampstead; the honour of Eye in East Anglia; a Midland estate extending into Northamptonshire, Rutland, Huntingdonshire and Lincolnshire; and a northern estate centred on Knaresborough. In all there were some sixty demesne manors with a gross yield of around £4,700 and a net yield of £3,100 in 1296–97. Similar in dimensions were the contemporary estates of the Bigod Earls of Norfolk. They had about thirty-three demesne manors in Norfolk, Suffolk, Cambridgeshire, Essex, Hertfordshire, Berkshire, Sussex and Gloucestershire; a Welsh marcher lordship centred on Strigoil castle and including the borough of Monmouth and some dozen dependent hamlets; and Irish property the gross value of which was around £750 annually.[57] It was an endowment which put the Earl of Norfolk into the £3,000–£4,000 a year class. If the Cornwall and Norfolk estates were similar in size, however, there were marked differences between them. By the end of the thirteenth century the Earls of Cornwall had reduced the scale of their demesne enterprise to very small proportions, so that sales of produce (even when timber and garden crops are brought into the account) represented only about 10 per cent of their manorial receipts. The Earls of Norfolk, on the other hand, were still engaged in demesne cultivation on a considerable scale, and to this end exploiting villein services, at least on their manors in eastern England; and even in far away Wexford they were engaged in agricultural enterprise very similar to that conducted for them at Earl's Soham or Lopham or Kennett in East Anglia (see pp. 202–3).

These examples may suggest some of the determinants governing the structure of lay estates. Some of the very small estates, though not all, seem to contain a very high proportion of demesne, probably because they were conducted principally to supply the household of their lord and because the latter was so placed that he could easily superintend in person the management of his property. Where this was not so, the reason may be that the estate was on the way to dissolution (was this the case with William Jake's?), or, as with the lands of Henry Clerbek and Nicholas Cheyney, estates were so scattered geographically that management was extremely difficult. On the other hand, it is evident that even landowners of similar standing pursued different policies, the Earl of Norfolk showing a preference for conventional demesne cultivation and the Earl of Cornwall a preference for rents. Possibly one explanation of that particular difference is the stability of the Bigod inheritance over many generations while the Cornwall lands were a chance agglomeration that had suffered many vicissitudes. It is also evident that all estates were, to one degree or another, heterogeneous if they extended over any considerable space. This heterogeneity might be a product of the particular history of manors gradually assembled into the inheritance of a particular landlord. It might also reflect marked regional differences in social structure. The idiosyncrasies of the north, the Danelaw, East Anglia, Kent and the far south-west controlled in considerable measure the courses open to a man in exploiting his properties. To a lesser extent regional characteristics probably governed many of the other minor contrasts between the components of the same estate which superficially are not easily explicable.

Ecclesiastical estates had a similar variety of structure, with some special characteristics of their own. The lands of the greater prelates had much in common with those of the lay magnates. Episcopal estates were often very extensive, including many manors in which demesne agriculture was conducted on a large scale. The marketable produce of the Bishop of Winchester's fifty or so demesne manors was at times worth £4,000 yearly or more in the thirteenth century. Villein labour was available on most of these manors in large quantities, although wage labour was used increasingly as the thirteenth century progressed. At the same time, the availability of unfree services was also governed by regional differences,[58] as it was on the Archbishop of Canterbury's estate: villein services were much used on his Sussex manors outside the Weald, but not in Kent where traditional freedom made services light. None the less he had in all nearly 7,000 acres under grain in 1273–74.[59] The Bishops of Ely had likewise to accommodate themselves to circumstances. Most of their manors had large demesnes and numerous villeins; but most of the inhabitants of their colonizing fenland manors were free rent-payers, and at Bramford (Suffolk) they acquired by purchase a typical East Anglian 'soke' with a dependent free tenantry scattered over many villages.[60]

The estates of the old Benedictine abbeys were those consisting of units corresponding most closely to the 'classical' notion of the manor, precisely because they were old and so many of them lay in the old settled core of England, and also because they had to provide continuity of supplies for a relatively large community of monks and servants. To this end, various expedients were adopted. Domesday, on occasion, reveals an arrangement whereby some manors provided liveries of food while others were assigned to provide cash for the monks' clothing. Later, on some estates, there was a division between a 'home' group of manors, principally used for the supply of the house, and the more distant properties that were managed in the main in order to produce a cash revenue.[61] However their estates were organized, the needs of monasteries made for manors with large or largish demesnes, and the greater monasteries at least were the organizers of arable production on a very large scale. Even as late as 1322 the monks of Canterbury Cathedral Priory were cultivating more land than the archbishop a generation earlier: they had 8,373 acres actually under crops.[62] Large-scale cultivation entailed the mobilization of much labour and, while Kentish liberty made services light on the Kentish manors of Christ Church, on many monastic manors labour services were substantial and relatively heavy.

The newer monastic estates, on the other hand, were often organized very differently from those of the old Benedictine houses. The endowments of twelfth-century foundations were commonly far more heterogeneous than those of pre-conquest establishments. The units of property belonging to the Augustinian abbeys of Leicester and Owston, for example, were varied in character and most of them relatively small; the profits of demesne agriculture were of relatively limited importance; and income from rents and tithes was relatively large. At Leicester Abbey in 1297–98, for instance, rents, the profits of churches, and the sale of corn (almost all from tithe) amounted to £366 out of a total of £612 received by the treasurer of the abbey. This total, moreover, was swollen by £220 received for the sale of wool of which an unknown proportion had been bought up by the abbey from smaller producers. This was at a time when about two-thirds of the Archbishop of Canterbury's manorial revenues came from sales of agricultural produce.[63]

Another variant type of monastic property unit calls for mention: the compact granges that were especially characteristic of Cistercian estates. They were not, however, exclusive to the Cistercians. In Yorkshire, as the Cistercians of Rievaulx or Fountains had their granges, so had the Gilbertines of Malton Priory, the Augustinians of Guisborough Priory and the Benedictine monks of St Hilda's Abbey at Whitby.[64] The main features of granges were that the greater part of a church's land in any given place was consolidated for its sole use, and that it was cultivated by lay brothers or paid labourers rather than by villein services. A grange might be created *de novo* in an uninhabited

area or by depopulating a village to accommodate it. Byland and
Rievaulx Abbeys established granges by reclamation in Bilsdale, as
Guisborough Priory did in Eskdale; but Byland Abbey itself and the
grange associated with it involved the clearing out of the villagers,
although they were permitted to settle elsewhere *ubi dicti homines
inceperunt unam villulam* (where the said men founded a small
hamlet).[65] Most granges, however, were neither located in the
wilderness nor made at the cost of destroying villages: they were
established in the already settled lowlands, and were mainly arable
enterprises, built up by the purchase or gift of existing holdings and
enlarged by assarting. They were particularly numerous in Yorkshire
where twelfth-century circumstances were especially favourable in that
there were many wholly or partially 'waste' villages awaiting reclamation.[66] In these conditions the formation of granges could be
expeditious, but the process might also be prolonged. The monks of
Newminster acquired the nucleus of their grange at Chopwell
(Northumberland) in the mid-twelfth century, but they were still
working in the early decades of the fourteenth century to extinguish the
common rights enjoyed by the Earl of Angus and others.[67]

Manors

Of course, not all the properties of the new monasteries were granges.
Newminster and Guisborough Priories possessed land held by tenants,
detached grazing rights, and even tithe (whatever the original Cistercian
rule might say). After all, the creation of a grange required either an
absence of initial obstacles to consolidation or great persistence in
carrying that process through. In any case, with granges we have passed
from estates to their constituent elements, amongst which granges were
exceptional. When medieval men spoke of the common run of
agricultural properties the word which came most naturally to them was
the word 'manor'. There was a time when scholars spoke of a 'manorial
system' as a basic feature of medieval times, but in these days we are
more prone to stress the almost infinite variety of manorial forms and
the almost complete absence of any system. In particular, what used to
be regarded as the 'typical' manor, an agricultural community
coincident with the village and composed of a home farm with attached
villein tenements providing labour and free tenements from which rents
were drawn, has been pushed out of the centre of the picture. In the East
Midlands, a manorialized area enough, manors which coincided with
villages were characteristic only of Oxfordshire, a county in which small
villages and hamlets are numerous.

Even when the coincidence of village and manor as a characteristic of the medieval countryside is abandoned, we are still not done with exceptions.[68] Some of them are discernible within the single village of Thriplow in Cambridgeshire. The Bishop of Ely had a manor there which conformed in many ways to the 'classical' type. When it was surveyed in 1251 there was a home farm of 372 acres of arable as well as meadow and pasture, a wind and a water mill, and a demesne flock of 960 sheep. Some twenty-four *libere tenentes* paid mainly money rents, though some of them also owed a few occasional services; twenty-four villein half-virgaters paid small rents but worked three days every week on the demesne, to say nothing of performing extra works at ploughing, hay and harvest times; and four cottars worked two days a week with extra works in the the harvest field. The other manors in the village were very different. William Muschet's was mainly demesne, for he kept 130 acres in his own hand, let out about 50 acres to free tenants, and had only a solitary villein with 2½ acres who owed two days work a week. Agnes de Barenton, too, exacted the same amount of week-work from her three villeins and five cottars, but these tenants together with four freeholders had only 45 acres between them, the lady having kept 120 acres in demesne. Agnes de Scalers, on the other hand, had no unfree tenants at all; indeed, her only tenants were six little freeholders with 14 acres amongst them. Essentially her manor consisted of a home farm of 114 acres.[69]

The same sort of contrasts, and a few others, emerge when we look not at a village but at an estate. The possessions of the Engaine family were surveyed by the king's escheators on three occasions between 1248 and 1297. They had a fair amount of demesne land in a good number of their manors, but these manors were very variously provided with villein labour for their cultivation. Services were relatively light at Upminster(Essex) and Hunsdon (Herts), and most of them in any case had been commuted by the mid-thirteenth century. Commutation had also largely dissipated the far heavier services which had once been owed at Dillington (Hunts) and Pytchley (Northants), and there is no sign that labour dues had ever been owed at White Notley (Essex). By contrast there was extensive villeinage at Great Gidding (Hunts) and Blatherwick (Northants) and fairly heavy services were owed to the demesnes of these manors. Laxton and Bulwick in Northamptonshire, on the other hand, were manors without any demesne at all. Free tenants were equally variously distributed, for while they were numerous at Upminster, Hunsdon and White Notley they were an insignificant part of the tenantry of Blatherwick.[70] Ralf Cameys's estate in 1277 displays a similar diversity Most of his manors had fairly large demesnes, although that at Tansor (Northants) was very small; free tenants were altogether absent at Tansor and Great Stewkley (Hunts); at Great Stewkley the demesne accounted for 90 per cent of the value of the manor and at Hardingham (Norfolk) there were apparently no tenants at all.[71]

Even in the central core of medieval England what was once regarded as the typical manor (a community conjoining demesne, villeinage and free tenancies) was not ubiquitous, accounting only for about 75 per cent of the manors surveyed in the hundred rolls of 1279. If manors comprising demesne and villeinage but no free tenancies are added, the proportion rises to somewhere about 80 per cent. A fifth of the manors still remain, some containing demesne only or demesne with an insignificant amount of tenant land; some demesne and freeholdings only; and some free and villein tenures only or free tenures only or villein tenures only.

Beyond the Midland area diversity had special forms of its own. In East Anglia many manors were composed of a central estate (often with most of the 'typical' manorial features, including numerous villeins owing quite heavy services) to which were attached groups of dependent freeholders, frequently scattered over several villages.[72] Analogous structures are found elsewhere. Huntingdonshire was a highly manorialized county, but tenants in seven villages straddling the boundary with Bedfordshire owed rents and suit of court at Kimbolton, and Somersham was the centre of a 'soke' comprising the dependent hamlets of Colne, Bluntisham, Pidley, Fenton and Earith.[73] Again, throughout the Northern Danelaw, from Northamptonshire north to the Vale of York, although heavy labour services were generally absent, we again find manorial centres that were ringed by satellite 'berewicks', detached portions of the home farm cultivated by the lord, and clusters of free tenants (often widely scattered) paying rents and doing suit at the court of the central manor.[74]

Kent, too, was a region of decentralized manors and of peasants linked to manorial centres by rent and suit rather than service (although, especially on ecclesiastical estates, carrying services might assume some importance). In many ways, however, the Kentish manor was *sui generis*: its demesnes were made up of scattered blocks of arable with appurtenant and sometimes distant pasture in marsh or forest, while the tenements of the dependent peasantry lay 'remote from the *curia* and from each other'.[75] This regime is in some ways the furthest from the nucleated characteristics which 'Midland' manors were apt to share with Midland villages.

Finally northern England had its own particular variant upon this theme, although it has close analogies with social patterns to be found in Scotland and Wales. The basic group was not so much the manorial group but rather the inhabitants of a much larger territory sometimes described as a 'shire'. Heighingtonshire in Durham, as it was described in 1183, is an example bringing out some of the essential characteristics of these northern 'shires'. The original centre was obviously Heighington, with its *aula* and *curia*, a demesne which was leased out in 1183, some of the mills of the 'shire' which were worth in total £8 yearly, and doubtless a court at which the men of the 'shire' owed suit. Heighington, however, was the focus of a group of satellite settlements: Killerby, Middridge, Redworth and the three hamlets called Thickley. The villeins in each of these places owed seasonal boon services on the bishop's demesne together with quite heavy rents in kind and a variety of other miscellaneous services, including carrying services. Week-work was provided by the cotmen (though they might hold up to 15 acres) and both villeins and cotmen made the bishop's hay, and fenced the *curia* and the copse at Heighington.[76] In some places, too, the 'shire' had its pastures over which the stock of all the settlements intercommoned, like the 'shire moor' which provided pasturage for the villages of 'Tynemouthshire'.[77] By the time we first see them these groupings were often dissolving. Even in Heighingtonshire the development of another demesne in Middridge was probably a complication of the original scheme; and in most of the north by the thirteenth century the older regime was rapidly being broken up by the subinfeudation of satellite hamlets and the development of demesnes in the outlying villages.[78]

The diversity of manorial forms in the medieval countryside has been much discussed and many explanations of it have been offered. Some part may have been played by the different traditions of different regions, so that the forms of manors as well as of villages owed something to the Jute in Kent, the Celt in Northumbria, the Dane in eastern England and perhaps even the Frisian in East Anglia.[79] Topography, too, played a part. Districts where the peasantry had access to ample reserves of reclaimable land were apt to have a looser manorial structure than older-settled regions; and the pastoral uplands were unfavourable ground for the development of anything like the 'typical' manor, a fact which may well explain some of the manorial peculiarities of the north.[80] The force of lordship, too, had its influence: 'typical' manors are more likely to be found on Benedictine than on Augustinian estates, on large rather than small lay estates.

At the same time it is also possible to regard the 'deviant' types of manorial structure as variants on a single theme. More or less deformed as most of them were by the twelfth century, they yet preserve the outlines of an older lordship exercised over federal groups of settlements and exacting from their inhabitants tribute more than service.[81] Long before 1066 a more positive landlordship had been 'making manors' either in new settlements or in the units of these federal estates; that work continued in the aftermath of the conquest and in the centuries which followed. It enabled lords to extract more from the land and perhaps more from its inhabitants. It enabled them to seize more fully the opportunities for gain that economic expansion offered. Their work, however, was never completed, for clear vestiges of ancient systems were firmly embedded even in the thirteenth-century landscape. By that time, moreover, even where the 'classical' manorial structure had been most firmly implanted, there were in some places signs of 'the beginning of the disintegration of the manorial system'.[82] These symptoms of decay added yet further to the diversity of manorial forms.

Diversity makes it near impossible to devise a technical definition for the manor on the basis of certain essential traits. Indeed, about all that can be said was said by Maitland: 'A lord may have many manors lying side by side, and yet they are separate manors because he treats them as separate'.[83] They are, so to speak, units of convenience for the administration of his estate, however much they differ in structure and in form. Because they are management units, and despite the fact that Bracton warns us that manor and *mansio* must be clearly differentiated, manors may be expected to have some sort of centre: perhaps a house or 'hall', perhaps farm buildings, at the very least some building where rents could be collected or tithes garnered or a court held. Details have survived of how a Northamptonshire man, Henry de Bray, equipped with buildings the composite manor he slowly accumulated at Harlestone as the base for his rise into the gentry. In 1289 he built a hall and north chamber, in 1291 a south chamber, in 1297 a herb garden, in 1298 a pigsty and fowl house (there seems already to have been a byre), in 1301 a new barn, in 1302 a bakehouse, in 1303 a new kitchen and dovecote, in 1304 a granary and sheepfold, and in 1307 a cartshed.[84]

Henry de Bray, of course, was a resident small landlord cultivating a substantial part of his property; but early in the thirteenth century similar facilities were provided for the lessee of the St Paul's manor at Acton (Middlesex). The buildings there comprised a tiled hall containing a dispensary, buttery, chamber and solar; another tiled house containing a kitchen, bakery and brewery; and a barn, a stable and a cow-byre.[85] Even Merton College's manor at Cuxham, though the Warden and Fellows were only occasional visitors, had a walled *curia* containing hall and chamber, a kitchen, bakehouse, hayshed, straw-shed, granaries, pigsty, byre, stable, cartshed and dovecotes, as well as an extensive garden and orchard. This fairly ample provision may have owed its origin to the fact that Cuxham had been a residence for the Chenduits before the manor passed to Merton; but the college kept it in being as the administrative centre for its property in the village.[86]

Estate management

The equipment of the *curia* at Cuxham, Acton and Harlestone remind us that lordship entailed problems of management. About the way in which small landlords managed their property we know very little. Obviously the man with only a manor or two had nothing like the elaborate officialdom that is found on large estates. As Henry de Bray's estate book testifies, he played a much more active part in the detailed running of his property than great lords did. The same impression derives from Walter of Henley's treatise on husbandry. Walter wrote from the standpoint of a manorial lord, but as 'one who owns a single estate of moderate size' and in terms of 'the squire farming his own land'. His advice is aimed at the lord of the manor himself, who is 'directed to oversee minutely the day-to-day working of his estate'.[87] For the most part, however, only the elaborate administrative apparatus of larger estates has left any great stock of evidence regarding land management. What can be said about the ways in which estates were managed, therefore, is the story of very large estates – the story, in other words, of medieval lordship in its most highly organized form.

The system of administration had two tiers: one concerned with the estate as a whole or its major subdivisions, and the other with affairs at the manorial level. Both in their various ways changed with the passing of time. Originally the administration of the estate was articulated by the household of its lord. In principle, the household staff provided their master with a set of domestic services, as the list of 'ministers' attesting a charter of Archbishop Theobald of Canterbury in the early 1150s makes clear: they were Robert the butler, Richard the dispenser, Gilbert the chamberlain, Odo the steward, William the master cook, Lawrence the usher, William the porter and Baylehache the marshal.[88] Nor is there doubt that these officers performed domestic duties. The narrative of the foundation of Byland Abbey mentions incidentally how the steward of Roger de Mowbray had to borrow food for the great multitude of guests entertained by his lord; and even at the beginning of the thirteenth century, when the Abbot of Westminster visited his manor at Deene (Northants), he was preceded by seven of his household and the specific responsibility of each of them in the various 'departments' of his house there were laid down in careful detail.[89]

At the same time, like the royal *domestici*, the household officers of a great lord formed a collective board of management for his estates which, even as early as the mid-twelfth century, might be described as his council;[90] and individually they could be set to any task the management of his estates demanded. Of these officers the steward often emerged as a kind of chief executive official of the estate, but any of them could be used for whatever purpose the exigencies of the moment required. It was also natural for lords to reward their principal domestics in the current coin of the feudal age, by enfeoffing them in a steward's fee, a chamberlain's fee and so forth. This territorialisation tended to make the offices themselves hereditary; and the heredity of offices, offering no certainty that its holder would be apt to serve, ultimately conspired to make them more or less ceremonial. By the end of the twelfth century, in fact, 'feudal' ministers were ceasing to provide the essential personnel of estate management.

The tendency towards changes in the administrative pattern was furthered by other influences. The transition from 'farming' manors to direct exploitation (see pp. 210–13), the increased technical expertise required in the management of estates mirrored in the agricultural treatises of the thirteenth century, and the possession by most great lords of judicial and administrative franchises in the conduct of which they were closely scrutinized by the government apparatus of the Angevin kings, all called for officials different from the amateur feudal *domestici* of Anglo-Norman honours. The signs of the times can be read before the twelfth century was over. As Samson returned to Bury St Edmunds after his election as abbot,

a multitude of new kinsmen went to meet him, desiring to be taken into his service. But to all of them he made answer that he was content with the prior's servants . . . but one knight he kept with him, an eloquent man and skilled in the law, not so much for his kinship as for his usefulness, for he was accustomed to secular business.[91]

About the same time, St Hugh of Lincoln was 'convinced that without the assistance of highly trained men he could not really be of much use to the clergy and people under his authority'. His estate was equipped with an exchequer, and he took care to staff it with 'men renowned for their honesty and prudence'.[92]

Within a few years, moreover, the great series of Winchester pipe rolls began, consolidated financial records detailing the income and expenditure of the many manors of that see. In the course of the thirteenth century, at least on the larger estates, financial management was everywhere placed on the basis of written record; the rare estate surveys of the twelfth century became common documents; charters and title deeds were systematically collected into registers; and at the latest by the mid-thirteenth century rolls of proceedings in manorial and franchisal courts began to be kept. The original purpose of the court roll may have been financial, to give information about the pecuniary penalties the bailiff or reeve ought to collect; but very soon the rolls developed into 'a chronicle of all that happens in the court' and even into a register of the changes in land occupancy amongst manorial tenants, copies of the entries providing the latter with their title deeds. In this sense copyhold tenure was an ultimate product of the placing of estate management on the basis of writing.[93]

New methods of estate management called for new men even if they often used old titles for their offices – men 'skilled in the law', 'highly trained men', men renowned for prudence if not always for honesty. The greater estates developed a veritable administrative apparatus. On many of them, as on the vast properties of Isabella de Fortibus which in the later thirteenth century stretched from Cumberland to the Isle of Wight, the key figure continued to bear the title of steward. He enjoyed the support of a receiver-general with mainly financial duties and a chamberlain in charge of the household secretariat (in the household of the Earls of Norfolk at this time this last official was given the title of chancellor). Each of these departmental heads was backed in turn by a clerical staff and there were local officers responsible for geographical groupings of manors (sub-seneschals, local receivers, bailiffs of fees and so forth). Sometimes the chief officials acted as a collective audit committee for the accounts of the various household and local officials; sometimes, as on the Ely estates, the auditors were distinct and important officials. Stewards, chamberlains, auditors and the rest, moreover, had this in common, that they spent much of their time out of the household travelling from manor to manor. Their achievement was that attributed to the stewards of Crowland Abbey: they welded 'the heterogeneous collection of private territories into a uniform system of organization and law, much as the Plantagenet itinerant justice welded the kingdom as a whole'.[94]

The Crowland Abbey stewards at this time were monk-stewards; and many monks played their part in estate administration as custodians of manors or much more commonly as obedientiaries in charge of one of the internal offices of their house. On lay estates, too, including the estate of the Earls of Norfolk, chaplains served their lord in a secretarial or financial capacity as well as by attending to his spiritual needs. Even on ecclesiastical estates, however, many officers were laymen and many of them came from knightly or gentle families; but they were men differently equipped to their predecessors in the Norman age. Abbot Samson's knightly kinsman was skilled in the law and the Northamptonshire new man, Henry de Bray, had probably received some legal education and certainly served St Andrew's Priory in Northampton as steward. This may make it less surprising that he wrote his book with his own hand, ordaining it 'as evidence for his heirs, namely transcripts of charters and memoranda arising from the time of the said Henry'.[95] He was not only literate; he had learned the value of the written word for validating title to land.

Henry was in many ways representative of a whole class of men, drawn from or rising into the gentry, that provided great lords with many of their estate and household officials. Their service was often well rewarded. John la Warre acquired the manor of Whitchurch by serving Isabella de Fortibus from 1268 to 1274, and he went on to be sheriff of Herefordshire. Robert Hereward, too, after starting as a mere bailiff of the Bishop of Ely, ended his life with manors at Ovington (Essex), Chesterfield (Herts) and Guilden Morden (Cambs), and he served the King in various capacities including the sheriffdoms of Cambridgeshire, Huntingdonshire, Norfolk and Suffolk.[96] Men like these, in fact, were a managerial class serving indifferently and in turn both private lords and the king. It is also characteristic that the Robert of Madingley whom we have already met (see p. 172), after leaving the Bishop of Ely's service for the King's, yet continued to be one of the Bishop's counsellors.

The elements of the private councils of the thirteenth and fourteenth centuries have been distinguished by Miss Levett: a group of the lord's larger tenants, neighbouring landowners and fellow magnates; the lord's permanent officials; some expert men, lawyers particularly, occasionally a judge or well-known counsel in the king' courts.[97] Counsellors were normally paid a fee for their service, his council costing the Earl of Gloucester £31 a year as early as 1273. What is most interesting, however, is the professional and expert character of the governing bodies of great estates. Counsellors appear in the role of policy-makers, advisers on difficult external relations (like important pleas in the king's courts) and solvers of problems that defeated manorial courts or the officials in charge of manors. Important tenants and neighbouring landowners had experience relevant to tackling this sort of problem; *jurisperiti* and officials could bring to bear trained minds and technical knowledge. Seignorial councils summarize and exemplify the bureaucratic tendencies at work in estate management in the generations after 1200.

When stewards, chamberlains and counsellors had fulfilled their offices, however, much detailed executive work remained to be done, most of it at the manorial level. Manors, therefore, also needed their officialdom. In many places, in the thirteenth century, a salaried bailiff exercised a general oversight, frequently over more than one manor. Within the manor the principal responsibility commonly rested with a reeve, sometimes assisted by a beadle for the collection of rents and by a hayward for managing the harvest work. These officials were normally unfree tenants obliged to serve because they held servile tenements; sometimes they were 'elected' annually by their fellow villeins. Their payment took the form of remission in whole or in part of their rents and services, a few perquisites and perhaps food provided by the lord in harvest time.[98] Among these servile officers the reeve was pre-eminent. One thirteenth-century treatise informs us that he should be chosen as the best husbandman in the township, and doubtless this justified lords in penalizing the general body of their tenants when they elected a man who turned out be be 'insufficient'. As for the reeve's duties, he had to see that farm servants got up betimes for their work, that the land was well ploughed and cropped, and that the lord's sheep were properly folded to ensure that the demesne was adequately manured. He had to see that the sheep were well kept, that grain was efficiently threshed and properly stored, that flocks and herds were culled for sale, that farm servants got no more than their proper pay and allowances. He had to look to the good order of farm buildings and implements and, subject to instructions, sell farm produce. At the end of the year he had to account for the proceeds of the manor, not excluding money paid in lieu of labour services. The final advice was that 'no reeve ought to remain reeve longer than one year unless he has proved himself very capable, just in his actions, and well able to further his lord's interests'.[99]

These were comprehensive and onerous tasks for a man who was a part-time, temporary and amateur farm manager, however closely he was supervised by stewards and auditors and local bailiffs. At the same time, it was evidently not out of the question that a profitable and faithful reeve would serve for more than a year; and the frequency of men surnamed 'the reeve' suggests that long service was by no means unusual even from an early date. By the late thirteenth and early fourteenth centuries, certainly, semi-professional reeves were far from uncommon. On the Crowland estates, three reeves at Dry Drayton served for twenty-nine, seventeen and twenty-one years respectively; William Kille was reeve of Oakington for sixteen years; and Nicholas was reeve of Elmington for forty-seven years from 1267 to 1314. Nor was this something peculiar to Crowland administration, for there were only two reeves on Merton College's manor of Cuxham between 1288 and 1349.[100] The professionalism marking the central administration of estates was also creeping into their constituent manors, and the reeveship was becoming a profession rather than an incident of tenure. Men like Nicholas of Elmington were the real-life prototypes of Chaucer's reeve – 'There was noon auditour coude on him winne' – precisely because they were men whose expertise was rooted in long experience.

The reeve of course did not operate without checks. He was under the eyes of stewards and auditors and bailiffs, and his most searching examination came sometime after Michaelmas, the end of each farming and financial year, when he would be called upon to account for the yield of his manor. It was in this way that the Ministers' Accounts, one of the most valuable sources for the agrarian historian, were produced. On a well run estate of substantial proportions a scribe would first draw up an account from details supplied by the reeve and other manorial officials. The front of the parchment roll was usually devoted to cash transactions, and the first part dealt with receipts from rents, sales of pannage and pasture, the commutation of labour services, the sale of agricultural produce, the profits derived from the manorial court, and so on. A sum total of receipts would then be calculated. The next part of the account was devoted to expenses and allowances, including such items as the customary allowance of rent to the reeve, allowances for vacant holdings, the costs of hiring labour, of repairing buildings or purchasing farming equipment, of buying seed corn and livestock, and the like. The sum of the allowances and expenses would then be deducted from that of receipts and finally a further deduction would be made for the money which the reeve had remitted to higher officials during the course of the year. On manors where the demesne was still being cultivated by the lord the dorse of the roll was devoted to grain and stock statistics. Therein were recorded the quantities of grain sown and harvested, consumed, bought and sold; the numbers and types of livestock bought and sold, born and died; the quantities of dairy produce and wool sold and consumed. The account was then submitted to the auditors who subjected each item to scrutiny. They might argue, for example, that the price the reeve obtained for the wheat he sold was too low, while the sum that he paid for the sheep he purchased was too high; the number of labourers he hired at harvest might be thought excessive, and the wages paid to them too high. In this way the auditors picked their way through the account, passing this item, refusing that, and surcharging the reeve for negligence on a third. As we can imagine the reeve may well have contested a number of their decisions, and it would only have been after much wrangling that the sum he still owed was finalized.

While the scrutiny of the auditors was sometimes searching, the reeve was even more continuously under the eye of jealous neighbours who were in a position to tell what they saw in the manor courts. A fourteenth-century treatise gives instruction how to present the reeve for

always haunting fairs and taverns and that he is negligent in all his duties. Therefore be he removed . . . and . . . put in the stocks upon a pining stool in the custody of his neighbours. . . . Then shall the steward command that the late reeve do come to the bar and that the beadle do proclaim that if anyone will complain against him . . . he should do so at once.[101]

This was merely one of the ways in which manor courts were used as part of the apparatus of estate management. They were used also to enforce the payment of customary dues and the performance of labour services; to control the market in peasant land and the succession to customary tenements, thus preserving the territorial basis of dues and services; to restrict the mobility of labour so that the lord would have workers at need; and to pronounce on details in the reeve's account, thus participating in the work of the auditors. In brief, manor courts were indispensable to the running of agricultural estates precisely because they could impose penalties on tenants and officials alike when they failed in their obligations or contravened the lord's interests.[102]

By the thirteenth century, at least on larger estates, the manorial tenant was faced in the manor court and in his daily round not so much by his lord as by a new managerial class ranging from long-serving reeves to itinerant stewards and auditors. The appearance of this class presented problems as to how accountability was to be ensured which preoccupied thirteenth-century legislators; but it also made lordship more effective. The lord's tenant faced a professional steward at the bar of the manorial court; in court the lord's bailiff might act as prosecutor and outside it he was the guardian of the lord's interests. Within the manor, the reeve was often hardly less of a professional than the steward or the bailiff, and was charged to see in detail that the tenant's obligations were fulfilled. This apparatus of officialdom, full-time and part-time, gave a new dimension to lordship. At the same time, human nature being what it is, and the supervision of local officials being inevitably intermittent, there were many times when the latter abused their powers. A precedent book for the holders of manorial courts provides for the occasions when tenants alleged that the bailiff persecuted them against all right and reason. These, of course, were 'bad and villain words', but the tenants might be justified in using them all the same, even if they made their case no better when one of them 'took a bow of yew in his hands . . . and pursued the bailiff to beat him'.[103]

Unscrupulous reeves aroused resentment as well as high-handed bailiffs. Michael the reeve of Elton in 1278 was said to have had his hay led, his harvest reaped and his land ploughed by the works of his lord's customary tenants; and it was further alleged that he released villeins from their works provided they let some of their land to him for a low rent.[104] Reeves were also charged with accusing men wrongfully of having refused to do labour services, with discriminating for money between rich and poor, and with taking bribes from those with little to pay them; and the complaint Alice the widow made about the reeve of Littleport is pathetic in its implications. He had impounded her cow because it had strayed in the lord's corn and refused to release it until she paid him 6s8d, 'for which she sold two quarters of corn'. She might well be hungry in the spring for her cow's straying.[105]

Bureaucratic tendencies and bureaucratic abuses, of course, are the particular feature of the great estate. They must have been less marked on smaller properties, but even on larger ones the lord does not quite disappear behind a curtain of officialdom. The registers of the council of Edward the Black Prince provide numerous examples of poor tenants presenting petitions on relatively minor matters and of personal intervention by the prince himself. After dealing with a petition from Reynold Trenansaustel of Tewington, Cornwall, concerning a dispute over 10s, it was recorded that

the prince marvels greatly that Reynold and other such poor folk are importuning him and his council so much, bringing their suits to him from such distant parts and upon such petty matters, although he has charged the steward to do right to all his subjects and tenants in all matters which can be tried and determined without the advice of him and his council.[106]

At Wakefield in the late thirteenth century men accused of poaching in the Earl of Warenne's forest were remanded until their lord came to those parts; so were whole townships which had grazed his meadow, a parker who had been inefficient in his office, men who maliciously accused the earl's foresters or refused to grind corn at his mills, a miller who stopped the water course to the new mill at Sandal, and a reeve who allowed a merlin's nest which was in his care to be stolen.[107] If the Earl of Warenne's interests in his property sometimes verged upon the esoteric, the same can hardly be said of an anonymous lord to whom an estate official wrote in 1309 reporting that he had fulfilled his lord's commands as well as he could, having sold his corn at prices he lists in detail. He had bought some livestock and sent some of the best to travel to London, doubtless for the lord's table; he had also sent forty pigs and, despite competition from the King's purveyors, 'the larder will be filled in time with God's help'. One reeve was greatly in arrears and another owed much money, and both had little of their own to meet their deficits. He had audited the accounts of another manor, but he still needed his lord's instructions on matters which touched his profit.[108] This is prosaic stuff, but it shows that for all the progress of bureaucracy lordship still entailed personal responsibility and a need for personal decision.

None the less, bureaucratic tendencies made a great progress in thirteenth-century England and created problems of their own for the owners of great estates. Urgent decisions might be shelved because the men on the spot preferred to take no risks, and a top-heavy apparatus of control was needed to oversee the officials in the manors. There was a direct relation between the fact that no auditor could get the better of Chaucer's reeve and that other fact that 'Ful riche he was astored prively'. Lords as well as tenants suffered from the machinations of reeves and bailiffs. We have seen how the reeve of Elton used on his own land labour services due to the Abbot of Ramsey; and almost every draft manorial account roll reveals emendations which testify to reeves understating the prices at which they sold produce and overstating the prices at which they had bought. More than that, Robert Carpenter in the course of the thirteenth century actually compiled a treatise giving instructions on how to 'cook' accounts, if only to show how such falsifications could be detected. He was a man with experience as a bailiff and, likely enough, he had been 'an astute and dishonest fellow who did not scruple to cheat his master'.[109] Thus, if the emergence of a managerial class helps to explain some of the successes of high-farming landlords during the thirteenth century, the difficulties of controlling that class may also have tempted some landlords to show a 'preference for rents'. For the great landlord demesne farming could, when markets were buoyant, produce great emolument; but the problems of managing widely scattered demesnes were very great, and in some ways became all the greater as the administration of great estates became more professional and more complex. These problems may have been one of the influences, though doubtless only a minor one, contributing to the contraction of demesne agriculture which set in well before the Black Death gave a new bargaining power to tenants.

Chapter 8

Landlords and the land

The overwhelming majority of medieval Englishmen were peasant villagers, but everywhere they were grouped into manors and even those of them whose obligations were nominal were still the tenants of the lords of those manors. Lords of manors, moreover, possessed powers the exercise of which basically affected the economic situation of the peasant majority; and, at least in the twelfth and thirteenth centuries, most of them kept a direct lien on some of the land subject to their lordship. Landlords and the officials who served them, therefore, had a profound influence both directly and indirectly on the economic development of the medieval countryside. It is time to look at the objectives they set themselves.

Objectives of estate management

The first objective was a very simple one: manors ought to contribute to the basic needs of their lord. The contribution might be straight-forward: when Monkton was described as *manerium monachorum et de cibo eorum*, the phrase may be understood literally as implying that manorial produce furnished the tables in the monastic refectory. On the other hand, when Sandwich was said to be *de vestitu monachorum* the implication is that it furnished the money used for purchasing the habits of the monks.[1] The ideas implicit in these Anglo-Norman formulae are echoed, in a more sophisticated form perhaps, in the thirteenth-century 'rules' that Robert Grosseteste compiled for the dowager Countess of Lincoln. The fourth of his rules 'teaches how lord or lady . . . can live throughout the year off their demesne lands'; and the twenty-sixth (in fact the tenth) spelled out the routine a lord or lady should follow.

Every year at Michaelmas when you will know the estimate of all your corn then plan your sojourn for the whole of the coming year and for how many weeks in each place; . . . and in no way burden the places where you stay . . . with too long a residence, but arrange your sojourn in such a way that the place at your departure does not remain in debt; (but) that something is left on the manor so that it can continue to

increase yields, especially of cows and sheep, until in the end your stock
will pay for your wine, your robes, your wax, and all your wardrobe.[2]

The purpose of this good advice is clear. The countess's manors, like
the monastic manors surveyed by the Domesday commissioners, served
two purposes. They provided provender for the lady with her attendants
and their horses; but they also provided a cash revenue for buying wine
and robes and wax – those things, in other words, that the English land
did not readily provide. This was true whether a landowner was large or
small. Lionel de Bradenham was 'a very minor light amongst the
English landlords of his day'; his only manor was Langenhoe (Essex)
and, in the generation before the Black Death, he had only around 165
acres under crops each year. About two fifths of the wheat grown,
moreover, was used for seed and wages in kind paid to agricultural
workers; and nearly a further quarter of the wheat harvest, as well as
variable quantities of other grains, were consumed by Lionel's
household. Even so, almost a third of the wheat crop was marketed and
cash also came from sales of wool and livestock and, of course, from
rents and dues. Lionel obviously did not live by wheaten bread alone.[3]
At the same time, because his residence was in the village, provisioning
it entailed no complicated arrangements. It was another matter for
greater lords with more scattered properties. They had to face the
problem of ensuring that provender was concentrated where they
needed it and that, at the appropriate time, they found themselves where
provender was concentrated.

This was one, though one only, of the reasons for the wanderings of
medieval landowners. The perambulations which Grosseteste assumes
that the Countess of Lincoln will make each year were prandial
perambulations. It was also the reason why the saintly Wulfstan,
Bishop of Worcester, had a humble dwelling in each of his manors, and
why more worldly prelates like Lanfranc of Canterbury and Roger of
Salisbury built on their properties more splendid houses to accommodate themselves and their successors.[4] The need to travel to eat also
explains the terms on which William of Warenne, lord of an honour
which stretched from Lewes to Conisbrough, granted the manor of
West Walton in Norfolk to Lewes priory. He reserved 'two *hospicia*
each year for myself and my heirs, one when going into Yorkshire and
one when returning'.[5] He assumed, in other words, that he would make
an annual tour of his widely scattered manors, with West Walton as one
of the stopping places of his itinerary; when he gave the manor away he
retained this necessary facility for his yearly pilgrimage.

A monastic community, of course, could not travel to its sources of
supply. Supply had to come to the monastery and, both early and late,
customary tenants had to cart the produce of demesne manors to the

house which owned them. Norfolk and Suffolk sokemen holding of Ely Abbey in the 1070s carried 'the food of the monks to the monastery';[6] around 1300 the bailiffs and reeves of Staines and Islip sent grain to Westminster Abbey, and poultry and livestock on the hoof sometimes came from even further away, from the abbot's manors in the west country;[7] and on the Canterbury Priory estates at the beginning of the fourteenth century, when most other services had disappeared, the carrying services of the customary tenants were retained to ensure the provisioning of the house.[8]

The centralization of the flow of produce on monastic estates was exceptional, deriving from the very special character of monastic communities. At the same time, other landlords had favourite or principal residences, and a good deal of demesne produce needed to be concentrated there to sustain their households. The Bishop of Winchester in 1210–11 made many calls on his manors: they supplied his larder with large quantities of grain, with fowls, pigs, cider, cheese, eggs and eels. At one time and another he consumed these commodities at Marwell, High Clere, Bishop's Waltham, Downton and Farnham; but evidently the great bulk of them (even some of the bacon cured at the centralized plant at Bishop's Waltham) went to his palace at Wolvesey.[9] Eighty years later Bishop Swinfield of Hereford likewise made much use of manorial produce. Hay, flour, eels and salmon for his household came from his estates; venison was taken in his parks and chases; beer was brewed and charcoal made at Prestbury against Christmas; and Harpin the falconer caught patridges for the bishop. The manor of Bosbury was evidently a favourite autumn residence and the Bishop's stay there called for the despatch of cattle, sheep and pigs from Sugwas, Tupsley, Ledbury, Colwall, Prestbury, Ross and even from the distant Berkshire manor of Earley.[10] Nor was this manner of living a habit only of prelates. The Earl Marshal possessed in the reign of Edward I a manor at Kennett in Cambridgeshire. He did not often visit it, though both he and the Countess came with their retinue in 1299 and ate up much of its produce. On the other hand, he drew upon it for supplies for his own and the Countess's larders at Earl's Soham and Framlingham; once wheat was sent from Kennett to the Earl in Scotland; and in 1296 victuals were sent to London for the Earl against the parliament. The supplies drawn from Kennett included only a little grain, the occasional calf and a few fowls and pigeons; rabbits from the warren were more numerous, on one occasion being taken as far as London; most frequently of all, however, pigs and sheep were the contributions this manor made to its lord's domestic needs.[11]

The structure of seignorial revenues

Even at the end of Edward I's reign, then, one of the great earls of England, as well as the Bishop of Hereford and the Abbot of Westminster, still drew a good deal of subsistence from their manors. On the other hand, the growth of markets made it easier for peripatetic landlords to buy what they needed on the spot and so avoid the cumbersome administrative problem of directing the flow of manorial produce to the right place at the right time. To the extent that they reduced the consumption demands they made upon their manors the surplus for sale there was enlarged; and in any case, as Grosseteste pointed out, a lord or a lady had need of cash for wine, robes, wax and many other things. Much of the revenues of landowners, therefore, was in the form of cash rather than liveries in kind. The sources of this cash revenue were diverse: during the vacancy of the bishopric of Ely in 1298–99 about £1,400 out of a total of £3,500 came from demesne agriculture, £1,700 from rents paid by the bishop's tenants, and £400 from tallages, fines and amercements imposed by manorial courts, entry fines and so forth. Since this last group of payments was likewise a charge on peasant enterprise they can be lumped together with rents as quasi-rents, so that in sum the cash revenues of the bishop at this time were composed of 40 per cent demesne profits and 60 per cent tenant renders. The fact that the bishopric was vacant makes this a very rough and ready computation of the Bishop of Ely's normal income; but it is not altogether out of line with the composition of the Bishop of Winchester's income from his estate in a bad year like 1288 when, towards a total of £3,600, his tenants contributed 53 per cent and his demesnes 47 per cent. On the other hand, the proportions were very different on the Winchester estates in years of high prices. Tenants contributed 28 per cent and demesne profits 72 per cent of the £6,100 the bishop received in 1258; and in 1317 the shares of a total revenue of £6,400 were 35 per cent and 65 per cent respectively.[13]

It has to be added that, on these episcopal estates, there were also signs of changes in the composition of seignorial revenues through time. On the Ely estates demesne profits fell in relation to income from other sources in the second half of the thirteenth century; and on the Winchester estates there was a downward trend in grain sales after about 1270, with a corresponding increase in revenue from charges on the peasantry. Rents rose in total amount – on the Winchester estates due at first to assarting which created new tenements, then to a combination of assarting and leasing portions of the demesne, and finally to an increase in demesne leaseholds alone. On the Ely estates an increase in the volume of competitive rents for leaseholds, tenancies at will and the like was also particularly noticeable. A further contribution came from the increasing conversion of labour services into money renders, income from this source rising more than sevenfold on the Winchester estates between 1253 and 1348 and by 60 per cent on the Ely estates between 1256 and 1298. Finally, on the Winchester estates, at the end of the thirteenth and the beginning of the fourteenth centuries, there was a particularly notable expansion of revenue from entry fines as mortality speeded up the turnover of tenements and overpopulation sharpened the scramble for land. In brief, even on estates that were representative of conventional, high-farming enterprise, the rentier element in revenues was expanding at the latest from the mid-thirteenth century.

The pattern of management evident on these episcopal estates did not prevail everywhere. Some monastic estates possibly depended more heavily than bishops did on supplies from their 'home' manors; some small landholders, with a very limited tenantry, can have enjoyed very little income from rents or quasi-rents. At the same time everything goes to show that there were some large landowners, and in all probability a good number of not so large landowners, receiving revenues structured in a way that is comparable to the revenues of the Bishops of Ely and Winchester. Lionel of Bradenham, by substituting leaseholds for customary tenures, increased his seignorial income from rents and courts from around £8.10s yearly to nearly £15 in the generation before the Black Death, about 30 per cent of the cash income he derived from his sole manor of Langenhoe.[14] A little earlier, in 1297, John Engaine, if the values attributed to his estate in Northamptonshire, Huntingdonshire, Hertfordshire, Essex and Suffolk can be taken to furnish a rough guide, drew 41 per cent of his cash income from his demesnes, 56 per cent from rents and 3 per cent from the profits of lordship.[15] Finally, at the very opposite end of the social scale to Lionel of Bradenham, manorial accounts permit an analysis of the revenues of seventeen of the Earl Marshal's manors in the year 1295–96.[16] Thirteen of the manors lay in Norfolk and Suffolk, being in some sense his 'home' manors, and they may therefore emphasize unduly the element of direct management and entrepreneurship on this estate. The manors were, none the less, very varied in their character. Large grain sales are found at Kennett and Weston as well as on some of the 'home' manors; a large income from rents was received in some of these 'home' properties (especially at Caister, Framlingham and Little Framlingham); and court profits and tallage furnished a particularly large proportion of receipts from Staverton, Hanworth, Lopham and Walsham. For what the figures are worth, on these manors, the Earl drew 51 per cent of his receipts from his demesnes, 33 per cent from rents and 16 per cent from the issues of lordship. This is the same world in which the contemporary bishops moved.

At the same time there is no doubt whatsoever that there were landowners, both large and small, who depended a good deal less than the bishops or the Earl Marshal did on the profits of their demesnes. The Earl of Cornwall in 1296–97 had a gross income from his widely scattered manors of just under £4,700. The sale of demesne produce contributed only 10 per cent of this total, the balance coming from rents of various sorts (67 per cent) and from court and other seignorial revenues (23 per cent). The Earl had many special assets: the Cornish stannaries, forges at Knaresborough, the custody of the alien priory of Eye, and a variety of important franchises (including the Chiltern Hundreds, the county of Rutland and the county and hundred courts of Cornwall). Even so demesne agriculture was notably insignficant on this estate. Sales of produce were of any importance only in three bailiwicks. They provided 29 per cent of receipts in Berkhamstead bailiwick, 24 per cent in the bailiwick of Howden and 28 per cent in the bailiwick of Mere. Their contribution to revenue in Wallingford and Knaresborough bailiwicks, on the other hand, was under 10 per cent, and only about 3 per cent in the honour of St Valery and Oakham bailiwick. In the honour of Eye and in Devon and Cornwall, counties producing nearly one-third of the issues of the estate, these receipts were negligible or non-existent.[17] The Earl by 1296 was near enough to being a rentier.

From these particular estates we must return to the needs of landlords. They and their households had a need for food and drink. Demesne manors might provide much of what they needed as Weston in Hertfordshire did for the Earl Marshal in 1292–93, when large quantities both of grain and animals were despatched to his household: 111½ quarters of wheat, 64½ quarters of malt, 2¼ ox carcases, a steer, 114 muttons, 36 pigs to say nothing of calves, geese, cheese, butter, milk and 2 tuns of cider.[18] But even fare as ample as this did not fully satisfy great men's demands. The expenditure of the Earl of Lincoln's household in 1304–05 amounted to £2,642, and his Countess's household cost £623 over and above. Some of this expenditure was a consequence of the Earl's political position – provisioning castles on the Welsh March, providing horses and liveries for knights in Scotland, and so forth; and of course there were wages and fees paid to many servants. Fine textiles were also bought: cloths of gold, a coverlet pointed with red, red hangings for the Earl's bed, cloth of Tarsus and cloth of Cyprus (subsequently decorated with gold thread), red and purple saddle cloths embroidered with the Earl's arms for his palfrey, even a green tent and robe for when he went hunting in the greenwood. But the heaviest cost of all, over £1,800, was the expense of pantry, buttery and kitchen. It included the purchase of spices, of Gascon and Rhine wine and of wax: but some of this charge no doubt represented a supplementation of supplies that the Earl drew from his manors.[19]

The fact is that, at least for the rich, consumption demands could be satisfied only when land provided cash as well as foodstuffs. The situation of the great landowner, moreover, changed over time. First, the development of markets made it easier in 1300 for a baronial household to buy a larger part of the provisions it required than might have been the case in 1100. Lords were offered a greater measure of flexibility as to whether they cultivated to any significant extent at all. At the same time, large as the appetites of medieval rich men were, they were not capable of being satisfied solely from manorial agriculture. Their expectations embraced a whole range of desirable goods which, once again, almost certainly greatly expanded between 1100 and 1300. If these conditions modified (or might modify) the ways in which landlords managed their estates, so did other circumstances: the market demand for the produce of their land and the price that would be paid for it, or the demand for land itself and the rent that would be offered for it. The interaction of these circumstances modified the objectives of estate management and the methods by which lords sought to realise them. These changes are an important chapter in the history of medieval rural society.

The farming of manors[20]

This subject may be introduced by reverting to Domesday terminology. Domesday and its satellites described particular manors belonging to Ely Abbey with some indifference as a demesne vill of the abbot, a manor which had lain always in demesne, or a manor which had lain always in 'demesne farm'. The word 'farm', with its association with the Anglo-Saxon word *feorm*, had a specific connotation at this time. It implied that the property concerned had been handed over to a third party and that, for the duration of his 'lease' (the word may be in a sense inappropriate, but it is as near as our modern vocabulary comes to an apt description) the 'lessee' would render to the 'lessor' a fixed rent, possibly but by no means necessarily in kind. This kind of arrangement was ubiquitous in Anglo-Norman England, and leaves many traces in Domesday both on the royal estates and on the estates of other landholders.

Subsequent records, in the nature of things most of them from ecclesiastical sources, fill out the characteristically enigmatic phrases of Domesday. One of the clearest descriptions is that contained in a

twelfth-century 'statute' of Ramsey Abbey which makes provision for
the food and clothing of the monks of that house. The manors of the
estate, either singly or two or more of them together, were burdened
with the obligation to provide what was needed by the monks for a
fortnight in the form of flour, bread, malt, honey, lard, cheese, sheep,
geese, fowls, eggs, butter, beans and money. The provisioning year
began on 1 October, when the manor of Ellington provided completely
for the needs of the abbey for a week. On 8 October Therfield took over,
on 15 October Burwell, on 22 October Houghton, on 29 October
Warboys and on 5 November Knapwell and Cranfield jointly. So the
list runs on throughout the year, *currens per singulas ebdomadas anni,
scilicet per quinquaginta duas ebdomadas* (running for every week of
the year, namely for fifty-two weeks).[21] St Albans, too, had a system of
weekly farms, though there were fifty-three of them, one being reserved
to provide the utensils needed in the kitchen.[22] Similar arrangements
had been adopted for the provisioning of Ely Abbey, again with a little
to spare; and seemingly (so a list probably of the late eleventh century
suggests) for the supply of the canons of St Paul's.[23] At Bury St
Edmund's, on the other hand, various manors or groups of manors each
rendered a month's farm, and the same system appears to have
prevailed on the Rochester estates.[24] The details of the arrangements are
less important, however, than their basic similarities.

Our knowledge of these arrangements is based almost exclusively on
monastic records, and it may well be asked how typical they were of
contemporary estate management. Large monastic communities had,
after all, needs that could very appropriately be met by more or less
fixed liveries in cash and kind from their manors. At the same time, it is
clear that the farming of manors was not restricted to monastic estates.
In 1086 it was found not only on the royal estates but on the lands of
Odo of Bayeux, bishop across the Channel but Earl of Kent in England.
Bishops as well as abbots adopted the device, for Lanfranc ordained
farms for the Canterbury estates; and how widespread it was becomes
evident once the evidence of the pipe rolls is available in the reign of
Henry II. In the 1170s and 1180s it is attested on the episcopal estates of
Lincoln, Ely, Winchester and Canterbury; the lands of the Bishop of
Chester were probably all at farm in 1195; some Durham lands were still
at farm in 1196; and on the Winchester estates Bishop's Fonthill was still
farmed in 1209, and Rimpton, Bentley and North Waltham had been
recently at farm.[25]

The evidence for lay estates is sparser, but exists none the less: there is
testimony to the farming of the manors (or some of the manors) of the
honour of Haughley (1184), the honour of Rayleigh (1181), the honour
of Chester (1182), the lands of William de Curci (1187) and the honour

of Boulogne (1196). The list makes no pretence of completeness, but at least it may suggest that the leasing of manors to farmers was no occasional device. This is not to say that landowners necessarily leased all their manors in this way or that all landowners farmed out their manors. Great landowners may sometimes have kept in hand manors attached to their principal residences; and the farming system may have been unnecessary on the estate of small landowners, who were close enough to their property to manage it themselves. The farming system looks essentially like a solution to the problems posed by estates that were both large and composed of widely scattered manors. On such estates it assured a lord of a fixed return from his lands and at the same time made minimum demands on central administrative supervision.

Monastic records permit a little more to be said about the nature of these arrangements. In 1152, for example, the canons of St Paul's granted their manor of Kensworth in Hertfordshire to Humfrey Bucvinte. He was to hold it for life rendering a farm of £5 in the first six years, and thereafter £10 yearly. The lease also laid down in precise terms how many cattle and sheep were to be on the manor, and how much land should be sown and how much fallow, when the lease ended.[26] Again, in or before 1200 Abbot Samson of Bury granted to Solomon of Whepstead for life the manors of Ingham and Elveden, with the farm buildings, implements and livestock, which were enumerated in great detail. For Elveden he paid a rent of barley and wheat together with 40*s* to the abbey kitchen and smaller sums to the abbey's baker and brewer. He was also to provide six servants to brew for one week in the year. For Ingham the main consideration was a money farm of £23 yearly, together with the provision of hay for the abbey dormitory.[27]

These instances are not untypical. First, the leases convey to lessees working agricultural concerns equipped with stock, implements and so forth, and one must presume with the rights the lord possessed to call on the labour of tenants. Secondly, they were for a fixed term – for the lessee's life in both the examples quoted, but in the early Norman period leases for two or even three lives were not unknown and a generation before Solomon of Whepstead got Ingham and Elveden they had been leased to Ralf Brian for a period of twelve years.[28] Finally, for the duration of the term, the return the lessee made was normally fixed. The lessees themselves included men of various sorts. On the Ely estates at the end of the eleventh century some seem to have been reeves who were probably men of no great standing. On the other hand, Abbot Richer was alleged to have used the manors of St Benet of Holme as a source of outdoor relief for his relatives of both sexes, although he leased South Walsham to a clerk,[29] and the farmers of other manors seem to have been men who might be described as gentry.[30] The Rochester manor of Haddenham, on the other hand, was in the charge of a monk.[31] Other lessees were men of considerable standing. Before 1100 the Bishop of Lincoln demised Ascott-under-Wychwood to Nigel d'Oilly, presumably Henry I's constable; and about the same time a Domesday baron, Ranulf brother of Ilger, held Dillington, and Henry I's dispenser held Ellington at farm from Ramsey abbey.[32]

One other matter deserves mention. The Ramsey and Elveden farms included a money payment as well as renders in kind. In the Ramsey scheme the cash paid by farmers was said to be for *compadium*, a word apparently equivalent to *companagium*, meaning anything which goes with bread. What went with bread might be wine or comestibles which a lord's manors could not produce; but monks also needed shoes and clothing and furnishings for their domestic buildings and their choir. Thus, when the pre-conquest farming system at Ely was said to provide a sufficiency for the abbey, that purpose could only be realized if cash was rendered as well as provisions. At Canterbury, too, the farms ordained by Lanfranc were from 'manors which render grain and pence and those which render pence only'. To what extent there was a trend for money farms to take the place of farms in kind during the twelfth century is not easily determined. The conversion of food rents into money payments had gone a long way on the royal estates before 1066; and after the conquest it went further, for kings with commitments on both sides of the Channel could scarcely conveniently be tied to a routine of prandial perambulations. To a hardly less extent this inconvenience must have been felt by the greater barons and even by bishops, so many of whom were civil servants as well as prelates. Money farms soon became the norm on the Canterbury estates and apparently also on the Ely estates by 1171; and on the monastic estate of Bury St Edmund's a change from food to money farms may have begun even in the eleventh century. On the Rochester estates, on the other hand, the twelfth-century trend was possibly the other way round, and on the Christ Church and Ramsey estates farms in kind persisted well into the thirteenth century, even though their importance diminished. By that time, however, they were something in the nature of survivals, preserved in an attenuated form by the special supply requirements of large monastic communities.

In one sense what is important, however, is not whether manorial farms were in cash or in kind, but whether or not manors paid a farm at all – a payment, that is, which was 'firm and unchangeable'.[33] In so far as they did so there seems every indication that they were being managed in a traditional way originating long before 1066. Here, as in so many other respects, Norman barons and churchmen stepped into the shoes of Saxon *antecessores*. The system was, in many respects, a good deal less inflexible than it sounds. Lanfranc evidently rearranged the version of it he found at Canterbury, although he had the advantage of being a new broom in circumstances when it was easier than usual to sweep clean. The same observation may apply to the division of Ely Abbey's food supply between abbot and monks before 1100; but it is more significant that, on the Ramsey estate, the returns from manors doubled in value between 1086 and 1135.[34] Here at least the abbey, while retaining the system of farming its manors, nevertheless so manipulated the system that it secured a share (and perhaps a considerable share) of the proceeds of agricultural expansion.

This is not to say that the device of farming manors was exempt from possible dangers. There was, in the first place, the chance that farmers would establish a hereditary lien on the land, and particularly farmers holding for one or more lives. At best the outcome would be that it would be more difficult to adjust the rents they paid to take account of the expansion of production or of rising prices; at worst that lords would lose control of their properties altogether. Twelfth-century leases frequently show consciousness of this particular danger in the stress they place on the temporary nature of the concession. Abbot Hugh of St Augustine's grant of land at Medegrave to William de Tichesi for life included a waiver of any claim being laid after his death by William's kinsmen or friends.[35] The Bishop of Lincoln's grant of Ascott to Nigel d'Oilly contained a similar saving clause barring Nigel's heir, and the Abbot of Ramsey's grant of Dillington to Ranulf brother of Ilger insisted that the manor was to be returned to the abbey after Ranulf's death, with all the possessions thereon.

Such precautions were not always effective, especially against great men. The Abbot of Ramsey in 1088 demised Over (Cambs) for £6 yearly to William Pecche and his wife for their lives, and the limits of their tenure were later formally recognized before Henry I's court. Geoffrey, William's grandson, however, still held the manor in 1187 when he acknowledged the abbot's right to it, but recovered it for his life for a rent increased to £7 yearly. Once again, however, Over passed with the rest of Geoffrey's estate to his brother Gilbert, and from Gilbert to his son Hamon, who claimed that it was his inheritance. Not until 1237, after nine years of litigation, did Hamon acknowledge the abbot's right to the manor. By then a farm for life established soon after the Norman Conquest had lasted for 149 years.[36]

These, perhaps, were extreme cases, but other disadvantages for the lord could arise from the farming of manors. When Ralf Brian took Elveden from the Abbot of Bury in 1160, he did so for 'the customary service', and the abbey's manors in 1181 were farmed according to 'the ancient assize'.[37] There was a real danger that the rents paid by lessees would achieve a customary stability, a serious matter for landlords when prices began to rise dramatically late in the twelfth century. How serious was indicated by another example from this same estate. Abbot Samson refused an offer of a £20 fine from a knight who sought to take Tilney at farm for the 'ancient service' of £4 yearly. His refusal was justified when, by keeping the manor in hand, the revenues from it amounted to £25 the first year and £20 the second.[38] But even when manorial receipts were not frozen in perpetuity, so long as the lease lasted the lessee enjoyed whatever unearned increment arose from expanding settlement, increased production or rising commodity prices. As inflation became more rapid the disadvantage of this whole system of management became more evident.

There might be yet other dangers inherent in it. There is a great deal of evidence from very many twelfth-century estates of contracting or even dissolving demesnes.[39] Time and time again there are records of men holding small parcels of the home farm, sometimes the result of successive alienations over time as on the St Paul's estate at Navestock where portions both of the demesne and the 'new demesne' had been alienated.[40] In some cases, although admittedly they were rare, the situation might be potentially worse: on Glastonbury's manor at Grittleton in 1189 the vill was leased to the homage, and in 1183 the men of Ryton farmed their vill 'with the demesne and assized rents and the mill and the labour services and the implements . . . and a fishery'.[41] It is easy to see how in such circumstances a manor might fall into dissolution. Even piecemeal alienation of portions of the demesne, however, had another consequence: it made redundant some of the arrangements existing to supply it with labour. The contraction of demesnes, therefore, was accompanied by some commutation of labour services. On the St Paul's manor at Beauchamp in 1181, for example, 130 acres of demesne had passed into the hands of tenants, and some tenements which had owed labour services no longer did so. A free tenant paid 8s for a virgate half of which had previously owed services; two holders of 'work-lands' paid money rents for half their holdings; and another paid money instead of works for the whole of his virgate.[42] On this estate, moreover, there is explicit testimony to the fact that the dismemberment of demesnes was, in many cases, the work of farmers: Richard the farmer granted land *de dominico* at Sandon to Richard the forester and at Navestock a series of farmers had alienated parcels of 'new demesne' to tenants.[43] On the Glastonbury estate, too, a tenant's labour services at Berrow-on-Shore were commuted by the farmer.[44] These 'depredations of farmers' were perhaps in the long run more serious than their more obvious misdeeds of selling timber, running down equipment and stock, or allowing the buildings to lapse into ruin.[45]

The reasons why farmers behaved as they did are not difficult to imagine. They had limited managerial resources at their disposal and the supervisory resources of their lords were inadequate to exercise regular control over them. Again, the fixed terms on which they held were an encouragement to accommodate members of an expanding village population on rented land since this was the least taxing way of managing the manor; and, as prices rose, they might find that less demesne land was needed to produce money farms or the money component of farms. If there was also a tendency for money farms to take the place of farms in kind, moreover, the necessary reliance of farmers on direct demesne cultivation would be still further reduced. In such circumstances the line of least resistance for farmers may have been capitulation to the demand of the peasantry for land as village populations increased, as evidently they were increasing. Some such explanation as this would seem best to fit the signs of crisis on larger estates, managed after the traditional fashion, as the twelfth century drew to its close.

The course landlords adopted in the face of that crisis was to abandon the traditional system. The reasons why they did so, however, went further than attempts to recover control over manors and to prevent a collapse of their structure. They sought, in fact, radically to transform their revenue position. There is, from one point of view, little that is surprising in the fact that 'it is only from 1184 that any general trend becomes visible' that would replace the farming of manors by a more profitable regime, or that the process was brought to completion by the early years of the thirteenth century.[46] This was, after all, the period during which the rate of inflation was at its most rapid during the medieval centuries (see pp. 64–9). The response of landlords may have owed a good deal to a recognition that soaring commodity prices offered new opportunities for profit, particularly since the home market for foodstuffs and raw materials was growing as towns grew and overseas outlets for wool and grain and dairy produce were expanding simultaneously. To the extent that this was so the inflation of the years around 1200 had major psychological consequences: it transformed a traditional class of landlords into entrepreneurs.

At the same time the possibility must be faced that the primary result of inflation was not so much to awaken consciousness of opportunities as to undermine the standards of living of those classes who were consumers par excellence. This happened, moreover, precisely at the moment when an expanding western commerce was diversifying available consumer goods and intensifying desires to take advantage of them. The static character of revenues from manors at farm, and the fall in the real values of money farms in such circumstances, cut into living standards established by custom and denied opportunities to raise them to levels new circumstances made possible. An attempt to ride the storm by borrowing might be a temporary recourse, and indeed the many signs of difficulty and indebtedness afflicting many landlords of all types in the late twelfth century were likely enough a further indication of the ravages of inflation. Borrowing might, as at Bury St Edmunds under Abbot Hugh, 'maintain the honour of his house' for a brief time; but debts filled Abbot Samson with anxiety. In the end his solution was radical: 'when Michaelmas came round, he took all his manors into his own hand',[47] thus ending at one blow the traditional system of management on the abbey's estate.

What replaced that traditional system may be illustrated by the accounts of the Bishop of Winchester's manor of Downton for the year beginning at Michaelmas 1208. The accounting officer was not a farmer but a reeve, and he accounted not for a fixed render but in detail for a great variety of receipts. They included rents, pannage payments for grazing pigs, and charges for pasturage. Then there were the proceeds of the sale of the lord's livestock, hides, wool, pork fat, cheese and grain. Finally, there were the profits of the bishop's court, entry fines and marriage fines paid by tenants, together with a tallage of £40 levied on customary tenants. Against these receipts, minutely itemized and totalling £165 1s 5½d, the reeve was allowed £25 1s 11d expenses to cover the cost of maintaining manorial ploughs, carts and buildings; of ditching and digging the garden; of food supplied for harvest workers; of wages paid to regular farm workers and to casual labourers hired to weed, thresh and spread manure; and of purchasing stock and canvas to make woolsacks. Subjoined to this cash account are accounts of the yield and disposal of grain and livestock on the lord's demesne. Once again everything is itemized: the grain and stock sold and used in the running of the manor, the grain sown for the following year's harvest, the oats used to feed the bishop's horses when he came to Downton, the stock which died or which went in tithe, the cow killed for the bishop's use and taken to Cranbourne, the cheese and pigs and fowls which went to his kitchen.[48]

The nature of the change is clear enough. Instead of accounts dealing with round amounts of provender and round sums of money, accounts like that for Downton ran to the last halfpenny, the last half bushel and the last lamb. The reeve was not a lessee who bore the risks but also gathered to himself any unearned increment; he was a manager who was allowed his expenses after their justification had been carefully scrutinized. The risks were now the lord's, but so were the windfalls and the profit when rising prices or a swelling rent roll augmented the income from a manor. A corollary of these changes in management is also suggested by the Winchester pipe rolls: lords set about reconstituting manors which had shown signs of dissolution during the twelfth century. The 1210–11 roll shows tenements formerly held for rent being 'drawn' into the bishop's demesne on fifteen of his manors; at Brightwell, Witney, Adderbury and Fareham villeins who had paid money in lieu of agricultural services were set to work once more; and at Wycombe villeins who attempted to prove they were freemen paid heavily for their presumption.[49]

This 'manorial reaction'[50] is now recognized as being a general feature of the opening years of the thirteenth century. The tendencies which had undermined manorial structure during the preceding century were checked. Some demesne land which had been alienated was resumed and some claims to agricultural services which had been released for money were revived; and these endeavours were also associated with a closer definition of villeinage and the obligations it entailed. It was hardly an accident that the lawyers devoted much time to this task precisely at this time. The reconstitution of manors, however, cannot be severed from the change from indirect to direct management: that change as well as the reassembling of demesnes and the reimposition of labour services was required to create the 'classical' manorial regime which bulked almost as large in the early thirteenth-century countryside as it does in our textbooks.

Two things remain to be added. First, if the system of farming manors had been principally characteristic of great estates, the changes which took place around 1200 mainly affected these large agglomerations of property. It is not impossible that, in adopting the course they did, larger landowners were following practices developed on some of the smaller estates by the class of 'rustic knights', the emergence of which had been a feature of the twelfth century. The large landowners did so at an opportune moment. The economic tide was running in their favour, for markets were expanding, prices continued to climb, and labour supply was eminently favourable to employers. In such circumstances the managerial revolution taking place around 1200 may conceivably have strengthened the position of greater vis-à-vis smaller owners. Be that as it may be, one other condition came to the aid of great men. The progress of education during the twelfth century, and not least the wider spread of lay literacy which had become evident by the reign of Henry II, provided them with the supervisory staff necessary if they were to take the fullest advantage of opportunities.[51] Secondly, if the basis of the prosperity of landlords was provided by 'classical' manors directly managed by reeves and bailiffs supervised by something like an estate bureaucracy, this regime must not be transformed into a constant of the medieval agrarian scene. It was preceded by the system of manors at farm; it was succeeded, during bleaker days for landowners in the later Middle Ages, by new moves on their part towards a rentier position; it was, in fact, 'hardly more than a substantial interlude in an age-long system of leasehold farming'.[52]

The high-farming era

To put the 'classical' manorial regime in its place in no way detracts from its significance, for it was the basis of agrarian organization at a time when medieval English agriculture reached the limits of its expansion. One aspect of it was the attempt, already noted on the Winchester estates in 1210, once more to augment demesne acres which had been shrinking on many estates in the twelfth century. On the Winchester lands the expansion of the demesne went on until after 1250, and much the same was happening elsewhere. During the same period the Bishops of Ely bought out military tenants at Northwold, Totteridge and Tydd, turning their fees into demesne manors; and they also added fenland and forest assarts to their demesnes in the Norfolk Marshland, Huntingdonshire, Hertfordshire, Essex and the Isle of Ely. The canons of St Paul's, too, bought out the farmer of Kensworth manor, and they did not disdain to purchase for £4 ten acres of arable and five acres of meadow at Heybridge;[53] and Matthew Paris found it worthy of mention that Prior Richard of Binham added to the endowments of his house some 600 acres of arable, 10 acres of wood and pasture rights in five villages.[54] In a very different terrain Whalley Abbey expanded its hold on the Pennine slopes of Rossendale. It acquired pasture rights there from Roger Lacy in the reign of King John, but at that time there was 'neither manor nor mansion' there. It was in the ensuing reign (so a jury said in the fourteenth century) that 'a certain abbot . . . first constructed and built a house . . . and enclosed a great part of the waste which is now called the manor of Brandwood'.[55]

Most of the information about this sort of enterprise comes from the larger estates, but some smaller men were also engaged in it. William of Abington in 1274 had 130 acres in demesne at Abington Piggots (Cambs) to which he had added three other parcels totalling 11 acres. These were not all of his acquisitions, for his wife tells of 48½ acres in Abington and 9 acres in Steeple Morden 'which William obtained in his life time from divers persons in small parcels'. Twenty years later when William's son died, there were said to be 166 acres in demesne together with 40 acres in additional parcels acquired from ten different people.[56]

Purchase of land was one form of seignorial investment; another was expenditure on manorial equipment. Prior Richard not only added to the demesnes of Binham priory but built a 'noble hall and barn' at Westley at a cost of more than £20; and his activities were paralleled by those of many high-farming landlords. One of the best known (and he too was a buyer of land) is Prior Henry of Eastry of Canterbury Cathedral Priory. Agriculture on the priory estate under his rule was conducted in a systematic way: seed grain was sown more intensively and new seed was bought in to improve yields, while even the value of the manure produced by the priory sheep flocks was calculated in pounds, shillings and pence. At the same time Henry invested in improvements. He engaged in a good deal of drainage work; he sought to promote fertility by the extensive use of lime and marl, promulgating a solemn ordinance *de terra marlanda* at the beginning of the fourteenth century; medicines were bought to treat livestock suffering from diseases; and reeves were strictly enjoined to maintain the manorial buildings and fences. There was also much expenditure on new buildings, carefully catalogued by the priory. The record begins at Monkton with a new wardrobe and a new gate in 1287, continues with a new grange, sheepfold, dovecote, granary and so forth, and ends in 1317 with a new ox-byre and a new salt-pan. There are similar lists for Eastry, Lyden, Adisham, Ickham, Chartham, Godmersham and Brooke, the total expenditure during Henry's thirty-seven years as prior for buildings and repairs on divers manors amounting to £3739.[57]

It may be significant in this connection that a number of the manuscripts of Walter of Henley's *Husbandry* and other didactic treatises were written at Canterbury. These 'highly technical discourses on planning and costing', with their assumption of an almost scientific approach to management and the routine of agriculture, are a counterpart of the high-farming that developed on great estates during the thirteenth century and of the professional approach to the managerial problems to which high farming gave rise.[58] Their advice contributed to the many steps that were taken to improve yields and ultimately to enhance profits. The change from a two-course to a three-course cycle of crops in some places was one of them (see p. 90); and an increase in the amount of legumes grown, a crop which improved fertility by fixing nitrogen in the soil, or the application of marl to combat acidity and infuse nitrates, were others. Some lords, too, followed Walter of Henley's injunction to change at least part of their seed corn each year; and some carefully culled their stock and brought in new animals (especially rams) to improve the quality of their flocks and herds.

At the same time, while these efforts at improvement were real enough, it must also be admitted that their impact was less than dramatic. The proportion of arable under legumes, for example, certainly expanded: on the Bishop of Winchester's estate it grew from under 1 per cent in 1208 to over 8 per cent in 1345, and in 1322 about 18 per cent of the arable of the Christ Church, Canterbury, estate was sown with these crops.[59] On some Holderness manors, indeed, by the mid-fourteenth century legumes occupied an even larger share of the cornfields, but in very many places they continued to be sown on a restricted acreage only. Marling, too, although widely practised both by lords and peasants, was all too often on a very small scale. Even on the Christ Church manors the acreage treated on any one of them in a given year was frequently in single figures, for the good reason that the cost of marling was high – invariably over 1*s* an acre and sometimes very much more. The cost of digging in seaweed or sand in coastal regions, or of burning the pared-off sward ('beat-burning') in the south-west, similarly restricted these devices for augmenting fertility.[60] In the last resort, most landlords were unwilling to spend heavily from current revenue upon improvements; and even Prior Henry of Eastry's impressive range of investments amounted in fact only to a very modest proportion of the average annual income of his house during his long years of office (see p. 232).

Grain yields illustrate well enough the technical limitations under which even the most enterprising of thirteenth-century landowners operated. Any attempt to demonstrate what these were in bushels per acre is virtually frustrated by the prevalence of customary measures both of area and volume; it is therefore safer to look at yields in terms of the ratio between seed sown and the crop subsequently harvested. Walter of Henley was not optimistic on this score: 'If the sum content of thy barn do answer only three times so much as the seed was, thou gainest nothing by it unless corn bear a good price.' Another treatise was somewhat more hopeful, putting the yield of oats at fourfold, of wheat at fivefold and barley at eightfold.[61] Estate records do not permit us to err too much on the optimistic side. The order of fruitfulness proposed by the last writer is indeed born out by the data assembled in Table 4: barley in many places did yield the best, although only in Durham and in Holderness did it even approach the eightfold harvest that was his hope. Wheat, in a few places, did attain a fivefold return, but generally the average was lower (sometimes much lower); the yield of oats everywhere fell below his fourfold expectation and was generally very much less. If the facts are disappointing in the light of medieval assumptions, moreover, they are much more disappointing in the light of modern expectations. Wheat and barley yielded less than one-third of today's returns on seed, oats less than one-fifth.

Table 4   Yield ratios of grain (per seed)[62]

County or region	Manors or estate	Period	No. of years	Wheat	Barley	Oats
Durham	Billingham	1328–38	5	5·5	7·25	—
	Westoe	1328–32	4	4·1	5·66	—
	Wardley	1329–35	6	4·3	—	—
Cumberland	Birkby and Cockermouth	1266–68	2	3·3	4·9	1·8
Yorkshire	Harewood	1266–89	4	3·5	3·5	2·1
	Keyingham	1263–91	16	4·6	5·2	2·8
	Little Humber	1263–91	16	5·4	7·8	2·9
	Easington	1263–91	16	3·2	6·0	2·4
	Bolton	1301–14	14	4·8	4·9	2·7
	Malham	1301–14	14	4·1	4·7	2·5
S. England	Winchester estates	1200–49	—	3·8	4·4	2·6
		1250–99	—	3·8	3·5	2·3
		1300–49	—	3·9	3·6	2·2
Norfolk	Forncett	1290–1306	6	5·0	4·0	3·5
Cambs	Crowland manors	1271–1320	—	5·0	4·75	2·64
Wilts	Sevenhampton	1273–88	16	4·3	5·3	3·0
Devon	Ottery	1335–42	3	4·7	—	4·3

This matter of yields prompts certain other observations. First, they varied sharply from manor to manor. In a very good year like 1309 the wheat ratio on the Winchester estates ranged from 8·6 at Ecchinswell to 2·5 at Esher, and in a moderate year like 1310 from 5·4 at Ivinghoe to 1·29 at Cheriton. Secondly, they varied equally sharply from year to year. At Ecchinswell, following the ratio of 8·6 in 1309, came 3·5 (1310), 4·5 (1311), 3·7 (1312), 4·5 (1313), 4·1 (1314), 2·5 (1315), 1·0 (1316) – the last two years being the years of the great famine. Thirdly, the relatively high yields of wheat and barley on some northern manors might reflect the fact that acreages under these crops were relatively small compared with the acreages under oats: they could, therefore, be confined to the very best land. Conversely it was very common for oats and to a lesser extent barley to be sown more heavily than wheat. On the Winchester estates, while wheat was sown at from 2½ to 3 bushels per acre, barley and oats were sown at a rate of 4 to 6 bushels: consequently, while wheat yielded up to 14 bushels per acre, oats yielded up to 16 bushels and barley almost 28 bushels. In the north, where up to 8 bushels of oats per acre were sometimes sown, this may have gone far to compensate for the very low yield-ratios. Even so 16–18 bushels per acre was the order of the oat harvest in these places. Once again these figures need to be compared with modern harvest results: 90 bushels per acre or more for barley, 105 bushels for oats, 136 bushels or more for wheat.[63]

There remains a final impression conveyed by the figures set out in Table 4. By far the largest body of evidence summarized there is that derived from the Winchester manors scattered over Hampshire,

Somerset, Wiltshire, Oxfordshire, Berkshire, Buckinghamshire and Surrey. If anything, yields, and especially wheat yields, were rather low on these manors; and if the latter held up over the whole period 1200 to 1350, the yields of barley and oats tended to fall. If account is taken of the fact that the arable acreage was shrinking from the mid-thirteenth century as poorer land was jettisoned, a reasonable inference seems to be that, while wheat yields could be maintained by concentrating this crop on the best land, barley and oat crops suffered as the fertility of the bishop's acres declined. The fact that much of his land lay in old manors, situated in some of the oldest settled parts of England, gives force to this supposition. If it is true it points to the fact that even highly organized and superficially efficient estates were failing in one quite basic requirement of good husbandry: the keeping of the land in good heart.

The likelihood that livestock farming was in any significant respect more efficient than arable farming is not high. The milk yields of cows are difficult to calculate, but were probably of the order of 120–150 gallons per cow, a sixth or less of the modern figure; and while Walter of Henley hoped for 90 lb of butter and cheese per cow, the target for the Yorkshire dairy herd of Bolton Priory was only 72 lb. The fact that ewes were treated as dairy animals probably did little to improve their stamina or the size of the various breeds. One result was that, by contrast with modern fleeces which average around 4½ lb in weight, those of medieval sheep ranged from 1 lb to around 2½ lb.[64] Fertility, too, was very low and was further reduced by the ravages of disease. On ten Winchester manors in 1210–11, 1,186 out of 2,990 lambs died during the year; the average number of surviving lambs at Sevenhampton from a flock of 181 ewes was 117 in the period 1269–81; and on this last manor in a bad year like 1279–80 nearly a third of the sheep flock of 809 died of murrain.[65] At times losses were even worse than that, rising to 55 per cent of the Holderness flock of Isabella de Fortibus in the time of 'common mortality' in the mid-1280s and to two-thirds of the Bolton Priory flock in 1315–17.[66] Until the second and third decades of the fourteenth century cattle diseases were somewhat less lethal, but there again the level of fertility was low, at least in northern herds. The small herd of twenty-five cows at Harewood did well to produce an average of seventeen calves yearly in the 1260s and 1270s; but the Bolton priory herd managed only one calf per two cows and the Lacy vaccaries in Blackburnshire did worse than that at two calves per five cows.[67]

These mortalities afflicting stock were not helped by defective feeding. True, hay was stacked beside the Holderness sheepfolds for winter feed and milk (and at Harewood ale) was bought to feed lambs; peas and oats were fed to draught animals. For the most part, however, livestock picked up what it could on the manorial pastures. Nor was the situation ameliorated by the state of veterinary knowledge. A good deal of pitch, quicksilver and other medicaments was bought to treat animal diseases, but it may be optimistic to assume that Eynsham Abbey's prescription for treating murrain would be effective. First a mass in honour of the Holy Spirit was sung and an offering of one penny made. Then the sheep were gathered together, extracts from the four Gospels were read to them, and they were sprinkled with holy water. Finally a hymn was sung, and the paternoster said thrice followed by the Ave Maria and a collect.[68] The inefficacy of this sort of treatment is perhaps evident in the figures for animal mortality.

These technical limitations of medieval agriculture must be stressed as well as the efforts of landlords and their officials to expand production. None the less, on many estates, a higher volume of production was achieved. Despite murrains Adam of Stratton at Sevenhampton increased his flock of ewes from 91 in 1269 to 306 a decade later, even though disease cut it back again to 212 by 1280. During the same period the sale of produce (and of grain in particular) accounted for 53 per cent on the average of the gross yield of the manor. In the same century, in good years, the proceeds of demesne farming contributed over £4,000 towards a total manorial income of over £6,000 accruing to the Bishops of Winchester. Rising prices explain some part of their soaring revenues, but so did the growth of their demesnes at least until some time after the mid-century.[69] Augmenting the lands they cultivated was no monopoly of the Bishops of Winchester: as we have already seen, the Bishops of Ely were likewise doing so until some time after 1251; so were a knightly family like the Abingtons in the second half of the century and Prior Henry of Eastry into the fourteenth century; and so were Elizabeth de Burgh and the Bohuns as late as the 1320s.[70]

It is possible, however, that in some parts an expansion of stock-farming was an even more important aspect of the expansion of production than the increase of arable demesnes. In this connection there seems little doubt that the rising scale of sheep-farming was the most ubiquitous: for it appears alike on moorland slopes and high and dry wolds, on pastures recovered from fen and marsh, and on manors (of which those in East Anglia were typical) combining arable and sheep in a sheep–corn husbandry. Whatever the circumstances, sheep were in many places very big business. Meaux Abbey had a flock of 11,000; Thomas of Lancaster kept 5,500 in the Peak District; in the west Winchcombe had 8,000 and Gloucester Abbey had 10,000; in the south the Bishop of Winchester had 29,000 in 1259 and, in the early fourteenth century, Canterbury Cathedral Priory had 14,000 and St Swithun's

Priory 20,000; in the far north Holm Cultram Abbey sold the wool of some 10,000 sheep.[71] All in all, the export trade alone in the reign of Edward I absorbed the fleeces of some 8 million sheep, no small proportion of which must have been provided by demesne flocks.

In some parts of the country, too, cattle farming was similarly organized on a large scale, particularly in the uplands of the south-west, on some of the marsh pastures of south-eastern and eastern England, and perhaps most conspicuously in the northern hill country. At Barnard Castle (Durham) in 1326 there were 300 cattle and calves in the demesne vaccary alone, and there were six other vaccaries; the Earl of Lancaster's Wyresdale vaccaries in Lancashire were stocked with over 800 cattle in 1313; and in 1305 the Earl of Lincoln's cattle farms in Blackburnshire accommodated 2,400 head of stock, half of them breeding cows.[72] The expansion of agriculture was in no way limited to the expansion of arable.

It was the expansion of arable, however, that caused another characteristic feature of the thirteenth century. The increase in demesne acreages, and possibly the application of a greater amount of labour to the same amount of land,[73] intensified and diversified the demand for labour on great estates and likely enough on smaller estates. A few instances make it clear that this demand was satisfied in a variety of ways. On the Ely manors at the end of the thirteenth and beginning of the fourteenth century, for example, the demesnes almost everywhere depended on three different sources of labour: customary tenants performing labour services, full-time workers paid in cash and kind, and casual labour hired for specific tasks and often paid at piece-rates.[74] Much the same was true of the Earl Marshal's Cambridgeshire manors. Both at Kennett and Soham his customary tenants owed substantial labour services and, while varying amounts of these were 'sold', usually a high proportion of them were performed. Some casual labour was employed not only for the garden and vineyard at Kennett and to repair buildings, but to harvest part of the corn at Soham in 1271–72. In both manors, however, much of the burden of cultivation fell on full-time labourers. The staff at Kennett in 1270 consisted of eight ploughmen, a carter, a dairymaid, a cowman, a swineherd, a warrener and two shepherds.[75] In 1343–44, when Soham had passed to the Earls of Lancaster, the customary tenants still weeded the corn, mowed part of the hay and did much harvest work; the threshing was done by casual labour; and the rest of the requirements of the demesne were met by four ploughmen, a carter, a dairymaid, a shepherd and a swineherd, augmented by a second shepherd and a lad during the lambing time.[76]

There are, of course, variations on this pattern. Labour services played little part in the cultivation of what demesne manors were retained by the Earls of Cornwall at the end of the thirteenth century; the freedom of Kent made them a negligible asset for the monks of Christ Church on their Kentish manors; and the Engaines in 1272 and 1297 had no services upon which to call at White Notley (Essex) and had commuted what had been owed at Dillington (Hunts).[77] At the same time, the mixed labour force evident on the Ely manors and the Earl Marshal's estate at the end of the thirteenth century was no recent innovation. As early as 1208 both casual and full-time labour, as well as the labour services of villeins, were prominent on the Winchester manors. At Downton, where labour services were certainly performed, casual labour did much of the ditching, building, walling, threshing and winnowing, and some of the manure spreading and weeding. At the same time there was a full-time staff of ploughmen, carters and shepherds, together with a swineherd, an oxherd, a dairymaid and a carpenter. This additional labour was paid in various ways. Casual labour was rewarded in cash only; the carters, oxherd and carpenter received both a money wage and a livery of barley; the dairy maid was paid only in kind; and the ploughmen were customary tenants excused their rents and services for serving their lord full-time.[78]

Certain conclusions seem to follow. First, even where it existed unimpaired, the villeinage met only a part of the labour requirements of the 'classical' manor in the thirteenth century. Demesne agriculture also needed men with particular skills like carpenters and building workers, often for a particular task and hired to do that job; but it also needed workers for tasks which required continuous application, like looking after the stock or the dairy, or keeping up the routine of ploughing throughout the year (the natural provinces of the full-time workers), and men to carry out seasonal tasks like weeding and threshing. These last tasks could conveniently be done by casual labourers, provided they were available. Secondly, it cannot be postulated that the full-time farm worker was a novelty of the thirteenth century. He was present, in fact, in Domesday Book in the person of the slave; but by the twelfth century the slave had generally gone and been replaced by the *bovarius*, a man seated on a tenement (possibly the descendant of a slave quartered out on some part of the lord's land) in return for which he worked full-time for the lord. By the thirteenth century, perhaps because a need for full-time service had increased, on some estates ordinary villein tenants were taken into service and excused the obligations incident upon their tenements in return for acting as ploughmen, carters or shepherds.

Even more typical of the full-time labour force of that century, however, was the *famulus*, a man who worked for a wage in cash or in kind or both. This change to full-time labour must be associated with the growth of village populations, creating a reserve of men for whom wages were not an extra to be added to the profits of a tenement, but a necessity of existence. The continued growth of population, moreover, helped to keep wage rates relatively stable, so that with rising prices the real cost of this sort of labour (at least the cost of the cash component of wages) even tended to fall. Conversely, the rising value of land made tenements appreciating assets, so that to pay labourers by excusing the service due from land would have raised the cost of labour. It was in this circumstance that the *bovarius* with a service tenement was replaced by the wage-earning *famulus*; and that on the Westminster Abbey estates in the 1290s orders were given that the *famuli* were no longer to be paid in the form of sown acres in the fields but in cash, as neighbouring lords paid their *famuli*.[79]

Something remains to be said, however, about the labour of villeins. It need hardly be repeated that the availability of servile labour varied greatly from region to region. It was substantial in parts of the Midlands and the south, but negligible in the north, the west and Kent. On the other hand, even in districts where villeins were numerous there was much variety in their obligations: on the Crowland estate, for example, the villeins of Dry Drayton owed only thirty-nine week-works a year, but those of Gedney theoretically owed 255.[80] For the moment, however, what is more important is the nature of villein works, and this may be illustrated by a specific example. On the Bishop of Ely's manor at Linden End Ralf Tony held a 20 acre tenement for which he paid 1*s*7*d* cash rent and various Easter eggs and Christmas hens. His main obligation, however, was to work three days each week between Michaelmas and harvest time and five days a week during harvest. Over and above, he did various additional days of ploughing and harrowing and brought a varying number of additional hands to three harvest 'boons', extra days of work to get in the corn. He was also obliged to do carrying service for the bishop when called on, although this might be counted against his week work if it fell on a day when such work was demanded of him.[81]

Ploughing and harvest labour evidently bulked large amongst Ralf's obligations; but he might be called on for many other tasks – harrowing, weeding, haymaking, leading hay or corn, cutting brushwood and rushes and thatch, threshing, ditching, and leading and spreading manure. The principal value of the villeinage to a lord, however, lay in the fact that it provided a reserve for those seasonal crises of the agricultural year which, the English weather being what it is, called for the flexible mobilization of large amounts of labour for the main ploughings in autumn and spring, harrowing and haymaking, harvesting and perhaps threshing, the carriage of the produce of the lord's fields to his residences or to markets. It was, so to speak, the safety factor in the labour organization of the manor, supplementing regular manorial workers and casually hired hands at those times when the demand for labour was at its highest in the medieval countryside.

The intensification and expansion of the scale of demesne exploitation during the first half of the thirteenth-century, therefore, almost automatically entailed endeavours on the part of lords to augment available supplies of villein labour. The area of villeinage was in many cases increased; the services owed by the holders of villein tenements were more closely defined, generally in an upward direction; and where villein tenements were divided the sum of the services owed by the two parts was usually greater than those which had been owed from the undivided whole. A strange legal treatise may refer to this trend when, after referring to imaginary endeavours by Edward the Confessor to protect cultivators against excessive customs, it argued that 'many of these men were driven by tortious distresses to do their lords . . . many arbitrary customs'.[82] There is nothing surprising in a tradition of peasant depression still being alive at the end of the thirteenth century, for the peasant had a long memory. Even in Edward I's time the men of Abbot's Ripton were able to recall that under Henry II the Abbot of Ramsey had distrained their ancestors to do ploughings and reapings and other undue customs.[83]

At the same time, it is dangerous to exaggerate either the extent or the durability of the thirteenth-century manorial reaction. The Bishop of Ely's estates were typical enough of the trends of the century, but there the villeinage was only increased to a limited extent before 1250 and hardly at all thereafter. Again, on that estate and on the estates of Ramsey Abbey and the bishopric of Winchester, an increasing proportion of labour services were being 'sold' (i.e. relaxed in return for a money payment on an ad hoc basis) in the century after 1250; and on the St Albans estates, perhaps because subdivision of tenements made services hard to exact, week-work hardly existed as early as the second half of the thirteenth century.

How far the tendency to dispense with labour services had gone generally by the opening of the fourteenth century is the subject matter of an ancient controversy. It was long ago suggested that, by 1349, only slight traces of them remained.[84] This assertion was rebutted so far as it applied to eastern, southern and Midland England;[85] but that rebuttal loses some of its force from the fact that it is based almost exclusively on evidence drawn from monastic estates, which tended to be conservative in their organization and management. A more detailed survey has suggested that services had virtually disappeared north and west of the line from Boston to the Severn, but that they were still widely prevalent south-eastwards of it (with the usual exception of Kent).[86] Even this proposition can be questioned. It is a conclusion drawn for the most part from manorial surveys, documents that are likely to state a lord's maximum claims to services rather than what in fact he exacted. Account rolls show, on the other hand, how widespread the practice was for lords to 'sell' at least part of the services owed to them; and it can also be demonstrated that, in Wiltshire for example, commutation was complete on many lay manors and on some ecclesiastical manors by the early fourteenth century.[87] In brief, there is much evidence for the progressive abandonment of villein services, in fact if not in theory, even in Midland and southern England during the generations prior to the Black Death.

Two examples may give a little concreteness to this trend. The Earl Marshal's manor at Tidenham (Glos) was not ill provided with labour services at the end of the thirteenth century, for the villeinage owed 3,604½ week-works, 276 hay-works, 783 ploughing-works and 1,692½ harvest-works – a total of 6,356. Of these, in 1294–95, 617 were excused to manorial officials and others, and 3,169 were performed in fencing, harrowing, weeding, threshing, leading manure, a little ploughing, making and leading hay, harvesting and stacking grain; but 2,570 works (some 38 per cent of those due) were 'sold' (i.e. excused for a payment in lieu) to those who owed them. What might have been done by villein labour may have been done in part by a full-time staff of eleven, but also by a good deal of casual labour, especially in harvest. There were indications in the next few years, moreover, of a more permanent relinquishment of some services. Two customary tenants had their works definitively commuted in 1296 for an annual payment of 7s7¼d, and they were joined by a third in 1300. A further stage in the same process can be observed on the Bishop of Ely's manor at Great Shelford in the heart of traditional Cambridgeshire. Here again the demesne was well provided with about 4,620 works yearly and, in addition, the tenants did 180 acres of ploughing. In 1327–28 the ploughing was still being done and only some 1,420 works were 'sold' for rather under £3. In 1340–41, on the other hand, neither works nor ploughing were done and the bishop's tenants paid nearly £13 in place of services.[88]

The reasons for this trend are not always self-evident. In many cases, of course, it simply reflected a fall in the demand for labour as demesnes contracted. Sometimes, however, lords commuted labour services without abandoning their demesnes, as the Engaines did at Dillington; and here, and on manors when lords stopped short of commutation but were willing to 'sell' each year some proportion of the services their villeins owed, the main influence at work was probably supply rather than demand factors. There was labour available in overpopulated villages both for full-time work and casual hire at wages favourable to the hirer, a situation encouraging lords to turn labour services into rents by either commuting or selling them. Often they clung longest to harvest works, since harvest was the time when the demand for labour was at its most intense both on demesne farms and peasant tenements. Even in harvest, however, village bye-laws seem more concerned to prevent labourers going elsewhere in search of higher wages, or to ensure that strangers were dragooned to work, than about the services of customary boon-workers. Everything suggests, in fact, that the contraction of demesne production in the century after 1250 was rather less rapid than the replacement of the villein *operarius* by men who laboured full-time or part-time for a lord's wages. This was the situation which, after 1349, called for ordinances and statutes of labourers.

The disposal of demesne produce

Whatever the character of a lord's labour force the hallmark of the high-farming estate was, at least by contrast with the peasant holding, production of agricultural commodities on a large scale. What became of them takes us back to Ralf Tony of Linden End and the carrying services he owed. The places to which he had to carry the bishop's goods were carefully specified. They included the bishop's residences at Ely, Somersham and Little Downham; they included other demesne manors of the lord's estate; they included local market towns like Huntingdon and Cambridge; and they included the international fair at St Ives and the port of King's Lynn, at once an outlet to the English coastal trade and to the export markets of western Europe. In other words carrying services might be used to provision a lord's household, to exchange seed or stock between manors, and to link manors with markets. They are testimony to the extent to which the high-farming estate took advantage of commercial opportunities as well as contributing to its lord's subsistence.

Commercial opportunities were of divers sorts. On the Earl Marshal's manor at Kennett sales of produce accounted for £53 out of total receipts of £69 in 1270–71 and £81 out of £94 in 1305–06. In the latter year sales of wool accounted for more than one third of the profits of the demesne; contributions were made by sales of livestock, fowls, pigeons, butter, cheese, and rabbits from the warren; but even on this manor, with its considerable sheep flock, the largest item was the sale of grain which in both years provided nearly half the total receipts from the sale of produce.[89] Demesne farming, in fact, was biased almost as much towards cereal production as peasant farming, and cereals bulked large in that part of demesne produce directed towards the market. At

Kennett in the reign of Edward I a third to a half of the barley was sold and two-thirds to three-quarters of the wheat; while at Soham in 1271–72 more than half the wheat, three-quarters of the rye and two-thirds of the barley went to market. Only oats were, for the most part, used in the manor.[90]

These random instances from Cambridgeshire can be paralleled from elsewhere.[91] Adam of Stratton at Sevenhampton derived on the average 53 per cent of his income from the sale of produce and, of the revenues of his demesne, two-thirds came from the sale of grain. On a grander scale much the same was true of the Winchester estates where again sales contributed between one-third and two-thirds of the receipts from the bishop's demesne in the thirteenth century, making fluctuations in grain prices the major determinant of fluctuations in his revenue. Concentration on grain production for sale was evident as early as 1208 and was still more evident at the end of the century: in 1300 sales accounted for nearly three-quarters of the wheat, two-thirds of the rye, two-fifths of the barley and one-third even of the oats grown on the bishop's manors. Some of these sales doubtless took place in local markets, but others probably contributed to the export trade from Southampton, for the bishop's tenants at Crawley certainly owed carrying services to that port.[92] At the same time, even at an early date, a significant part found its way to the London market. The bishop's mills at Southwark were in full operation in 1210–11, receiving no less than 644 quarters of wheat (as well as some oats and mixed corn) to be turned into flour for Londoners' bread.

If cereal production took pride of place in the business dealings of most great estates, other branches of farming (even the Earl Marshal's rabbit warren and dovecote at Kennet) also contributed to the cash incomes of landlords. Of these branches sheep-farming was evidently the most important and, on some estates with a heavy pastoral bias, it may even have been pre-eminent. In the years 1273–75 grain sales on the principal Holderness manors of Isabella de Fortibus totalled less than £100, but wool sales produced a revenue of about £460.[94] This sort of proportion was certainly unusual, for on the Winchester estates wool sales never exceeded 10 per cent of manorial receipts and, at Sevenhampton, they accounted only for 13 per cent of Adam of Stratton's returns. In aggregate, none the less, wool revenues were anything but insubstantial. The demand from Flanders had intensified from the twelfth century onwards; by the late thirteenth century some 30,000 sacks yearly were being exported, worth possibly in the region of £200,000 yearly; and overseas sales reached their peak in the early fourteenth century, over 40,000 sacks yearly being exported in the years 1304–7.[95]

This booming export market explains why wool was a major cash crop for many landowners, and the fact that wool was principally an export crop was one good reason for the fact that sheep-farming was highly organized, often on an inter-manorial basis. This was certainly the case on the Crowland estates between 1276 and 1313, during which time the abbey's flock was built up from around 4,000 to over 7,000. The stock on particular manors was kept up to strength by drafts from the central sheep farm at Crowland; the wool clip was stored centrally there and prepared for sale; and the whole enterprise was controlled and accounted for by a head shepherd and a staff which increased from two in 1277 to twenty-four in 1307.[96] This highly centralized system of management is not found everywhere, but centralized selling of wool is very common. Eynsham Abbey, for instance, was able to enter into an agreement with a Witney merchant for the disposal of its wool from seven Oxfordshire and two Gloucestershire manors as well as from one in Buckinghamshire.[97] These bulk transactions between large land-owners and export merchants are the practice which is presupposed by Pegolotti's list of vendors and the amounts of wool they had to vend in early fourteenth-century England.

Centralized marketing and the careful preparation and grading of wool which it made possible, as well as the care with which they managed their flocks, were probably the major reasons for the high reputation enjoyed by Cistercian wool among international merchants. Their share of the export trade was not all that high, possibly no more than 4 per cent, but it is notable how relatively high Pegolotti set the price of the best wool they marketed.[98] At the same time centralized marketing was in no sense a peculiarity of monasteries. Some, indeed, never adopted it, at least in our period, including Westminster and Battle; and Canterbury Cathedral Priory only did so in 1289. At the same time, other landowners were certainly pursuing a policy of centralized sales by the second half of the thirteenth century, including the Bishops of Winchester in the south and Isabella de Fortibus in Holderness.[99] On the Lacy estates in Yorkshire, too, the constable of Pontefract castle gathered up the wool from the manors and sold it in bulk for a sum which, in 1305, totalled £116.[100] The advantage to merchants over buying in penny packets wool of doubtful and varying quality is obvious enough.

After the revenues from grain and wool had been entered in the accounts, other proceeds of demesne husbandry were normally more miscellaneous and individually less important. The sale of a few livestock and poultry, and occasionally some dairy produce or cider or garden crops, might yield modest sums; and in the wooded regions timber and brushwood were apt to provide a welcome addition to income. In certain parts of the country, however, livestock other than sheep were managed in such a way that they, too, made a significant contribution to seignorial incomes. As might be expected some great landowners were horse-breeders, both to provide riding and pack animals for themselves and their retinues and to show a profit on the side. Down to about 1300 the Crown had a stud based on Hope and Castleton in Derbyshire; the Abbots of Welbeck and Basingwerk also had studs in the High Peak; and that of Thomas of Lancaster at High Duffield was stocked with 113 mares and 112 yearlings or older horses in 1322.[101] The Lancaster stud at Blansby Park, near Pickering in the North Riding, was a smaller affair, and its 40–50 horses were far outnumbered by the 1,300 deer for hunting in this same place.[102] None the less, these too were instances of enterprise on some scale, and produced their modicum of profit.

In general, however, cattle were commercially more important than horses if only because, apart from a market for dairy produce, oxen remained the principal draught animals in every part of England. Their replacement was therefore a necessary and continuous process and the production of oxen was almost certainly the major concern of the larger cattle farms. Here again, in some places, the management of cattle herds was placed on a centralized basis. The Earl of Warenne in 1274 had all the Sowerby cattle that were to be offered for sale sent down to Wakefield, where the central officers of his Yorkshire estate could check that they had been marked with the Earl's mark and sell them to his best advantage.[103] The 400 strong Bolton priory herd (it included 189 cows in 1297) was likewise under the control of a central stockman and so was the Earl of Lincoln's much larger herd in Blackburnshire.[104] The canons of Bolton valued their cows for the dairy produce they provided for the priory as well as for their calves; but the former object had no place in the Lacy management of their herds. If dairy produce was made it must have been part of the perquisites of the keepers of the twenty-nine vaccaries which were essentially breeding units. The revenue received by the chief stockman, who supervised this whole enterprise, came solely from the sale of animals: £90 for 4 bulls, 72 cows, 11 calves and 140 oxen in 1295–96 and in 1304–05, £173 for 5 bulls, 165 cows, 2 calves and 213 oxen. These are sums of the same order of magnitude as those the Earl's constable of Pontefract got for wool.

In the thirteenth century, therefore, the organization of agricultural production for sale on some considerable scale is a familiar part of the rural scene. It is a feature of the times that is documented most particularly by the greater estates, precisely because such estates were run by a professional managerial staff that kept records of its management. Professional management, too, may well have helped to raise levels of efficiency; but, to the extent that something like a maximization of seignorial incomes was achieved, even more was probably owed to the expansion of market opportunities, buoyant prices, and plentiful supplies of cheap labour. These advantages were equally enjoyed by smaller landowners, but evidence about how they profited from them is seldom forthcoming. Some may have consumed a higher proportion of their demesne produce than great men did, and to that extent gained less benefit from the rise of producer prices; while the fact that many of them were likely to have been more personally engaged in the day-to-day running of their estates than the magnate, with his large managerial staff, might tell in more than one direction. The efficient small landowner might be even more successful than his betters; but if he was inefficient or feckless or extravagant, disaster might come very rapidly. The fortunes of individual gentry families are therefore likely to have fluctuated wildly in the thirteenth-century circumstances, when prosperity had come to depend upon an agriculture efficient by the standards of the day, efficient management, and efficient marketing. The virtues Walter of Henley preached did not necessarily come naturally to a class bred originally for war and politics.

It seems certain, however, that some of them (like those men, often of this same class, who staffed the offices of great estates) were capable of embracing these virtues. Some we have already met, even if it is hardly possible to know them with any particular intimacy. Lionel de Bradenham, for example, managed Langenhoe in part for self-supply and in part he depended upon rents and seignorial profits to maintain his station, but he depended even more heavily on the revenue he earned from the sale of produce. Again, the Abington family accumulated capital enough to invest fairly steadily in additional parcels of land. The fact that in 1294 their demesne was valued at £22 and rents and other perquisites at only £6 suggests that a main source of their capital is likely to have been the sale of demesne produce (see p. 213). Henry de Bray, too, that pushing Northamptonshire new man, may have had an income in which rents and demesne profits were nearer parity; but at least he used a surprisingly large share of his income, up to 20–25 per cent on average, for investment even when expenditure on the purchase of land is excluded.[105] He can hardly be denied an access of the economic virtues, and if he started as a freeholder he was thriving into the gentry.

Businesslike qualities, then, even though they may have been far from universal, appeared more and more frequently in the management of estates; and even accountancy and auditing took on a new purpose. Beginning with the objective of seeing that officials did not cheat their lord, the financial officers of many estates extended their concern to enquiries about profitability. Such enquiries appeared as early as 1224 at Canterbury Cathedral Priory; and at Norwich Cathedral Priory they developed from calculations of the profit of a manor as a whole, already being made in the 1250s, to calculations of the profit of demesne production generally (including livestock), and ultimately to calculations of the profits of arable husbandry alone. In one form or another this practice was very widespread: in the thirteenth or first half of the fourteenth century it was adopted by St Albans and St Benet of Holme, Osney and Beaulieu Abbeys, the Bishops of Worcester and Norwich, the Lady of Clare and the Earl Marshal.[106] How scientifically the information was used is another matter, but at least some landlords could have given a precise answer to the question Robert Grosseteste thought must be asked: 'How well are my ploughs and stock doing?'.

The rising level of demesne production, the increasing volume of demesne product that was marketed, and in many instances an increasingly rational attitude to the management and conduct of husbandry on large estates are, then, central features of the thirteenth-century economy. These are matters not of praise or blame[107] but of fact. What may be of greater moment is the limits beyond which medieval estate owners did not go. Time and time again we encounter the primacy which consumer motives occupied in their minds. The move to direct management of manors in the generation around 1200 was probably an attempt by earners of fixed incomes to escape the consequences of severe inflation. It was eminently successful, since every aspect of the market for commodities and the labour market made for its success. It was a time when failure to make profits for the landowner of any substance was difficult.

As seignorial incomes expanded rapidly so did seignorial expenditure; indeed the propensity of landlords to live up to, and often beyond, their incomes was a feature of the age. We have already noted the Lucullan proportions of consumption by Henry de Lacy's household (see pp. 203–4), but compared with that of his son-in-law and successor, Thomas of Lancaster, 'the household of Henry Lacy was a model of economy and practical efficiency'.[108] The potential value of Thomas's estates was around £11,000 annually in the second decade of the fourteenth century. The sum he actually received after deductions for expenses and arrears is likely to have been significantly less than that, but his income was still considerably greater than that received by any of his peers. Yet Thomas's expenditure regularly exceeded his income, and examination of his accounts shows exactly why this should have been so. Both in 1313–14 and in 1318–19, the cost of running the households of the Earl and his Countess exceeded £7,500. Of this sum more than £5,000 was spent on food, drink and lighting; clothing for the Earl and his retinue cost nearly £1,080 in 1313–14 and the purchase and sustenance of horses a further £734. In the same year fees and rewards to servants and retainers totalled £624, not including those which were charged directly to the accounts of particular manors. In addition Thomas spent almost £2,000 on the erection of new buildings (of which £1,202 went towards the costs of constructing a castle at Melbourne in Derbyshire), not including the expenses of normal repairs and maintenance paid out of local receipts. The net result of such colossal expenditure was a substantial deficit, which in the short term could only be made good by borrowing and in the long term by intensified exploitation of the Lancaster estates.

To modern eyes it might appear a relatively simple task to make Lancaster's budget balance or even produce a surplus, perhaps by pruning the household and restraining its appetites, or by resisting the temptation to build new castles, but such an assumption would display an ignorance of the social, military and political pressures upon the nobility. Although Edward II drew attention to Lancaster's 'retainings. . . for unusual and excessive wages', the essential difference between the expenditure of the earl and that of his peers was quantitative rather than qualitative. The power and prestige of the nobility were to a large extent determined by the size of their retinues, the scale of their patronage, the magnificence of their households, and the number and strength of their castles. In an age when private as well as national and international wars and feuds were a frequent occurrence economy in these matters could easily prove false.

Nor were conspicuous consumption and indebtedness confined to great lay nobles. It was also normal for ecclesiastical institutions to live to the fullest extent of their incomes and where necessary to meet current expenses by borrowing. There was, after all, a close similarity between the households of barons and prelates. The households of most bishops included not only many ecclesiastical attendants and estate administrators, but squires, valets, servants, grooms, pages, foresters, huntsmen, and even soldiers, all drawing wages and livery as well as food and drink.[109] The standard of living enjoyed by most monks, too, whatever the original rule of their order might say, seems rarely to have sunk much below that enjoyed in the great lay households. In addition to ample supplies of good food and drink, they were liberally supplied with servants: in most monasteries more of them than monks.[110] In Edward I's reign over £1,400 was spent in a year on the sustenance of the eighty monks of Bury St Edmund's Abbey, their 111 servants, eleven chaplains, the nuns of Thetford and the guests of the house.[111] Again, we can be certain that the cost of building was a drain on the resources of many ecclesiastical institutions. True, the costs of construction were shared with countless benefactors, but the magnificence of surviving structures leaves no doubt as to the large sums that were invested in them. In the years 1278–80 over £1,500 was spent on the Abbey of Vale Royal in Cheshire, and between 1391 and 1394 Henry Chillenden, Prior of Christ Church Canterbury, spent well over £5,000 on building works, mainly in the cathedral.[112]

If household and building expenses can be viewed as 'ordinary', there were 'extraordinary' expenses in the form of royal and papal taxation and the costs stemming from litigation, fees and straightforward bribery. The scale of such charges is illustrated by the records of Canterbury Cathedral Priory in the late thirteenth century: between 1270 and 1280 £1,160 was paid in taxation; between 1270 and 1273 the election of a new prior cost over £1,000; and in 1293–94 over £1,300 was spent on the election of a new archbishop. In addition the priory was involved in extensive litigation in both England and Rome, the expenses of which could be met only by large loans from Italian merchants.[113] The death or resignation of the head of a religious house often provoked a severe financial crisis, for it might suffer exploitation of its estates by royal officials during the period of vacancy and the successor usually had to pay heavily to get his election ratified. In 1302 John Maryns, the newly elected Abbot of St Albans, spent £1,707 to obtain papal confirmation, and his successor, Hugh de Evresdone, had to spend over £1,000 for the same purpose.[114]

Even high and rising incomes did not necessarily provide adequate security in the face of such massive expenditure, and yet the indebtedness of most ecclesiastical institutions was chronic rather than acute. Impressive as the debts may appear when baldly listed,[115] they rarely exceeded one or two year's income and were invariably covered many times over by assets. The problem most houses faced was not impending bankruptcy but persistent shortage of cash, and few could resist the temptation to solve it by anticipating future revenues. Borrowing was one means by which this could be achieved, the sale of corrodies and the future yields of wool and grain were others. Even when, through profligacy or mismanagement, indebtedness reached critical proportions, a decade or so of modest frugality was often sufficient to restore financial equilibrium. It took Abbot Samson of Bury St Edmund's only the twelve years after 1183 to pay off debts in excess of £3,000; and Kirkstall Abbey, nearly £5,250 and fifty-nine sacks of wool in debt in 1284, and possessed of little more than 100 cattle, had got this debt down to £160 by 1301 and built up its livestock to over 600 head of cattle and 4,000 sheep.[116]

The expenditure of ecclesiastical establishments might be more easily pruned than that of lay lords, since that course did not necessarily lead to loss of prestige or political power; but even for churchmen parsimony was tolerated only in exceptional circumstances. Raised standards became an expectation. In this respect there is much to be learned from the more or less unique account book of Bolton Priory covering the period 1286–1320. Throughout that period the priory had a running debt, but down to 1315 this was very largely employed to assist in financing an expanding economy and the purchase of additional assets. With the famine years of 1315–17 and Scottish raids that did substantial damage to its property, however, the priory had to pay heavily for food supplies that would normally have come from its manors, and the expense of sustaining the community of the priory sharply increased. To preserve as far as possible customary standards of consumption cuts had to be made elsewhere: in expenditure on building and labour and gifts and alms and on estate running costs.[117]

This cautionary tale pinpoints one of the major limitations of economic development in the age of high-farming. Capital investment usually depended on a combination of exceptionally favourable circumstances; where those circumstances ceased to exist or were undermined investment was curtailed, sometimes to vanishing point; and even in good times calls for capital formation had to compete with a propensity for conspicuous consumption or even conspicuous waste. Capital investment is a matter as yet inadequately studied,[118] but everything suggests that the rate of saving of Henry de Bray was quite exceptional, not least among those whose resources were far larger than Henry's. On the basis of the work so far done, it would appear that most landlords invested 5 per cent or less of their gross revenues each year. Even Henry of Eastry's investment on the Canterbury Cathedral Priory estate may have averaged, when land purchases are excluded since they transfer rather than create capital, less than 5 per cent of the total cash returns from the priory manors. The rate of investment on the Peterborough Abbey and Winchester Cathedral estates appears likewise to have been of the order of 5 per cent. Adam of Stratton's investment at Sevenhampton in the reign of Edward I was a little higher at 6·5 per cent; but Crowland's investment at Wellingborough was less than 4 per cent, as was the rate of investment on the estates of St Swithin's priory at Winchester and Glastonbury Abbey. Lowest of all was the Earl of Cornwall's capital expenditure on the manors of his vast estate in 1297, which was only 1·5 per cent of his substantial revenues.

These figures are, without exception, far below the investment rates of modern business enterprises, but one may ask whether calculations based upon gross revenues are the best method of tackling the problem. The greater medieval landlords generally combined at least three main roles, those of agricultural producers, rentiers and dispensers of justice. If we distinguish between the revenues from each activity and the investment in each, a somewhat different picture emerges. In the first place, such investment as took place was principally directed towards demesnes and to only a very limited extent, often not at all, towards the improvement of tenant lands. If income from and investment in the demesnes is isolated from other income and investment, much higher rates are obtained. The most dramatic result of such a recalculation would occur on the estate of the Earl of Cornwall where very few demesnes were being cultivated, but on all estates the investment rate would rise sharply. If the calculation were to be based on demesne profits the rate would be higher still and possibly as high as was necessary in the light of the technical limitations of the age.[119] So far as the individual landlord was concerned, the purchase of additional land might frequently prove a more profitable course of action.

Where investment was undoubtedly deficient, however, was on peasant farms. It was on the tenant himself that the responsiblity for maintaining and improving his holding fell. That the peasantry contributed towards capital formation in the medieval centuries is undoubted, even if their contribution cannot be quantified. The fact that colonization was above all a small man's enterprise is the most striking illustration of the peasant's part in economic expansion, and it is likely that there were many among the richer free tenants and villeins who were capable of saving and investing at something of the same sort of rate as Henry de Bray. All the same, the picture grows increasingly unfavourable in many or most parts of the country as the thirteenth century passes into the fourteenth. The age of colonization was coming to a close, indeed in some places the arable frontier was beginning to retreat. The tendency was for the average amount of land per family among the peasantry to decrease and their charges were very often increasing. There was less and less chance of compensation from new land for the low rate of investment by landlords, a rate which may well have been further reduced by the catastrophes and difficulties of the time. This was in many respects the most serious flaw behind the flourishing façade of the high-farming great estate.

Rents in the high-farming era

The high-farming era, none the less, was the great age of the direct exploitation of their manors by medieval landlords. The lords of large estates, in particular, were encouraged in these circumstances to employ professional skill in managing their lands, at times to mobilize considerable capital resources, and to show a willingness to wait until investment yielded a return. They also disposed of ample reserves of labour and could concentrate commodities in sufficient quantities to attract the export merchant. They controlled transport facilities in the form of villein carrying services which helped them to seek out merchants and markets. Finally, they shared with others the favourable conditions created by population growth and inflation: low real wages and prices which were moving upwards. In these respects high-farming was the child of a very special environment.

At the same time landlords did not rely exclusively on demesne production for their incomes. In 1322–23 the Bishop of Ely was heavily engaged in agricultural enterprise in his manor of Great Shelford. Sales of produce accounted for £89 out of a total cash revenue of £115. A margin of £26 remained, however, derived from rents, payments for pasture, the farm paid by the lessee of the mill, the sale of 891 labour services, entry fines and the profits of the manorial courts. Three years later, moreover, rent income was increased by leasing 6 acres of demesne and an order was given to lease a further 36 acres in the following year 'in Hellifeld and Hungridole and Stoklode . . . because it is worth nothing to the lord and will profit him more if it is leased'.[120]

In some places the non-agricultural element in landlords' incomes during the thirteenth century was very small; it amounted, for example, only to £3 on Osney Abbey's manor at Water Eaton at a time when demesne returns were £112.[121] On the Winchester estates in 1208–09, on the other hand, two-thirds of the bishop's income came from rents, tallage, payments for pasture, and court profits (including entry fines). Here the situation was modified in the course of the thirteenth century by efforts to maximize agricultural revenues, but that was not the whole of the story. The volume of money rents increased fairly steadily between 1209 and 1348, entry fines yielded more as the demand for land intensified, and from the 1260s there was a growth in the proceeds of the sale of labour services. In fact the rentier element in the bishop's revenues increased by some 25 per cent during the century after 1258. Nor was this tendency in any way unusual. The Bishop of Ely's income from rents was significantly augmented in the second half of the thirteenth century and, even before 1250, the Abbots of Ramsey were as much concerned to add rent-paying tenements to their manors as they were to acquire tenements rendering labour services.

Kosminksy's studies of the data provided by the hundred rolls of 1279, in fact, put the trends of the high-farming age into perspective. In the area covered by these records over two-thirds of the land was in the hands of the peasantry rather than of landlords; and the predominant payment peasants made for their land took the form of money rents rather than labour services. This was true even of the villeins, for they paid, on average, more than half their dues in money.[122] Even these calculations almost certainly underestimate the rentier element in seignorial revenues, for the surveys on which they are based do not always provide adequate information about the profits lords drew from leasing mills and pasture, from entry fines or tallages, and from the sale of labour services. When these are taken into account the non-agricultural element in seignorial incomes usually bulks very large: the high-farming Bishops of Ely and Winchester were 60 per cent and 35 per cent rentiers respectively by the end of the thirteenth century; and the Earls of Cornwall by that time drew 90 per cent of their income from sources other than the exploitation of their demesnes.[123]

There is no single explanation of the growing rentier element in the revenues of landlords from the land. The category normally called assized rents – rents which, once established, tended to be fairly stable – might be enlarged in a variety of ways: through purchase of rented land, sometimes by the commutation of services into rents, and most commonly until at least well down the thirteenth century through colonization. Assarts provided the greater part of the additional income from *gabulum* received by the Bishops of Winchester down to about 1270: the profits of intakes from the woodlands at Witney and in the Thames valley manors, from the open downs in Wiltshire and Somerset, and from the wastes in Hampshire. For the same reason, on the Ely estates, rents increased most spectacularly in the Norfolk and Cambridgeshire marshland where fen was being reclaimed on a vast scale. In part, in other words, the growth of money rents reflected the expansion of settlement, which contributed far more to the enlargement of tenures than it did to the augmentation of demesnes.

Other means were found to expand the volume of rents, especially in the century after 1250. New types of rent contract were adopted (leases for a term or tenancies at will) which could be more easily revised to take account of the falling value of money or the rising demand for land. If these were applied at first mainly to mills, fisheries and pasturage they soon began to invade demesnes. The Winchester demesnes were already contracting by the 1270s; by 1300 there were small leaseholds in half a dozen of the Ely manors and most of the demesnes at Pulham and East Dereham were leased; and in 1295 the stewards of the Earls of Cornwall were ordered, if possible, to lease out the whole of Sundon and Glatton and the demesne park at Beckley.[124] As demesnes contracted, moreover, so did the area of villeinage required to service them. At Pulham and East Dereham villein holdings were turned into tenancies at will, and not much later some bondlands on the Tavistock estates were converted into leaseholds.[125] These tenures, compared with the older type of customary holdings for rent, were more precarious and their terms could be adjusted at longer or shorter intervals. Indeed, by the end of the thirteenth century a forty-year lease was considered an abuse, since 'continuance of seisin and lapse of time' might easily convert a temporary bargain into a contract hallowed and made immutable by custom.[126]

In a less definitive way (at least in principle) the 'sale' of labour services also contributed to the growth of rent incomes. The Bishop of Winchester received £248 from this source in 1348, ten times the sum of one hundred years before; one-third of the labour service due on the Bishop of Ely's manors in 1299 were sold; and on the Ramsey estates after 1293 the sale of services has been called a 'systematic project'.[127] Nor was this the end, for quasi-rents added to the burden of rents properly so-called. Tallages on some estates became an annual impost of no small weight. On the Prior of Ely's manor at Sutton they represented an average surcharge on rents of 2s per head; and in 1350, on the Abbot of Tavistock's manor at Werrington, they added £20 to a rent roll of £35.[128] Entry fines to take over customary tenements also reached levels which were almost impossibly high in places where the shortage of land was particularly acute. These supplementary payments not only added to the burdens of tenants: they expanded that part of their lord's revenues which had nothing to do with high-farming.

Indeed, by the early years of the fourteenth century, there are signs of a change of emphasis in the English countryside. During most of the thirteenth century the incomes of landlords from rents and from agricultural profits seem to have expanded concurrently on most estates, but at some point before or after 1300 this ceased to be true. On the Ramsey estates the period from the 1290s onwards has been described as one of 'retrenchment and organized stability';[129] and on many others a decline in demesne cultivation became much more marked about this time. Between 1297 and 1347 nearly 2,000 acres were lopped from the acreage sown with grain on the Winchester demesnes; on six Ely manors alone over 1,000 acres of demesne were leased during the same period; and between 1320 and 1345 income from demesne leases on the great manor of Wisbech Barton increased from £3 to £48. This was also a time when demesnes were contracting on the English manors of the Abbey of Bec; when the Abbot of Tavistock was leasing in whole or in part the demesnes of his outlying manors, a practice he proposed to extend to some of the central manors in 1339; and when Henry de Lacy's successors as lords of Clitheroe were handing over to lessees the Lancashire vaccaries which Henry had exploited as a veritable cattle ranch. Just slightly later, too, the attempts to expand the demesnes of the Clare, Bohun and Beauchamp estates came to an end.[130] The year 1325 very roughly marks the point in time when these secular lords changed their direction and their policies.

There were other signs of the times as well as the physical contraction of demesnes. On the Ramsey estates labour seems to have been used less intensively and a greater proportion of demesne produce was directed towards the abbey's own consumption rather than to the market. Household supply also appears to have been the main objective of demesne agriculture in the bailiwick of Clare at this time, and on the Ely estates investment in the capital equipment of manors was cut back. Furthermore, the retreat of demesne farming encouraged still further the sale of surplus labour services and, at least on some estates, their definitive commutation. At the latest by the second quarter of the fourteenth century, and sometimes even earlier, the days of endeavour to maximize the returns from demesne agriculture seem to be passing away.

To put the matter so may in some places be to put it too strongly, but the modification of manorial revenues is still clear in the account rolls. The Duchy of Lancaster manor at Soham (Cambs) was still an active agricultural enterprise in 1342–43. The sale of grain and stock that year produced an income of about £61; but the details of rents are interesting. The assized rents, which may be taken to be for the most part the traditional peasant renders, totalled just short of £30. Added to these were 'farms', leases of one sort or another. Not all were of land: some were of fisheries; half the market (presumably the tolls therefrom) at Fordham was 'farmed'; and under this head men paid to have their own sheepfolds or *pro communa habenda* (for having common rights). Certain tenements, customary land and other plots of land were likewise 'farmed' and so was land in divers fields for £16 yearly out of a total of nearly £22 from farms. Much of this sum gives an impression of relative novelty compared with the assized rents, and the same may be true of labour services sold for over £3. The rentier trend is there at Soham.[131]

One task remains: to draw up some sort of balance sheet of the age of high-farming. From the start, of course, landlords had a measure of choice between different ways of realizing the potentialities inherent in their properties. On the one hand they could seize the opportunities presented by expanding markets and rising prices by intensifying demesne production; on the other, they could take advantage of the rising demand for land created by a growing population and reflected in a rising level of rents, entry fines and fines for leases. In fact, during the thirteenth century, most landlords had the best of both worlds and exploited both avenues of opportunity. At the same time, the adoption of a high-farming policy was not everywhere straightforward. Sometimes it was not easy to reconstitute manors which had disintegrated during the twelfth century. Sometimes formidable traditions of peasant freedom set barriers to a lord's liberty of action, a circumstance which may help to explain why the expansion of the new revenues of the lordship of Canterbury during the thirteenth century was less than dramatic.[132] High management or production costs may also have been a disincentive to cultivation,[133] and the problems of efficient administration must have been particularly acute on very large and scattered estates. The fact that the Earl of Cornwall's manors stretched from Yorkshire to remotest Cornwall may well have played its part in making him mainly a rentier by 1296.

Somewhat paradoxically, the most effective force of all pushing landlords in a rentier direction was the continued growth of population. It created demands for land that pushed up the level of rents and therefore the attractions of being a rentier; at the same time it provided the dynamic for what was essentially the peasant enterprise of colonization. It was for this good reason that the main colonizing areas like the Lincolnshire fens or the Arden and Wealden forests were regions of rent-paying tenants. Even in the old-settled parts of the country, however, the insistent demand of more people for land surrounded the core of demesne and villeinage with a periphery of *censuarii* seated on intakes from waste and wood and common. The growth of money rent was not an alternative to high farming but an accompaniment of it, to the extent that by 1279 money was the predominant return which the peasantry made for land.

To stress the expansion of rents in the high-farming era in no way denies the reality of the 'manorial reaction' which took place in the generations around 1200, or of the contribution made by landlords to the expansion of agricultural production during the thirteenth century. The decision which many of them took during that century to maximize the yield of their demesnes may have owed something to the traditions of great ecclesiastical estates, used from time immemorial to regarding their demesnes as the source of large-scale supply for episcopal or monastic 'families'. It was not all that difficult to shift some part of that supply into new and expanding commercial channels. At the same time the growth of a more or less professional class of estate agents facilitated a more systematic exploitation of seignorial properties. The willingness of lords to pursue this course, however, was also conditioned by the fact that the trend of prices made commercial agriculture profitable, all the more so because circumstances conspired to depress the large element represented by labour costs in the total cost of agricultural production. Many lords could rely on substantial labour services to fulfil their needs at the peak periods of the farming year; but the growth of population created reserves of 'free' labour competing for jobs and driving down the levels of real wages. This alternative supply of labour was large enough to permit some labour services to be dispensed with as the thirteenth century progressed, either through *ad hoc* 'sales' of services or by definitive commutation. In this way another element was added to the rent income which, along with demesne profits and seignorial perquisites, made up the revenues of medieval landlords.

All the same, there was a certain balance between rents and demesne profits in the high-farming age, but at various points in time from the second half of the thirteenth century onwards there are signs that this balance was being upset. Demesne land, by choice or by necessity, began to be abandoned; in consequence, some villein services became surplus to requirements, while others might be relinquished in favour of paid workers; and the tendency was for the scale of seignorial activity to narrow down. The obverse of these trends were indications that some landlords were showing up a positive 'preference for rents'. The Earl of Cornwall appears to be doing so in 1296 and so does the Bishop of Worcester in 1312. He instructed his steward to 'increase the rents of our manors' by reclaiming and letting waste, by leasing demesne arable and pastures and meadows remote from manorial centres, and by remitting the services due from villein holdings which were to be 'set at an annual rent at their true value'.[134] A 'preference for rents' could hardly be more explicit, even though it was by no means total.

These trends, already evident before 1300, continued afterwards. In the generation before the Black Death demesnes were still contracting, villein services were still being 'sold', and villein tenures were still being turned into copyhold or leasehold. They did not yet constitute a wholesale process. Demesne production was preserved by forces of inertia, by the call of seignorial households for supplies, and perhaps by a feeling that some of the difficulties landlords faced need not necessarily endure for ever. The nature of these difficulties will be a matter for enquiry in the last chapter of this book; but for the present there is one final observation to be made. When the English countryside came to face the demographic crisis of the half century after 1349 the landlord's situation was deeply affected by what had happened in the age of high-farming. Their demesne profits were undermined by the eventual contraction of markets and downward drift of prices, all the more because long before 1349 demesne production had come to rely heavily upon wage labour. Recurrent plague made labour scarce and dear, large-scale enterprise became virtually impracticable. At the same time, during the generations when population had been increasing, the peasant's demand for land and the price he would pay for it had already habituated some lords in some places to display a preference for rents over the tribulations of direct exploitation. In that habit they continued after 1349, but with this difference: before that date landlords had been able to compel the peasantry to pay dearly for their land; after it the bargaining positions were all but reversed.

Chapter 9

King Edward's England

When, after a series of melodramatic events, the young Edward III was put in the place of his father in January 1327, economic as well as political troubles lay in the background of the succession crisis. There had been famines in the previous decade; there had been disastrous attacks of livestock diseases; and landowners, or at least some of them, were restricting the scale of their entrepreneurial activity and the rate of their investment in maintenance and improvements. Nor were troubles confined to the agrarian sector. The wool trade, England's greatest trade, which had reached its highest level in the first decade of the new century, had subsequently suffered extreme vicissitudes mainly through government intervention aimed at political or diplomatic advantage. In towns, too, there were many signs of underemployment and the constitutional crisis of 1326–27 was accompanied and preceded by urban social movements indicating an underlying malaise in various places. One chronicler of the times was filled with despair: 'Alas, poor England! You, who once helped other lands from your abundance, now poor and needy are forced to beg.'[1]

The long-term significance to be attributed to the tendencies evident as the second quarter of the fourteenth century opened is not easily determined. In a sense what happened in those years, catastrophic as events appeared to contemporaries, was overtaken by later events more catastrophic still, which lingered longer in popular memory and have been correspondingly more influential in shaping the views of historians. Of these the most important by far was the coming of plague in 1348. At the same time even the fullest appreciation of the immediate and longer-term consequences of the Black Death does not necessarily mean that we must discount the effects of circumstances a generation and more earlier. True, there had been famines and harvest failures before 1315–17, and the dearth of 1258 provoked lamentations as eloquent as those of Edward II's biographer from the chroniclers of that time. There had also been earlier outbreaks of disease amongst livestock like the 'common mortality' that afflicted the sheep flocks of Holderness in the 1280s. King John, too, had manipulated the wool trade before Edward I did so and the social conflicts in London in 1263–65 had been not dissimilar in intensity to those of 1326–27.[2] None the less, certain basic changes in the English economy do appear to be taking place in the generation around 1300 and to have generated something like a new economic balance in the two or three decades before 1348. These changes and that balance are the proper conclusion of this study of the central Middle Ages.

Land and people

Many influences governed the economic developments of the twelfth and thirteenth centuries, but it has been a central argument of this book that the growth of population occupied a key place in the successive transformations which turned King William's England into the England which faced the famines of the early fourteenth century. No one writing in the midst of the great drought of 1976 will be inclined to underrate the disastrous effects that exceptional and 'accidental' weather conditions can have; and in an underdeveloped society those effects were obviously far more severe than in a society equipped with modern resources and techniques, and with access to world markets. There are, however, many indications that the multiplication of people, a constant theme in English history from a time well before 1066 to around 1300, was by the latter date creating basic structural problems. These problems, as we have seen, had numerous manifestations. High (and rising) charges were paid for holdings which were often too small to sustain a family; in many cases cultivation had spread to poor and intractable soils; in some places grain-growing had expanded excessively at the expense of stock-farming; on the whole attempts to increase crop yields had failed and it seems probable that, even on demesnes, they had sometimes declined; and rising prices, sluggish wages and the difficulty of finding work made the rewards of labour low. In the last resort the mortalities that accompanied dearths, and above all the mortalities of 1315–17, were the measure of this increasingly unfavourable balance of land and people.

At the same time the consequences which flowed from changes in this balance were sometimes contradictory and sometimes differed at different points in time. If we start at the beginning, King William's England was already dominated by landowning classes relying principally on the rents and labour of the dependent peasantry to provide them with income and produce. For the ensuing three or four generations these landowning classes were able, for the most part, to support or even improve their exalted life by a mainly passive exercise of their rights and powers. They managed their manors indirectly through lessees; they even let some demesne lands go and, with them, some of the labour services that had been needed for their cultivation. They were, in other words, for the most part rentiers in an old style inherited from the Saxon past. It was their good fortune that the apparently steady growth of population and settlement in varying measure expanded their incomes by augmenting the acres of land and numbers of men subjected to their lordship.

The great inflation of the years around 1200 and the subsequent steady, if less rampant, inflationary trend upset this balance. Cash incomes from rents and from leases were held down by custom or contract and, at least in the short run, fell rapidly in real value under the impact of inflation. To escape the erosion of their incomes landowners were pushed into becoming entrepreneurs, making the thirteenth century the great age of direct demesne exploitation. Demesne land relinquished in the twelfth century was taken back into hand and sometimes new land was added to it; and labour on a large scale was mobilized to cultivate the lands of lords. *Famuli* and casual labourers in the employ of landlords also multiplied; at the same time obligations from which villeins had been released were often reimposed and the servile implications of villeinage were more stringently defined.

This 'manorial reaction' took place in circumstances in which the tide was running for landlords: against a background of rising producer prices, expanding markets at home and abroad, and a continuing growth of population. About prices enough has been said in an earlier chapter; but for a proper understanding of the thirteenth-century agrarian situation the importance of increased outlets for agricultural products both in growing towns at home and in markets overseas can hardly be overstressed. No reader of manorial account rolls, when they begin to be available to us in that century, can fail to note the large contribution made by grain sales (mainly in home markets) and wool sales (mainly for export) in the structure of seignorial revenues. In this sense commerce was not so much a solvent of manorialism and serfdom in this period as it has sometimes been thought to be: it encouraged an expansion of demesne production and the intensification of servile obligations on which, in part, demesne production depended.

The gains that accrued from commerce, however, are not the only lesson the account rolls teach. The abundant supply of labour, whether that of villeins willing to accept the onerous services incident on their holdings or that of wage workers receiving payments which tended to fall in real terms, is a pointer to a population continuing to grow at a rate which increasingly outstripped the gains of colonization. At the same time the gains of colonization and desperate competition for land pushed up the income lords could expect from rents and other charges.

This feature of the landlord's boom of the thirteenth century offered an alternative to the way of entrepreneurship into which the great inflation had pushed so many lords of manors. At the very least they were encouraged to discard less productive demesne land and to cease to cultivate distant manors that were difficult to manage effectively. In the process the peasant's share of the marginal soils that had increasingly been brought into cultivation was probably unduly magnified as wornout demesne acres were added to marginal peasant assarts.

Increasing mortality in the villages was merely one aspect of the economic problems which reached an acute stage as the thirteenth century closed and the fourteenth century opened. Peasant impoverishment implied a low level of domestic purchasing power, for most Englishmen were peasant villagers; and that, in turn, cramped the continued potentialities for expansion in the urban sectors of the economy. The England of 1300, moreover, had few manufactured exports, and the fact that export outlets were repeatedly interrupted by war and political interference had the effect of further undermining the expanding markets on which the earlier phases of the landlord's boom had depended. In these circumstances landowners were less assured that enterprise would be profitable, with the result that the temptation to surrender to the clamour of wouldbe tenants became more compelling. Especially on less profitable manors or manors presenting management difficulties some lords by the opening of the fourteenth century were displaying a more and more positive 'preference for rents'. The attraction of this policy was that, given the intensity of the demand for land, the rental value of land might be high.

Adjustment in the villages

Such demographic data as exist for the late thirteenth and early fourteenth centuries has not yet been systematically investigated; but from a sample of Winchester manors we have evidence of mortality rates which may perhaps be regarded as symptomatic, though not necessarily as typical. The numbers of heriot payers in the famine years of 1315–17 averaged 142 annually compared with 95 in the three years of above average death rates in the previous decade and 48 in the worst years of the late 1270s. These figures, of course, appear low when set against a death toll of 1,429 in the same manors in 1349, topping 200 at Waltham alone or Wargrave alone and at Taunton exceeding 700;[3] but that does not make the mortality of 1315–17 insignificant. The famines of these years were an episode in an era of high mortality that persisted until the Black Death raised it to heights beyond all precedent. The precise significance of the trends in mortality evident on these Winchester manors can only be judged from indirect indicators, but it seems probable the long upward movement of the national population curve was first checked and then reversed. It looks as though the increased death rate may have reduced, however marginally, the intensity of consumer demand, and done something to damp down both competition for land and competition for employment by stabilizing or thinning the number of competitors. It was by no means the only influence at work, but, in the establishment of a new equilibrium in the thirty years or so before the 'great pestilence' came, the modified ratio of men to land was of prime significance.

The responses of landlords to the new cirumstances were very varied, but in general their watchwords were retrenchment, endeavours at cost cutting and the concentration of demesne enterprise where it would yield the best returns. Those of them who cultivated their demesnes directly faced from the 1320s onwards a tendency for most producer prices to fall and for real wages to rise somewhat above the miserable levels that had prevailed before 1315. On the other hand the demand for land among the peasantry, although less undiscriminating than it had been a generation before, was still keen enough to maintain, nearly maintain or occasionally increase the price at which it could be let. In these circumstances there was every encouragement for the prudent landlord to divest himself of his less productive demesnes, so that the contraction of seignorial enterprise continued and was even speeded up in the second quarter of the fourteenth century. The Bishops of Winchester reduced their demesne acreage by a further 17 per cent in the period 1325–49. By 1349 not far short of 5,000 acres had been shed by the bishop's home farms over a period of some eighty years.[4]

The contraction or abandonment of demesne production mitigated for landlords the effects of rising labour costs; and by concentrating cultivation on the better land or by increasing the acreage under legumes they might also be rewarded by a modest improvement of yields. The principal recourse of landowners in this period, however, may have been a new flexibility, a willingness to shift their responses to circumstances, showing how well they had learned to gauge the market for commodities and the market for land. They not only let land go when its cultivation seemed unprofitable: they switched their options as the probable advantage changed or appeared to change, or sometimes as financial necessity dictated. In 1330 a need for cash forced the Abbot of Ramsey to lease two of his wealthiest manors, but in the 1340s an improvement in the prospect of profits caused land to be drawn back into demesne on some manors and more intensive cultivation to be resumed.[5] On the Titchfield Priory manors, while a reduced arable demesne was kept in good heart by the application of marl, manure and seaweed, the sheep flock was built up again after disastrous losses in 1315–17; and at Langenhoe in Essex Lionel de Bradenham adjusted his grain crops both to the quality of his land and the state of the market. At the same time Lionel increased his income from rents by substituting new leases for old customary contracts: like most lords of manors he was by no means solely an entrepreneur.[6]

Seignorial estates faced many problems in the post-famine decades. By and large the cost of labour and the profits of cultivation had turned somewhat against them; and the charge of rebuilding flocks and herds, to say nothing of plough teams, decimated by disease forced many to discriminate between investment that could be undertaken or that might be postponed. On the other hand, there are signs of a new equilibrium being achieved by the 1330s and 1340s even if, as on the Ramsey estates, 'the attraction which agrarian production held for the convent was now restricted to even fewer manors, and to still less demesne land on these manors, than in the first decade of the century'.[7] The new balance achieved through retrenchment, however, also depended in a measure on the continued demand of the peasantry for land – both established tenant holdings and relinquished demesne acres – and their willingness to pay for it. This is an area in which there are many seeming contradictions, although here once again there are some signs that a new balance was being struck.

The evidence that some land was lapsing from cultivation altogether, or at least from arable cultivation, has already been discussed, and also the unwillingness of tenants except under compulsion to take up land of poorer quality. These features of the land market, together with the tendency of prices to drift downwards and wages upwards, may reflect a less intense demand from a population reduced, or at the very least stabilized, by rising levels of mortality. At the same time, this summary of the situation and the influences which shaped it are in certain respects inadequate. There are clear signs in some places of a very active peasant land market;[8] and on the whole one gets the impression (and until further research is undertaken it can be little more than an impression) that rent levels were reasonably well maintained, although some other customary charges may have been mitigated. Indeed, as we have seen, the Langenhoe tenants were even willing to accept higher leasehold rents in place of their old customary renders. In some parts of the country, too, continued pressure on resources is suggested by continued assarting.

The seeming contradiction between abandoned tenements and an active peasant market for land can, in the light of our present knowledge, only be resolved by hypothesis. We have already suggested that one explanation may be that the peasantry were now better placed to show discrimination between better and worse land. In some districts, this capacity to choose, may have owed something to the readier availability of alternative earnings from textile manufacture, mining and the like. Perhaps, too, the improvement of real agricultural wages made life as a labourer more acceptable to some, thus relieving pressure on the land. Most important of all may have been the not inconsiderable amount of land of which lords divested themselves. Admittedly not all the land discarded by lords was taken up by tenants, but a very large part of it was: for, even if it was not the best land, it might well be acceptable to peasants who were insulated from some of the rising costs (especially for labour) which demesne cultivation entailed. Admittedly, too, the letting out of demesne land was not something new in the second quarter of the fourteenth century; but now it was taking place after the prolonged upward movement of population had been checked or even reversed. For that reason putting demesne land on the market is likely to have represented a net addition to the resources available to the peasantry and to have modified the element of desperation that appears to attend the search for land of the late thirteenth-century peasant.

The process of adaptation to new circumstances, of course, was an imperfect one. Lords did not easily, after so many generations when conditions had been consistently in their favour, take easily to a situation in which they were favourable no longer. On the Winchester estates net profits which had fluctuated between £3,050 and £5,350 in the years 1221–83 were down to the £3,700 to £3,800 bracket in the years 1335–44.[9] The achievement of this much stability of income represented a not unsuccessful adjustment to new conditions, but others may have been less fortunate or less skilful. The religious houses in Bishop Grandisson's diocese of Exeter in 1338, for example, appear almost uniformly beset by difficulties.[10] While landlords found that the days of easy profits were over, the fact that the peasantry were still vulnerable to influences beyond their control is demonstrated by the impact on their fortunes and the viability of some of their holdings of Edward III's measures to finance his war with France (see p. 151). The new equilibrium, moreover, might have proved temporary. The check to population growth might conceivably have been impermanent, like the consequences of the mortality caused by the famine in 1258. In the event this did not happen, so that the long-term growth of population was not resumed; and the influence that would have had on the somewhat more equitable distribution of land that underlay the new equilibrium was never put to the test. Instead, the second quarter of the century closed with the coming of the 'great pestilence' involving mortality of a different order to that occasioned by any preceding catastrophe. In its wake there was no question either of preserving intact the economic pattern coming into being after 1325 or of returning to that prevailing before 1315.

Manufacturers and traders

Adjustment to new circumstances in the decades before the Black Death was not restricted to villages: in some ways the tentative and faltering changes that were taking place in other sectors of the economy were even more significant. These changes have been even less adequately explored than the short-term movements in the rural economy, but in one or two areas their direction appears clear enough. This is most obviously true of the manufacture of textiles.[11] The English industry, and in particular its urban branch, had been progressively undermined during the thirteenth century by Flemish competition both in the foreign markets it had been serving in 1200 and in the English home market itself. By the opening of the fourteenth century, however, the tide was turning and, in East Anglia, the south and south-west, and the West Riding, a mainly country industry was producing relatively cheap kerseys and worsteds and aylshams and mendips on an increasing scale. At the same time the revival did not stop in the villages or villages growing into little country towns. It also touched Norwich and Colchester, Salisbury and Winchester, Beverley and York; and it was in no small measure due to the growth of its cloth industry that Coventry in 1362 was in a position to bear the cost of building its 'formidable town wall'.[12] By this time, moreover, revival had extended to the manufacture of broadcloths as well as cheaper fabrics; furthermore, imports of foreign textiles were down and English cloth had captured both a large part of the home market and new markets overseas. In the 1350s England imported only about half the 12,000 cloths imported by foreign merchants alone at the beginning of the century (the proportion had been even lower in the late 1330s when war made trading hazardous); and on the eve of the Black Death exports of broadcloths and worsteds combined amounted to the equivalent of 5,000–6,000 cloths a year.[13] Industrial growth since the opening of the century was already significant even if it was not yet spectacular.

The extent to which similar development was present in other fields of industry is harder to determine and more difficult to measure. There are some indications of increased activity in the coal-mining region along the Tyne: for coal was exported to Pontoise in 1325 and to provision Scottish castles in 1338; Tynemouth Priory was opening new collieries at Elswick in 1330 and 1334; and in 1356 the Bishop of Durham leased out five mines at Wickham for £333. 6s8d a year. True this figure is quite unusual: the £2–£5 yearly for leases of the Elswick mines is far more typical; but coal, too, was appearing on the industrial horizon.[14] About tin-mining we are better informed. Production in Cornwall had begun to increase at the opening of the century and had almost reached a million pounds annually by 1323–24. Thereafter there was 'a burst of exceptional expansion' and output in 1331–32 reached the unprecedented level of 1,643,000 lb.[15] Once again new opportunities were being grasped in the pre-plague generation.

Whether or not the same was true in the 'typical' industries of the time – the handicrafts that served the ordinary and everyday needs of Englishmen – is far more difficult to determine and certainly must await closer study than has yet been undertaken of short-term movements in the prosperity of English towns. The upward trend in the number of freemen admitted at Colchester in the 1330s and 1340s and at York in the period 1307–49 is possibly significant in this connection; but the records of admissions to town franchises were governed by rules that are ill-known and by changes in qualification that make them a dangerous guide.[16] At best the data drawn from them indicate that, at least in some towns, a recovery or modest advance of fortunes is not out of the question.

If the bread-and-butter industries directed towards the domestic market are in large measure unknowable, so for the most part is the course of domestic trade. On the other hand, the customs accounts enable us to follow in somewhat more detail the fortunes of some branches of overseas trade.[17] The clearest indications relate to the wool trade: the total volume of exports fell away (as did the corresponding import of manufactured textiles) from the medieval peak of over 41,000 sacks annually in the years 1304–09 to around 24,000 sacks in the years 1333–42. Secondly, the share of English merchants in this trade, which may already have increased substantially over the previous thirty years, increased from around 55 per cent in the early years of the century to around 65 per cent in the 1330s. It looks as though the export boom with which the century opened was English-led and that, in the subsequent shrinkage of wool exports, English merchants retained a much larger share than foreign interests. Other branches of trade display a certain consistency with these trends. In the new export trade in English cloth English merchants shipped four-fifths or more of the textiles exported; and English gains in the Bordeaux wine trade matched gains in the wool trade. Wine imports appear to have been remarkably stable down to the opening of the Hundred Years War, but at the beginning of the fourteenth century Gascon importers handled at least two-thirds of the

20,000 tuns or so coming in each year. By the mid-1320s, on the other hand, Gascon imports had been halved and the trade was now preponderantly in denizen hands. In 1330 the King's Butler's view was that Englishmen were importing as much in one year as the Gascons did in two.

The new economic equilibrium of the 1330s and 1340s, then, is not something confined to the countryside: there are also signs that a change in the structure of the medieval economy was taking place. In the first place a measure of industrial development both in town and country was diversifying, however modestly, the employment opportunities available. Secondly, in a country in which external commerce had been dominated by the foreign merchant, denizens were assuming the dominant role and, in the process, generating resources of commercial capital of a new magnitude. Indeed, in order to finance the French war in the 1340s, Edward III, after he had ruined his foreign merchant-bankers, turned to Englishmen for banking services for the provision of which the monarchy had relied upon Italians since the time of Edward I. The English wool merchants and others who responded got little joy from their new role, but the economic changes of the previous generation had done much to make it possible for them to assume it.

Conclusion

A full account of the industrial and commercial developments in the pre-plague decades belongs to a second volume of this work in which their background can be fully sketched. At the same time, those developments are explicable in part by reference to the rural society with which the present volume has been principally concerned. In one sense, that context appears unpromising. Viewed from the demesnes of landlords, the dominant impression is one of contraction and retrenchment; and, in a countryside in which cultivation had been expanding over so many generations, even in colonizing areas the scale of reclamation was slowing down and some marginal settlements had already become lost villages by the opening of the fourteenth century.[18]

Paradoxically, however, the overcrowding of villages and even the poverty of villagers may have contributed to new economic developments. The poverty of villagers first created a market for 'slump' products like worsteds and other cheaper fabrics, often country-made, the manufacture of which initiated the revival of the textile industry. True, the subsequent expansion of this industry, and of the commercial stake of English merchants in it, may have owed even more to the opening of new export opportunities and a measure of improvement in the purchasing power of which ordinary Englishmen disposed by the second quarter of the fourteenth century; but the growth of cloth manufacture, and of mining and other country crafts, was also largely made possible by the reserves of cheap labour available in so many villages. When, in the generation preceding the Black Death, village populations had ceased to grow the country labourer may even have had a genuine degree of choice in some places between industrial and agricultural employment. If that were so, it would help to explain the tendency for agricultural wages to rise at this time;[19] and the complaint of the bailiffs of the Winchester manors in 1332, for all the reduction of demesne acreages, that reapers, mowers and harvest workers were in short supply seems to suggest that the wheel had come at least part circle.[20]

In this context, one is also bound to ask what the effects may have been of some improvement of the real wages earned by labourers and some shift of productive assets to the peasantry. In this area there is no possibility of measuring or calculating; but in principle the effect must have been to increase the purchasing power available in the rural mass market. The development of rural industry, by diversifying country-men's sources of earnings, would have the same effect. These influences are likely to have been marginal, and they were probably offset at least in part by Edward III's taxes; but they are a possible explanation of some signs of urban recovery in the decades before 1348, and they may have done something to encourage a growth of manufacture and mining.

The plague, however, was a radical break in what otherwise might have been an evolutionary trend; yet in one sense it did not basically alter certain of the directions of economic change established in the second quarter of the fourteenth century. For landlords there was no longer any question of reviving demesne production on the thirteenth-century scale: on the contrary they were forced to retreat even from the positions to which they had withdrawn in the pre-plague generation. Plague mortality, on the other hand, raised once more the wages of labourers and increased still further the availability of land to tenants, augmenting yet again the purchasing power of the mass market. This redistribution of wealth, in turn, is likely to have been one influence making for a relative advance in the share of manufacturing industry in total economic activity; and, at the same time, English merchants retained a great part of their increased share of English trade won in the years preceding 1349. In brief, the economy of the later Middle Ages developed on the more diversified foundations which were being established during the pre-plague generation. Those foundations, moreover, were more soundly laid than the bases of the older medieval economy that made its failings manifest in the famines and mortalities at the opening of the fourteenth century.

Notes and references

(Publication details of books cited in the notes are given in the Bibliography.)

Introduction

1. Ohlin, 'No safety in numbers: some pitfalls of historical statistics', *Essays in Quantitative Economic History*, ed. Floud, pp. 64–6; Postan and Titow, 'Heriots and prices in Winchester manors', *Econ. H.R.*, 2nd ser., **11** (1958–9), 394–6, 414–15. By contrast, according to the *United Nations Year Book,* in 1951 the life expectancy of English males at birth was 65·8 years, at twenty = 49·1 years and at thirty = 39·7 years.
2. Powicke, *Henry III and the Lord Edward*, ii, 686.
3. Hilton, *A Medieval Society: the West Midlands at the end of the thirteenth century*, pp. 248–61; and for levels of violence in medieval society see also Bellamy, *Crime and Public Order in the Late Middle Ages*, pp. 1–36.
4. Stubbs, *Select Charters*, pp. 466–7.
5. Hilton, *op. cit*, 250.
6. Hurnard, *The King's Pardon for Homicide before A.D. 1307*, pp. 247–50.
7. *Gesta Stephani*, pp. 101–2; *Chronica Rogeri de Houedene.*
8. Bishop, 'The Norman settlement of Yorkshire', in *Essays in Economic History*, ed. Carus-Wilson, ii, 1–11; J. Scammell, 'Robert I and the North of England', *E.H.R.* **74**, (1958), 385–403.
9. Maitland, *Domesday Book and Beyond*, p. 170.
10. Together perhaps with wisdom in counselling his lord: Painter, *William Marshal*, pp. 284–5.
11. *Northumberland County History*, i, 124.
12. *English Historical Documents, c. 500–1042*, pp. 853–4.
13. *Anglo-Norman Political Songs*, pp. 118–19.
14. Bartholomaeus Anglicus, *De Proprietatibus Rerum*, Bk. vi, ch. 12.
15. Titow, *English Rural Society, 1200–1350*, p. 93; Postan, *The Medieval Economy and Society*, p. 38.
16. Russell, 'The pre-plague population of England', *Journal of British Studies*, **5** (1966), 1; Hallam, 'The Postan thesis', *Historical Studies*, **15** (1972), 222.

Chapter 1. King William's England

1. H. R. Loyn in the preceding volume of this series, *Anglo-Saxon England and the Norman Conquest*, deals much more fully with the evidence of Domesday both for the period before and immediately following 1066.
2. *The Charters of the Borough of Cambridge*, p. 2; *D.B.*, i, 298b, 337.
3. Lennard, *Rural England, 1086–1135*, ch. 1.
4. For what follows see generally the five regional volumes of the *Domesday Geography* by H. C. Darby and his colleagues.
5. Hallam, *Settlement and Society,* p. 7; Darby, *Medieval Fenland,* p. 18.
6. Harley, 'Population trends and agricultural developments from the Warwickshire Hundred Rolls', *Econ. H.R.*, 2nd ser., **11**, (1958), 8–12.
7. The Wiltshire geld roll, quoted *Domesday Geography of South-East England*, p. 337.

8. Bishop, 'The Norman settlement of Yorkshire', *Essays in Economic History*, ed. Carus-Wilson, ii, 1–11

9. *V.C.H. Durham*, ii, 179.

10. See M. M. Postan's observations in *Cambridge Econ. Hist.*, i, 560–63 (2nd edn.), prompted by the estimates contained in Russell, *British Medieval Population*, pp. 34–54.

11. Regarding the differences between east and west, which are 'visible to the natural eye', Maitland's discussion is still central: *Domesday Book and Beyond*, pp. 15–22.

12. *D.B.*, i, 184b.

13. Hoskins, *Devon*, pp. 48–50.

14. The totals are those provided by the *Domesday Geography* volumes for east and south-west England.

15. Trow-Smith, *History of British Livestock Husbandry*, pp. 79–80.

16. *Ibid*, 73–4.

17. *Ibid*, 73, 75–6; *The Kalendar of Abbot Samson of Bury St Edmunds*, pp. 157–8.

18. Tait (*Medieval English Borough*, p. 69) points out that bordars were not necessarily agricultural tenants; at Norwich in 1086 they may have been impoverished burgesses.

19. *Cartulary of Darley Abbey*, i, xlvi–xlvii; see also Stenton in *V.C.H. Derbyshire*, i, 309.

20. Tait, *op. cit.*, 71–4.

21. Maitland, *Township and Borough*, p. 54.

22. *V.C.H. York*, 20.

23. Biddle, 'Winchester: the development of an early capital', *Abhandlungen der Akademie der Wissenschaften in Göttingen*, 1973, pp. 257–8; 'The Winton Domesday', *Die Stadt in der Europäischen Geschichte: Festschrift Edith Ennen*, p. 38.

24. Hurst, 'Saxo-Norman pottery in East Anglia', *Proc. Cambridge Antiquarian Soc.*, **51**, (1958), 57–65.

25. Loyn, *op. cit.*, 92–7.

26. Maitland, *Domesday Book and Beyond*, pp. 178–9.

27. *D.B.*, i. ff. 310, 321, 325.

28. E.g. storage vessels made at Thetford: Hurst and West, 'Saxo-Norman pottery in East Anglia', *Proc. Cambridge Antiquarian Soc.*, **50** (1957), 55.

29. Even so mills had only partially replaced the hand quern, for example in Devon where in 1086 they were much less numerous than in neighbouring Somerset: Hodgen, 'Domesday Water Mills', *Antiquity*, **12** (1939), 261ff; Finberg, *Tavistock Abbey*, p. 53.

30. *D.B.*, ii, f. 224b; Finn, *Introduction to Domesday Book*, p. 109.

31. Lennard, *Rural England 1086–1135*, pp. 351–6.

32. Payne, 'The plough in early Britain', *Arch. Journal*, **104** (1948), 103–8; *Agrarian History of England and Wales*, I (ii), 409–10; one example is reproduced in Kendrick, *Late Saxon and Viking Art*, plate xxiv (a wheeled plough drawn by four oxen).

33. *The Bayeux Tapestry*, ed. Stenton *et al.*, plate 12.

34. *Studies of Field Systems*, pp. 360–1.

35. *Agrarian History of England and Wales*, I (ii), 489–90.

36. *Inquisitio Comitatus Cantabrigiensis*, p. 97.

37. *Cambridge Medieval History*, v, 507 ff. In what follows the incomes of the Conqueror's half-brothers (Robert of Mortain and Odo of Bayeux) have been transferred from the provision made for the royal family to that made for the lay barons, since this better expresses the role and status of these men in early Norman England.

38. Wolffe, *The Royal Demesne in English History*, pp. 33–4.

39. Southern, 'The place of Henry I in English history', *Proc. Brit. Acad.*, xlviii (1962), 157–69.

40. Robinson, *Gilbert Crispin*, p. 38.

41. See also the grant of Holme Lacy to Roger de Lacy in 1085: Galbraith, 'An episcopal land-grant of 1085', *E.H.R.*, xliv (1929), 353–72.

42. *Documents illustrative of Medieval Kentish Society*, ed. Du Boulay (Kent Arch. Soc. Rec. Pubns., xviii, 1964), 4–5.

43. *Domesday Monachorum of Christ Church, Canterbury,* ed. Douglas, pp. 71–2; Painter, *Studies in the History of the English Feudal Barony,* pp. 17, 22.
44. *Cartulary of the Priory of St Gregory, Canterbury,* no. 1; Harvey, 'The knight and the knight's fee in England', *P. and P.,* **49** (1970), 11.
45. *D.B.,* i, 26–27b, 47, 148, 157b, 196–196b, 205b, 211b, 321, 351b; ii, 36–38, 157–172b, 398–400b.
46. *Inquisitio Comitatus Cantabrigiensis,* pp. 50–1.
47. Miller, *Abbey and Bishopric of Ely,* pp. 46–8; but see also the criticism of this argument by R. Lennard in *Econ. H.R.,* 2nd ser., **5** (1952), 133.
48. Maitland, *Domesday Book and Beyond,* pp. 56–7; *D.B.,* i, 180.
49. *V.C.H. Suffolk,* i, 369 ff.
50. *Domesday Book and Beyond,* p. 149.
51. *Inquisitio Comitatus Cantabrigiensis,* pp. 88–9; *D.B.,* i, f. 198.
52. Population figures have been taken from the volumes of Darby's *Domesday Geography* and those for the stake of the various classes in the soil from Inman, *Domesday and Feudal Statistics,* p. 2. Any figures drawn from Domesday must have many imperfections, and those from Inman cannot be claimed to offer more than the very roughest order of magnitude. The population figures exclude Lancashire and the north-west since the Domesday data here preclude any remotely accurate counting of heads.
53. Maitland, *Domesday Book and Beyond,* pp. 62–3; *V.C.H. Bedfordshire,* ii, 75.
54. *D.B.,* i, 3–4b.
55. The available figures have been tabulated and analysed by R. Lennard, in three articles in the *Economic Journal,* **56** (1946), **57,** (1947), **61** (1951).
56. Domesday assumes the virgate to be 30 acres, but this is a fiscal convention. In terms of real acres it doubtless varied, as in later times, according to local custom, available supply of land, fertility, etc.
57. *Histoire de Guillaume le Conquérant,* pp. 222–4.
58. Quoted in Matthew, *The Norman Conquest* (1966), pp. 17–18.
59. In general see Sawyer, 'The wealth of eleventh-century England', *T.R.H.S.,* 5th ser., **15** (1965), 145 ff.; and for a critical review of attempts to calculate the volume of coin in circulation, Grierson, 'The volume of Anglo-Saxon coinage', *Econ.H.R.,* 2nd ser., **20** (1967), 153 ff.

Chapter 2. Land and people

1. The (probably) early eleventh-century tract on wergilds and dignities in *English Historical Documents c. 500–1042,* p. 432.
2. *Dialogus de Scaccario,* p. 40, but see also Round, *Commune of London,* pp. 66–75 for a comment on the dating of the change to cash payments.
3. Duby, *Rural Economy and Country Life in the Medieval West,* pp. 119 ff.
4. Halperin, 'Les transformations économiques au xiie et xiiie siècles', *Revue d'histoire économique et sociale,* **38** (1950), 25.
5. For recent commentaries see M. M. Postan in *Cambridge Economic History,* i, 561–5 (2nd edn.); Titow, *English Rural Society,* pp. 66–8; and *New Historical Geography of England,* pp. 45, 143–4.
6. Russell, *British Medieval Population.*
7. Hatcher, *Plague, Population and the English Economy,* pp. 21–5.
8. For example, Russell at one end of the spectrum argues for a population of 1·1 million in 1086 and 3·7 million in 1347, and Postan at the other for 2 million or more in 1086 and around 7 million at the turn of the thirteenth century.
9. J. Z. Titow, 'Some evidence of the thirteenth-century population increase', *Econ. H.R.,* 2nd ser., **14** (1961).
10. The first systematic analysis of manorial extents was published by Russell in 1948 (*British Medieval Population,* pp. 55–91).

11. Hallam, *Settlement and Society*, pp. 197–222; 'Some thirteenth-century censuses', *Econ.H.R.*, 2nd ser., **10** (1958); 'Population Density in Medieval Fenland', *Econ.H.R.*, 2nd ser., **14** (1961); R. E. Glasscock, 'England *circa* 1334' in *A New Historical Geography of England*, pp. 78–83.
12. J. B. Harley, 'Population trends and agricultural developments from the Warwickshire Hundred Rolls of 1279', *Econ.H.R.*, **11** (1958).
13. Searle, *Lordship and Community*, pp. 21–3; Donkin, 'The Cistercian Order and the settlement of the north of England', *Geographical Review*, **59** (1969), 403–16.
14. P.R.O. C133/15/2; *Northumberland County History*, vi, 178–80, 202–3; xii, 168, 178; *Archaeologia Aeliana*, 4th ser., **3** (1927), no. 6.
15. *Curia Regis Rolls*, xiii, pl. 1103; Hoskins, *Making of the English Landscape*, pp. 70–1; Raftis, *Ramsey Abbey*, p. 72; J. Z. Titow, 'Some differences between manors and their effects on the condition of the peasants in the thirteenth century', *Agric. Hist. Rev.*, **10** (1962), 8.
16. Searle, *Lordship and Community*, p. 59; *Studies of Field Systems*, p. 423; Hoskins and Finberg, *Devonshire Studies*, pp. 140, 320–1.
17. M. L. Bazeley, 'The extent of the Royal Forest in the thirteenth century', *T.R.H.S.*, 4th Ser., **4** (1921); *Dialogus de Scaccario*, p. 57.
18. Stenton, *English Society in the Early Middle Ages*, pp. 109–10; *Registrum Antiquissimum*, i, nos. 153, 180, 184, 199, 205, 211; Harleian MS. 391, f. 50; for assarting on the Essex estates of St Paul's see also *Early Charters of St Paul's Cathedral*, nos. 36, 39, 276.
19. *Cartulary and Terrier of the Priory of Bilsington, Kent*, p. 41. For the *consuetudo marisci*, which was a matter of *communis provisio*, see *Curia Regis Rolls*, xiii, pl. 313 (1227). For the adoption of this code of customs in Holderness see Lythe, 'The organization of drainage and embankment in medieval Holderness', *Yorkshire Arch. Journ.*, **34** (1939), 282.
20. Salzmann, 'The inning of Pevensey levels', *Sussex Arch. Coll.*, **53** (1910), 32–60; Williams, *The Draining of the Somerset Levels*, pp. 25–81; Hoskins and Finberg, *Devonshire Studies*, pp. 105–17; *Oxford Dictionary of Place Names*, pp. 121, 194, 325.
21. Miller, *Abbey and Bishopric of Ely*, pp. 95–7, 119–20, Hallam, *Settlement and Society*, pp. 38–9.
22. *The Place-Names of Westmorland* (English Place-Name Society, xlii–xliii), *passim*.
23. For a review of the evidence of the expansion of settlement in south-west England see Hatcher in *Agrarian History of England and Wales*, ii, ch. 3.
24. Tupling, *Economic History of Rossendale*, pp. 17–27; *Yorkshire Inquisitions*, i, nos. 81, 130; Moore, *A Short History of the Rights of Common upon the Forest of Dartmoor*, pp. xix, 9 ff.
25. Ramm, *et al, Shielings and Bastles*, pp. 3, 36: the latter settlement is associated with the name Scale (= shieling) farm.
26. *Northumberland County History*, i, 310; vi, 314–5; *Studies of Field Systems*, p. 141; *Archaeologia Aeliana*, 4th ser., **3** (1927), no. 111; *Early Yorkshire Charters*, xi, no. 143; *Coucher Book of Furness Abbey*, i (2), no. 224.
27. Hoskins, *Local History in England*, p. 113; Dudley and Minter 'The medieval village at Garrow Tor, Bodmin Moor, Cornwall', *Medieval Arch.*, **6–7** (1962–3), 272–94; Linehan, 'Deserted sites and rabbit-warrens on Dartmoor, Devon', *Medieval Arch.*, **10** (1966), 113–44.
28. Hatcher, *Duchy of Cornwall*, pp. 82–5; Finberg, *Tavistock Abbey*, pp. 32–4, 105–7.
29. T. A. M. Bishop, 'Assarting and the growth of the open fields', *Econ. H.R.*, **6** (1935), 13 ff.
30. Rennell of Rodd, *Valley on the March*, p. 98.
31. Beresford and St Joseph, *Medieval England*, pp. 91–2.
32. Muniments of St John's College, Cambridge, Drawer III, nos. 2, 13.
33. Quoted in Hallam, *Settlement and Society*, p. 166.
34. Colonization also resulted in many quarrels between religious houses over rights to

tithes from assarted land. See, for example, *Cartulary of Tutbury Priory*, nos. 16, 47, 48, 49, 220, 265–8, 330 G.

35. Hoskins, *English Landscape*, p. 83; Darby, *The Medieval Fenland*, pp. 75–80.
36. *Close Rolls, 1227–31*, p. 8.
37. Pluknett, *Legislation of Edward I*, pp. 83–5.
38. For some instances see pp. 213–14.
39. *A Terrier of Fleet*, p. lxxvi; Hallam, *Settlement and Society*, pp. 16, 102–4.
40. Miller, *Abbey and Bishopric of Ely*, pp. 119–20; Hilton, *A Medieval Society*, pp. 20–3; Raftis, *Ramsey Abbey*, pp. 72–3; King, *Peterborough Abbey, 1086–1310*, pp. 72–85; and the 1340 entries for Chobham and Frimley in *Chertsey Abbey C.R. Abstract*, nos. 1111–1125.
41. For example, *Pipe Roll, 10 Richard I*, pp. 17, 73, 104–5.
42. *New Historical Geography*, pp. 100–1; Searle, *Lordship and Community*, pp. 61–2.
43. B. L. Cotton MS. Tiberius B ii, ff. 147b–8, 242b–4; Caius College MS. 485/489, ff. 74b–5, 78b–81, 334–334b.
44. B. L. Cotton MS. Tib. b ii, ff. 107d–9d; Caius College, Cambridge MS. 485/489, ff. 53–8d; *Cambridgeshire and the Isle of Ely: Lay Subsidy for the Year 1327*, pp. 81–2.
45. Raftis, *Tenure and Mobility*, pp. 135–6, 141; Raftis, *Warboys: Two Hundred Years in the Life of an English Village*, pp. 150–1; *Cartularium Monasterii de Rameseia*, iii, 246.
46. *Cambridgeshire and the Isle of Ely: Lay Subsidy for the Year 1327*, p. 304.
47. Powell, *A Suffolk Hundred in the Year 1283*, Table 2.
48. *Accounts and Surveys of the Wiltshire Lands of Adam of Stratton*, pp. 4–14.
49. *Leger Book of Stoneleigh Abbey*, pp. 50–4.
50. *Northumberland County History*, viii, 252, 330, 342–3; xii, 221–3.
51. Davenport, *The Economic Development of a Norfolk Manor*, pp. 37–43, 45–6.
52. Postan, *Cambridge Economic History*, i, 624.
53. Hatcher, *Duchy of Cornwall*, pp. 98, 220–1; P.R.O. SC6/811/1–812/1, 816/11, 12; Duchy of Cornwall Office, Rolls 1–3.
54. An impression of the differences between manors in this respect can be derived from the records of chevage payments on scattered estates like those of the earldom of Cornwall or the bishops of Winchester: *Ministers' Accounts of the Earldom of Cornwall*, and Levett, *The Black Death on the Estates of the See of Winchester*, pp. 29, 171–7.
55. Raftis, *Tenure and Mobility*, pp. 141–3.
56. H. E. Hallam, 'Some thirteenth-century censuses', *Econ. H.R.*, 2nd ser., **10** (1958), 354–6.
57. Davenport, *Economic History of a Norfolk Manor*, pp. 45–6; *The Court Baron*, ed. F. W. Maitland, p. 112.
58. *Feudal Documents from the Abbey of Bury St Edmunds*, pp. 25–44; Miller, *Abbey and Bishopric of Ely*, pp. 107–8.
59. Du Boulay, *The Lordship of Canterbury*, pp. 178–80.
60. P.R.O. SC6/1145/21; *Ancient Petitions Relating to Northumberland*, nos. 96–7.
61. Titow, *English Rural Society*, pp. 77–8; Raftis, *Estates of Ramsey Abbey*, pp. 238, 248–9; Hilton, *A Medieval Society*, p. 145: King, *Peterborough Abbey*, p. 166.
62. Titow, *English Rural Society*, pp. 73–6; Postan, *Cambridge Economic History*, i, 533. See also p. 136.
63. Titow, 'Some differences between manors', *Agric. Hist. Rev.*, **10** (1962), 5.
64. *Ministers' Accounts of the Earldom of Cornwall*, 2 vols, *passim*.
65. *C.R. of . . . Wakefield*, i, 106, 108; *Some C.R. . . . Lancaster*, *passim*; for examples of similar fines in the north see Harvey, 'Population trend in England between 1300 and 1348', *T.R.H.S.*, 5th ser., **6** (1966), 26; Kershaw, *Bolton Priory*, p. 28. Fines in Durham were often higher: *Halmota Prioratus Dunelmensis*, pp. 4–5, 7.
66. King, *Peterborough Abbey*, pp. 166–7, 182–8; Morgan, *English Lands of the Abbey of Bec*, p. 109; *C.R. Chalgrave Manor*, pp. 16, 22, 24.
67. *Chertsey Abbey C.R. Abstract*, 2 vols. *passim*; *Court Rolls of the Wiltshire Manors of Adam de Stratton*, nos. 45, 201, 209.

68. Titow, *English Rural Society*, pp. 74–6; Hilton, *A Medieval Society*, p. 145; King, *Peterborough Abbey*, pp. 166–7; Page, *Estates of Crowland Abbey*, pp. 50, 116.

69. Page, *op. cit.*, 106; Hatcher, *Duchy of Cornwall*, pp. 81–9.

70. Caius Coll., Cambridge, MS., 485/489, f.273.

71. *Accounts and Surveys of the Wiltshire Lands of Adam of Stratton*, pp. 52, 54; *Ministers' Accounts of the Earldom of Cornwall*, 1296–7, i, 62, 66; *Select Documents of the English Lands of the Abbey of Bec*, pp. 164–6.

72. Beveridge, 'Wages in the Winchester manors', *Econ. H.R.* **7** (1936).

73. Beveridge 'Westminster wages in the manorial era', *Econ. H.R.*, 2nd ser., **8** (1955).

74. Beveridge, *Econ. H.R.*, 2nd ser., **8** (1955), 21.

75. Phelps Brown and Hopkins, 'Seven centuries of the prices of consumables compared with builders' wage-rates', in *Essays in Economic History*, ii, 179–96.

76. Postan and Titow, 'Heriots and prices on Winchester manors,' *Econ. H.R.*, 2nd ser., **11**(1959), 392–411.

77. This appears to be the case at Sevenhampton between 1269 and 1288.

78. Postan, *The Famulus*, p. 37; Raftis, *Estates of Ramsey Abbey*, p. 205; Page, *Estates of Crowland Abbey*, p. 251.

79. *V.C.H. Wiltshire*, iv, 9–10.

80. Hoskins, *Midland Peasant*, pp. 30, 63–4.

81. This matter, and the industrial developments mentioned above, will be discussed in detail in the second volume of this work.

82. Searle, *Lordship and Community*, pp. 67–8; Brandon, 'Demesne arable farming in coastal Sussex during the later Middle Ages,' *Agric. Hist. Rev.*, **19** (1971), 117–18.

83. *Yorkshire Inquisitions*, i, nos. 97, 131; iii, no. 53; *Yorkshire Arch. Soc. Miscellanea*, iv, 1–3, 28–30.

84. For a fuller discussion of landholding in northern England see E. Miller in *Agrarian History of England and Wales*, ii.

85. For example, Miller, *Abbey and Bishopric of Ely*, p. 93; Morgan, *English Lands of the Abbey of Bec*, pp. 92–3; Hilton, *The English Peasantry in the Later Middle Ages*; pp. 132–3; Postan, *Essays on Medieval Agriculture and . . . Economy*, pp. 117–22.

86. *The Court Baron*, p. 112.

87. Powicke, 'Observations on the English freeholder in the thirteenth century', *Wirtschaft und Kultur*, pp. 338–9.

88. Miller, *Abbey and Bishopric of Ely*, pp. 95–6; Smith, *Canterbury Cathedral Priory*, pp. 178–9.

89. Cf. Postan in *Cambridge Economic History*, i, 550–2.

90. E. Miller, 'Farming in northern England during the twelfth and thirteenth centuries', *Northern History*, **11** (1976), 10.

91. Postan in *Cambridge Economic History*, i, 556–9.

92. Analysed by Titow in *Winchester Yields*.

93. Matthew Paris, *Chronica Majora*, v, 660, 690, 701–2, 710–12, 728.

94. *V.C.H. Bedfordshire*, ii, 83–4.

95. For this and what follows see Postan and Titow, 'Heriots and prices on Winchester manors', *Econ. H.R.*, 2nd ser., **11** (1959), 392–411; the essay has been republished in Postan, *Essays on Medieval Agriculture and . . . Economy*, pp. 150–78.

96. We are grateful to Dr D. L. Farmer for this information.

97. Ohlin, 'No safety in numbers: some pitfalls of historical statistics,' in *Essays in Quantitative Economic History*, ed. Floud, 61–6; Russell, *British Medieval Population*, pp. 186, 232–4, 259, 274.

98. Searle, *Lordship and Community*, pp. 179–80.

99. Calculated from the date provided by Postan and Titow, in 'Heriots and Prices on Winchester Manors'.

100. Raftis, *Estates of Ramsey Abbey*, p. 217; Miller, *Abbey and Bishopric of Ely*, p. 100; Titow, *Winchester Yields*, p. 10 note.

101. For what follows in this paragraph see the important study by Kershaw, 'The great famine and agrarian crisis in England, 1315–22', *P. and P.*, **59** (1973), 3–50.

102. *Ibid.*, pp. 40–3.

103. Baker, 'Evidence in the *Nonarum Inquisitiones* of Contracting arable lands in England', *Econ. H.R.*, 2nd ser., **19** (1966), 518–32.
104. See p. 151 and also Maddicott's important monograph, *The English Peasantry and the Demands of the Crown, 1294–1341.*

Chapter 3. Markets

1. Many of the subjects discussed in this chapter will be discussed more thoroughly in the second volume of this study, but some preliminary account of them is required to provide a context for the development of rural England.
2. Rogers, *History of Agriculture and Prices in England*, 6 vols.
3. 'The yield and price of corn in the Middle Ages', in *Essays in Economic History*, i, 13 ff.
4. For what follows see Lloyd, *The Movement of Wool Prices in Medieval England;* and Farmer, 'Some price fluctuations in Angevin England', *Econ. H.R.*, 2nd ser., **9** (1956), 34–43; 'Grain price movements in thirteenth-century England', *ibid.*, **10** (1957), 207–20; 'Livestock price movements in thirteenth-century England', *ibid.*, **22** (1969), 1–16.
5. *English Hist. Docs. c. 500–1042* pp. 388–90; *Domesday Book*, i, ff. 117b, 179a; Farmer, 'Some price fluctuations in Angevin England', *loc. cit.*, 41.
6. Figures taken from Farmer, 'Some price fluctuations in Angevin England', *Econ. H.R.*, 2nd ser., **9** (1956), 37, 41.
7. Miller, 'War, taxation and the English economy', in *War and Economic Development*, ed. Winter, p. 24; Miskimin, 'Monetary movements in fourteenth- and fifteenth-century England', *J. Econ. Hist.*, **24** (1964), 477; Mayhew, 'Numismatic evidence and falling prices in the fourteenth century', *Econ. H.R.*, 2nd ser., **27** (1974), 1–15.
8. Harvey, 'The English inflation of 1180–1220', *P. and P.*, **61** (1973), 27.
9. Our price evidence at this time comes solely from royal purveyances.
10. For descriptions of adverse weather, see *Flores Historiarum*, ii, 123, and Roger de Wendover, *Flores Historiarum*, i, 312.
11. *Borough Customs*, ed. Bateson, i, 247–8.
12. Billson, *Medieval Leicester*, pp. 144–5; and see also p. 141 for a similar range of recruitment of the body of burgesses at an earlier date as revealed by the rolls of gild members.
13. Ekwall, *Studies on the Population of Medieval London*, pp. xlii ff.
14. Bridbury, *Economic Growth: England in the later Middle Ages*, p. 55.
15. Thornton, 'A study in the history of Clare, Suffolk',. *T.R.H.S.*, 4th Ser., **11** (1928), 83–111.
16. Beresford and St Joesph, *Medieval England*, pp. 161–4; Raftis, 'Rent and capital at St Ives', *Medieval Studies*, **20** (1958), 79–92.
17. Beresford and St Joseph, *op. cit.*, pp. 167–8; Hilton, *A Medieval Society*, pp. 190–2.
18. Hill, *Medieval Lincoln*, pp. 315–20.
19. Hoskins, *Local History in England*, pp. 81–3.
20. Beresford, *New Towns of the Middle Ages*, pp. 506–8.
21. *Ibid.*, pp. 328, 417–26, 441–50, 513–14.
22. *Northumberland County History*, i, 248–52; v, 139–51.
23. *Register of John de Halton*, i, 115–16.
24. *Monumenta Juridica*, ii, 184 ff.
25. Billson, *op. cit.*, 117; *V.C.H. Leicestershire*, iv, 46–8.
26. Page, *Estates of Crowland Abbey*, pp. 138–9; Levett, *Studies in Manorial History*, pp. 295–6; *Annals of Cambridge*, i, 101, 163, 173.
27. *Rotuli Litterarum Clausarum*, i, 620.
28. *Documents illustrative of the Rule of Walter de Wenlock, Abbot of Westminster, 1283–1307*, p. 63.

29. *Cal. Charter Rolls*, i, 279, 294, 329, 475; ii, 252, 262, 356; iii, 469; iv, 339; *Cal. Patent Rolls, 1247-58*, 379, 453; *Rotuli Hundredorum*, ii, 529, 570-1.
30. *Cal. Charter Rolls*, i, 2-28.
31. See one of the few systematic discussions of medieval markets and fairs by B. E. Coates, 'The origin and distribution of markets and fairs in medieval Derbyshire', *Derbyshire Archaeological J.*, **85** (1965), 92 ff.
32. *Ministers' Accounts of the Earldom of Cornwall, passim.*
33. Levett, *Studies in Manorial History*, pp. 181-2, 357.
34. *Records of the Borough of Leicester*, i, 14, 24-5, 29-33, 43-4, 74-85, 95-6, 98-9, 114, 180-85, 207, 216, 226, 262, 321, 395, 397.
35. Gras, *Evolution of the English Corn Market*, pp. 42-55.
36. *Laws of the Kings of England from Edmund to Henry I*, pp. 70-73.
37. Hill, *Medieval Lincoln*, 173-7; *Foedera*, i(i), 149; *Close Rolls, 1231-4*, 242, 247, 532; *1234-7*, 426-7; *1242-4*, 538.
38. Weinbaum, *London unter Eduard I und II*, ii, 29 ff.; William of Malmesbury, *Gesta Pontificum*, 140.
39. Holmes, 'Florentine merchants in England', *Econ. H.R.*, 2nd ser., **13** (1960), 199.
40. What follows is drawn from the customs accounts printed by Gras in the appendices of his *Early English Customs System* where no other reference is given.
41. Prologue to *The Canterbury Tales*, lines 447-8.
42. As indicated by records of piracy at sea: Cuttino, *English Diplomatic Administration, 1259-1339*, 162, 165, 167.
43. James, *Studies in the Medieval Wine Trade*, pp. 9-10.
44. Veale, *The English Fur Trade in the Later Middle Ages*, p. 19.
45. *Chronicon Walteri de Gyseburne*, p. 293.
46. The details are tabulated by ports in Carus-Wilson and Coleman, *England's Export Trade, 1275-1547.*
47. Gras, *op. cit.*, p. 111.
48. *Monumenta Juridica*, ii, 184 ff.
49. Carus-Wilson, ed., *The Overseas Trade of Bristol*, pp. 168-77.
50. *Cal. Patent Rolls, 1313-17*, 266, 370, 371, 373, 380, 382, 386, 397, 399-400, 450, 459, 466-7, 501-2, 558, 622, 624.
51. E.g. *Close Rolls, 1227-31*, 219.
52. Hatcher, *English Tin Production and Trade*, p. 23.
53. We return to this matter in greater detail in the final chapter of this book.

Chapter 4. Villages

1. See the order of 1109-11 for the holding of shire and hundred courts: Stubbs, *Select Charters*, p. 120.
2. *Cambridgeshire and the Isle of Ely: the Lay Subsidy for the Year 1327*, pp. 47-8.
3. *Northumberland County History*, iii, 32-4; v, 207, 224, 254, 273, 298.
4. At Amble, for example, there were 40 landholders in 1295 and 9 taxpayers in 1296; at Hungry Hatley, if the number of landholders in 1327 had changed little since 1279 (*Rot. Hundr.*, ii, 539-40), 32 landholders correspond to 14 taxpayers in 1327. This is merely one illustration of the pitfalls of the lay subsidy rolls for a comparative study of village populations.
5. P.R.O. E.120/1; Duchy of Cornwall Office, Roll 471.
6. Hoskins and Finberg, *Devonshire Studies*, pp. 265-88; Hoskins, *Local History in England*, p. 133.
7. Oliver, *Monasticon*, pp. 367-9.
8. *Sussex Custumals*, ii, xxxi-ii.
9. Levett, *Studies in Manorial History*, pp. 180-2; Hallam, *Settlement and Society*, p. 3.
10. Beresford and St Joseph, *Medieval England: an Aerial Survey*, pp. 125 ff.

11. Hilton, *A Medieval Society*, p. 90.
12. *Danelaw Documents*, nos. 12, 18, 336.
13. Rahtz, 'Holworth: a medieval village excavation', *Proc. Dorset Arch. Soc.*, **81** (1959), 127 ff.
14. Beresford and St Joseph, *op. cit.*, 62–4 and cf. p. 141 (Warkworth, Northumberland) where again the crofts stretch away from the steep main street down to the river on the west and to Emery, the back lane, on the east.
15. *Vetus Registrum Sarisberiense,* i, 239.
16. Seebohm, *English Village Community*, pp. 1–16.
17. The boundaries of the 'Midland' system are still accepted as lying more or less where H. L. Gray placed them: see the map based on his material in *New Historical Geography of England*, p. 82. In recent years historical geographers have made a major contribution to the study of field systems and, in what follows, the main source is Baker and Butlin, ed.; *Studies of Field Systems*.
18. Hoskins and Finberg, *Devonshire Studies*, pp. 265–88.
19. Harvey, *A Medieval Oxfordshire Village*, pp. 3, 17–22, 29–31, 99–100.
20. Joan Thirsk, 'The common fields', *P. and P.,* **29** (1964), 1–2. Cuxham, of course, also had in its manor court the necessary tribunal to regulate communal interests.
21. Gray, *English Field Systems*, pp. 70–1; Baker and Butlin, ed., *Studies of Field Systems*, pp. 222, 347–8.
22. Gray, *English Field Systems,* espy. p. 73.
23. Baker, 'Howard Levi Gray and English field systems: an evaluation', *Agric. Hist.*, **39** (1965), 88.
24. *V.C.H. Berkshire*, ii, 170; iv, 505; *V.C.H. Wiltshire*, iv, 14–15.
25. *V.C.H. Oxfordshire*, ii, 171.
26. For the constitution of the open fields see the description of the even better known example at Laxton (Notts): Orwin and Orwin, *The Open Fields*, pp. 69–85.
27. Postgate, 'The open fields of Cambridgeshire', pp. 49 ff.
28. *Cart. Osen.*, v, no. 730.
29. The question of balks between strips has generated controversy: Orwin *op. cit.*, 46–7, has denied their existence, but they have been rehabilitated by Kerridge, 'A reconstruction of some former husbandry practices', *Agric. Hist. Rev., 3* (1955), 32 ff. In Cambridgeshire, certainly, there is evidence of these 'minor balks' in at least thirty-six villages: Postgate, *op. cit.*, 69 ff.
30. *Registrum Antiquissimum*, ii, no. 319; *Cart. Osen.,* v, nos. 673A, 880A.
31. *Ibid.*, v, no. 730.
32. Harvey, *op. cit.*, 3; Hoskins, *The Midland Peasant*, p. 63.
33. Beresford and St Joseph, *op. cit.*, p. 22.
34. Gray, *op. cit.*, p. 369.
35. *Coucher Book of Whalley Abbey*, iii, 647.
36. *Sussex Custumals*, i, 127–9; for, 'a complex three-course arable system' in another 'multi-field setting' in Cheshire, see Sylvester, 'Medieval three-course arable systems in Cheshire', *Trans. Hist. Soc. of Lancashire and Cheshire*, **110** (1958), 183–6.
37. Hoskins, *Midland Peasant*, p. 70.
38. On the other hand, even closes held in severalty did not necessarily escape all communal claims; at Alverthorpe in 1308 the whole township had right of common in open time in the assart Richard Brown held in severalty; *Wakefield C.R.*, ii, 191.
39. For the cultivation of the waste in the south-west see J. Hatcher in *Agrarian History of England and Wales*, ii.
40. Thirsk, *art. cit.*, 7.
41. See the important discussion by T. A. M. Bishop, 'Assarting and the growth of the open fields', *Econ. H.R.*, **6** (1935), 13–29.
42. J. A. Sheppard, in *Geografiska Annaler*, **48** (1966) summarised in Baker and Butlin, *Studies of Field Systems*, pp. 176–8.
43. Chatsworth MSS, Bolton Coucher Book, f. 38.
44. B.L. Add. MS. 40010, f. 20.
45. For this period as the crucial one in the development of the 'first common field systems', see Thirsk, *art. cit.*, 23.

46. Titow's observations on this matter are pertinent: 'Medieval England and the open-field system', *P. and P.*, **32** (1965), 86–102.
47. Even when the main part of the arable lay in some sort of open fields, however regular or irregular, tenants might be empowered to enclose plots of assart situated on the margins of these fields: *Chertsey Abbey C.R. Abstract*, nos. 801, 1117–20, etc.
48. P.R.O. DL 29/1/1–2; *Lancashire Inquisitions*, ii, 8.
49. *Northumberland County History*, xv, 244–5.
50. *Danelaw Documents*, no. 47.
51. *Custumals of the Manors of Laughton, Willingdon and Goring*, p. 1.
52. *Registrum Antiquissium*, ii, no. 319; *Cart. Osen.*, v, no. 730.
53. *Chertsey Abbey C.R. Abstract*, nos. 1085, 1275.
54. *Cart. Osen.*, v, no. 665.
55. E.g. *C.R. of the Manor of Hales*, i, 126, 130.
56. Thirsk, *art. cit.*, 16–19.
57. *Sir Christopher Hatton's Book of Seals*, no. 18.
58. *C.R. of the Manor of Hales*, i, 162.
59. Vinogradoff, *Villainage in England*, p. 262; *Early Yorkshire Charters*, xii, no. 67.
60. *Ibid.*, nos. 44, 56.
61. Harvey, *op. cit.*, 101–2.
62. Postan, 'Village livestock in the thirteenth century', *Econ. H.R.*, 2nd ser., **15** (1962), 248.
63. *Danelaw Documents*, nos. 32–4, 36, 40, 42–3, 45–7.
64. Stubbs, *Select Charters*, pp. 362–5 (for the date see Cam, *The Hundred and the Hundred Rolls*, p. 189).
65. Pollock and Maitland, *History of English Law*, i, 688.
66. *Inquisitio Comitatus Cantabrigiensis*, p. 97.
67. Stubbs, *Select Charters*, p. 170.
68. For some of these developments, see Powicke, *Military Obligations in Medieval England*.
69. *Cal. Inquisitions Miscellaneous*, i, nos. 1654, 1711, 1726, 1754, 1946, etc.
70. Another example may be the ale-tasters appointed to enforce the assize of ale.
71. *Parliamentary Writs*, i, 62–3.
72. E.g. *C.R. of the Manor of Hales*, i, 17, where it is recorded that all had judicially declared that a man might enclose a plot in the common field to make a curtilage without leave either from the lord or his neighbours.
73. *C.R. of the Manor of Chalgrave*, pp. 49, 62, for common swineherds at Chalgrave and Toddington and a common gooseherd at Chalgrave.
74. Homans, *English Villagers of the Thirteenth Century*, pp. 64, 288.
75. Hoskins, *The Medieval Peasant*, p. 97.
76. Vinogradoff, *Villainage in England*, pp. 233–5, 457–8.
77. Page, *Estates of Crowland Abbey*, pp. 25–7, 164–5.
78. Homans, *English Villagers*, p. 273.
79. Hilton, 'Peasant movements in England before 1381', in *Essays in Economic History*, ii, 90.
80. Ault, *C.R. of the Abbey of Ramsey and of the Honor of Clare*, p. 201, n. 35.
81. For examples, see Hilton, *op. cit.*; Homans, *op. cit.*, pp. 275–84; Morgan, *Abbey of Bec*, pp. 105–8.
82. The story is told by Hilton, *A Medieval Society*, pp. 159–61.
83. *Estate Book of Henry de Bray*, p. 87.
84. Ault, *Open-Field Husbandry and the Village Community*, pp. 55–9; in this book Professor Ault has summed up his pioneering work on this matter.
85. *The Court Baron*, pp. 143, 145; Caius College, Cambridge MS. 485/489, f. 49; and see also Ault, *op. cit.*, p. 50.
86. Hoyt, *The Rural Demesne in English Constitutional History*, pp. 104–5, 136–40; Lennard, *Rural England, 1086–1135*, pp. 153–4.
87. *Cartularium Monasterii de Rameseia*, ii, 244–6.
88. Raftis, *Estates of Ramsey Abbey*, p. 125.

89. *Danelaw Documents*, pp. lxx–lxxi and no. 465; Owen, *Church and Society in medieval Lincolnshire*, p. 13.
90. Hoskins,*Midland Peasant*, pp. 15–16.
91. Lennard, *op. cit.*, pp. 300–3.
92. Hoskins, *Devon*, p. 224.
93. *Northumberland County History*, v, 294–5, 376; x, 380, 389.
94. Homans, *English Villagers of the Thirteenth Century*, p. 383.
95. Moorman, *Church Life in England in the Thirteenth Century*, pp. 144–5.
96. For examples in Lincolnshire see Owen, *op. cit.* pp. 140–1.
97. *Ibid,* 121; Hilton, *Medieval Society*, pp. 263–6.
98. *Danelaw Documents*, no. 270.
99. Bennett, *Life on the English Manor*, pp. 321–8.
100. Homans, *English Villagers of the Thirteenth Century*, p. 353 ff., in particular, has brought out this relationship.
101. *Court Roll of the Ramsey manor of St Ives*, quoted Homans, *op. cit.*, 458

Chapter 5. Villagers: 1. status and tenure

1. *Rot. Hundr.*, ii, 407 ff.
2. Hallam, *Settlement and Society*, pp. 202–6.
3. *Eng. Hist. Docs, 1042–1189*, p. 814.
4. 'Freedom and villeinage in England', *P. and P.*, **31** (1965), 6–19.
5. *The Mirror of Justices*, 77; for the procedure of suit of kin, see Hyams, 'The proof of villein status in the common law', *E.H.R.*, **89** (1974), 721–49.
6. *Curia Regis Rolls*, ii, 93.
7. *Earliest Lincolnshire Assize Rolls*, pl. 423.
8. *Curia Regis Rolls*, iv, 195–6.
9. Hyams, *art. cit.,* 728 ff., and see pp. 132–3.
10. Dean and Chapter of Ely, Sutton court roll, Nativity of St John, 20 Edw. I.
11. *Cartulary of Winchester Cathedral*, no. 331.
12. *Cartularium Monasterii de Rameseia*, iii, 246, 248, 257.
13. For the development of the procedures of the royal courts in this regard see, *Royal Writs in England from the Conquest to Glanville*, pp. 336–40.
14. *Cart. Osen.*, iv, 405–6.
15. *Curia Regis Rolls*, xiv, pl. 969.
16. *Cartularium Prioratus de Colne*, no. 73; *Curia Regis Rolls*, v, 49–50, 94–5; *Cart. Osen.*, iv, nos. 316, 316A; vi, p. 140; *Early Charters of St Paul's*, nos. 256–60, 262, 267; *Eynsham Cartulary*, no. 102.
17. *Registrum Antiquissimum*, v, 2–3.
18. *Great Chartulary of Glastonbury*, i, no. 328.
19. *Coucher Book of Furness Abbey*, ii (2), 549; B. M. Lansdowne MS. 402, ff. 17–7d; *Guisborough Chartulary*, ii, no. 1147; *Chartulary of Cockersand*, iii (2), 1056–66.
20. *Select Bills in Eyre*, no, 40; *Curia Regis Rolls*, i, 264; vi, 349–50.
21. *Ibid.*, i, 22, 264; iii, 324–5, vi, 106–7; *Rolls of the Justices in Eyre for Yorkshire, 1218–1219*, pl. 1024.
22. *Notes on the Religious and Secular Houses of Yorkshire*, i, 109.
23. Glanville, *Tractatus de Legibus*, p. 57 and cf. *Bracton's Note Book*, pl. 1256.
24. *Earliest Lincolnshire Assize Rolls*, pl. 531.
25. Bennett, *Life on the English Manor*, pp. 145–7; Hilton, *English Peasantry in the Later Middle Ages*, pp. 234–5; Hatcher, *Rural Economy in the Duchy of Cornwall*, p. 63.
26. *Bracton's Note Book*, pll. 485, 574, 632 and see also Poole, *Obligations of Society in the Twelfth and Thirteenth Centuries*, pp. 14–15.
27. Page, *Estates of Crowland Abbey*, pp. 373–4.
28. *Gesta Abbatum Monasterii S. Albani*, i, 453–5.
29. *Chertsey Abbey C.R. Abstract*, nos. 240–1; *Court Roll of Chalgrave Manor*, pp. 42, 46.

30. *Curia Regis Rolls*, xiv, pl. 1492.
31. See generally Pollock and Maitland, *History of English Law*, i, 359–60; Vinogradoff, *Villainage in England*, pp. 43–8.
32. Pollock and Maitland, *op. cit.*, i, 371, 377.
33. *Chron. Monasterii de Abingdon*, ii, 25; *Cirencester Cartulary*, i, nos. 36, 40; *Earliest Lincolnshire Assize Rolls*, pp. 11, 312–3.
34. E.g. *Merchet*, tallage, *leyrwite*: Hilton, 'Freedom and villeinage', *P. and P.*, no. 31 (1965), 10.
35. *Curia Regis Rolls*, i, 16; x, 62.
36. Caius College, Cambridge MS. 485/489, f. 136d; the holding had paid the same rent in 1222: B.L. Cotton MS. Tiberius B ii, f. 215.
37. B.L. Cotton MS. Julius A i, f. 126.
38. *Bracton's Note Book*, pl. 1210; *Curia Regis Rolls*, vii, 240–1.
39. *Leger Book of Stoneleigh Abbey*, pp. 100–108.
40. Pollock and Maitland, *History of English Law*, i, 393–4.
41. McIntosh, 'The privileged villeins of the English ancient demesne', *Viator*, **8** (1976).
42. N. Neilson, 'Custom and the common law in Kent', *Harvard Law Review*, xxxviii (1924–5), 482–98.
43. *V.C.H. Kent*, iii, 325–6; Du Boulay, *Lordship of Canterbury*, pp. 180–1.
44. Hatcher, *Duchy of Cornwall*, pp. 52–79; Finberg, *Tavistock Abbey*, pp. 249–52.
45. Kominsky, *Studies in the Agrarian History of England*, pp. 205–6.
46. See especially 'The free peasantry of the northern Danelaw', *Bulletin de la société royale des lettres de Lund* (1925–6), pp. 83–4.
47. *Cartulary of Darley Abbey*, i, 25.
48. Douglas, *Social Structure of Medieval East Anglia*, pp. 2–3; Dodwell, 'Holdings and inheritance in medieval East Anglia', *Econ. H.R.*, 2nd ser., **20** (1967), 59.
49. Du Boulay, *Lordship of Canterbury*, 183.
50. It should, however, be remembered that very often a 'day's' work, while beginning at daybreak, ended at noon.
51. *Rot. Hundr.*, ii, 472, 510.
52. *Domesday of St Paul's*, pp. 3–6, 17; *Documents . . . of the Abbey of Bec*, 29, 43; *Registrum . . . Prioratus Beatae Mariae Wigornensis*, 10b, 33b.
53. Miller, *Abbey and Bishopric of Ely*, p. 88.
54. *Liber Henrici de Soliaco*, pp. 54, 103, 117.
55. Page, *Estates of Crowland Abbey*, pp. 102–3; Morgan, *English Lands of the Abbey of Bec*, pp. 79–80.
56. For references see below, Ch. 8, notes 84, 85, 86.
57. Kosminsky, *Studies in the Agrarian History of England*, ch. 3.
58. Hilton, *English Peasantry in the Late Middle Ages*, p. 129; *Northumberland County History*, viii, 223.
59. *Eng. Hist. Docs, c. 500–1042*, p. 371; *Eng. Hist. Docs, 1042–1189*, pp. 812–14, 816–18; see also *Agrarian History of England and Wales*, i (2), 507–25.
60. P.R.O. C135/11/13; Cambridge University Library, Downham Account Roll, 13–14 Edw. II. For a much fuller discussion of commutation and the sale of works, see pp. 222–4.
61. Postan, *Essays on Medieval Agriculture . . .*, pp. 89–106; Poole, *Obligations of Society*, pp. 24–8; Stenton, *English Society in the Early Middle Ages*, pp. 139–40.
62. Raftis, *Estates of Ramsey Abbey*, p. 115, note 68.
63. Postan, *op. cit.*, 105; Miller, *op. cit.*, 101–2.
64. Hilton, 'Freedom and villeinage in England', *P. and P.*, **31** (1965), 13.
65. As Stenton observed, *Anglo-Saxon England*, p. 475.
66. Postan, *Essays on Medieval Agriculture . . . Economy*, p. 94.
67. King, *Peterborough Abbey 1086–1310*, p. 142.
68. *Liber Henrici de Soliaco*, p. 21; Poole, *Obligations of Society . . .*, pp. 27–8; *Cartulary of Cirencester Abbey*, i, no. 20.
69. Vinogradoff, *English Society in the Eleventh Century*, p. 143; *Eng. Hist. Docs 1042–1189*, p. 814.

70. *Boldon Buke*, pp. 3–4.
71. Caius College, Cambridge MS. 485/489, f. 173b.
72. Homans, *English Villagers in the Thirteenth Century*, pp. 112–13.
73. *Bracton's Note Book*, pl. 691; *C.R. of the Manor of Hales*, i, 104–5.
74. *Chertsey Abbey C.R. Abstract*, no. 291.
75. Bennett, *Life on the English Manor*, pp. 146–7.
76. *Bracton's Note Book*, pl. 784.
77. *C.R. of . . . Ramsey and . . . Clare*, p. 208; *Bracton's Note Book*, pl. 1228.
78. Maitland, *Collected Papers*, ii, 369–80.
79. *Curia Regis Rolls*, xiii, pl. 1760.
80. *Ibid*, iv, 128, 305: *Bracton's Note Book*, pl. 702; *Rolls of the Justices in Eyre at Bedford, 1227*, pl. 106.
81. *Curia Regis Rolls*, i, 95–6; xi, pl. 1733; *Rolls of the Justices in Eyre . . . for Gloucestershire, Warwickshire and Shropshire* (1221–22), pl. 615.
82. Cam, *Liberties and Communities of Medieval England*, p. 134.
83. *The Court Baron*, pp. 110, 113.
84. Miller, *Abbey and Bishopric of Ely*, pp. 150–1.
85. Hyams, 'The proof of villein status in the common law', *E.H.R.*, **89** (1974), 730.

Chapter 6. Villagers 2. Family and fortunes

1. *Crown Pleas of the Wiltshire Eyre, 1249*, pl. 203.
2. Homans, *English Villagers of the Thirteenth Century*, pp. 133–4; there were, of course, other customs: for instances in the north and south-west where a lord had more extensive rights over the chattels of dead villeins; see above.
3. Faith, 'Peasant families and inheritance customs in Medieval England', *Agric. Hist. Rev.*, **14** (1966), 79–81.
4. *Chertsey Abbey Court Rolls Abstract*, nos. 1047, 1053, 1055, 1058.
5. D. and C. of Ely, Sutton Court Rolls, St Barnabas 23 Edward I and St Luke 31 Edward I; Titow, 'Some differences between manors', *Agric. Hist. Rev.*, **10** (1962), 6–9.
6. Raftis, *Tenure and Mobility* p. 36; *Chertsey Abbey Court Rolls Abstract*, p. xxvii.
7. *Court Rolls of the Abbey of Ramsey and the Honour of Clare*, p. 211; Homans, *op. cit.*, 188.
8. It is interesting to note that such men sometimes took their spouse's surname: *Chertsey Abbey Court Rolls Abstract*, p. xxxix.
9. Titow, *art. cit.*, 7–8.
10. *Court Roll of Chalgrave Manor*, p. 18; *Chertsey Abbey Court Rolls Abstract*, no. 1369.
11. *Chertsey Abbey Court Rolls Abstract*, no. 533; *Court Roll of Chalgrave Manor*, p. 10; Dean and Chapter of Ely, Sutton Court Rolls, Easter 26 Edward I.
12. *Halmota Prioratus Dunelmensis*, p. 9; for a similar entry, see *Wakefield Court Rolls*, i, 286.
13. *Court Rolls of the Manor of Hales*, i, 166–8.
14. *Chertsey Abbey Court Rolls Abstract*, no. 93; *Wakefield Court Rolls*, ii, 210; *Court Rolls of the Wiltshire Manors of Adam de Stratton*, pp. 104–5.
15. Dean and Chapter of Ely, Sutton Court Rolls, St Matthew, 3 Edward II; *Crown Pleas of the Wiltshire Eyre*, no. 166.
16. *Chertsey Abbey Court Rolls Abstract*, no. 468; *Crown Pleas of the Wiltshire Eyre*, no. 508.
17. Page, *Estates of Crowland Abbey*, pp. 110–11.
18. *Court Roll of Chalgrave Manor*, p. 9; Pollock and Maitland, *History of English Law*, i, 380.
19. Taken from the four volumes of the *Wakefield Court Rolls* covering the period 1274–1316.

20. *Chertsey Abbey Court Rolls Abstract*, no. 933.
21. *Wakefield Court Rolls*, iv, 106.
22. *Chertsey Abbey Court Rolls Abstract*, no. 776.
23. King, *Peterborough Abbey*, p. 124.
24. Miller, *Abbey and Bishopric of Ely*, p. 87n; *Historia et Cartularium Monasterii S. Petri Gloucestriae*, ii, 48, 54.
25. *Cartulary of Newnham Priory*, ii, no. 475.
26. *Eynsham Cartulary*, i, no. 148.
27. *Cartularium Monasterii S. Petri Gloucestriae*, ii, 35 ff., 41 ff.
28. *Carte Nativorum*, ed. C. N. L. Brooke and M. M. Postan, p. liii.
29. For the 'habit of regarding land as a vendible commodity' in this region, see Stenton, *Danelaw Charters*, p. lii.
30. For some discussion of this matter, see Hyams, 'Origins of the peasant land market in England', *Econ. H.R.*, 2nd ser., **23** (1970), 18–31.
31. *Court Rolls of the Abbey of Ramsey and the Honour of Clare*, p. 259.
32. Page, *Estates of Crowland Abbey*, pp. 112–13.
33. *Court Rolls of The Abbey of Ramsey and the Honour of Clare*, pp. 216, 218.
34. *Chertsey Abbey Court Rolls Abstract*, no. 647.
35. *Gesta Abbatum Monasterii S. Albani*, i, 435.
36. *Court Rolls of the Abbey of Ramsey and the Honour of Clare*, pp. 216, 230, 278.
37. *Chertsey Abbey Court Rolls Abstract*, nos. 648–53, 828.
38. *Medieval Customs of the Manors of Taunton and Bradford on Tone*, p. 86.
39. *Stoneleigh Leger Book*, p. xii; Page, *op. cit.*, pp. 84–7.
40. Harley, 'Population trends and agricultural developments from the Warwickshire Hundred Rolls', *Econ. H.R.*, 2nd ser., **11** (1958), 17; B. L. Cotton MS. Claudius, C xi, ff. 82d–5d, 89–93.
41. Kosminsky, *Studies in the Agrarian History of England*, esp. tables on pp. 216 and 223.
42. *Cambridge Economic History of Europe*, i, 619–20.
43. Above, p. 54–5; Kosminsky, *Studies in the Agrarian History of England*, pp. 216, 221–3; the size of holdings in the south-west and north of England will be treated in greater detail in our contributions to *Agrarian History of England and Wales*, ii.
44. B. L. Cotton MS. Tiberius B ii, ff. 215–8 (1222); B. L. Cotton MS. Claudius C xi, ff. 127–31 (1251); *Rot. Hundr.*, ii, 544–5 (1279).
45. It may be significant that in 1251 the Bishop of Ely, although quite well provided with some 55 acres of meadow, had only 26 acres of pasture, and even that might be ploughed if the lord liked: B. L. Cotton MS. Claudius C xi, f. 127b.
46. *D.B.*, i, 191.
47. *Collected Papers*, ii, 370.
48. *Northumberland County History*, v, 363–5; some 70 acres appear to have been lost in the course of time, but the reduction in the size of holdings is clear.
49. M. M. Postan, *Carte Nativorum*, p. xi and cf. the Glastonbury manor of Damerham in the thirteenth century where 'there are also 32 cottagers holding of the villeins': Titow, *English Rural Society*, pp. 86–7.
50. Moore, *A Short History . . . upon the Forest of Dartmoor*, pp. 156–9; Oliver, *Monasticon*, pp. 367–9.
51. M. M. Postan, in *Cambridge Economic History of Europe*, i, 603.
52. Bennett, *Life on the English Manor*, pp. 85 ff; Kosminsky, *Studies in the Agrarian History of England*, p. 230 ff; Hilton, *A Medieval Society*, pp. 114–15; Titow, *English Rural Society*, p. 79 ff.
53. Miller, 'War, taxation and the English economy', *War and Economic Development*, ed. Winter, p. 18.
54. Homans, *English Villagers*, p. 287; the likelihood is, however, that most of them did not: Postan, *The Famulus*, pp. 39–41.
55. *Chertsey Abbey Court Rolls Abstract*, no. 533; *Court Rolls of the Abbey of Ramsey and the Honour of Clare*, p. 236.

56. *Chertsey Abbey Court Rolls Abstract*, nos. 25, 1299, 1434, 1436, 1521, 1842; Miller, *Abbey and Bishopric of Ely*, pp. 148–51; Levett, *Studies in Manorial History*, pp. 187–8.

57. *Halmota Prioratus Dunelmensis*, pp. 14–16.

58. King, *Peterborough Abbey*, pp. 137–9.

59. Hatcher, *Rural Economy . . . in the Duchy of Cornwall*, pp. 235 ff.

60. See the important observations by M. M. Postan in *Cambridge Economic History of Europe*, i, 618–22.

61. *Ibid.*, p. 622.

62. Maddicott, *The English Peasantry and the Demands of the Crown, 1294–1341*, 75.

63. *Wakefield Court Rolls*, iv, 148–56.

64. *Halmota Prioratus Dunelmensis*, p. 2; *Northumberland County History*, ii, 85. The Tweed salmon fisheries were even more productive of revenue: in 1313 they were leased for £35 1s yearly: P.R.O. DL 29/1/3.

65. N. S. B. and E. C. Gras, *Economic and Social History of an English Village*, pp. 69–74.

66. *Court Roll of Chalgrave Manor*, pp. 10–11.

67. The figures for the first three districts are taken from Postan 'Village livestock in the thirteenth century', *Econ. H.R.*, 2nd ser., **15** (1962), 219ff; the others are calculated from *The Taxation of 1297*, ed. A. T. Gaydon, printing assessment rolls for Barford, Biggleswade and Flitt hundreds (Beds), and from *The Yorkshire Lay Subsidy, 25 Edward I*, ed. W. Brown. The Bedfordshire figures exclude all demesne stock.

68. Postan, *op. cit.*, 244.

69. *Liber Henrici de Soliaco*, pp. 28, 103, 141.

70. *Selected Pleas in Manorial Courts*, iii; B. L. Cotton Tiberius B ii, f. 112d; Homans, *op. cit.*, pp. 80–1.

71. Fuller, 'The tallage of 6 Edward II', *Trans. Bristol and Gloucestershire Arch. Soc.*, **19** (1894–95), 196–8.

72. It was none the less an offence when a man, who had hired a heifer for her milk and calf, harnessed her to the plough : *C.R. of the Manor of Wakefield*, ii, 7; but the incident shows that cows might be used for ploughing.

73. *Accounts and Surveys of the Wiltshire Lands of Adam de Stratton, passim.*

74. Kershaw, 'The great famine and agrarian crisis in England', *P. and P.*, **59** (1973), 26–9.

75. Powell, *A Suffolk Hundred in 1283*, pp. 78–80, presumably the half cows and calves point to shared ownership.

76. *Magna Vita Sancti Hugonis*, ed. D. L. Douie and H. Farmer, i, 62.

77. *Rotuli Parliamentorum*, i, 228–38, 243–65; Barley, *The English Farmhouse and Cottage*, pp. 18–20.

78. Barley, *op. cit.*, p. 13; Biddle, 'The deserted medieval village of Seacourt, Berkshire', *Oxoniensia*, **26–27** (1961–62), 92–6.

79. *Estate Book of Henry de Bray*, pp. 49–51, six out of the eight cottages he provided cost between 10s and 18s each.

80. Tester and Caiger, 'Medieval buildings in Joyden's Wood', *Arch. Cantiana*, **72** (1958) 18–40; Rahtz, 'Holworth: a medieval village excavation', *Proc. Dorset Arch. Soc.*, **81** (1959), 127 ff.

81. Field, 'Worcestershire peasant buildings, household goods and farming equipment in the later Middle Ages', *Medieval Archaeology*, **9** (1965), 115.

82. Hilton, *A Medieval Society*, pp. 100–102; Hilton and Rahtz, 'Upton, Gloucestershire', *Proc. Bristol and Gloucestershire Arch. Soc.*, **85** (1966), 94–107.

83. *Medieval Archaeology*, **7** (1964), 289; **9** (1969), 214–5; **13** (1969), 167–203.

84. Beresford, *The Clayland Village: excavations at Barton Blount and Goltho.*

85. Hilton, *A Medieval Society*, p. 96.

86. For recent discussions of peasant chattels, see *ibid.*, pp. 100, 104–5 and Hatcher and Barker, *A History of British Pewter*, pp. 32–4, 57–9.

87. *Rotuli Parliamentorum*, i, 228–38, 243–65.

88. Calculated on the basis that a quarter of grain would produce approximately 400 lb of bread: see A. S. C. Ross, 'The Assize of Bread', *Econ. H.R.*, 2nd ser., **9** (1956), 333.

89. Kershaw, *Bolton Priory*, p. 158.
90. *Mirour de l'Omme*, 11, 26, 450–60: adapted from the translation by Coulton, *The Medieval Village*, p. 237 from the text in *Complete Works of John Gower*, ed. G. C. Macaulay, i, 293.
91. Hilton, *op. cit.*, 111–13.
92. Rogers, *Six Centuries of Work and Wages*, p. 63.
93. Giraldus Cambrensis, *Itinerary through Wales*, ed. Llewellyn Williams, p. 166.
94. I. Kershaw, 'The great famine and agrarian crisis in England, 1315–22', *P. and P.*, **59** (1973), 12; and see above, pp. 51–2.
95. Quoted Homans, *English Villagers in the Thirteenth Century*, pp. 144–5.
96. *Court Rolls of the Abbey of Ramsey and the Honour of Clare*, p. 269, 270.
97. *Ibid.*, p. 249.
98. *Rotuli Parliamentorum*, i, 156–7; *Rot. Hundr.*, i, 317.

Chapter 7. Lords

1. *Liber Rubeus de Scaccario: The Red Book of the Exchequer*, pp. 378, 385.
2. *Sir Christopher Hatton's Book of Seals*, no. 213.
3. *Cartularium Monasterii de Rameseia*, i, 248.
4. *Chronicon Monasterii de Abingdon*, ii, 90.
5. *Cal. Inq. Misc.*, i, 168–71; Stenton, *English Feudalism*, p. 66 note.
6. *Leges Henrici Primi*, lv (1), ed. L. J. Downer, 173.
7. *Leges Henrici Primi*, lv (3); Glanville, *Tractatus de Legibus: Treatise on the Laws and Customs of the Realm of England*, ed. Hall, p. 107.
8. *Liber Rubeus . . .*, pp. 395–7, 402.
9. *Chronicon Monasterii de Abingdon*, ii, 4–5; the details are untrustworthy, but they can be collated sufficiently closely with Domesday to give a general indication of the distribution of property: Round, *Feudal England*, pp. 221, 305–6.
10. Stenton, *First Century of English Feudalism*, pp. 56–7, 59, 84.
11. Constitutions of Clarendon, c.11: Stubbs, *Select Charters*, p. 166.
12. Miller, *Abbey and Bishopric of Ely*, p. 178.
13. *Early Yorkshire Charters*, v, 17–19.
14. *Chronicon Monasterii de Abingdon*, ii, 3; *Liber Eliensis*, 217; Orderic Vitalis, *Historia Ecclesiastica*, Bk XI, chpt. 3.
15. Sanders, *English Baronies*, pp. 49–50; Miller, *op. cit.*, 179; Bean, *Estates of the Percy Family*, pp. 5–6.
16. Miller, *op. cit.*, 180–81.
17. Perroy, 'Social mobility among the French *noblesse*', *P. and P.*, **21** (1962), 31; and see, for a later period, McFarlane, *Nobility of Later Medieval England*, pp. 142–71 and his conclusion that 'the higher ranks of the nobility rarely deserved the epithet old', although political catastrophe as well as dynastic failure contributed to that fact.
18. Altschul, *A Baronial Family in Medieval England*, pp. 17–23; Sanders, *op. cit.*, pp. 19–20.
19. *Sir Christopher Hatton's Book of Seals*, nos. 84, 105; *Early Yorkshire Charters*, i, 426–8.
20. B. L. Harleian MS. 391, ff. 40, 77.
21. The story is recounted by Richardson, *The English Jewry under the Angevin Kings*, pp. 89–90, 95–7, 281–4.
22. Especially M. M. Postan in *Cambridge Economic History of Europe*, i, 592–5 and Hilton, *A Medieval Society*, pp. 51–3.
23. For some of the evidence see King, *Peterborough Abbey, 1086–1310*, pp. 66–9; Miller, *op. cit.*, pp. 175, 177, 185–6; Altschul, *op. cit.*, pp. 210–13; Powicke, *Henry III and the Lord Edward*, pp. 703–12.
24. King, *Peterborough Abbey*, pp. 41–4.

25. For some examples see below pp. 213, 228 and also King, 'Large and small landowners in thirteenth-century England', *P. and P.,* **47** (1970), 26–50 for an important discussion of this whole question.
26. Miller, *Abbey and Bishopric of Ely,* pp. 267–8.
27. King, *Peterborough Abbey,* pp. 130–31.
28. *Political Songs of England,* p. 230 and cf. Mann, *Chaucer and Medieval Estates Satire,* pp. 87–91.
29. See the remarks of Hilton, *op. cit.,* pp. 52–6.
30. Lapsley, *Crown, Community and Parliament,* pp. 63–110.
31. Denholm-Young, *Collected Papers,* pp. 56–67.
32. The basic outlines of John's estate are set out in Chancery Inq. p.m., Edward I, File 34/2.
33. *Cart. Osen.,* v, no. 666.
34. Quoted Barlow, *The Feudal Kingdom of England, 1042–1216,* p. 440.
35. Stenton, *op. cit.,* 178.
36. J. O. Prestwich, 'War and finance in the Anglo-Norman state', *T.R.H.S.,* 5th ser., **4** (1954), 19–43.
37. Robert de Monte or de Torigni in Stubbs, *Select Charters,* pp. 152–3.
38. *Chronicle of Jocelin of Brakelond,* pp. 85–6; *Magna Vita S. Hugonis,* pp. 99–100.
39. Sanders, *op. cit.,* p. 126.
40. These developments and others are comprehensively discussed by Powicke, *Military Obligations in Medieval England.*
41. Chancery Inq. p.m., Edward II, File 30/10.
42. Henry I's coronation charter in Stubbs, *Select Charters,* 118; *Cartulary of Tutbury Priory,* no. 103.
43. See the important article by S. J. Thorne, 'English feudalism and estates in land', *Cambridge Law Journal,* 1959, pp. 193–209; and for 'heritability and the canons of inheritance themselves slowly hardening in feudal jurisdictions', Milsom, *Historical Foundations of the Common Law,* pp. 91–3.
44. For the development of 'enfeoffment to uses' to serve these purposes, see Bean, *Decline of Feudalism in England,* pp. 104–26.
45. Holmes, *Estates of the Higher Nobility in Fourteenth-Century England,* pp. 40–1.
46. See the figures given by McFarlane, *Nobility of Later Medieval England,* p. 175.
47. Chancery Inq. p.m., Edward I, File 2/1.
48. *Curia Regis Rolls,* xiii, pl. 943.
49. *Cart. Osen.,* v, no. 572C.
50. Quoted by Hilton, *The English Peasantry in the Later Middle Ages,* p. 21.
51. *Pipe Roll, 14 John,* 3–4.
52. *Rot. Hundr.,* ii, 407–8, 511–14.
53. Chancery Inq. p.m. Edward I, File 53/5.
54. Chancery Inq. p.m. Henry III, File 3/6; Edward I, File 75/13; Edward II, File 103/2.
55. *Ibid.,* Edward I, File 50/24.
56. *Ibid.,* Edward I, File 16/9.
57. *Calendar of Inquisitions post mortem,* i, no. 744; iv, no. 434 and for the value of the Irish estates, Denholm-Young, *Seignorial Administration in England,* p. 46.
58. Titow, 'Land and population on the Bishop of Winchester's estates, 1209–1350', and 'Some differences between manors', *Agric. Hist. Rev.,* **10** (1962), 1–13.
59. Du Boulay, *Lordship of Canterbury,* pp. 169, 208.
60. Miller, *Abbey and Bishopric of Ely,* pp. 115–20.
61. E.g. the Ely and Canterbury estates: Miller, *Abbey and Bishopric of Ely,* p. 76; Smith, *Canterbury Cathedral Priory,* p. 119.
62. Smith, *op. cit.,* p. 141.
63. Hilton, *Economic Development of some Leicestershire Estates in the 14th and 15th Centuries,* pp. 25–33; Du Boulay, *The Lordship of Canterbury,* p. 244.
64. Waites, 'The monastic grange as a factor in the settlement of north-east Yorkshire', *Yorkshire Archaeological Journal,* **40** (1959–62), 627 ff.
65. *Monasticon Anglicanum,* v, 351 quoted Waites, *op. cit.,* 652.

66. Donkin, 'The Cistercians in medieval England', *Trans. and Papers of the Institute of British Geographers*, 1963, pp. 186–7; and for a wide-ranging discussion of granges see Platt, *The Monastic Grange in Medieval England*, chs 1–4.
67. *Newminster Chartulary*, pp. 45–6, 50–1.
68. For these matters see Kosminsky, *op. cit.*, pp. 68–151.
69. Caius College, Cambridge MS. 485/489, ff. 141–44b; *Rot. Hundr.*, ii, 442–4.
70. Chancery Inq. p.m., Henry III, Files 9/3, 42/2; Edward I, File 80/2.
71. *Ibid.*, Edward I, File 16/9.
72. Douglas, *Social Structure of Medieval East Anglia*, esp. ch. 3.
73. *V.C.H. Huntingdonshire*, i, 332–3; *Rot. Hundr.*, ii, 605–7.
74. The classic account is F. M. Stenton, *Types of Manorial Structure in the Northern Danelaw*.
75. Jolliffe, *Pre-feudal England: the Jutes*, p. 9.
76. *Boldon Buke*, pp. 20–3; Jolliffe, 'Northumbrian institutions', *E.H.R.*, **41** (1926), 8–9.
77. *Northumberland County History*, viii, 412.
78. For an example, *Cal. Documents relating to Scotland*, i, no. 1712.
79. For this last possibility, see Homans, 'The Frisians and East Anglia', *Econ. H.R.*, 2nd ser., **10** (1957), 189–206.
80. Cf. M. M. Postan, *Cambridge Economic History*, i, 576–7.
81. Barrow, *The Kingdom of the Scots*, pp. 9–28; Miller, 'La société rurale en Angleterre, Xᵉ–XIIᵉ siècles', *Agricoltura e Mondo Rurale in Occidente nell'Alto Medioevo*, pp. 111–34.
82. Kosminsky, *op. cit.*, 87.
83. Pollock and Maitland, *op. cit.*, i, 604.
84. *Estate Book of Henry de Bray*, pp. 48–51.
85. *Early Charters of St Paul's*, no. 301.
86. Harvey, *op. cit.*, pp. 32–9.
87. Denholm-Young, *Collected Papers*, pp. 229–30.
88. Saltman, *Theobald, Archbishop of Canterbury*, p. 482.
89. Quoted by F. M. Stenton, *First Century of English Feudalism*, pp. 72, 74.
90. *Ibid.*, pp. 74–5.
91. *Chronicle of Jocelin of Brakelond*, p. 24.
92. *Magna Vita S. Hugonis*, i, 110; ii, 152.
93. *Select Pleas in Manorial Courts*, pp. xiii ff.
94. Page, *Estates of Crowland Abbey*, p. 30; and for the general picture of estate administration given above, see Denholm-Young, *Seignorial Administration in England*, pp. 6–31.
95. *Estate Book of Henry de Bray*, p. 3.
96. Denholm-Young, *Seignorial Administration*, pp. 75–6; Miller, *Abbey and Bishopric of Ely*, p. 268; *Feudal Aids*, ii, 114, 430; *Cal. Close Rolls, 1302–7*, p. 41.
97. Levett, *Studies in Manorial History*, p. 26.
98. Denholm-Young, *Seignorial Administration*, pp. 32–6; Bennett, *Life on the English Manor*, pp. 151–92.
99. *La Seneschaucie* in *Walter of Henley*, ed. Oschinsky, pp. 274–80.
100. Page, *op. cit.*, p. 71; Harvey, *op. cit.*, p. 64.
101. *The Court Baron*, pp. 103, 105.
102. Denholm-Young, *Seignorial Administration*, pp. 148–51.
103. *The Court Baron*, p. 30.
104. *Select Pleas in Manorial Courts*, p. 98.
105. *The Court Baron*, p. 105.
106. *Registers of Edward the Black Prince*, ii, 22.
107. *Court Rolls of the Manor of Wakefield*, ed. W. P. Baildon, i, 86, 91–3, 103–4, 144, 151, 160, 187, 202.
108. *Cal. Documents relating to Scotland*, iii, no. 107.
109. Denholm-Young, *Collected Papers*, p. 100.

Chapter 8. Landlords and the land

1. *Domesday Monachorum of Christ Church, Canterbury*, p. 89; see also above, p. 183.
2. *Walter of Henley*, pp. 390–1, 396–9.
3. Britnell, 'Production for the market on a small fourteenth-century estate', *Econ. H.R.*, 2nd ser., **19** (1966), 380–7.
4. William of Malmesbury, *Vita Wulfstani*, p. 30; Kealey, *Roger of Salisbury*, pp. 86–90; Lennard, *Rural England 1086–1135*, p. 210.
5. *Monasticon Cluniacense Anglicanum*, i, 48–53.
6. *Inquisitio Comitatus Cantabrigiensis*, pp. 193–4.
7. *Documents illustrative of the Rule of Walter of Wenlock, Abbot of Westminster*, pp. 136, 138.
8. Smith, *Canterbury Cathedral Priory*, p. 122.
9. *Pipe Roll of the Bishopric of Winchester, 1210–11, passim.*
10. *Bishop Swinfield's Household Book*, esp. i, 3–4, 7–8, 12; ii, cvii–viii, cxv.
11. P.R.O. SC6 768/5–23.
12. Miller, *Abbey and Bishopric of Ely*, p. 93 and for some of the material which follows, pp. 73–112.
13. For these figures and what follows, see Titow, 'Land and Population on the Bishopric of Winchester's Estates, 1208–1350', esp. pp. 10, 36–41, 55–8, 61–2.
14. Britnell, *op. cit.*, pp. 381, 386.
15. P.R.O. Chancery Inq. p.m., Edward I, File 80/2.
16. The manors are: Kennett (Cambs); Dovercourt (Essex); Tiddenham (Glos); Weston (Herts); Caister, Little Framlingham, Hanworth, Lopham, Walsham (Norf); Dunningworth, Framlingham, Hollesley, Hoo, Peasenhall, Earl's Soham, Staverton and Stonham (Suff): see P.R.O. SC6/768/18, 840/9, 859/25, 873/17, 932/25, 935/55, 937/3, 938/9, 944/31, 995/22, 997/11, 998/29, 999/15, 1003/20, 1004/11, 1005/17, 1006/3.
17. Calculated from *Accounts of the Earldom of Cornwall, 1296–7*; see also above, p. 181.
18. P.R.O. SC6/873/14.
19. P.R.O. DL29/1/2.
20. The point of departure here must be Lennard, *Rural England 1086–1135*, pp. 105–212. The material on which the following paragraphs are based is more fully set out in Miller, 'The twelfth and thirteenth centuries: an economic contrast?', *Econ. H.R.*, 2nd ser., **24** (1971), 1–14 and in Harvey's meticulous examination of the Pipe Roll evidence: 'The pipe rolls and the adoption of demesne farming in England', *ibid.*, **27** (1974), 345–59.
21. *Cartularium Monasterii de Rameseia*, iii, 230–6.
22. *Gesta Abbatum Monasterii S. Albani*, i, 74.
23. *Domesday of St Paul's*, p. 152.
24. *Anglo-Saxon Charters*, ed. A. J. Robertson, pp. 195–7; *Registrum Roffense*, p. 119.
25. *Pipe Roll of the Bishopric of Winchester, 1208–9*, pp. 72, 80; *1210–11*, pp. 46, 52.
26. *Domesday of St Paul's*, pp. 128–9.
27. *Kalendar of Abbot Samson*, Charters no. 77.
28. *Feudal Documents from the Abbey of Bury St Edmund's*, no. 145.
29. *Register of the Abbey of St Benet of Holme*, i, nos. 148–9; Ralf Brian, who took up Ingham and Elveden from the abbot of Bury was also a clerk.
30. *Ibid.*, i, nos. 184, 187–8, 235, 250, 271.
31. *Registrum Roffense*, p. 119.
32. *Registrum Antiquissimum*, i, no. 6; *Cartularium Monasterii de Rameseia*, i, 128, 237.
33. *Dialogus de Scaccario*, p. 30.
34. *Liber Eliensis*, p. 220; Raftis, *Estates of Ramsey Abbey*, pp. 82–5.
35. *Register of St Augustine's Abbey, Canterbury*, ii, 385.
36. *Cartularium Monasterii de Rameseia*, i, 120–27; *Chronicon Abbatiae Ramesiensis*, p. 228; *Regesta*, ii, no. 1629.

37. *Pipe Roll*, 28 Hen. II, 73.
38. *Chronicle of Jocelin of Brakelond*, p. 33.
39. Postan, 'Chronology of Labour Services', *T.R.H.S.*, 4th ser., **20** (1937), 173–85.
40. *Domesday of St Paul's*, pp. 77, 79.
41. *Liber Henrici de Soliaco*, p. 107; *Boldon Buke*, p. 38.
42. *Domesday of St Paul's*, pp. 114–17.
43. *Ibid.*, pp. 14–15, 79.
44. *Liber Henrici de Soliaco*, p. 69.
45. For examples see *Chronicle of Jocelin of Brakelond*, pp. 1, 32.
46. Harvey, *op. cit.*, p. 353.
47. *Chronicle of Jocelin of Brakelond*, p. 32. For the much more protracted resumption of the Worcester priory lands, see Hilton, *A Medieval Society*, pp. 79–80.
48. *Pipe Roll of the Bishopric of Winchester, 1208–9*, pp. 20–23.
49. *Pipe Roll of the Bishopric of Winchester, 1210–11*, pp. 9, 17, 26, 38, 55–6, 63, 68, 78–9, 88, 93, 104, 107, 112, 121, 130, 139, 163–4.
50. The phrase is Postan's, *art. cit.*, 187.
51. For lay literacy in the twelfth century, see the important discussion by Richardson and Sayles, *The Governance of Mediaeval England from the Conquest to Magna Carta*, 269–84.
52. Du Boulay. *The Lordship of Canterbury*, p. 197.
53. *Early Charters of St Paul's*, nos. 124, 320.
54. *Chronica Majora*, vi, 85–7.
55. Tupling, *Economic History of Rossendale*, pp. 5–6.
56. P.R.O.Chancery Inquisitions post mortem, Edward I, Files 5/6, 68/6.
57. Extracts are printed by Knowles, *The Religious Orders in England*, i, 324.
58. Oschinsky's edition replaces all previous versions of these texts: *Walter of Henley and other Treatises on Estate Management and Accounting*, esp. p. 190; and see also Smith, *Canterbury Cathedral Priory*, pp. 134–5.
59. Titow, *English Rural Society*, pp. 41–2; Smith, *op. cit.*, pp. 140–1.
60. Smith, *op. cit.*, 136–7; Finberg, *Tavistock Abbey*, pp. 92–4.
61. *Walter of Henley*, ed. Oschinsky, pp. 325, 418.
62. Titow, *Winchester Yields*, pp. 14, 48–9, 148
63. The sources of this table are: Ugawa, *Lay Estates in Medieval England*, p. 143; Morimoto, 'Arable farming of Durham Cathedral Priory in the 14th century', *Nagoya Gakuin University Review*, **11** (1975) 273–4; Kershaw, *Bolton Priory*, p. 41; Titow, *Winchester Yields*, p. 4; Davenport, *Economic History of a Norfolk Manor*, pp. 29–31; *Accounts and Surveys of the Wiltshire Manors of Adam de Stratton*, pp. 39–185; P.R.O. SC6/824/6-7, 1077/26-9; Finberg, *Tavistock Abbey*, pp. 110–12.
64. Trow-Smith, *History of British Livestock Husbandry*, pp. 120–2, 166–8; Kershaw, *op. cit.*, p. 102.
65. *Pipe Roll of the Bishopric of Winchester, 1210–11; Accounts and Surveys of the Wiltshire Lands of Adam of Stratton.*
66. Ugawa, *op. cit.*, pp. 177–8; Kershaw, *op. cit.*, pp. 83–4.
67. Kershaw, *op. cit.*, pp. 97–103; P.R.O. SC6/824/6-7; Tupling, *Economic History of Rossendale*, p. 25.
68. *Eynsham Cartulary*, i, 18.
69. Titow, 'Land and Population on the Bishop of Winchester's Estates'.
70. See above p. 213, and Holmes, *Estates of the Higher Nobility in the XIVth Century*, p. 113.
71. Power, *Wool Trade in Medieval English History*, pp. 28, 34; Smith, *op. cit.*, 151–3; Trow-Smith, *op. cit.*, 135–42; Hilton, *A Medieval Society*, pp. 81–4; *Holm Cultram Register*, no. 367E.
72. P.R.O. SC6/835/1 and DL29/1/2-3.
73. As Postan suggests, 'The chronology of labour services', *T.R.H.S.* 4th ser., **20** *(1937)*, 186; and in general for what follows see his essay, *The Famulus*.

74. Miller, *op. cit.*, pp. 87–93.
75. P.R.O. SC6/768/5-16, 770/1.
76. P.R.O. DL29/288/4716.
77. P.R.O. Chancery Inquisitions P. M., Hen. III, File 42/2; Edw. I, File 80/2.
78. *Pipe Roll of the Bishopric of Winchester, 1208-9*, pp. 20–22.
79. *Documents illustrating the Rule of Walter de Wenlock, Abbot of Westminster*, pp. 147–8; compare also the manor of Bray where, in the reign of Henry III, the farm servants were still half-virgaters, but were paid in cash and kind by 1297: *V.C.H. Berkshire*, ii, 175–6.
80. Page, *op. cit.*, 102–3.
81. Caius College, Cambridge MS. 485/487, ff. 54a–56b.
82. *The Mirror of Justices*, pp. 80–1; and for the development of the villeinage in the thirteenth century, see Postan, 'Chronology of labour services', *op. cit.*
83. *Select Pleas in Manorial Courts*, p. 100.
84. Rogers, *History of Agriculture and Prices*, i, 91.
85. Page, *The End of Villeinage in England*, esp. p. 41.
86. Gray, 'The commutation of labour services'. *E.H.R.*, **29** (1915), 627 ff.
87. *V.C.H. Wiltshire*, iv, 37.
88. P.R.O. SC6/1132/15, 1133/1, 859/24-5, 27.
89. P.R.O. SC6/768/5, 23.
90. *Ibid.*, SC6/766/14, 768/5-23.
91. What follows is based upon the accounts of Adam de Stratton's manors and Titow, 'Land and Population on the Bishop of Winchester's Estates'.
92. Gras, *Social and Economic History of an English Village*, p. 61.
93. *Pipe Roll of the Bishopric of Winchester, 1210-11*, pp. 57–8, 62, 86, 153–8.
94. Ugawa, *op. cit.*, pp. 118, 196.
95. Miller, 'War, taxation and the English economy', in Winter, ed., *War and Economic Development*, p. 13; Carus-Wilson and Coleman, *England's Export Trade*, 40–41.
96. F. M. Page, 'Bidentes Hoylandie', *Economic History*, **1** (1926-9), 603 ff.
97. *Eynsham Cartulary*, i, 251.
98. Donkin, 'Cistercians in medieval England', *Trans. and Papers of Inst. of British Geographers* (1963), 194–5, and for Pegolotti's list, Cunningham, *Growth of English Industry and Commerce*, i, 628–41.
99. Lloyd, *Movement of Wool Prices in Medieval England*, pp. 6–7, 37.
100. P.R.O. DL29/1/2.
101. Blanchard, 'Economic change in Derbyshire during the later middle ages', pp. 164–8.
102. Waites, 'Monasteries and the medieval development of north-east Yorkshire', pp. 254 ff.
103. *Wakefield Court Rolls*, i, 18.
104. Kershaw, *Bolton Priory*, pp. 97–103; P.R.O. DL29/1/1-2.
105. Hilton, *English Peasantry in the Later Middle Ages*, p. 200.
106. Stone, 'Profit-and-loss accountancy at Norwich Cathedral Priory', *T.R.H.S.*, 5th ser., **12** (1962), 25–48.
107. In this respect the approach of Bridbury, *Economic Growth*, pp. xii-iv, adds little to our understanding of the thirteenth century.
108. Baldwin, 'Household administration of Henry Lacy and Thomas of Lancaster', *E.H.R.*, **42** (1927), 189; and for what follows see also Maddicott, *Thomas of Lancaster*, esp. ch. 1.
109. Moorman, *Church Life in the Thirteenth Century*, p. 175 ff.
110. *Ibid.*, pp. 265–6, 334 ff.
111. Snape, *English Monastic Finances*, pp. 168–9.
112. Knoop and Jones, *The Medieval Mason*, p. 4; Smith, *Canterbury Cathedral Priory*, p. 194.
113. Mate, 'The indebtednesss of Canterbury Cathedral Priory, 1215-95', *Econ. H.R.*, 2nd ser., **26** (1973), 183–94.
114. Snape, *op. cit.*, pp. 102–3.
115. As by Moorman, *op. cit.*, pp. 302–5.

116. Snape, *op. cit.*, pp. 102–3.
117. Kershaw, *Bolton Priory*, pp. 161–74.
118. See the important exploratory studies by Hilton, 'Rent and capital formation in feudal society', in Hilton, *English Peasantry*, pp. 174–214 and Postan, 'Investment in medieval agriculture', *J. Econ. Hist.*, **27** (1967), 576–87.
119. As Titow suggests, *English Rural Society*, p. 50.
120. P.R.O. SC6/1132/14.
121. *Cart. Osen.*, iv, 97.
122. *Studies in the Agrarian History of England in the Thirteenth Century*, pp. 90–1.
123. Here and in what follows the Ely material is derived from Miller, *Abbey and Bishopric of Ely* and the Winchester data from Titow, 'Land and Population on the Bishop of Winchester's Estates'.
124. *Earldom of Cornwall Accounts, 1296–7*, i, 54, 150; ii, 185.
125. Finberg, *Tavistock Abbey*, p. 249.
126. *The Mirror of Justices*, p. 164.
127. Raftis, *Estates of Ramsey Abbey*, p. 222; and see above, p. 222.
128. Finberg, *op. cit.*, p. 254.
129. Raftis, *op. cit.*, p. 217 ff.
130. Morgan, *English Lands of the Abbey of Bec*, pp. 113–18; Finberg, *op. cit.*, 249–50; Shaw, *Royal Forest of Lancaster*, p. 375; Holmes, *Estates of the Higher Nobility in XIVth Century England*, pp. 113–14.
131. P.R.O. DL29/288/4716.
132. Du Boulay, *The Lordship of Canterbury*, p. 244.
133. At Wootton in 1242–50 the average net return from the demesne was 51s annually; if it had been let at the same rate per acre as the customary tenants of the dependent vill of Stonesfield paid for demesne land there, it would have produced almost double that amount: Ballard, 'History of an Oxfordshire manor', *Vierteljahrschrift fur Sozial- und Wirtschaftsgeschichte*, **6** (1908), 457.
134. *Register of Walter Reynolds, Bishop of Worcester, 1308–13*, p. 34.

Chapter 9. King Edward's England

1. *Vita Edwardi Secundi*, p. 70.
2. The story of these conflicts is told by Gwyn Williams, *Medieval London*.
3. Postan, *Essays on Medieval Agriculture and . . . Economy*, pp. 177–8.
4. Calculated from Titow, *Winchester Yields*, pp. 136–44.
5. Raftis, *Estates of Ramsey Abbey*, pp. 246–51.
6. Watts, 'A model for the early fourteenth century', *Econ. H.R.*, 2nd ser., **20** (1967), 544, 547; Britnell, 'Production for the market on a small fourteenth-century estate', *ibid.*, **19** (1966), 380–7.
7. Raftis, *op. cit.*, pp. 240–1.
8. Watts, *art. cit.*, p. 544.
9. Titow, 'Land and Population on the Bishop of Winchester's Estates', pp. 66–8.
10. Finberg, *Tavistock Abbey*, pp. 261–2.
11. For what follows see Miller, 'Fortunes of the English textile industry during the thirteenth century', *Econ H.R.*, 2nd ser., **18** (1965), 64–82.
12. Platt, *The English Medieval Town*, p. 95.
13. Carus-Wilson, *Medieval Merchant Venturers*, pp. 242–5; Gray, 'Production and export of English woollens in the fourteenth century', *E.H.R.*, **39** (1924), 21.
14. Welford, *History of Newcastle and Gateshead*, i, 63, 74, 86, 102; Salzman, *English Industries of the Middle Ages*, p. 17.
15. Hatcher, *Rural Economy and Society in the Duchy of Cornwall*, pp. 92–3, 288–9.
16. Bridbury, *Economic Growth*, p. 65; Miller in *V.C.H. City of York*, 114–16; but see the cautionary remarks of Dobson, 'Admissions to the Freedom of the City of York', *Econ. H.R.*, 2nd ser., **26** (1973), 1–22.

17. For what follows, see Carus-Wilson and Coleman, *England's Export Trade*; Carus-Wilson, *Medieval Merchant Venturers*, pp. 239–45; James, *Studies in the Medieval Wine Trade*, pp. 1–36.
18. Beresford, *Lost Villages of England*, pp. 155–8.
19. As suggested by Harvey, 'The population trend in England between 1300 and 1348', *T.R.H.S.*, 5th ser., **16** (1966), 37–8.
20. Postan, *Essays on Medieval Agriculture and . . . Economy*, p. 170.

Bibliography

The lists of books and articles which follow are not intended as a comprehensive bibliography of the subjects touched upon in this book, but rather as a guide to further reading and as a means of providing full details of those works which have been most frequently cited in the text. For a more comprehensive and systematic bibliography the reader is referred to C. Gross, *A Bibliography of English History to 1485: Based on the Sources of Literature From the Earliest Times to About 1485*, ed. E. B. Graves, Oxford U.P., 1975.

Sections of the bibliography

Primary sources

Public records
Chronicles and biographies
Estate records
 (i) Cartularies and registers
 (ii) Accounts, surveys and court rolls
Collections of local records etc.
Legal treatises and records

Secondary works

General studies
Estate and regional studies
Estate management, farming practices and settlement
Population and the standard of living
Villages and villagers
Lords and knights
Markets and towns

Printed primary sources

Public records etc.

Anglo-Norman Political Songs, ed. I. S. T. Aspin, Anglo-Norman Text Society, Oxford, 1953, vol. xi.
Calendar of the Close Rolls, 1272–1485, 45 vols, 1892–1954
Calendar of Documents relating to Scotland, 1108–1509, ed. J. Bain, 4 vols, Edinburgh, 1881–88
Calendar of Inquisitions Miscellaneous, preserved in the P.R.O. (Henry III – Henry V), 7 vols, 1916–68
Calendar of Inquisitions Post Mortem and other analogous documents in the P.R.O. (Henry III – 7 Rich. II), 15 vols, 1904–70
Calendar of the Patent Rolls, 1216–1509, 54 vols, 1891–1916

Curia Regis Rolls, preserved in the P.R.O., 1922– , in progress
Dialogus de Scaccario, ed. C. Johnson, 1950
Domesday Book seu Liber Censualis Willhelmi Primi Regis Angliae, ed. A. Farley and H. Ellis, 4 vols, 1783–1814
English Historical Documents, Eyre & Spottiswoode: vol i. *c. 500–1042*, ed. Dorothy Whitelock, 1955; vol. ii. *1042–1189*, ed. D. C. Douglas and G. W. Greenaway, 1953
Foedera, Conventiones, Litterae etc, ed. T. Rymer, ed. A. Clarke, etc., Record Commission, 1816–30
Inquisitions and Assessments relating to Feudal Aids, 1284–1431, 6 vols, 1899–1920
Liber Rubeus de Scaccario: the Red Book of the Exchequer, ed. H. Hall, 3 vols, Rolls Ser., 1896
Monumenta Juridica: the Black Book of the Admiralty, ed. T. Twiss, 4 vols, Rolls Ser., 1871–6
Parliamentary Writs and Writs of Military Summons (Edw. I–Edw. II), ed. F. Palgrave, 2 vols in 4, 1827–34
Political Songs of England from the Reign of John to that of Edward II, ed. T. Wright, Camden Soc., old ser., 1839
Publications of the Pipe Roll Society, 1884 – in progress
Regesta Regum Anglo-Normannorum, 1066–1154, ed. H. W. C. Davis, C. Johnson, H. A. Cronne and R. H. C. Davis, 4 vols, Oxford, 1913–69
Rotuli Hundredorum Temp. Hen. III et Edw. I, ed. W. Illingworth and J. Caley, 2 vols, 1812–18
Rotuli Litterarum Clausarum in Turri Londinensi Asservati, 1204–27, ed. T. D. Hardy, 2 vols, 1833–44
Rotuli Litterarum Patentium in Turri Londinensi Asservati (1201–16), ed. T. D. Hardy, 1835
Rotuli Parliamentorum, 1278–1503, 6 vols.
Royal Writs in England from the Conquest to Glanville, ed. R. C. van Caenegem, Selden Society, **77**, 1959
Stubbs, W. *Select Charters and other Illustrations of English Constitutional History from the Earliest Times to the Reign of Edward the First*, Oxford U.P., 1913 edn

Chronicles and biographies

Bartholomaeus Anglicus, *De Proprietatibus Rerum*, ed. R. Steele 1907
Chronica Rogeri de Houedene (A.D.732–1201), ed. W. Stubbs, Rolls Ser., 4 vols, 1868–71
The Chronicle of Jocelin de Brakelond, ed. H. E. Butler Nelson, 1949
Chronicon Abbatiae Rameseiensis, ed. W. D. Macray, Rolls Ser., 1886
Chronicon Monasterii de Abingdon (A.D. 201–1189) ed. J. Stevenson, Rolls Ser., 2 vols, 1858
Chronicon Walteri de Gyseburne, ed. H. Rothwell, Camden Ser., 89, 1957
Flores Historiarum (from the Creation to 1326), ed. H. R. Luard, Rolls Ser., 3 vols, 1890.
Gesta Abbatum Monasterii S. Albani A Thoma Walsingham (A.D. 793–1401), ed. H. T. Riley, Rolls Ser., 3 vols 1867–69
Gesta Stephani: the Deeds of Stephen (1135–54), ed. K. R. Potter, Nelson, 1955
Giraldus Cambrensis, *Itinerary through Wales*, ed. W. L. Llewellyn Williams, 1908
Histoire de Guillaume le Conquérant, ed. R. Foreville, Paris, 1952
Magna Vita Sancti Hugonis, ed. D. L. Douie and H. Farmer, Oxford U.P. (Medieval Texts), 2 vols, 1961–2
Matthew Paris, *Chronica Majora (from the creation to 1259)*, ed. H. R. Luard, Rolls Ser., 7 vols, 1872–83
Ordericus Vitalis, *Historia Ecclesiastica*, ed. M. Chibnall, Oxford U.P. (Medieval Texts), 5 vols, 1968–75 (in progress)
Roger de Wendover, *Flores Historiarum*, ed. H. G. Hewlett, Rolls Ser., 3 vols, 1886–89
Vita Edwardi Secundi, ed. N. Denholm-Young, Nelson, 1957
William of Malmesbury, *Vita Wulfstani*, ed. R. R. Darlington, Camden Soc., 3rd Ser.

xl (1928)
William of Malmesbury, De Gestis Pontificum Anglorum Libri Quinque, ed. N. E. S. A. Hamilton, Rolls Ser., 1870

Estate Records

1. Cartularies and registers

Anglo-Saxon Charters, ed. A. J. Robertson, Cambridge, 1939

Carte Nativorum: a Peterborough Abbey cartulary of the fourteenth century, ed. C. N. L. Brooke and M. M. Postan, Northants Rec. Soc., xx, 1960

Cartularium Monasterii de Rameseia, ed. W. W. Hart and P. A. Lyons, Rolls Ser., 3 vols, 1884–93

Cartularium Prioratus de Colne, ed. J. L. Fisher, Essex Archaeol. Soc., Occasional Pubns. no. 1, 1946

Cartularium Prioratus de Gyseburne, ed. W. Brown, 2 vols, Surtees Soc., lxxxvi (1889), lxxxix (1894) (Cited in notes as *Guisborough Chartulary*).

The Cartulary of Cirencester Abbey, ed. C. D. Ross, 2 vols, Oxford U.P., 1964

The Cartulary of Darley Abbey, ed. R. R. Darlington, Derbys. Archaeol. and Nat. Hist. Soc., 2 vols, 1945

Cartulary and Terrier of the Priory of Bilsington, Kent, ed. N. Neilson, Brit. Acad. Records of Soc. and Econ. Hist., vii, 1928

The Cartulary of Newnham Priory, ed. J. Godber, 2 vols, Beds. Hist. Rec. Soc., xliii, 1963–64

Cartulary of Oseney Abbey, ed. H. E. Salter, 6 vols, Oxford Hist. Soc., lxxix, xc, xci, xcvii, xcviii, ci, 1929–36 (Cited in notes as *Cart. Osen.*)

Cartulary of the Priory of St Gregory, Canterbury, ed. A. M. Woodcock, Camden Society, 3rd Ser., lxxxviii, 1956

Cartulary of Tutbury Priory, ed. A. Saltman, Staffs. Rec. Soc. and Hist. MSS Comm., 1962

Charters of the Borough of Cambridge, ed. F. W. Maitland and M. Bateson, Cambridge, 1901.

Chartularium Abbathiae de Novo Monasterio Ordinis Cisterciensis, ed. J. T. Fowler, Surtees Soc., lxvi, 1878

The Chartulary of Cockersand Abbey of the Premonstratensian Order, ed. W. Farrer, Chetham Soc., 3 vols in 7 pts, Manchester, 1898–1909

Chartulary of Winchester Cathedral, ed. A. W. Goodman, Winchester, 1927

The Coucher Book, or Chartulary, of Whalley Abbey, ed. W. A. Hulton. Chetham Soc., 4 vols, Manchester, 1847–49

The Coucher Book of Furness Abbey, ed. J. C. Atkinson and J. Brownhill, Chetham Soc., 2 vols in 6 pts, new ser. ix, xi, xiv, lxxiv, lxxvi, lxxviii (1886–1919)

Domesday Monachorum of Christ Church, Canterbury, ed. D. C. Douglas, Royal Historical Society, 1944

Domesday of St Paul's of the Year 1222, ed. W. H. Hale, Camden Soc., old series, 1858

Early Charters of St Paul's Cathedral, ed. M. Gibbs. Camden Society, 3rd ser. lviii, 1939

The Estate Book of Henry de Bray of Harleston, Northants, c. 1289–1340, ed. D. Willis, Camden Soc., 3rd ser. xxvii, 1916

Eynsham Cartulary, ed. H. E. Salter, Oxford Hist. Soc., xlix, 1909; li, 1908

Feudal Documents from the Abbey of Bury St Edmunds, ed. D. C. Douglas, Brit. Acad. Rec. Soc. Econ. Hist., viii, 1932

The Great Chartulary of Glastonbury, ed. A. Watkin, 3 vols, Somerset Rec. Soc., lix, lxiii–iv, 1947–56

Historia et Cartularium Monasterii S. Petri Gloucestriae, W. H. Hart, Rolls Ser., 3 vols, 1863–67

Kalendar of Abbot Samson of Bury St Edmunds and Related Documents, ed. R. H. C. Davis, Camden Soc., 3rd ser. lxxxiv, 1954

Liber Eliensis, ed. E. O. Blake, Camden Soc., 3rd ser., xcii, 1962

Liber Henrici de Soliaco Abbatis Glastoniensis, ed. J. E. Jackson, Roxburghe Club, 1882

Monasticon Cluniacense Anglicanum or Charters and Records among the Archives of the Abbey of Cluni, 1077–1534, ed. G. F. Duckett, 2 vols, Lewes, 1888

Register and Records of Hulm Cultram (c. 1236), ed. F. Grainger and W. G. Collingwood, Cumb. and Westm. Antiquarian and Archaeol. Soc. Rec. ser., vii, 1929

Register of the Abbey of St Benet of Holme, 1020–1210, ed. J. R. West, 2 vols, Norfolk Rec. Soc. ii, iii, 1932

Register of John de Halton (1292–1324), ed. W. N. Thompson, Canterbury and York Soc. and Cumb. and Westm. Antiquarian and Archaeol. Soc., 2 vols, 1913

Register of St Augustine's Abbey, Canterbury, ed. G. J. Turner and H. E. Salter, Brit. Acad. Rec. Soc. Econ. Hist., 2 vols, 1915–25

Register of Walter Reynolds, Bishop of Worcester, 1308–13, ed. R. A. Wilson, Worcestershire Hist. Soc., 1927, and Dugdale Soc., 1928

Register of Edward the Black Prince preserved in the Public Record Office, 4 vols, H.M.S.O., 1930–33

Registrum Antiquissimum of the Cathedral Church of Lincoln, ed. C. W. Foster and K. Major, 10 vols, Lincoln Rec. Soc., 1931–68

Registrum Roffense, ed. J. Thorpe, 1769

Registrum Sive Liber Irrotularius et Consuetudinarius Prioratus Beatae Mariae Wigornensis, ed. W. H. Hale, Camden Soc., xci, 1865

Sir Christopher Hatton's Book of Seals, ed. L. Loyd and D. M. Stenton, Northants Rec. Soc. and Oxford, 1950

The Stoneleigh Leger Book, ed. R. H. Hilton, Dugdale Soc., xxiv, 1960

Vetus Registrum Sarisberiense: alias dictum registrum S. Osmundi episcopi, ed. W. H. R. Jones, 2 vols, Rolls Ser., 1883–84

2. Accounts, surveys and court rolls

Accounts and Surveys of the Wiltshire Lands of Adam of Stratton, ed. M. W. Farr, Wilts. Archaeol. Soc. Rec. Ser., xiv, 1959

Bishop Swinfield's Household Book; see *Roll of the Household Expenses of . . .*

Boldon Buke: a survey of the possessions of the see of Durham, 1183, ed. W. Greenwell, Surtees Soc., Durham, 1852

Chertsey Abbey Court Rolls Abstract, ed. E. Toms, Surrey Rec. Soc., nos. 38 and 48, 1937–54

The Court Baron, ed. F. W. Maitland and W. P. Baildon, Selden Soc., iv, 1891

Court Roll of Chalgrave Manor, 1278–1313, ed. M. K. Dale, Beds. Hist. Rec. Soc. Pubns., xxviii, 1950

Court Rolls of the Abbey of Ramsey and the Honour of Clare, ed. W. O. Ault, Yale Historical Pubns., ix, Yale U.P., 1928

Some Court Rolls of the Lordships, Wapentakes, and Manors of Thomas, Earl of Lancaster, in the County of Lancaster, 1323–4, ed. W. Farrer, Lancs. and Ches. Rec. Soc., xli, 1901

Court Rolls of the Manor of Hales (Halesowen), 1270–1307, ed. J. Amphlett and S. G. Hamilton, 2 pts, Worcs. Hist. Soc., 1910–12

Court Rolls of the Manor of Wakefield, 1274–1331, ed. W. P. Baildon, J. Lister and J. W. Walker, 5 vols., Yorks Archaeol. Soc. Rec. Ser., xxix, 1901; xxxvi, 1906; lvii, 1917; lxxviii, 1930; cix, 1945

Court Rolls of the Wiltshire Manors of Adam de Stratton, ed. R. B. Pugh, Wilts Archaeol. Soc. Rec. Ser., xxiv, 1970

Custumals of the Manors of Laughton, Willingdon and Goring, ed. A. E. Wilson, Sussex Rec. Soc., 1, 1961

Custumals of the Sussex Manors of the Archbishop of Canterbury, ed. B. C. Redwood and A. E. Wilson, Sussex Rec. Soc., lvii, 1958 (Cited in notes as *Sussex Custumals*).

Documents illustrative of the Rule of Walter of Wenlock, Abbot of Westminster, 1283–1307, ed. B. F. Harvey, Camden Soc., 4th ser., ii, 1965

Halmota Prioratus Dunelmensis, ed. W. H. D. Longstaffe and J. Booth, Surtees Soc., lxxxii, 1889

Medieval Customs of the Manors of Taunton and Bradford on Tone, ed. T. J. Hunt, Somerset Rec. Soc., lxvi, 1962

Ministers' Accounts of the Earldom of Cornwall 1296–1297, ed. L. M. Midgley, 2 vols, Camden Soc., 3rd ser., lxvi and lxviii, 1942–45

Pipe Roll of the Bishopric of Winchester, 1208–9, ed. H. Hall, 1903

Pipe Roll of the Bishopric of Winchester, 1210–11, ed. N. R. Holt, Manchester U.P., 1964

Roll of the Household Expenses of Richard de Swinfield, Bishop of Hereford, 1289–90, ed. J. Webb, 2 vols, Camden Soc., lix, lxii, 1853–55 (Cited in notes as *Bishop Swinfield's Household Book*)

Select Documents of the English Lands of the Abbey of Bec, ed. M. Chibnall, Camden Soc., 3rd ser., lxxiii, 1951

Select Pleas in Manorial Courts, Hen. III – *Edw. I,* ed. F. W. Maitland, Selden Soc., ii, 1889

A Terrier of Fleet, Lincolnshire, ed. N. Neilson, Brit. Acad. Rec. Soc. Econ. Hist., iv, 1920

Walter of Henley and other Treatises on Estate Management and Accounting, ed. D. Oschinsky, Oxford U.P., 1971

Collections of Local Records etc.

Ancient Petitions relating to Northumberland, ed. C. M. Fraser, Surtees Soc., 1966

Annals of Cambridge, ed. C. H. Cooper, 5 vols, Cambridge, 1842–1908.

Cambridgeshire and the Isle of Ely: the lay subsidy for the year 1327, ed. J. Muskett and C. H. Evelyn White, n.d.

Crown Pleas of the Wiltshire Eyre, 1249, ed. C. A. F. Meekings, Wilts. Archaeol. and Nat. Hist. Soc. Rec., xvi, 1961

Documents illustrative of Medieval Kentish Society, ed. F. R. H. Du Boulay, Kent Archaeol. Soc. Rec., xviii, 1964

Documents illustrative of the Social and Economic History of the Danelaw, ed. F. M. Stenton, Brit. Acad. Rec. Soc. Econ. Hist., v, 1920 (Cited in notes as *Danelaw Documents*)

The Earliest Lincolnshire Assize Rolls, A.D. 1202–1209, ed. D. M. Stenton, Lincoln Rec. Soc., xxii, 1926

Early Yorkshire Charters, ed. W. Farrer, Yorks. Archaeol. Soc. Rec. Ser., extra ser., 3 vols, 1914–16

Inquisitio Comitatus Cantabrigiensis subjicitur Inquisitio Eliensis, ed. N. E. S. A. Hamilton, 1876

Miscellanea, iv, ed. T. A. M. Bishop and E. W. Crossley, Yorks. Archaeol. Soc. Rec. Ser., xciv, 1937

Monasticon diocesis Exoniensis: records illustrating the ancient foundations in Cornwall and Devon, ed. G. Oliver, Exeter, 1846

Notes on the Religious and Secular Houses of Yorkshire, ed. W. P. Baildon, Yorks. Archaeol. Rec. Ser., xvii, 1895; lxxxi, 1931

Records of the Borough of Leicester, 1103–1603, ed. M. Bateson, 3 vols, Cambridge, 1899–1905.

Rolls of the Justices in Eyre being the Rolls of Pleas and Assizes for Gloucestershire, Warwickshire and Staffordshire, 1221–2, ed. D. M. Stenton, Selden Soc., lix, 1940

Rolls of the Justices in Eyre being the Rolls of Pleas and Assizes for Yorkshire in 3 Henry III (1218–19), ed. D. M. Stenton, Selden Soc., lvi, 1937

A Suffolk Hundred in the year 1283, ed. E. Powell, Cambridge, 1910

'The tallage of 6 Edward II', ed. E. A. Fuller, *Trans. Bristol and Gloucestershire Arch. Soc.*, 19 (1894–95)

Yorkshire Inquisitions (1241–1316), ed. W. Brown, Yorks. Archaeol. Soc. Rec. Ser., xii, 1892; xxiii, 1898; xxxi, 1902; xxxvii, 1906

Legal treatises and records

Bracton, *De Legibus et Consuetudinibus Angliae*, ed. G. E. Woodbine, 4 vols, Yale, 1922; same ed., Bracton, *On the Laws and Customs of England*, trans. S. E. Thorne, 2 vols, Harvard U.P., 1968

Bracton's Note Book, ed. F. W. Maitland, 3 vols, 1887

Glanville, *Tractatus de Legibus: Treatise on the Laws and Customs of the Realm of England*, ed. G. D. G. Hall, 1965

Laws of the Kings of England from Edmund to Henry I, ed. A. J. Robertson, Cambridge, 1925

Leges Henrici Primi, ed. L. J. Downer, Oxford U.P., 1972

The Mirror of Justices, ed. W. J. Whittaker, Selden Soc., vii, 1893

Select Bills in Eyre (1292–1333), ed. W. C. Bolland, Selden Soc., xxx, 1914

Secondary works

General studies

Agrarian History of England and Wales, vol. 1, pt 2, ed. H. P. R. Finberg, Cambridge U.P., 1972

Beresford, M. W. and **St Joseph, J. K. S.** *Medieval England: an aerial survey,* Cambridge U.P., 1958

Bridbury, A. R. *Economic Growth: England in the later Middle Ages,* 2nd edn, Harvester Press, 1975

Cam, H. M. *Liberties and Communities of Medieval England: collected studies in local administration and topography*, Cambridge U.P., 1933; repr. Merlin Press.

Cam, H. M. *The Hundred and the Hundred Rolls: an outline of local government in medieval England*, Methuen, 1930; repr. Merlin Press

Cambridge Economic History of Europe, Cambridge U.P., vol. i. *The Agrarian Life of the Middle Ages*, ed. M. M. Postan, 2nd edn, 1966; vol. ii. *Trade and Industry in the Middle Ages*, ed. M. M. Postan and E. E. Rich, 1952; vol. iii. *Economic Organization and Policies in the Middle Ages*, ed. M. M. Postan, E. E. Rich and E. Miller, 1963.

Carus-Wilson, E. M. ed. *Essays in Economic History,* 3 vols, E. Arnold, 1962.

Cunningham, W. *The Growth of English Industry and Commerce,* vol. i, 6th edn, Cambridge U.P., 1915

Darby, H. C. ed. *New Historical Geography of England,* Cambridge U.P., 1973

Darby, H. C. *et al.*, ed. *The Domesday Geography of England,* 6 vols, Cambridge U.P., 1952–67 (*Eastern England, Midland England, South-east England, South-west England, Northern England,* and *Gazetteer*).

Darby, H. C. *Domesday England*, Cambridge U.P., 1977.

Denholm-Young, N. *Collected Papers on Medieval Subjects,* Oxford, Blackwell, 1946

Domesday Geography of England: see Darby, H. C. *et al.*

Duby, G. *Rural Economy and Country Life in the Medieval West*, trans. C. Postan, E. Arnold, 1968

English Place-Name Society publications, Cambridge 1924–   (in progress)

Essays in Economic History: see Carus-Wilson, E. M., ed.

Finn, R. W. *An Introduction to Domesday Book*, Longmans, 1963

Halperin, J. 'Les transformations économiques au XIIe et XIIIe siècles', *Revue d'histoire économique et sociale*, **38** (1950)

Inman, A. H., *Domesday and Feudal Statistics*, with a chapter on agricultural statistics, 1900

Lennard, R., *Rural England 1086–1135: a study of social and agrarian conditions*, Oxford U.P., 1959

Levett, A. E., *Studies in Manorial History*, Oxford U.P., 1938

Loyn, H. R., *Anglo-Saxon England and the Norman Conquest*, Longmans, 1962

Maitland, F. W. *Domesday Book and Beyond: three essays in the early history of England,* Cambridge, U.P., 1960 edn

Maitland, F. W. *Collected Papers*, ed. H. A. L. Fisher, 3 vols, Cambridge U.P., 1911

Miller, E. 'The English economy in the thirteenth century, implications of recent research', *P. and P., **28** (1964)

Miller, E. 'La Société rurale en Angleterre, Xe–XIIe siècles', *Agricoltura e Mondo Rurale in Occidente nell' Alto Medioevo* (Spoleto, 1966)

Miller, E. 'The twelfth and thirteenth centuries: an economic contrast?", *Econ., H.R.*, 2nd ser., **24** (1971)

Milsom, S. F. C. *The Historical Foundations of the Common Law*, Butterworth, 1969

New Historical Geography of England: see Darby, H. C. ed.

Oxford Dictionary of English Place-Names, ed. E. Ekwall, 4th edn, Oxford U.P., 1960

Pollock, F. and **Maitland, F. W.** *The History of English Law before the time of Edward I*, 2 vols, Cambridge U.P., 1968 edn

Postan, M. M. *Essays on Medieval Agriculture and General Problems of the Medieval Economy*, Cambridge U.P., 1973

Postan, M. M. *Essays on Medieval Trade and Finance*, Cambridge U.P., 1973

Postan, M. M. *The Medieval Economy and Society: An Economic History of Britain in the Middle Ages,* Wiedenfeld & Nicolson, 1972

Postan, M. M. and co-editors: see *Cambridge Economic History*

Richardson, H. G. and Sayles, G. O. *The Governuance of Medieval England from the Conquest to Magna Carta*, Edinburgh U.P., 1963

Round, J. H. *Feudal England: historical studies of the eleventh and twelfth centuries*, 1895

Sawyer, P. H. 'The wealth of eleventh-century England', *T.R.H.S.* 5th ser., **15** (1965)

Stenton, D. M. *English Society in the Early Middle Ages,* new edn, Penguin Books 1952

Stenton, F. M. *Anglo-Saxon England, c. 550–1087*, Oxford U.P. (Oxford History of England), 3rd edn, 1971

Titow, J. Z. *English Rural Society, 1200–1350*, Allen & Unwin, 1969

Victoria History of the Counties of England, Oxford U.P. for the Institute of Historical Research, 1900–ᅠ(in progress)

Winter, J. M. ed. *War and Economic Development: essays in memory of David Joslin*, Cambridge U.P., 1975

Estate and regional studies

Bean, J. M. W. *The Estates of the Percy Family 1416–1537*, Oxford U.P., 1958

Britnell, R. H. 'Production for the market on a small fourteenth-century estate', *Econ. H.R.*, 2nd ser., **19**, 1966

Darby, H. C. *The Medieval Fenland*, Cambridge, 1940; 2nd edn. David & Charles, 1974

Davenport, F. G. *The Economic History of a Norfolk Manor (Forncett) 1086–1565*, Cambridge, 1906

Donkin, R. A. 'The Cistercian Order and the settlement of the north of England', *Geographical Review*, **59** (1969)

Douglas, D. C. *Social Structure of Medieval East Anglia*, Oxford U.P. (Oxford Studies in Social and Legal History, vol. ix), 1927

Du Boulay, F. R. H. *The Lordship of Canterbury, an essay on medieval society*, Nelson, 1966

Finberg, H. P. R. *Tavistock Abbey: a study in the social and economic history of Devon*, Cambridge U.P., 1951

Gras, N. S. B. and **Gras, E. C.** *The Economic and Social History of an English Village: Crawley, Hampshire, A.D. 909–1928*, Cambridge, Mass., 1930

Hallam, H. E. *Settlement and Society: a study of the early agrarian history of south Lincolnshire*, Cambridge U.P., 1965

Harvey, P. D. A. *A Medieval Oxfordshire Village: Cuxham 1240–1400*, Oxford U.P., 1965

Hatcher, J. *Rural Economy and Society in the Duchy of Cornwall, 1300–1500*, Cambridge U.P., 1970

Hewitt, H. J. *Medieval Cheshire: an economic and social history of Cheshire in the reigns of the three Edwards*, Manchester U.P., 1929

Hilton, R. H. *A Medieval Society: the West Midlands at the end of the thirteenth century*, Weidenfeld & Nicolson, 1967

Hilton, R. H. *Economic Development of some Leicestershire Estates in the Fourteenth and Fifteenth Centuries*, Oxford U.P., 1947

Holmes, G. A. *Estates of the Higher Nobility in Fourteenth-Century England*, Cambridge U.P., 1957

Hoskins, W. G. *Devon*, Collins, 1954; new edn, David Charles, 1972

Hoskins, W. G. and **Finberg, H. P. R.** *Devonshire Studies*, Cape, 1952

Jolliffe, J. E. A. *Pre-Feudal England: the Jutes*, Oxford U.P., 1933

Jolliffe, J. E. A. 'Northumbrian institutions', *E.H.R.*, **41** (1926)

Kershaw, I. *Bolton Priory: the economy of a northern monastery, 1286–1325*, Oxford U.P., 1973

King, E. *Peterborough Abbey, 1086–1310: a study in the land market*, Cambridge U.P., 1973

Lennard, R. V. 'The demesnes of Glastonbury Abbey in the eleventh and twelfth centuries', *Econ. H.R.*, 2nd ser., **8**, 1956

Levett, A. E. and **Ballard, A.** *The Black Death on the Estates of the See of Winchester*, Oxford Studies in Social and Legal History, v, Oxford, 1916

Miller E. *The Abbey and Bishopric of Ely*, Cambridge U.P., 1951

Miller, E. 'Farming in northern England during the twelfth and thirteenth centuries', *Northern History*, **11**, 1976

Moore, S. A. *A Short History of the Rights of Common upon the Forest of Dartmoor and the Commons of Devon*, Plymouth, 1890

Morgan, M. *The English Lands of the Abbey of Bec*, Oxford U.P., 1946

Northumberland County History, 15 vols, ed. M. H. Dodds *et al.*, Newcastle, A. Read, 1893–1940

Page, F. M. *Estates of Crowland Abbey*, Cambridge U.P., 1934

Postan, M. M. 'Glastonbury estates in the twelfth century', *Econ. H.R.*, 2nd ser., **5** 1953 and **9**, 1956

Raftis, J. A. *The Estates of Ramsey Abbey: a study of economic growth and organization*, Toronto, 1957

Raftis, J. A. *Tenure and Mobility: studies in the social history of the medieval village*, Toronto, 1957

Raftis, J. A. *Warboys: two hundred years in the life of an English village*, Toronto, 1974

Rennell of Rodd, Lord, *Valley on the March: a history of a group of manors on the Herefordshire March of Wales*, Oxford U.P., 1958

Scammell, J. 'Robert I and the north of England', *E. H.R.*, **74** (1958)

Searle, E. *Lordship and Community: Battle Abbey and its banlieu*, Toronto, 1974

Smith, R. A. L. *Canterbury Cathedral Priory*, Cambridge U.P., 1943

Titow, J. Z. 'Land and population on the Bishop of Winchester's estates, 1209—1350', Cambridge University Ph.D. dissertation, 1962

Tupling, G. H. *Economic History of Rossendale*, Chetham Soc., new ser., lxxxvi, 1927

Ugawa, K. *Lay Estates in Medieval England*, Tokyo, 1966

Waites, B. 'The monastic grange as a factor in the settlement of north-east Yorkshire', *Yorkshire Arch. Journal*, **40** (1959–62)

Waites, B. 'Monasteries and the medieval development of north-east Yorkshire, London University M.A. dissertation, 1957

Estate management, farming practices and settlement

Ault, W. O. 'Open-field husbandry and the village community: a study in agrarian by-laws in medieval England', *American Philosophical Soc. Trans.* iv, pt 7, 1965

Baker, A. R. H. 'Evidence in the *Nonarum Inquisitiones* of contracting arable lands in England during the early fourteenth century', *Econ. H.R.*, 2nd ser., **19** (1966)

Baker, A. R. H. 'Howard Levi Gray and English field systems: an evaluation', *Agric. Hist.*, **39** (1965)

Baker, A. R. H. and **Butlin, R. A.**, ed., *Studies of Field Systems in the British Isles*, Cambridge U.P., 1973

Bazeley, M. L. 'The extent of the royal forest in the thirteenth century', *T.R.H.S.*, 4th ser., **4** (1921)

Beresford, M. W. and **Hurst, J. G.** ed. *Deserted Medieval Villages: studies*, Lutterworth Press, 1971

Bishop, T. A. M. 'Assarting and the growth of the open fields', *Econ. H.R.*, **6** (1935)

Bishop, T. A. M. 'The Norman settlement of Yorkshire', in Carus-Wilson, ed., *Essays in Economic History*, 1962, ii, 1–13

Brandon, P. F. 'Demesne arable farming in coastal Sussex during the later Middle Ages', *Agric. Hist. Rev.*, **19** (1971)

Denholm-Young, N. *Seignorial Administration in England*, Oxford U.P., 1937

Donkin, R. A. 'The Cistercian Order and the settlement of the north of England', *Geographical Review*, **59** (1969)

Donkin, R. A. 'The Cistercian Order in medieval England: some conclusions', *Trans. and Papers of the Inst. of British Geographers*, no. 33 (1963)

Drew, J. S. 'The manorial accounts of St Swithin's Priory', *E.H.R.*, **57** (1947)

Gray, H. L. *English Field Systems*, Harvard U.P., 1915

Hallam, H. E. 'The Postan thesis', *Historical Studies*, **15** (1972)

Harvey, P. D. A. 'The Pipe Rolls and the adoption of demesne farming in England', *Econ. H.R.*, 2nd ser., **27** (1974)

Kerridge, E. 'A reconsideration of some former husbandry practices', *Agric. Hist. Rev.*, **3** (1955)

Linehan, C. D. 'Deserted sites and rabbit-warrens on Dartmoor, Devon', *Medieval Archaeology*, **10** (1966)

Lythe, S. G. E. 'The organization of drainage and embankments in medieval Holderness', *Yorkshire Arch. Journal*, **34** (1939)

Mate, M. 'The indebtedness of Canterbury Cathedral Priory, 1215–95', *Econ. H.R.*, 2nd ser., **26** (1973)

Morimoto, N. 'Arable farming of Durham Cathedral Priory in the fourteenth century', *Nagoya Gakuin University Review*, **11** (1975)

Orwin, C. S. and **Orwin, C. S.** *The Open Fields*, 3rd edn, Oxford U.P., 1967

Page, F. M. 'Bidentes Hoylandie', *Economic History*, **1** (1926–29)

Payne, F. G. 'The plough in early Britain', *Arch. Journal*, **104** (1948)

Platt, C. *The Monastic Grange in Medieval England: a reassessment*, Macmillan, 1969

Plucknett, T. F. T. *The Medieval Bailiff*, Athlone Press: Constable, 1954

Postan, M. M. 'The chronology of labour services', *T.R.H.S.*, 4th ser., **20** (1937)

Postan, M. M. *The Famulus: the estate labourer in the twelfth and thirteenth centuries*, *Econ. H.R.* Supplement no. 2, Cambridge, 1954

Postan, M. M. 'Investment in medieval agriculture', *J. Econ. Hist.*, **27** (1967)

Postgate, M. R. 'The open fields of Cambridgeshire', Cambridge University Ph.D. dissertation, 1964

Power, E. *The Wool Trade in English Medieval History*, Oxford U.P., 1941

Raftis, J. A. 'Rent and capital at St Ives', *Medieval Studies,* **20** (1958)
Ramm, H. G., McDowall, R. W. and **Mercer, E.** *Sheilings and Bastles,* Royal Commission on Historic Monuments, 1970
Salzman, L. F. 'The inning of Pevensey levels', *Sussex Arch. Coll.,* **53** (1910)
Shaw, R. C. *The Royal Forest of Lancaster,* Preston, R. C. Shaw, 1956
Stone, E. 'Profit and loss accountancy at Norwich Cathedral Priory', *T.R.H.S.* 5th ser., **12** (1962)
Studies of Field Systems, see Baker above
Sylvester, D. 'Medieval three-course arable systems in Cheshire', *Trans Hist. Soc. Lancashire and Cheshire,* **110** (1958)
Thirsk, J. 'The common fields', *P. and P.,* **29** (1964) and **33** (1966)
Titow, J. Z. 'Medieval England and the open-field system', *P. and P.,* **32** (1965)
Titow, J. Z. *Winchester Yields: a study in medieval agricultural productivity,* Cambridge U.P., 1972
Trow-Smith, R. *History of British Livestock Husbandry,* 2 vols, Routledge, 1957–9
White, L. jr. *Medieval Technology and Social Change* Oxford U.P., 1962
Williams, M. *The Draining of the Somerset Levels* Cambridge U.P., 1970
Wretts-Smith, M. 'The organization of farming at Crowland Abbey', *J. Econ. and Business History,* **4** (1931)
Youd, G. 'The common fields of Lancashire', *Trans. Hist. Soc. Lancashire and Cheshire,* **118** (1961)

Population and the standard of living

Beveridge, M. W. 'The yield and price of corn in the Middle Ages', *Econ. H.R.,* **1** (1929)
Beveridge, M. W. 'Wages in the Winchester manors' *Econ. H.R.,* **7** (1936)
Beveridge, M. W. 'Westminster wages in the manorial era', *Econ. H.R.,* 2nd ser., **8**(1955)
Farmer, D. L. 'Some price fluctuations in Angevin England', *ibid.* **9** (1956)
Farmer, D. L. 'Grain price movements in thirteenth-century England', *ibid.,* **10** (1957)
Farmer, D. L. 'Livestock price movements in thirteenth-century England', *ibid.,* **22** (1969)
Grierson, P. 'The volume of Anglo-Saxon coinage', *Econ. H.R.,* 2nd ser., **20** (1967)
Hallam, H. E. 'Some thirteenth-century censuses', *Econ H.R.,* 2nd ser., **10** (1958)
Hallam, H. E. 'Population density in medieval Fenland, *ibid.,* **14** (1961)
Harley, J. B. 'Population trends and agricultural developments from the Warwickshire Hundred Rolls', *Econ. H.R.,* 2nd ser., **11** (1958)
Harvey, B. F. 'The population trend in England between 1300 and 1348', *T.R.H.S.,* 5th ser., **16** (1966)
Harvey, P. D. A. 'The English inflation of 1180–1220', *P. and P.,* **61** (1973)
Hatcher, J. *Plague, Population and the English Economy, 1348–1530,* Macmillan, 1977
Kershaw, I. 'The great famine and agrarian crisis in England, 1315–22' *P. and P.,* **59** (1973)
Lloyd, T. H. *The Movement of Wool Prices in Medieval England, Econ H.R.* Supplement no. 6, 1973
Mayhew, N. S. 'Numismatic evidence and falling prices in the fourteenth century', *Econ. H.R.,* 2nd ser., **27** (1974)
Miskimin, H. A. 'Monetary movements in fourteenth and fifteenth-century England', *J. Econ. Hist.,* **24** (1964)
Ohlin, G. 'No safety in numbers: some pitfalls of historical statistics', in Floud, ed., *Essays in Quantitative Economic History,* 1974
Phelps Brown, E. H. and **Hopkins, S. V.** 'Seven centuries of the prices of consumables compared with builders' wage-rates', in Carus-Wilson, ed., *Essays in Economic History,* vol. ii.
Postan, M. M. and **Titow, J. Z.** 'Heriots and prices on Winchester manors', *Econ. H.R.,* 2nd ser., **11** (1959)
Rogers, J. E. T. *A History of Agriculture and Prices in England, 1259–1793.* 7 vols, Oxford, 1866–1902
Rogers, J. E. T. *Six Centuries of Work and Wages: the history of English labour,* 2 vols, 1884

Ross, A. S. C. 'The Assize of Bread', *Econ. H.R.*, 2nd ser., 9 (1956)
Russell, J. C. *British Medieval Population*, Albuquerque, 1948
Russell, J. C. 'The pre-plague population of England', *Journal of British Studies*, 5 (1966)
Titow, J. Z. 'Some evidence of the thirteenth-century population increase', *Econ. H.R.*, 2nd ser., 14 (1961)
Titow, J. Z. 'Some differences between manors and their effects on the condition of the peasants in the thirteenth century', *Agric. Hist. Rev.*, 10 (1962)
Watts, D. C. 'A model for the early fourteenth century', *Econ. H.R.*, 2nd ser., 20 (1967)

Villages and villagers

Ballard, A. 'History of an Oxfordshire manor', *Vierteljahrschrift fur Sozial und Wirtschaftsgeschichte*, 6 (1908)
Barley, M. W. *The English Farmhouse and Cottage*, Routledge, 1961
Bennett, H. S. *Life on the English Manor: a study of peasant conditions, 1150–1400*, Cambridge U.P., 1938
Beresford, G. T. M. *The Clayland Village: excavations at Barton Blount and Goltho*, Society for Medieval Archaeology, Monographs, no. 6, 19
Biddle, M. 'The deserted medieval village of Seacourt, Berkshire', *Oxoniensia*, 26-27 (1961–62)
Coulton, G. G. *The Medieval Village*, Cambridge U.P., 1925
Dodwell, B.'Holdings and inheritance in medieval East Anglia', *Econ. H.R.*, 2nd ser., 20 (1967)
Dudley, D. and Minter, E. M. 'The medieval village at Garrow Tor, Bodmin Moor, Cornwall', *Medieval Archaeology*, 6-7 (1962–63)
Faith, R. J. 'Peasant families and inheritance customs in medieval England', *Agric. Hist. Rev.*, 14 (1966)
Field, R. K. 'Worcestershire peasant buildings, household goods and farming equipment in the later Middle Ages', *Medieval Archaeology*, 9 (1965)
Gray, H. L. 'The commutation of labour services', *E.H.R.*, 29 (1915)
Hilton, R. H. 'Freedom and villeinage in England', *P. and P.*, 31 (1965)
Hilton, R. H. 'Peasant movements in England before 1381', in Carus-Wilson, ed. *Essays in Economic History*, vol. ii
Hilton, R. H. *The English Peasantry in the Later Middle Ages*, Oxford U.P., 1974
Hilton, R. H. and Rahtz, P. A. 'Upton, Gloucestershire, 1959–1964', *Proc. Bristol and Gloucs. Arch. Soc.*, 85 (1966)
Homans, G. C. *English Villagers of the Thirteenth Century*, Harvard U.P., 1941
Homans, G. C. 'The Frisians and East Anglia', *Econ. H.R.*, 2nd ser., 10 (1957)
Hoskins, W. G. *Local History in England*, Longman 1959 (2nd edn, 1973)
Hoskins, W. G. *The Making of the English Landscape*, Hodder & Stoughton, 1957 (Penguin, 1970)
Hoskins, W. G. *The Midland Peasant: the economic and social history of a Leicestershire village*, Macmillan, 1957
Hyams, P. R. 'Origins of a peasant land market in England', *Econ. H.R.*, 2nd ser., 23 (1970)
Hyams, P. R. 'The proof of villein status in the common law', *E.H.R.*, 89 (1974)
Kosminsky, E. A. *Studies in the Agrarian History of England in the thirteenth century*, Oxford, Blackwell, 1956
McIntosh, M. K. 'The Privileged Villeins of the English Ancient Demesne', *Viator*, viii (1976)
Maddicott, J. R. *The English Peasantry and the Demands of the Crown, 1294–1341*, *P. and P.*, Supplement no. 1, 1975
Miller, E. 'War, taxation and the English economy in the late thirteenth and early fourteenth centuries', J. M. Winter, ed., *War and Economic Development*, Cambridge U.P., 1975

Neilson, N. 'Custom and the common law in Kent', *Harvard Law Review,* **38** (1924–25)

Owen, D. M. *Church and Society in Medieval Lincolnshire,* Lincolnshire Local History Society, 1971

Page, T. W. *The End of Villeinage in England,* New York, 1900

Poole, A. L. *Obligations of Society in the Twelfth and Thirteenth Centuries,* Oxford U.P., 1946

Powicke, F. M. 'Observations on the English freeholder in the thirteenth century', *Wirtschaft und Kultur* (Baden, 1938)

Rahtz, P. A. 'Holworth: a medieval village excavation', *Proc. Dorset Arch. Soc.,* **81** (1959)

Seebohm, F. *The English Village Community: an essay on economic history,* 1883

Stenton, F. M. *Types of Manorial Structure in the Northern Danelaw,* Oxford U.P., 1910

Stenton, F. M. 'The free peasantry of the Northern Danelaw', *Bulletin de la société royale des lettres de Lund* (1925–26)

Tester, P. J. and **Caiger, J. E. L.** 'Medieval buildings in Joyden's Wood', *Archaeologia Cantiana,* **72** (1958)

Thornton, G. A. 'A study in the history of Clare, Suffolk', *T.R.H.S.,* 4th ser. **11** (1928)

Vinogradoff, P. *English Society in the Eleventh Century,* Oxford, 1908

Vinogradoff, P. *Villainage in England: essays in English medieval history,* Oxford, 1892

Lords and Knights

Altschul, M. *A Baronial Family in Medieval England: the Clares, 1217–1314,* Johns Hopkins Press, 1965

Baldwin, J. F. 'Household administration of Henry Lacy and Thomas of Lancaster', *E.H.R.,* **42** (1927)

Bean, J. M. W. *The Decline of English Feudalism, 1215–1540,* Manchester U.P., 1967

Coss, P. R. 'Sir Geoffrey de Langley and the crisis of the knightly class in thirteenth-century England', *P. and P.,* **68** (1975)

Harvey, S. 'The knight and the knight's fee in England', *P. and P.,* **49** (1970)

Hoyt, R. S. *The Royal Demesne in English Constitutional History, 1066–1272,* Cornell U.P., 1951

Kealey, E. J. *Roger of Salisbury: Viceroy of England,* University of California Press, 1972

King, E. 'Large and small landowners in thirteenth-century England', *P. and P.,* **47** (1970)

Knowles, D. *The Religious Orders in England,* 3 vols, Cambridge U.P., 1948–59

Lapsley, G. T *Crown, Community and Parliament in the Later Middle Ages,* ed. H. M. Cam and G. Barraclough, Oxford, Blackwell, 1951

McFarlane, K. B. *The Nobility of Later Medieval England,* Oxford U.P., 1973

Maddicott, J. R. *Thomas of Lancaster, 1307–22: a study in the reign of Edward II,* Oxford U.P., 1970

Moorman, J. R. H. *Church Life in England in the Thirteenth Century,* Cambridge U.P., 1945

Painter, S. *William Marshall,* Johns Hopkins Press, 1933

Painter, S. *Studies in the History of the English Feudal Barony,* Johns Hopkins Press, 1943

Perroy, E. 'Social mobility among the French *noblesse*', *P. and P.,* **21** (1962)

Plucknett, T. F. T. *The Legislation of Edward I,* Oxford U.P., 1949

Powicke, F. M. *Henry III and the Lord Edward: The Community of the Realm in the Thirteenth Century,* 2 vols, Oxford U.P., 1947

Powicke, M. R. *Military Obligations in Medieval England: A Study in Liberty and Duty,* Oxford U.P., 1962

Prestwich, J. O. 'War and finance in the Anglo-Norman state', *T.R.H.S.,* 5th ser., **4** (1954)

Richardson, H. G. *The English Jewry under the Angevin Kings,* Methuen, 1960

Robinson, J. A. *Gilbert Crispin: Abbot of Westminster*, Cambridge, 1911
Saltman, A. *Theobald, Archbishop of Canterbury*, Athlone Press, 1956
Sanders, I. J. *English Baronies: a study of their origin and descent, 1086–1327*, Oxford U.P., 1960
Snape, R. H. *English Monastic Finances in the Later Middle Ages*, Cambridge U.P., 1926
Southern, R. W. 'The place of Henry I in English history', *Proc. Brit. Acad.*, **48** (1962)
Stenton, F. M. *The First Century of English Feudalism, 1066–1166*, Oxford U.P., 1932
Wolffe, B. P. *The Royal Demesne in English History: the Crown estate in the governance of the realm from the Conquest to 1509*, Allen & Unwin, 1971

Markets and towns

Beresford, M. W. *New Towns of the Middle Ages*, Lutterworth Press, 1967
Biddle, M. 'The Winton Domesday: two surveys of an early capital', *Die Stadt in der Europaïschen Geschichte: Festschrift Edith Ennen*, Bonn, 1972
Biddle, M. 'Winchester: the development of an early capital', *Vor- und Frühformen der Europaïschen Stadt im Mittelalter*, **1**, Abhandlungen der Akademie der Wissenschaft in Göttingen (1974)
Billson, C. J. *Medieval Leicester*, Leicester, 1920
Carus-Wilson, E. M. *Medieval Merchant Venturers*, Methuen, 1954
Carus-Wilson, E. M., ed. *The Overseas Trade of Bristol in the later Middle Ages*, Bristol Record Soc. Publications, no. 7, 1937
Carus-Wilson, E. M. and **Coleman, O.** *England's Export Trade, 1275–1547*, Oxford, 1963
Coates, B. E. 'The origin and distribution of markets and fairs in medieval Derbyshire', *Derbyshire Arch. Journal*, **85** (1965)
Dobson, R. B. 'Admissions to the freedom of the City of York', *Econ. H.R.*, 2nd ser., **26** (1973)
Ekwall, E. *Studies on the Population of Medieval London*, Stockholm, 1956
Gray, H. L. 'The production and export of English woollens in the fourteenth century', *E.H.R.*, **39** (1924)
Gras, N. S. B. *The Early English Customs System*, Harvard U.P., 1918
Gras, N. S. B. *Evolution of the English Corn market*, Harvard U.P., 1915
Hatcher, J. and **Barker, T. C.** *A History of British Pewter*, Longman, 1974
Hatcher, J., *English Tin Production and Trade before 1550*, Oxford U.P., 1973
Hill, J. F. W. *Medieval Lincoln*, Cambridge U.P., 1948
Hodgen, M. 'Domesday water mills', *Antiquity*, **13** (1939)
Holmes, G. A. 'Florentine merchants in England', *Econ. H.R.*, 2nd Ser., **13** (1960)
Hurst, J. G. and **West, S. E.** 'Saxo-Norman pottery in East Anglia', *Proc. Cambridge Antiquarian Soc.*, **50** (1957)
James, M. K. *Studies in the Medieval Wine Trade*, ed. E. M. Veale, Oxford U.P., 1971
Knoop, D. and **Jones, G. P.** *The Medieval Mason*, Manchester U.P., 1933
Maitland, F. W. *Township and Borough*, Cambridge, 1898
Miller, E. 'Medieval York', in *Victoria County History: City of York*, 1961
Miller, E. 'The fortunes of the English textile industry during the thirteenth century', *Econ. H.R.*, 2nd ser., **18** (1965)
Platt, C. *The English Medieval Town*, Secker & Warburg, 1976
Round, J. H. *The Commune of London and other Studies*, 1899
Salzman, L. F. *English Industries of the Middle Ages* (1913)
Tait, J. *The Medieval English Borough: studies on its origins and constitutional history*, Manchester U.P., 1936
Veale, E. M. *The English Fur Trade*, Oxford U.P., 1966
Weinbaum, M. *London unter Eduard I und II*, 2 vols, Stuttgart, 1933
Welford, R. *The History of Newcastle and Gateshead*, 3 vols, 1884–87
Williams, Gwyn A. *Medieval London: from commune to capital*, Athlone Press, 1963

Index of persons and places

Subject index